The Cross in the Johannine Writings

The Cross in the Johannine Writings

JOHN MORGAN-WYNNE

WITHDRAWN

PICKWICK *Publications* · Eugene, Oregon

THE CROSS IN THE JOHANNINE WRITINGS

Pickwick Publications
An Imprint of Wipf and Stock Publishers
199 W. 8th Ave., Suite 3
Eugene, OR 97401

www.wipfandstock.com

ISBN 13: 978-1-61097-251-2

Cataloging-in-Publication data:

Morgan-Wynne, J. E.

    The cross in the Johannine writings / John Morgan-Wynne.

    X + Y p. ; 23 cm. Includes bibliographical references and index.

    ISBN 13: 978-1-61097-251-2

    1. Jesus Christ—Crucifixion. 2. Bible. N.T. John—Theology. 3. Bible. N.T. Epistles of John—Theology. I. Title.

BT450 M67 2011

Manufactured in the U.S.A.

Contents

Preface / ix

PART I: THE GOSPEL OF JOHN

1. The Significance of "the Cross in the Fourth Gospel" in New
    Testament Scholarship from Bultmann to the Present / 3

2. An Examination of the Case that Salvation in the Fourth Gospel
    is by Revelation / 45

3. The Johannine Doctrine of Sin / 113

4. Jesus' Ministry up to the Cross in the Fourth Gospel / 124

5. The Cross in the Fourth Gospel / 132

6. Appropriation of what is Accomplished in the Cross / 192

PART II: THE JOHANNINE LETTERS

7. "The Death of Jesus in the Johannine Letters" in New Testament
    Scholarship from Bultmann to Painter / 212

8. The Situation Behind the Johannine Letters / 218

9. The Meaning of the Death of Jesus in the Johannine Letters / 241

10. Final Summary and Conclusions / 254

Select Bibliography / 263
Index of Authors / 281
Index of Ancient Documents / 287

Preface

This work has had a long gestation. A few days after I had completed my final examinations in the Honour School of Theology at Oxford (June 1960), the late Revd. Dr. George Beasley-Murray—then Principal of Spurgeon's College, London—graciously saw me and suggested as a possible topic for research "Atonement in the Gospel and First Epistle of John," an area which, he felt, merited examination. It made an immediate appeal as a topic which was both theological and relevant for preaching and teaching in future pastoral ministry.

I began reading commentaries, monographs and articles in the area of Johannine studies, and registered the topic for a proposed thesis for the Oxford BD (a research degree in Oxford, and, curiously, the only such one which an Oxford graduate can do without being in residence at Oxford). Officially, no supervisor is appointed, but one is advised to seek help and guidance. On returning to Oxford in September 1962 as minister of Botley Baptist Church and assistant minister at New Road Baptist Church, Oxford, I did consult the late Revd. Dr. George Caird, of Mansfield College. He was later appointed an examiner together with the Revd. Leslie Houlden, then chaplain-fellow of Trinity College, Oxford, and they recommended the award of the degree (Sept/Oct 1965). By this time, I had been appointed Tutor in New Testament at Regent's Park College, the Baptist college in Oxford University. Heavy teaching responsibilities and the demands of a growing family plus the endeavor to play a part in Oxford Baptist life, left little or no time for revising and updating the thesis.

In fact, it was not till the Spring of 1993, when recovering from a heart attack, that I set to and rewrote the original thesis, taking note of intervening Johannine scholarship. I accepted a call to become the

ix

minister of Ilkley Baptist Church, West Yorkshire, and commenced in January 1994. I continued work on the topic, and decided to change the title to "The Cross in Johannine Writings." Whether John has a "theology of the cross" still remained and remains an area of debate and discussion, and this is reflected in the amount of space devoted to it. There is far less controversy among scholars about the place of the cross/ death of Jesus in the First Epistle, and the treatment of the First Epistle has accordingly been briefer.

Once again, the work was put on hold, while I wrote the history of the church for its centenary (1899–1999) and co-authored "The Last Seven Days: the Story of Jesus and Holy Week" (1999) with the late Revd. Dr. G. Henton Davies, former Principal of Regent's Park College, Oxford. Fortunately, the late Mrs. Judith Lunan, a church member, typed my script and got it on to a floppy disc, and since then I have had the help of Mr. Graham Sunderland, and Amy and Michelle Marsden, both Computer Study graduates, when I ran into problems with the computer; and I am grateful to them all for their welcome help. Since I finally retired at the end of June 2002, I have had the time to take up this work again. Even when I had finished revising the work, two sets of events beyond my control conspired consecutively to delay still further its appearance. So what is at last here offered represents, I trust, a big improvement on the effort of 1965! More recently, my daughter, Leri-Anne Morgan-Wynne, and my elder son, David J. Morgan-Wynne, have been of great help in getting the work into the format required by Wipf and Stock, and I record my thanks to them. I also record my thanks to Dr. Robin Parry of Wipf and Stock for all his encouragement and Mr. Ian Creeger, my typesetter, for all his help in the final stages of preparing the work for publication.

My dear wife, Enid, has put up with my spending long hours in the study with remarkable cheerfulness and patience, and I thank her for all her love and support over the years.[1]

—J. E. Morgan-Wynne, February, 2011

---

1. While I have made my own translations of New Testament passages, for other quotations from the Bible and Apocrypha the text of the Holy Bible. New Revised Standard Version, copyright 1987, by the Division of Christian Education of the National Council of the Churches of Christ in the USA, is used by permission.

Abbreviations

AB	Anchor Bible
AnBib	Analecta Biblica
AGSU	Arbeiten zur Geschichte des Spätjudentums und Christentum
AThANT	Abhandlungen zur Theologie des Alten und Neuen Testaments
BBB	Bonner Biblische Beiträge
BDF	F. Blass and A Debrunner, *A Greek Grammar of the New Testament and Other Early Christian Literature*. Translated and revised by Robert W. Funk. Chicago: University of Chicago Press, 1961.
BEThL	Bibliotheca Ephemeridum Theologicarum Lovaniensium
Bib	*Biblica*
BJRL	*Bulletin of the John Rylands Library*
BNTC	Black's New Testament Commentary
BSR	Biblioteca di Scienze Religiose
BTS	Biblisch-Theologische Studien
BWANT	Beiträge zur Wissenschaft vom Alten und Neuen Testament
BZ	Biblische Zeitschrift
BZNW	Beihefte zur Zeitschrift für die neuentestamentliche Wissenschaft
CB	Coniectanea Biblica
CBET	Contributions to Biblical Exegesis and Theology

CJT	Canadian Journal of Theology
CNT	Commentaire de Nouveau Testament
EH	Europäische Hochschulschriften
EKKNT	Evangelisch-Katholischer Kommentar zum Neuen Testament
EQ	*Evangelical Quarterly*
ETL	Ephemerides Theologicae Lovanienses
EvTh	Evangelische Theologie
ExT	*Expository Times*
FRANT	Forschungen zur Religion und Literatur des Alten und Neuen Testaments
FzB	Forschung zur Bibel
GCT	Gender, Culture, Theory
HBS	Herders Biblische Studien
HTKNT	Herders theologsicher Kommentar zur Neuen Testament
IRT	Issues in Religion and Theology
ITS	Innsbrucker theologische Studien
JB	*Jerusalem Bible*
JBL	*Journal of Biblical Literature*
JTS	*Journal of Theological Studies*
JSNT	*Journal for the Study of the New Testament*
JSNTSS	Journal for the Study of the New Testament Supplement Series
KEK	Kritisch-Exegetischer Kommentar über das Neue Testament
KuD	Kerygma und Dogma
LSJ	H. G. Liddell, R. Scott, H. S. Jones, *A Greek-English Lexicon*. Oxford: Clarendon, 1968.
LD	Lectio Divina
MNTC	Moffatt New Testament Commentary
MTS	Münchener theologischen Studien
MTZ	Münchener theologische Zeitschrift
NA	Neutestamentliche Abhandlungen
NCB	New Century Bible

NICNT	New International Commentary on the New Testament
NIV	*New International Version*
NT	*Novum Testamentum*
NTD	Das Neue Testament Deutsch
NTS	*New Testament Studies*
NTTS	New Testament Tools and Studies
PBM	Paternoster Biblical Monographs
QD	Quaestiones Disputatae
SANT	Studien zum Alten und Neuen Testament
SBLDS	Society for Biblical Literature Dissertation Series
SBS	Stuttgarter Bibel-Studien
ScEc	Sciences Ecclésiastiques
SCHT	Studies in Christian History and Thought
SJT	*Scottish Journal of Theology*
SNT	Supplements to Novum Testamentum
TB	Theologische Blätter
TBC	Torch Bible Commentary
TDNT	*Theological Dictionary of the New Testament.* Edited by Gerhard Kittel and Gerhard Friedrich. 10 volumes. Grand Rapids: Eerdmans, 1977.
TU	Texte und Untersuchungen
TRE	Theologische Realenzyklopädie
WBC	Word Bible Commentary
WMANT	Wissenschaftliche Monographien zum Alten und Neuen Testament
WUNT	Wissenschaftliche Untersuchungen zum Neuen Testament
ZNW	*Zeitschrift für neutestamentliche Wissenschaft*
ZTK	*Zeitschrift für Theologie und Kirche*

PART I
THE GOSPEL OF JOHN

1

The Significance of "the Cross in the Fourth Gospel" in New Testament Scholarship from Bultmann to the Present[1]

1. Some explanation of the principles of arrangement may be in order. I have chosen Bultmann as a starting point because of his enormous influence in the area of Johannine studies. The last work chronologically speaking which I have mentioned is the monograph on the Johannine concept of glory and glorification, *Die Herrlichkeit des Verherrlichten* by Nicole Chibici-Revneanu published in 2007. Rather than a chronological survey I have opted for a thematic approach. Inevitably, some works do not always fit neatly into the sections in which they appear. I trust that this has not meant any serious misrepresentation of their viewpoints. The aim has been to let the authors speak for themselves rather than to engage in a dialogue directly (to have attempted the latter would have made a lengthy survey still longer and involved a good deal of repetition). The main "engagement" should, in any case, be with the text of the Fourth Gospel itself. I trust, however, that the survey is sufficiently comprehensive to show the major positions and approaches adopted in scholarly discussion. If I have missed any significant work, I apologise and can only plead my current distance from theological libraries. (Actually, given the veritable flood of material published on Johannine literature, never mind the whole of the New Testament, it is in all probability impossible for anyone to be completely abreast of the secondary literature. There comes a point where one simply has "to put pen to paper"!) I may also point out that there are some authors not mentioned in the survey, whose views are mentioned in the later discussion of passages (e.g., Barrett and Brown) and whose commentaries have greatly enriched us, but in whose section on the theology of the Gospel the cross is not specifically discussed.

3

A. REVIEW OF SCHOLARLY APPROACHES TO
THE CROSS IN JOHN'S GOSPEL

1. *The Death of Jesus has No Special Significance. Salvation is by Revelation in the Incarnate Ministry*

THIS, IN A NUTSHELL, is the interpretation of Rudolph Bultmann who set out his views on Johannine Theology conveniently in Volume 2 of his *Theology of the New Testament*.[2] Bultmann believed that in John the death of Jesus is subordinate to the incarnation (52): it has no special importance for salvation, but simply marks the accomplishment of the "work" which began with the incarnation (52, 55)—it is the last demonstration of the obedience which governs Jesus' whole life (14, 31). The common Christian interpretation of Jesus' death as an atonement for sins does not determine John's view of it (53–54). Salvation in John comes through Jesus' *word* or the truth mediated by Jesus' word (55. See John 8:32; 15:3; 17:17).

Even when Bultmann says that John has subsumed Jesus' death under his idea of revelation, what he means is that in his death Jesus is acting as the revealer and is not the passive object of a divine process of salvation (53). The Johannine passion story shows us Jesus not really suffering death but rather choosing it, not as the passive victim but as the active conqueror (53). Bultmann believed that John 1:29 applies to the whole ministry rather than only Jesus' death (53–54) and that John 6:51b–58 is an insertion by an ecclesiastical editor, as is also 19:34b which aimed to ground baptism and the Lord's Supper on Jesus' death (54).

In the end, Jesus—as the revealer of God—reveals nothing but that he is the Revealer (62, 66).[3] This revelation creates a crisis and demands a decision (38–39, 46–47). People must decide whether they will remain in the cosmos—the perversion of creation, which is existence in bondage (26–32)—or whether they will live from God, abandoning their self-created security and existing in creaturely dependence on God (75).

2. The German original was published in 1948. The English translation appeared in 1955. His commentary *Das Evangelium des Johannes*, Göttingen: Vandenhoeck and Ruprecht had, of course, been published earlier in 1941. The English translation by Beasley-Murray et al, did not appear till considerably later, in 1971.

3. Later, Meeks, "Man from Heaven," 151, sought to correct Bultmann's dictum by asserting that Jesus revealed that he was an enigma.

Around the time Bultmann published his commentary, the British scholar, Vincent Taylor, was producing a trilogy on the meaning of the death of Jesus. The second of these, *The Atonement in New Testament Teaching* (1945), has a section on the distinctive teaching of John (Taylor accepted the common authorship of Gospel and First Epistle). Taylor considered that John's "apprehension of the meaning of the Cross is much less profound" than Paul's (156) and speaks of "serious" or "notable limitations" in it (157, 159). "The evangelist never gives expression to the idea of the One great Sacrifice . . . no description of a self-offering of Christ for sinners with which they can identify themselves in their approach to God for pardon, reconciliation and peace other than the statement that He sanctifies Himself for His own that they too may be sanctified in truth (17:19) . . . From the negative point of view the Johannine writings are an impressive warning of the attenuated conceptions of the significance of the death of Christ which inevitably follow when the Incarnation is thought of predominantly in terms of revelation, of life and of knowledge" (159–60).

Although Taylor does say that "the death is itself a part, and indeed the crowning moment in the revelation in the Son" (153), it is in fact by no means clear that his exposition justifies the use of "crowning moment." Taylor does not engage in discussion with Bultmann, but it is clear that he is close to Bultmann's fundamental position of salvation-by-revelation.

Bultmann's view that Jesus' death was of no significance for salvation continued to be reiterated by scholars. S. Schultz, who was the author of two monographs on John's Gospel together with a commentary on the Gospel (1975), firmly asserted that while the fourth evangelist knew theological statements about Jesus' atoning death, he did not develop any pronounced theological interpretation of the cross. The cross is not expounded with the help of atonement motifs but is the redeemer's exit from the alien world (237–38). Jesus' cross has no special saving significance, and the Pauline theology of the cross must not be imported into John.

Also in 1975, U. B. Müller published an article on the meaning of Jesus' death on the cross in John's Gospel,[4] in *Kerygma und Dogma* 21 (1975). He asserted emphatically that salvation in John is not decided

4. "Die Bedeutung des Kreuzestodes Jesu im Johannesevangelium. Erwägung des Kreuzestheologie im NT."

at the cross (59–60): there is no concept of the cross as constitutive for salvation in the Gospel (57, 60). Statements like 1:29; 10:11, 15 are dismissed as "tradition" and not specifically Johannine, those in 10:11,15 being modified in any case by 10:17,18 (63–64). Müller goes so far as to link John in with the same theological spectrum as Paul's Corinthian opponents (69).

W. Loader, *The Christology of the Fourth Gospel: Structure and Issues*, is concerned with the saving event in John's theology. At its simplest, Jesus' death is a return to the Father, which authenticates his claim (John 16:10). Vicarious atonement is present, but only in an incidental manner (94–102). His death brings to a climax the issues of Jesus' life (revelation and judgment): it reveals the character of the relationship between the Father and the Son and of the Son's love for his friends and it reveals the world in all its lostness as it finally rejects Jesus. The dominant model of salvation in John's Gospel is the Son as the Father's envoy bearing revelation-information and making a relationship with the Father possible through encounter with himself (136, 206). The death and return only ensure the continuing and greater accessibility of the offer (16, 121).

It is indicative of how dominant Bultmann's approach has been that J. Ashton in his monumental and brilliant work, *Understanding the Fourth Gospel* (1991), did not engage in any discussion with representatives of viewpoints other than that of Bultmann and Käsemann. For Ashton, John's theology is first and foremost a theology of revelation (497, 545) and the idea of Jesus' death as atonement for sin is not central (491). The crucifixion is the re-ascent of the Son of Man to his true home in heaven (496), a departure, an exaltation, an ascent (545–46). Ashton discusses five summary passages (3:31–32; 3:16–21; 7:33–36; 8:21–27; 12:44–50)—in which significantly, in his opinion, the death of Jesus is not mentioned—to illustrate how in John revelation is delivered by the divine envoy and how its effect is divisive, leading to new life or to judgment (531–45).

In the volume *Kreuzestheologie im Neuen Testament*, edited by A. Dettwiler and J. Zumstein (2002), F. Vouga contributed two chapters, "Ist die Kreuzestheologie die hermeneutische Zentrum des Neuen Testaments?" and "Crux probat omnia: Der or ein Prüfstein der neutestamentlichen Hermeneutik? Dialog und Konsens mit Pierre Bühler." Voulga did not treat John in any detail in either chapter, but, in challenging the idea that the theology of the cross was the hermeneutical center of the New Testament, he revealed that he believed that the hermeneutical center of the New Testament is the absolute uniqueness of the revelation of the eternal God in the person of Jesus of Nazareth (334, 336); that the incarnation was the basic concept of John's Gospel (335); and that the concept of incarnation was as appropriate a model as the cross to set forth what Vouga sees as the hermeneutical center of the New Testament (335) (Voulga added "the absolute paradox" drawn from Kierkegaard to the cross and incarnation as appropriate models,—see 336–37). It is reasonable, therefore, to place Voulga in our first category.

2. *Salvation is by Revelation and Jesus' Death is Itself Revelatory*

Among those who consciously sought to modify Bultmann's position on the cross in John, while accepting that revelation is the central theme of Johannine theology, we may mention J. T. Forestell, whose *The Word of the Cross* appeared in 1974. Revelation began with the incarnation and culminated in the glorification of Jesus (17, 19, 165, 191, 198, 202). Jesus' death is proof of his love for his own (76). The elevation on the cross will have revelatory significance (John 8:28–29)—it reveals the Father's love for people. The cross is the external sign of the attraction of God's love (64, 112). Those who "see" the cross as the revelation of God's love are saved, because the sources of eternal life are opened for people by the cross (88, 192). Revelation is not the communication of propositional truths but an event that communicates life and is, therefore, saving (192).

Forestell argues that there is nothing in the context of John 10:11, 15; 15:13, which points to the cultic character of Jesus' death (74–75, 193–94, 202) nor do the other ὑπέρ texts demand a sacrificial interpretation of the cross (194). Even if they were to be so taken, they are entirely secondary and peripheral (9) to the primary theology of the Gospel which is revelation (202). The purpose of John 6:53–58 is to show contemporary Christians that it was in the eucharistic worship of the church that their faith in the word of God revealed in Jesus now found expression (144). Though John 1:29 was forged in an atmosphere of vicarious atonement and expiatory sacrifice, it was a liturgical formulation in the Johannine churches (163, 165).

In the end, "Jesus communicates his own divine and sinless life to men by the revelation of the word of God. This revelation culminates in his exaltation upon the cross" (165).

The Japanese scholar, Takashi Onuki, in his *Gemeinde und Welt im Johannesevangelium* (1984) was concerned with the nature of Johannine dualism. He argued, in criticism of many German scholars, that John's dualism resulted from his concept of revelation (and not vice versa, as in Gnosticism) and that this revelation culminated and was completed in the cross (a point he constantly stresses, e.g., 51, 59), and its true meaning revealed by the Spirit. This results in the founding of the church (58, 177) and is continued in the post-Easter preaching of the church (e.g., 51). The death of Jesus is the centre (Schwerpunkt) of the event of revelation and of the Johannine church's self-consciousness (59, 61–62, 210). The Passion Story is no mere appendix, but has constitutive significance for the Gospel of John and its portrait of Jesus, as it looked back from the vantage point of its Easter experience (205).

D. K. Regensberger, *Overcoming the World: Politics and Community in the Gospel of John* (1989), believed that John's Gospel was conceived as a Passion Gospel from the first, because there is an intimate connection in Johannine thought between the revelation of Jesus to the world and his Passion. "It is his revelation that leads to the Passion, and the Passion is the climax of his revelation" (76).

Josephine Massynbaerde Ford in her book, *Redeemer—Friend and Mother: Salvation in Antiquity and in the Gospel of John*, followed Forestell's approach and denied that salvation in John's Gospel was effected by Jesus' death seen as an expiatory sacrifice, but rather was effected through divine love (137, 175, 195). Jesus dies for his friends (John 15:1–15), and, like a woman, to give birth (so Ford takes John 16:16–24 and 19:34). Written from an avowedly feminist perspective, Ford seeks to find feminine texts in the Gospel which may appeal to women particularly, hence the stress on "mother" and "friend."

In her *"Er aber sprach vom Tempel seines Leibes."* (1998), Johanna Rahner works with the category of revelation as redemptive (e.g., 328). Jesus the Son is the place of God's presence mediating salvation and grace, and his life is definitively determined by his death (310). The willing surrender of his life is the real work of the Son (333). His death on the cross is the place of God's action which reveals salvation (338). The cross reveals not so much the unfathomable lostness of humanity but the unfathomable love of God for men and women (173). As the new place of God's presence, Jesus replaces the temple (309).

Cornelius Bennema's *The Power of Saving Wisdom: An Investigation of Spirit and Wisdom in relation to the Soteriology of the Fourth Gospel* (2002), is primarily concerned with how people are saved in the view of the Fourth Gospel, rather than specifically with the meaning of the cross/death of Jesus as such. Jesus' revelation contains saving wisdom, and this revelation culminates in the cross (177), which is the demonstration of God's love for the world (178–79). The Spirit enables men and women to understand this revelation, seen especially at the cross: he is the life-giving cognitive agent, and he brings about ethical renewal; he is also the affective agent (38). This spiritual understanding brings about the birth from above and the saving relationship with the Father and the Son (179–80). While Bennema believes that salvation was available before the cross, it is only available in the full Johannine sense after the cross (142–45), for the Spirit was not fully available before Jesus' glorification (195, 205, 212). The Spirit is a soteriological necessity (e.g., 150).

John Painter has written extensively on both the Fourth Gospel and the Johannine Epistles. In 2004, he contributed to the Festschrift for Johannes Beutler an essay germane to our theme: "Sacrifice and Atonement in the Gospel of John." Early on in his essay Painter remarks that insufficient attention had been given to the absence of overt atonement language in John (289) and that the category of sacrifice understood as an offering to God, in some sense, of the death of Jesus is not helpful for interpreting John (290). He immediately goes on to say that if atonement were used in the sense of overcoming the power of darkness, it could, however, be used fruitfully (290). Painter proceeds to examine various passages and finds nothing in John 1:29; 6:31–58; 10:11–18; or 11:51–52, to suggest that Jesus' death is seen as a sacrifice for sin. When he comes to 12:23–34, he significantly comments "The revelatory character of Jesus' work is quite critical for John's understanding of the mission and achievement of Jesus" (308). He believes that "lifting up" has overtones of revelation (309), and so in 8:28 and 12:32 the revelatory work of Jesus is portrayed as the light of God splitting the darkness (309–12). The death of Jesus, "in solidarity with and for humankind, has the power to enable the blind to see the reality of the love of God in the midst of the darkness and so to draw all people back to God" (309). The power of the uplifted Son is life-giving, and this was the purpose of the Father's sending him (308–9) It is the merit of Painter that he has linked the concept of revelation to that of overcoming the power of darkness.

3. Jesus' Death is the Return to the Father and the Establishment of Jesus as the Giver of Life

Since Jesus' death is the means of returning to the Father and of Jesus' enthronement, it establishes Jesus in his life-giving power. A. Vergote began his study "L'exaltation du Christ en Croix selon le quatrième Évangile," (1952), with the remark that the manifestation of Christ's divine glory on earth does not at first sight leave room for the passion and cross (5), whereas, in primitive Christianity, God glorified Jesus after his passion (6). Vergote maintains that on earth he only disposed his life-giving efficacy imperfectly; the elevation of Christ on the cross, in establishing him in the divine region which is his own, invested him with new spiritual power (7, 12, 22). Thus, John's theology of the cross perfects the theology of incarnation and revelation (23). The cross has fundamentally the same significance as the ascension and so establishes Christ in the fullness of his life-giving divinity (12. John 3:14–15).

C. H. Dodd, whose mature reflections on the Fourth Gospel were set forth in *The Interpretation of the Fourth Gospel* (1953), believed that for John Jesus' life "expresses the eternal thought of God, the meaning of the universe" (284). "Jesus gave to His disciples 'words of eternal life,' and they were born again" (284). However, Dodd clearly believed that Jesus' death and resurrection are seen by John as an integral part of the revelation. In a Platonising expression, he says that "in one single area of the universe of space and time phenomena have completely absorbed the reality of the eternal archetype, and . . . this area is coextensive with the life, death and resurrection of Jesus Christ" (295).

It is through death that Christ brings life to the world (339 on John 6:51; 360 on John 10:11, 14). Dodd uses the phrase "self sacrifice" of Jesus' death on the cross (360, 368, 373) or "self oblation" (402–3, 419), but it is clear that he does not have in mind the concept of expiatory sacrifice (e.g., 233, 236–38 on John 1:29; 233 on 11:50–52).

For Dodd, it is only through Jesus' actual death and resurrection that the life he brings is liberated for the life of the world (423). The love of God, released in history in the incarnate ministry, is perpetuated by the Son's return to the Father for disciples, and draws them "into the same unity of which the relation of Father and Son is the eternal archetype" (262, 379–79; cf. 418–19). By his return to the Father through death, Christ draws men and women into the sphere of eternal life which is union with God (419).

J. Blank, *Krisis Untersuchungen zur Johanneischen Christologie und Eschatologie* (1964), sees Jesus' death as both an end and completion, but equally as laying the foundation for his work to be open to the future. One can, therefore, never speak of a past of the event of eschatological revelation, Jesus Christ (280). Jesus' death is the beginning of his glorification. He has become the dispenser of eschatological life and mediator of salvation because he is not a dead person but the Living One (281).

In Christ, as the exalted one, the cross is abidingly present because the Exalted One is for all eternity the Crucified One and the Crucified One is the Exalted One. For Blank, the concept of lifting up serves the Johannine theology of actualizing: it makes present the cross as the abiding reality of the saving event.

In 1973, J. Riedl, *Das Heilswerk Jesu nach Johannes*, maintained that Jesus' history has entered into the divine transcendence of history in the Being of the Father (21). The time of Jesus' history has flowed once for all into the time of the sea of the Son of God's eternity (31, 150, 187, 414). Since Easter, the exalted Lord actualizes the past event of Jesus in and through his church in the power of his Spirit in word, Scripture and preaching (31, 187, 410, 423). It is the event of lifting up which bestows the character of what is abiding, final, definitive on the Christ-event (37). The Christ-event is the End event because in the cross and resurrection of Jesus the world has come to its end (38). The incarnate, crucified, and glorified is one (28). He has no future (163, 182). Jesus' earthly work has become the eschatological event through the hour of glorification (303, 376–77).

E. Ruckstuhl[5] contributed an essay "Abstieg und Erhöhung des johanneischen Menschensohns" to the Festschrift for Anton Vögtle (*Jesus und der Menschensohn*, 1975). The Son of Man descends to fulfill his unique task as revealer of the End Time (329, 335). He completes this revelation in the hour of his lifting up and glorification. It is God's will that the Son of Man should win the power to dispense life through his lifting up (330). The crucified One is the permanent presence and source of life, having been installed through the lifting up into the office of dispenser of eschatological life (331–33. John 3:14). Salvation proceeds from, and is linked with, the cross. Indeed, Ruckstuhl declares that no

---

5. He earlier had argued on stylistic grounds for the unity of the Fourth Gospel in *Die literarische Einheit des Johannesevangeliums* (1951).

Christian preacher or theologian before him, not even Paul, interpreted the saving meaning and power of Jesus' death on the cross as John did.

In his massive study of the Prologue of John's Gospel and its relation to the rest of the Gospel and to 1 John, *Die Fleischwerdung des Logos* (1988), M. Theobald makes sufficient statements to place him in this category. Jesus is the Word come from the Father as his envoy, reveals him (e.g., 388), and then ascends back to him. The cross is the saving completion of his work and his installation in lordship in heaven, while believers can receive a share in divine life by sharing in the destiny of the Son of Man (383–85). Faith sees, below the surface of Jesus' end on the cross, the real saving event (386). In his subsequent work, H*errenworte im Johannesevangelium* (2002), Theobald again referred to the death of Jesus as the decisive event of salvation in which God has involved himself for men and women and has opened up the way to life for them (588–89), for Jesus' death is his going to the Father (*als Hingang zum Vater* [italics in the original], 613) and this opens up the way to heaven and bestows the prospect of life (219).

K. Grayston published *Dying, We Live: A New Enquiry into the Death of Christ in the New Testament* in 1990. He maintained that in John God gave his Son that he should descend with illumination, sustenance, and life, and ascend by means of the cross to prepare a way for believers who are in him (294). The death of Jesus is not fortuitous or peripheral to his revealing work (301). It was necessary to complete his work (304). Through his death and ascension, death will no longer have the power to hinder life (309–10). The death of Jesus is his cessation of life and its resumption in heaven, thus making eternal life possible for believers (322). The descent of the Son of Man disclosed the possibility of eternal life and his subsequent ascent guaranteed possession of it (356). Thus far, Grayston might be classified with a salvation-by-revelation category, which the return to the Father perpetuates. But he goes further in actual fact, and believes that after baptism, subsequent sins committed by Christians can be forgiven through the blood of Christ (312), while he takes John 1:29 to mean that Christ removes the practice of sinning.

We have already mentioned F. Voulga in our first category. In addition to the revelation through incarnation, Voulga mentioned that in John's Gospel Jesus is the forerunner and redeemer, since his return to the Father has opened the way to heaven (336).

Into this category, we should also place D. F. Gniesmer, *In den Prozetz verwickelt. Erzähltextanalytische und pragmatische Erwägungungen zur Erzählung vom Prozetz Jesu vor Pilatus (Joh 18,28; 19,16a.b)*, which came out in 2000. He asserts that to speak of a Johannine theology of the cross is problematic and he sides with U. B. Müller (8, 25) against T. Knöppler (see below pp. 31–32) who defended the view that John attributes atoning value to the cross. The death of Jesus is more than a transition stage. Jesus' death is the confirmation of his commission and the demonstration of that unsurpassable love which gives its life for his own (John 15:13). It means that the gift of love and of the life which overcomes death is possible for the first time. The death stands *pars pro toto* for the whole of Jesus' sending—hence saving significance is attributed to it (183–94, esp. 193).

4. Jesus' Death as His Victorious Return to the Father

Although E. Käsemann, ever a provocative figure in New Testament scholarship, challenged his teacher Bultmann's approach to the Fourth Gospel in his *The Testament of Jesus* (the English translation appeared in 1968, two years after the German original), he remained with the basic position of salvation by revelation (e.g., "Jesus has no other function and authority apart from being the revealer of God . . . Jesus is nothing but the revealer . . . the only revealer of God," 11).

Käsemann argued that the center of Johannine theology was not "the Word became flesh" but "we beheld his glory" (9–10). In John, the glory of Jesus determines his whole presentation so thoroughly from the very outset that the incorporation and position of the passion narratives becomes problematical (7). (There is no humiliation followed by glorification in John.) The hour of the passion is for John the hour of Jesus' glorification because in it he leaves the world and returns to the Father (18, 20). The incarnation and the passion indicate the change of space—and thus, the scope—of the manifestation of Christ (20). The passion must be described in John as a triumphal procession, not a *via dolorosa* (18). "This cross is no longer the pillory, the tree of shame, on which hangs the one who had become the companion of thieves. His death is rather the manifestation of divine self-giving love and his victorious return from the alien realm below to the Father who had sent him." (10).

Jesus' obedience is the result of his glory and attests that glory in the situation of the earthly conflict (19).

Believers are friends of Jesus, sanctified through the Word (28). "The church is basically and exclusively the fellowship of people who hear Jesus' word and believe in him; in short, it is the community under the Word" (40). The heavenly Christ is still accessible but only in his Word (46). When the community under the Word confesses the divinity of Jesus, it has eternal life (55).

There is a slight lacunae in Käsemann's presentation because he does say that Jesus' death is "the manifestation of divine self-giving love" as well as his victorious return to the Father (20), but he never develops the former idea at all.

As is to be expected, Käsemann's influence is discernible in the work of his pupil, Mark L. Appold, whose work *The Oneness Motif in the Fourth Gospel* appeared in 1976. He argued that in John the cross is not a tragic catastrophe but Jesus' exaltation, ascent, and elevation to victory and glory—a confirmation of his oneness with the Father. Jesus' death does not represent the center of John's Gospel: his glory determines the meaning of the cross, and not vice versa (119). He denies that texts expressing vicarious atonement can be said to be a constitutive or central factor in John's proclamation—they remain distinctly on the fringe and peripheral (121 n.3, 194, 273). Jesus is the Sovereign Lord who is actively in control and determines his own death. The cross is the victorious action of a sovereign Jesus who returns to the heavenly world of glory. Death is understood as departure (273). Man's integration into the heavenly oneness of the Father and the Son constitutes the saving event (the oneness motif provides a theological abbreviation for soteriology, 284–86).

The New Zealand scholar, G. C. Nicholson, in *Death as Departure: The Johannine Descent-Ascent Schema* (1983), argued that the primary reference in the lifting up passages is the lifting up to heaven (which takes place by means of the crucifixion, 75–144). He takes John 12:33 as concerned with what kind of death is allowed for by talk of lifting up (136–37). The crucifixion receives its meaning by being understood as part of a larger schema of descent–ascent: the death is not ignominious but a return to glory (143–44, 163). John 13:1 should be used as the key to the hour passages. Basically, Jesus' death is his return to the Father. Jesus came to return rather than to die (167). It is clear that Nicholson is somewhat uncomfortable with Johannine Christology and soteriology (e.g., 165–66).

Käsemann's approach drew a critical response from G. Bornkamm in a review article published in *Evangelische Theologie* in 1968. It was translated by J. Ashton as "Towards the Interpretation of John's Gospel" in the collection of essays on John edited by Ashton, *The Interpretation of John* (1986).[6] Bornkamm denies that the passion story must have been an embarrassment to John (88). The Johannine picture of Christ is not in the first place grounded in the earthly Jesus but upon him who died on the cross (88). Any use of glory language prior to this is used in retrospect (88). Bornkamm defends his criticism by referring to the "hour" passages (John 2:3 (sic); 7:30; 8:20; 12:23; 13:1; 17:1) and to 2:13–22; 3:12–15; 6:62–63; 12:32–33 (lifting up and ascent). These allusions become clearer with the Shepherd Discourse, the raising of Lazarus, the anointing, and the saying at 12:24–25.

Käsemann maintains that there is no real antithesis between the earthly Jesus and the Jesus exalted on the cross (96) and alleges that "Bornkamm's statistics might seem rather to support me than to tell against me" (96) and maintains that none of these passages goes anywhere towards a theology of the cross (97).

Ashton felt that at some points Käsemann ought to be criticized, and he enunciated these in his work already referred to, *Understanding the Fourth Gospel*. The passion story is not a mere postscript, but the evangelist has made deliberate connections and allusions between chapters 1–17 and 18–20 (487). John's passion story "has been deliberately and skillfully integrated with the book of signs" (488). At the same time, he also felt that Käsemann's case "can be made even stronger" (487). John's vocabulary of Jesus' death seems to emphasize the reascent of the Son of Man to his true home in heaven (490–501). Later he says that death is conceived as departure (ὑπάγειν), exaltation (ὑψοῦν) or ascent (ἀναβαίνειν)" (546–47).

5. Jesus' Death as both Revelation and Atonement

(A) Despite the enormous influence of Bultmann, there has been still a large number of scholars, both Protestant and Catholic, who were prepared to maintain that the concept of Jesus' death on the cross as an *atoning sacrifice* was not foreign or marginal to John's thought.

---

6. At the end of the article, some notes by Käsemann, in response to Bornkamm, from the 3rd German edition of *Jesu Letzter Wille* (1971) were included.

F. Mussner, *ZΩH. Die Anschauung vom "Leben" im vierten Evangelium unter Berücksichtigung der Johannesbriefe* (1952), maintained that the incarnation is the essential presupposition for the accomplishment of the divine work of salvation, namely the death of Jesus which is the ontological ground of salvation (86, 110). While revelation and revealer are united in Jesus' being as Logos and his words are life-giving truth (100), his sacrificial death is the climax of his saving activity in this world of death. The giving up of flesh and blood in a bloody sacrifice makes the incarnate Logos into the Savior of the world (111). God wills a connection between Jesus' death and his gift of life (106).

In an influential article "Joh 6:51c—ein Schlüssel zur grotzen johanneischen Brotrede," which appeared in 1958, H. Schürman also expressed similar notions about the relationship between incarnation and cross (256). He argued that 6:51c links the universal giving of life to Jesus' sacrifice in death (259). The flesh to be eaten is given in death and the blood to be drunk is shed in death (261).

The early sixties were to see two challenges to Bultmann's position. W. Thüsing wrote *Die Erhöhung und Verherrlichung Jesu im Johannesevangelium* (1960).[7] He asserted that Jesus' death is central for salvation in John (289). It has atoning power (see, e.g., his discussion of John 19:34 on 167–68)—there is no eternal life without atonement (171, 174). Indeed, there is no saving significance of Jesus' earthly work as revealer when separated from his exaltation and glorification (164). The Spirit glorifies Jesus when he witnesses to and actualizes the saving significance of Jesus' death (174). More will be said on Thüsing's important work.

T. Müller's *Das Heilsgeschechen im Johannesevangelium*, 1961, bore the sub-title *Eine exegetische Studie, zugleich der Versuch einer Antwort an Rudolf Bultmann*. He argued that in John there was teaching on the atonement as well as revelation, and that a synthesis between the two was possible. Müller stressed the *extra nos* and *pro nobis* features of texts like John 1:29; 3:14–15; 10:11, 15; 11:50; 12:24, 31–32; 13:8; 16:33; 17:17, 19—see 38–75). Though there is no imposingly consistent presentation of the significance of Jesus' death in John, it does stand at the centre of salvation (73). The sacrifice on the cross has atoning significance and

---

7. A second edition appeared in 1970 which slightly altered the arrangement of material and added a fifth section entitled "On Newer Discussion: Reply and Correction," and a third edition in 1979 which added a small appendix.

secures victory over evil (114) and completes the revelation given in the ministry (132). The cross is in the true sense the unique saving event whose validity demands a decision from us (139).

George B. Caird set out his thinking in two articles: "Judgment and Salvation: An Exposition of John 12:31–32," and "The Will of God: In the Fourth Gospel."[8] Caird sees the saving will of God unfolding in three stages in John. Firstly, the man Jesus lives in unity with God—which is his glory. He reveals God's will to save, to take manhood into unity with the divine Logos (*ExT*, 115–16). This revelation arouses opposition and leaves Jesus alone with the Father (*CJT*, 233–34). Secondly, in the cross Jesus identifies himself with mankind in their sin and accepts for himself their condemnation and death. Because of this, the cross is the defeat of Satan. Mankind, released from Satan's power, is drawn into a unity with Jesus and, therefore, with the Father. At the cross, then, Jesus becomes representative man (*CJT*, 234–35; *ExT*, 116). Thirdly, after the cross, the Spirit and the disciples bear witness to what Jesus has already done: what exists as a divine achievement on the cross must also become a human experience (*CJT*, 235; *ExT*, 117).

Caird's posthumously published *New Testament Theology* (1995), touches briefly on these themes (79–80, 149–50). Caird was a pupil of W. D. Cadman and had edited his teacher's *The Open Heaven: The Revelation of God in the Johannine Sayings of Jesus* (1969), in which the same sort of approach is revealed. Caird says of Cadman "From him we learnt that the Cross was as central to the theology of St. John as to that of St. Paul" (viii).

J. Blank, *Krisis: Untersuchungen zur Johanneischen Christologie und Eschatologie* (1964), while speaking of the revelatory significance of Jesus Christ (e.g., 64, 68, 70, 114, 118–19, 216, 231–51—"Jesus himself as Son is the divine revelation," 114), also stresses that the cross is the divine event of revelation and salvation for John (84) and has definitive saving character (84). He refers to it as the "saving death" (138), though stressing that Jesus' death, glorification, return to the Father together make up "the hour of the saving event" (139). Blank described the lifting up of John 12:32 as the objective expression of God's *prius* of grace. "In the lifting up of the Son of Man, God Himself has, objectively and independently of any subsequent human decision, decided for the salvation and

8. These appeared in the *Canadian Journal for Theology* 2 (1956) 231–37 and the *Expository Times* 74 (1960–61) 115–17 respectively.

rescue of the world" (289; cf. 290). Jesus' death is the essential event in the gathering of a saved community (292).

R. Schackenburg's monumental commentary, *The Gospel according to St. John* stretched over three volumes.[9] He devoted several pages to the doctrine of salvation in his introduction (1:156–59). Jesus as the Word Incarnate unites the two worlds of darkness and of God to each other by his descent and ascent, to make the same way possible for believers (157). Schnackenburg sees John 1:18 as an addition by the evangelist to a hymn, and in this verse the evangelist stresses Jesus' action as revealer who speaks with authority because of his unique relation to God. The evangelist prepares the way for the revelation discourse of Jesus.

The power of the forces hostile to God is broken on the cross (1:157 on John 12:31–32; 16:33). Older thought of vicarious expiation is retained and incorporated (e.g., 6:51c). The incarnation makes the sacrifice of the cross possible (1:157). That the thought of expiatory sacrifice was genuinely part of Johannine theology is shown by John 1:29 (1:158). Faith means not only an existential decision at the summons of the revealer but also and above all union with him as the bringer of salvation, following him as the guide to, and mediator of, salvation (1:159).

In Volume 2, Schnackenburg devoted an important excursus to "The Exaltation and Glorification of Jesus" (2:398–410). The cross is the climax of Jesus' saving activity (2:403). The Johannine view removes the *scandalum crucis* by a process of theological reflection which regards what happened on the cross as the glorification of God or the ascent of Jesus into his glory and the beginning of his saving rule. John transforms the terrible end of Jesus' life into a dazzling success and victory, though admittedly only for the eyes of believers. Apparent humiliation is already exaltation, and the outward degradation of Jesus in reality is his glorification (2:408). In 4th Teil (111–15), Schackenburg compared different perspectives on the cross in Paul and John. He asserted that John overcomes the scandal of the cross and yet also holds fast to it insofar as only believers understand the deeper meaning of Jesus' lifting up (4:112). In John, the Logos has entered the earthly, transitory, and valueless sphere

9. The German edition, *Das Johannesevangelium*, Teile 1, 2, and 3, appeared in the HTKNT 4:1–3. Herder: Freiburg-Basel-Wien, in 1965, 1971 and 1975 resp. The first two volumes appeared in English translation published London: Burns & Oates, 1968 and 1980 resp. The third volume was published New York: Crossroad, 1982. A 4th Teil has appeared in German—*Ergänzende Auslegungen und Exkurse*, Freiburg-Basel-Wien: Herder, 1984.

and in the man Jesus can bestow life on humanity separated from God (4:113). The passion is the unavoidable event in the divine ordering of salvation (4:114).

Barnabas Lindars followed up his *The Gospel of John* (1972), in which he had asserted the centrality of the cross (1) and argued for a deliberate choice of "Lamb of God" in John 1:29 to point to Jesus' vocation to an atoning death (109), with "The Passion in the Fourth Gospel," a contribution to the Festschrift for N .A. Dahl, entitled *God's Christ and His People* (1977). He maintained that the sacrificial interpretation of Jesus' death, "although it is a secondary issue, . . . is not wholly unintegrated into his thought, and it is unsafe to try and excise it as due to the hand of a redactor" (72–73).

A little earlier than his WBC commentary on *John* (1987), George R. Beasley-Murray contributed an essay "John 12:31–34, The Eschatological Significance of the Lifting Up of the Son of Man," in *Studien zum Text und zur Ethik des Neuen Testaments* (which was the Festschrift for H. Greeven, piublished in 1986). He stated that "the sentence of judgment passed on this world is endured by the One Whom this world murders—the Son of Man" (74)—a clear indication that for him the cross is an atoning,

B. H. Rigsby published "The Cross as an Expiatory Sacrifice in the Fourth Gospel," in 1982. He also believed that "there appears to be ample room in the evangelist's Passover theology for both revelatory and expiatory themes" (53) and maintained that even if the exact relationship between Christ's death and the elimination of sin is not explicit, that death has the same decisive importance as elsewhere in the NT (63).

The American scholar, Marianne M. Thompson, *The Humanity of Jesus in the Fourth Gospel* (1988), sought to rebut Käsemann's charge that in John's picture of Jesus his divinity has completely swamped his humanity. She argues that for the fourth evangelist Jesus' heavenly and earthly origins are not mutually exclusive and that the death of Jesus is not an ill-fitting addendum but is the fitting climax of the ministry on earth of one who "became flesh." The death of Jesus is saving, revelatory, and exemplary (remarks on the footwashing on 102). "Although the benefits of Jesus' ministry and death can be viewed as identical (cf. e.g., 13:10; 15:3), nevertheless, Jesus' death is necessary to insure those benefits (13:8)" (103. See further 111–15).

In 1990, Max B. Turner published an article entitled "Atonement and the Death of Jesus in John—Some Questions to Bultmann and Forestell." Turner concentrated on these two scholars, presumably because Bultmann denied any soteriological significance to the death of Jesus in John, while Forestell argued that the cross was the supreme revelation of God's love and that this was its saving significance. After outlining the views of Bultmann and Forestell (100–113), Turner turns to his response. He believes that a combination of the cross as an objective atoning event and as redemptive revelation offer a more coherent explanation of the place of the cross in John than the focus entirely on the latter by Forestell. He maintains that Jesus' dying for the sake of others would be part of the presuppositions shared by reader and author (118), and that the ὑπέρ texts together with John 1:29, whose background is to be seen in Isaiah 53 (119–21), are the basis for believing that John held to the traditional concept of objective atonement in the cross.

Donald A. Carson in his commentary, *The Gospel according to John* (1991), also believed that the Fourth Gospel demands a both/and approach as regards the issue of salvation by revelation and redemption (97, 152–53).

Dorothy A. Lee in her book, *The Symbolic Narratives of the Fourth Gospel: The Interplay of Form and Meaning* (1994), while arguing strongly that for the evangelist in the incarnation, material reality (σα ρξ) is capable of bearing and disclosing the divine—because σάρξ and πνεῦμα are bound together (e.g., 159–60)—nonetheless asserted that in the end eternal life can only be given at the cost of the life of Jesus (54, 149–50, 225).

Otfried Hofius, in a book of essays written by himself and Hans-Christian Kammler entitled *Johannesstudien: Untersuchungen zur Theologie des vierten Evangeliums* (1996), also believes that the Fourth Gospel presents both Jesus as revealer—the absoluteness of his revelation being grounded in his divine nature and being (e.g., 24, 31)—and also the saving significance of Jesus' death (see 63 especially).

In a study of sin entitled *Das Verständnis der Sünde im Johannesevangelium* (2000), R. Metzner maintained that for John the concepts of representation, atonement and forgiveness of sins on the one hand and revelation and mediation of the new life through faith were not mutually exclusive but complementary matters in the evangelist's understanding of salvation (10); that the saving will of God was fulfilled in the cross (79, referring to John 4:34 and 19:30) and that the removal of sin takes place *extra nos* through the atoning death of Jesus on the cross (22, 111).

The American scholar, C. R. Koester, *Symbolism in the Fourth Gospel: Meaning, Mystery, Community* (2nd ed., 2003), combined revelation and redemption ideas in his understanding of the fourth evangelist's approach to the cross, though probably the weight falls on the former for him. He can state that Jesus' "death brings cleansing and atonement" (217), but more often we come across statements like "through his crucifixion, Jesus reveals the glory of the love of God that gives life to the world" (117).[10] Actually, Koester brings together the two ideas when he asserts that "if sin is estrangement from God, it is 'taken away' when it is replaced by faith, and faith is evoked by the love of God that is revealed through the crucifixion of Jesus" (245; cf. 133, 182, 205, 221, 224). So, for Koester "Divine love is the center around which the varied dimensions of meaning of the crucifixion revolve" (244).

In her massive monograph, *Die Herrlichkeit des Verherrlichten. Das Verständnis der δόξα im Johannesevangelium* (2007), Nicole Chibici-Revneanu's major concern is John's use of δόξα and δοξάζεσθαι. As she examines these terms in great detail, she maintains that they show that John links salvation and revelation together (e.g., 69, 73, 78, 268, 274). The passage John 1:12–14 indicates this close link between salvation and revelation, and that the self-mediation of the Logos in the incarnation is already represented under the soteriological outline of 1:12–13 (69). The revelation is the basis of the knowledge of God (307) and aims at taking men and women into the relationship which exists between the Father and the Son (276): thus salvation is less a possession and much more relational (562). John's idea of revelation is strongly impressed by his soteriology (557) and acceptance of it brings salvation/eternal life (558, 560, 571). In discussing the Cana miracle, she states that we find the thought that it will be first with the death of Jesus that the fullness of salvation will become accessible (82). And in a long footnote extending over two pages (609–10, note 351), in which she discusses whether atonement ideas are to be found in John, she states that John takes over atonement ideas but modifies them. A few aspects of atonement theology (new life, freedom from sin, renewed fellowship with God) are very important to

10. Similar statements can be found on 125, 133-34, 172, 184, 205-6, 237-38, 245, 264.

John, but others (like the regular accomplishment of sacrifice) clearly recede (610, note 351). It fits in with her stress on the relational aspect of salvation that for her the major stress in John's soteriology is the gathering of a community united to Jesus and through him with God (173 [here, in note 382, she quotes Bultmann, *John*, 424, to the same effect with approval], 176, 181, 575, 600, 603, 610, 619).

Within this section 5, it is necessary to mention the application of redaction criticism to the fourth gospel and the attempts to separate tradition and redaction, with the consequent assignment of an atonement interpretation of the cross to different stages in the development of the Johannine tradition. Of course, scholars have been seeking to disentangle the sources of the fourth evangelist for a considerable while. Bultmann was himself an example of this—he postulated a discourse source and a signs source, both of which the evangelist quarried and adapted, a passion narrative, plus an ecclesiastical redactor (John 3:5; 6:51–58; 19:34b). After the works of Conzelmann on Luke (1954), W. Marxsen on Mark (1956) and Bornkamm, Barth, and Held on Matthew (1960), however, the term redaction criticism seemed to enter scholars' vocabulary and to be applied to the Fourth Gospel also.[11]

The application of its techniques to the Fourth Gospel has produced very varying results in terms of what was tradition and what was redaction and at what stage the "evangelist" was to be placed. Here we shall review some contributions and their relevance to our study on the significance of the cross in Johannine thought.

W. Wilkens published *Die Entstehungsgeschichte des vierten Evangeliums* (1958), following it up a decade later with *Zeichen und Werke* (1969). In the first volume, he argued for a *Grundevangelium*, a sign gospel, expanded by the addition of the speeches, and finally revised (by means of references to the Passover at John 2:13; 6:4; 11:55 plus the cleansing of the Temple, the Eucharistic speech, the anointing at Bethany and 19:31–37) into a passion gospel (in dispute with gnosticism). In this final shape "The cross of Jesus is the centre of the Gospel" (171).

Wilkens adhered to this theory of development in his second volume, but concentrated on working out the theological emphases in the signs and speech sections of the Gospel. Irrespective of the correctness

---

11. E.g., The comment of Fortna, *Gospel of Signs*, ix, "This study is occasioned by the recent emergence of Redaktionsgeschichte as a method of Gospel research."

of his reconstruction of the rise of the Gospel, we may note that he makes certain assertions about the place of Jesus' death in the theology of the evangelist.

In his second volume, Wilkens maintained that the thought of representation (*der Stellvertretungsgedenke*) is expressly set forth in John 11:47–53 (52, 72, 79): Jesus' death is fundamental for the event of salvation (52, 72). On 19:31–39, he says "It will again be clear here that the cross is the culminating point of Johannine theology" (75). Jesus is the passover Lamb of the End Time, the atoning sacrifice for the sins of the world (79).

In the speeches, the lifting up and the glorification of Jesus are accomplished through Jesus' death on the cross but are not identical with his death (104). His death is his return to the Father (105, 145). The cross stands at the point of intersection between two periods of Jesus' work (105). The saving meaning of the cross lies in making his coming to his own possible in the sending of the Paraclete (109). The saving significance of Jesus' death is not in his death *per se*, but in Jesus' lifting up and glorification (112, 145, 155). Ecclesiology is linked to the saving event of the cross (159, commenting on John 12:24–25; 15; 17).

Thus, while the cross remains central for the evangelist[12] throughout the development of his work, different nuances emerge. Wilkens has no problem in attributing the new interpretation to the same author.

Sadly, G. Richter's premature death robbed us of many contributions, but he had published a monograph on the foot washing plus several articles. The latter were gathered together and edited posthumously in *Studien zum Johannesevangelium*, by J. Hainz in 1977, and these indicate Richter's approach. He believed that the Fourth Gospel in its present shape was the result of a lengthy process to which many hands contributed. He detected a christological-soteriological explanation of Jesus' death on the cross in the Fourth Gospel. Through giving up his life on the cross, Jesus effects salvation through the will of the Father. In fact, salvation can only be effected through the cross—a belief set forth symbolically in the foot washing as a bath which makes any further religious purification superfluous (293). The death of the Messiah is a saving death. In the cross, too, the Father is glorified because of the Son's

---

12. Olsson, *Structure and Meaning,* 66, signified his agreement with Wilkens' position: "The concentration on Jesus' death at Golgotha is rightly stressed by Wilkens 1969, passim."

obedience and love and because of the redemption worked by the cross (62). John wrote to strengthen faith in Jesus as Messiah and Son of God, a faith threatened by the fact that Jesus died on the cross (John 12:34).

The paraenetic interest in Jesus' death on the cross belongs to a later hand, in fact, the author of 1 John, (72–73): the community must imitate Jesus' act of love on the cross (62–64). Richter also attributed John 6:51c–58 to a later hand, challenging Borgen's attempt to defend the unity of 6:31–58 on the basis of a synagogue homiletical pattern. So, Richter does detect a redemptive understanding of Jesus' death, present from an early stage, within the Johannine churches.

J. Becker went in a different direction from Richter and took up an approach akin to Bultmann, in his *Das Evangelium des Johannes* (2 volumes, 1979, 1981). Volume 2 contained an excursus on "The Significance of Jesus' Death in John." Jesus' death, as the point of transition in the return to the Father, is not the abiding place of revelation (2:402). The exaltation as the conclusion of the sending is the real, abiding ground of redemption (2:403). The Son sent by the Father out of love enters the diabolical realm of darkness and death and brings divine life (2:403), though unbelief sees only a usual human life (2:404). In the dualism of John's Gospel, the world of death can only be offered life if a stranger comes to it. The Son's revelation creates the possibility of salvation (2:405). In his passion, Jesus demonstrates the nothingness of death (2:406 commenting on John 14:31 and 19:30).

A church redactor added traditional explanations of Jesus' death as vicarious for others (John 1:29; 6:51c; 10:11, 15; 11:51–52; 15:13; 17:19) and as a model of sacrifice for others which the church should follow (2.407 discussing 13:14–15; 15:13–14).

Becker sees in John's interpretation a far-reaching obliteration of earthly reality and a deterministic devaluation of history and creation.

Although E. Haenchen did not live to complete his commentary, his work was sufficiently far advanced to be edited by U. Busse for publication in 1980, and translated *A Commentary on the Gospel of John*, in 2 volumes in 1984. Haenchen followed Bultmann in distinguishing between sources used by the evangelist (to which e.g., he ascribed John 1:29); the evangelist; and a later redactor (to whom e.g., 3:5; 6:51b–58; 11:51 are attributed). The hour of the cross was the central event for the evangelist opening up the way to the Father (1:178–79).

Haenchen sees the foot washing as having great significance for the evangelist—it is the great token of love (2:105), "last and conclusive proof of Christ's love," "an anticipation of the cross," and "it expresses the meaning of the cross graphically as a deed of Jesus" (2:106–8). When Jesus goes to the cross, there is a victory of divine love (2:98). Haenchen dismisses the "all" of 12:32 as an error—Jesus only draws those given him by the Father—and he goes on to interpret this verse in an individualistic manner: the evangelist has now lost his fear of the lord of this world and his power; he has, therefore, lost his fear in the face of his own anxiety and despair, and in the face of injustice and suffering perpetrated on him, and is able willingly to say Yes to martyrdom (2:98).

Haenchen alleges that the redactor misunderstood the heart of the evangelist's proclamation and actually contradicted it by his introduction of references to the sacraments (1:299). He wanted a much more palpable connection with Jesus in the present (1:298). As the redactor conceived it, Jesus' flesh was sacrificed on the cross for the life and salvation of the world, but now men and women need to get a share in Jesus' redemptive flesh (1:299).

Thus, both Becker and Haenchen see conflicting theologies present within the Fourth Gospel. So far as I can see, neither of them addresses the question why a redactor allowed such conflicting passages to stand if he were actually setting out to correct them? Why not eliminate them altogether or start *de novo*?

We have already referred to the work of M. Theobald, *Die Fleischwerdung des Logos*. In his discussion of how what he calls an original "archaic" opening of the Gospel story, namely Jesus' baptism, has been transformed into a witness by John the Baptist to Jesus, Theobald argues that an original tradition consisted of John 1:29a, 30 (without the ὅτι clause), and 33, to which a redactor added vv. 29cd, 31b, 32, and 34. Theobald argues that 1:29cd interprets Jesus' death as an atonement for sins (276, 281) and forms an inclusion with the death of Jesus at the end of the Gospel. In other words, the atonement theology of the cross is the work of the redactor.

Martinus C. de Boer, *Johannine Perspectives on the Death of Jesus* (1996), believes that the Fourth Gospel reflects the story of Johannine Christianity. The Gospel is a result of a long process of composition which reflects four phases, namely before the first crisis, and then successively three crises. John Phase I consisted of miracles stories plus passion and resurrection. No saving significance is attributed to the death of Jesus, and it is "explained" by the OT quotations (83–95). John Phase II (following expulsion from the synagogue, the first crisis for the community) incorporated the discourse material. Jesus' death is the end of his earthly sojourn, whence he returns to the Father through resurrection and ascension (97–145). John Phase III (after martyrdoms, the second crisis), through using the Son of Man sayings, incorporates Jesus' death into the process of glorification (147–217). John Phase IV (after the schism, the last of the three crises), with the Epistles, stressed Jesus' sacrificial death (219–309). There is no one single theology of Jesus' death in the Gospel; nor is there any synthesis (311–15).

In 2004 a massive treatment of the death of Jesus appeared from H-U. Weidemann, a student of M. Theobald, entitled *Der Tod Jesu im Johannesevangelium: Die erste Abschiedsrede als Schlüssel für den Passions- und Osterbericht.* As the subtitle suggests, Weidemann saw the first farewell discourse (John 13:31—14:31) as offering a commentary or instructions to the reader how to read and understand the story of the passion and Easter. Especially he emphasized John 14:29 in this respect. His work analyzes John 13:31—14:31 and 18–20. He sees John 15–17 plus the passages about the Beloved Disciple, and of course 21, as later additions to the work by a redactor, who, however, recognized the importance of what the first farewell discourse was trying to do and, therefore, retained 14:30-31. It is because he distinguishes between a first form of the Gospel and a later enlarged form that we are placing Weidemann in the present category. In terms of a theology of the passion, Weidemann emphasizes what he calls the satanological and the pneumatological—new creation aspects of John's understanding of the cross. He believes (as revealed especially in his interpretation of 19:34b) that John on the one hand sees Jesus as the true Passover Lamb, whose blood wards off and defeats Satan and creates a sphere in which believers are protected, while, on the other hand, there comes from the crucified one the Spirit who effects the eschatological new creation. While not unique in pointing out the defeat of Satan as an important part of John's theology, Weidemann certainly stands out from other exegetes in the prominence which he gives to it and the way in which he uses the apotropaic effect of the Passover Lamb's blood in Exod 12 and subsequent Jewish interpretation.

It ought, of course, to be pointed out that many scholars seek to make sense of the Gospel as it stands in its present form and believe that it does make good sense Among commentators we might mention C. K. Barrett, *The Gospel according to St. John* (2nd ed., 1978);[13] Raymond E. Brown, *The Gospel according to John* (2 vols. in 1966 and 1971); Rudolf Schackenburg, *The Gospel according to St. John* (3 vols. 1968, 1980, and 1982); Barnabas Lindars, *The Gospel of John* (1972); and George R. Beasley-Murray, *John* (1987); not to mention many writers of monographs who adopt this position, from among whom C. H. Dodd's classic statement may be quoted: "I conceive it to be the duty of an interpreter at least to see what can be done with the document as it has come down to us" (*Interpretation*, 290).

6. Does John have a Two-Stage Glorification?

We have already mentioned the work of W. Thüsing. Here we need to mention a distinctive section of his work. Part II (by far the longest part, 41–253) deals with the glorification of Jesus. Thüsing believes that the evangelist sees two stages to this. The first stage comprises up to and including the hour. This is Jesus' work on earth which is completed by death (45–46, 48–49, 71–72). The earthly revelation is accomplished in the culmination of Jesus' death on the cross (100, 226). The cross, therefore, has a special place in "stage one" (75, 100). The second stage stems from the hour, i.e., it is the period after the cross. The Paraclete enables the effects of the lifting up to be brought about (97–154)—in "fruit bearing" (101, 105–7, 117–22, 141) and in the loving unity among believers (124–26).

In the second edition, Thüsing vigorously defended this two-stage idea against the criticism of especially J. Blank (cf. 201–5). He maintained that John does differentiate between "not yet glorified" and "glorified" (311–12 commenting on John 7:19 and 12:23) and claimed the support of Schackenburg's exegesis of 12:28 for the two-stage idea (313). He felt that it was possible for the cross to belong to Jesus' earthly work without its belonging to the complex of events of "the hour" being called in question, for John's theology has a wealth of differentiations (313).

---

13. Barrett's commentary has now been translated into German and published in 1990 in the KEK series as a special volume (Sonderband, 1990)—a rare accolade for a British scholar!

Although Käsemann in his *The Testament of Jesus* briefly rejected Thüsing's thesis on the grounds that he was too orientated to the pattern of Phil 2:6–11 (obedience rewarded by exaltation), which is not typical of John, and Ashton dismissed it in a terse remark in a footnote (*Understanding*, 495 n.22), Thüsing's main critics have been J. Blank, (*Krisis: Untersuchungen zur Johanneischen Christologie und Eschatologie*) and J. Riedl (*Das Heilswerk Jesu nach Johannes*), who agrees substantially with Blank's criticisms. Their case runs as follows. In the first place, they allege that Thüsing's two-stage theory does not really do justice to John's post-Easter standpoint. One cannot distinguish between past, present, and future: there is no before or after, no first or second (Blank, 267–68). The interpreted story of Jesus is lifted into an eternally valid revelation of what Jesus has become for the world (Blank, 140, 267–68). The Crucified and the Glorified are one (Blank, 273). Riedl maintains that for John the history of Jesus has entered into the divine transcendence of history in Jesus' being with the Father (e.g., 21, 31, 184, 187–88). It is only from a literary point of view, determined by the *Gattung* of a Gospel, that future tenses are used (e.g., 21 discussing 13:32). The Christ event is abidingly present (cf. 27, 185). Secondly, they maintain that Thüsing has not worked out the Christological foundation (specifically, he does not handle the Son of Man) of the glorification concept (Blank, 268–69 n.11; Riedl, 158–59, 161–62). Finally, for both Blank and Riedl the cross in John is both an end and yet not an end, but a transition, a beginning, an opening up or point of intersection. The glorification embraces Jesus' death but equally reaches beyond it. We cannot distinguish sharply between the death (as the condition) and the fruit bearing (as the consequence) (Blank 267, 273, 278; Riedl, 157). Rather than a second stage, Riedl prefers to speak of Jesus' saving work becoming fruitful or extending itself to faith (170, 181), but this does not mean any "increase" in the glorification completed in death (173, 183–86). The actualizing of Jesus' work is called its "social function" by Riedl (e.g., 155, 173, 185).

7. Did John have a Theologia Crucis?

In the 1970s and 1980s particularly, there was a series of articles, mainly by German scholars, which had as its main aim, or one of its aims, a discussion on whether John had a theology centered on the cross or not. Given the importance of the concept of *theologia crucis* in Lutheranism in general and in Pauline studies in particular, it is not surprising that scholars with a Lutheran background should use it as a yardstick by which to "measure" other writings in the New Testament.

H. Hegermann voiced criticism of Käsemann's views in "Er kam in sein Eigentum. Zur Bedeutung des Erdenswirkens Jesu in vierten Evangelium," a contribution to the Festschrift for J. Jeremias, *Der Ruf Jesu und die Antwort der Gemeinde* (1970). He believed that the Passion is a central piece in the Fourth Gospel (116). Jesus' word convinces and cleanses (117–19). Hegermann sees Johannine dualism as serving to show that salvation can only be a radical miracle of new creation (128). The cross completes the exposure of the world's lostness; its hostility to and distance from God. Jesus exposes and convinces the world in order to save it (126). Hegermann looks at chapters 3–4 and 7–8 as giving examples of the light exposing the lostness of darkness and pointing to the possibility of miraculous new creation (119–26). This process of convincing us of our lostness and changing us began in the earthly work of Jesus and was completed in his dying and is articulated anew in the church.

In 1974, Ulrich Luz contributed to the debate in his article "Theologia Crucis als Mitte der Theologie im Neuen Testament," which appeared in *Evangelische Theologie* for 1974. He denied that the alternatives *theologia crucis* or *theologia gloriae* were possible for John. Death and glorification are two aspects of the same fact but not two fundamentally different possibilities of theological thinking (118).

The following year appeared the already mentioned article of U. B. Müller, "Die Bedeutung des Kreuzestodes Jesu im Johannesevangelium," *KuD* 21 (1975) (He was to return to this topic over twenty years later in 1997—see below). As we have summarized it previously, suffice to say here that Müller denied that John had a *theologia crucis*. The passion is Jesus' withdrawal from the world and return to the Father (53–56); the cross is his exaltation and victorious return to the Father (56–58), an event on the way to life, over which the Son exercises complete control (61–63). For John as a believer there is no "offence" of the cross (64) and he writes to strengthen the faith of his community—Jesus did not lose his glory by death but was glorified by God through death (67).

H. W. Kuhn contributed to the debate with "Jesus als Gekreuzigter," in *Zeitschrift für Theologie und Kirche* (Vol. 72 for 1975). He maintained that John holds to the identity of the crucified and Risen One and can claim a *theologia crucis* in the strong sense (26–27; 23). On the other hand, P. von der Osten-Sacken, "Leistung und Grenze der johanneisch-en Kreuzestheologie," (in *Evangelische Theologie* 36 for 1976), while he felt that John was concerned to understand Jesus' appearance under the sign of the cross (e.g., John 2:13–22) and sees the passion as included in Jesus' work (160 on John 19:30), spoke of "the limitations" of John's understanding of the cross (173). The cross is the culmination point of an event which comprises the whole appearance of Jesus (161 discussing John 12:28; 13:31–32), *viz.* that Jesus belongs to God—his unity with the Father (162–63). Osten-Sacken is dismayed that John calls the Jews/the unbelieving world "children of the devil" and feels that he has fallen back into dualistic thinking (164). John has no vocabulary of hope—there is no hope for creation and for Israel.

F. Hahn affirmed John's *theologia crucis* and argued for its determin-ing the text of the Shepherd Discourse (his article, "Die Hirtenrede in Joh 10," appeared in the Festschrift for E. Dinkler, in 1979). A. Lindemann, "Gemeinde und Welt," in the Festschrift for Günther Bornkamm (1980), also believed that, if not explicitly, then in fact, John held firmly to as-pects of a *theologia crucis*. In the same volume, H. Thyen, in his "Das Heil kommt von den Juden" criticised P. von der Osten-Sacken for miss-ing John's theology of the cross.

In his monograph *Bedrängte Gemeinde und verherrlichter Christus: Der historische Ort des Johannesevangelium als Schlüssel zu seiner Interpretation* (2nd ed., 1983), K. Wengst strongly maintained that one could not understand Jesus apart from his cross and that one encounters God in Jesus' way to the cross in John (110–11). In another article ap-pearing in *Zeitschrift fur Theologie und Kirche*, (Vol. 82 for 1985), "Die Aufgabe einer theologischen Interpretation des 4. Evangeliums," W. Klaiber argued that the cross had an essential, indeed decisive, place in John's Gospel. The question is how far this leads to a theology of the cross in the sense of Paul's *theologia crucis* (311). Klaiber himself be-lieves that, while the terminology of Paul's teaching on justification is lacking in John, the basic elements of the saving event described by it are present (318).

The English translation of U. Schnelle's work appeared in 1992, *Antidocetic Christology in the Gospel of John* (the German original was published in 1987). Schnelle firmly believed that John had a *theo-logia crucis*. He sees the miracles in John as stages on the way to the cross—2:14–22 interprets the story of Jesus from the standpoint of the cross and resurrection (189–90). One glory links incarnation and glorification (95). John starts to develop his *theologia crucis* at the beginning of Jesus' public appearance (95). John's theology of the cross is not just a relic of tradition but a deliberate anti-docetic statement of the saving significance of Jesus' death (256).

Martin Hengel in his *The Johannine Question* (1989), while not dealing with any aspects of Johannine theology in detail, revealed that he considered that in John's Gospel Jesus' death on the cross was an atoning sacrifice. "From John 1:29 to 17:19 there is a whole series of statements in the Gospel which refer clearly to the vicarious atoning death of Jesus" (66).

Mention must be made of two books devoted to the theme of John's theology of the cross. The first of these is H. Kohler's *Kreuz und Menschenwerdung im Johannesevangelium,* which appeared in 1987. In the first part of his monograph, Kohler surveyed and criticized the approach to and interpretation of John by Bultmann, Käsemann, Schotroff, Richter, Thyen, Becker, and Wengst (1–155). Then he exegetes four passages (20:19–29; 13:1–17; 12:27–36; 3:14–21 in 157–270), from which emerges the importance of the cross for John. The Risen One wishes to be identified as the crucified One (177, 181). The foot washing symbolizes the movement of Jesus to the cross (198), the accomplishment of God's saving nearness (218). Kohler takes 12:31 as meaning the end of time when Jesus draws sin on himself and gathers it to himself like the Lamb (1:29) and so the cosmos and its ruler are divested of their destructive power (237, 239). Chapter 3:14–21 interprets the incarnation from the cross (230, 248), which discloses the true meaning of Jesus' sending (257), which makes known the Father as the principal giver (259).

When the lifting up is defined as Jesus' glorification, his death on the cross is defined as God's revelation in the most comprehensive manner (271). Kohler's thesis is basically that the concept of the cross as the lifting up of Jesus demands the idea of God's nearness to mankind in the sending of his Son into the world in incarnation (see esp. 9, 60, 154, 271). John holds cross and incarnation together (9).

In 1994 came T. Knöppler, *Die theologia crucis des Johannesevangelium: Das Verständnis des Todes Jesu im Rahman der johan-*

neischen Inkarnations- und Erhöhungschristologie.[14] Knöppler sought to show how important the death of Jesus is in the Fourth Gospel. As early as 1:14 with the occurrence of the word "flesh" there is an allusion to the death of Jesus—the Logos became a mortal man (26–66). Knöppler looked at the Lamb of God passage (67–101); the hour texts (102–15), the references to the Passover (116–21); the lifting up and glorification concepts (154–73); the idea of a work given to Jesus by God (174–83); the references to the opponents' wish and plans to kill Jesus (184–200). He has a chapter on the representative motif in John (the ὑπέρ passages, 201–16), though in his opinion only 6:51 has a clearly atoning reference (he concedes this may also color the sense of other texts with ὑπέρ). He examines the references to Judas' betrayal (217–27) and the various terms for Jesus' departure to the Father, of which ὑπάγειν certainly alludes to the cross (228–41). Finally, he looks at the passion story itself and the stress in chapter 20 on the Risen One's identity with the crucified Jesus (242–68).

With tremendous thoroughness Knöppler has certainly broadened the basis for believing that the cross dominates the Fourth Gospel. He has not looked in much detail at the meaning of the cross/death of Jesus for the evangelist, though he indicates that he thinks that for John Jesus' death procures atonement and cleansing from sin and the rescue of humanity imprisoned in death.[15]

The debate in Germany shows no signs of abating. Some of the further contributions may be noted. Jean Zumstein contributed an essay to the Festschrift for F. Neirynck in 1992 on "L'Interpretation johannique de la mort du Christ,"[16] and this was translated into German and included in his *Kreative Errinerung: Relecture und Auslegung im Johannesevangelium.*(2nd expanded ed., 2004), to which we shall refer. Zumstein is convinced that the Johannine narrative is directed to the cross which presents its theological climax (226, 228, 234). References to the hour, lifting up, and glorification prepare the way (Zumstein calls

---

14. Knöppler followed this work up with another entitled *Sühne im Neuen Testament,* of which 233–52 basically summarized his earlier work on the contribution of John's Gospel to this theme.

15. Söding, *Offenbarung des Logos,* 396, maintained that for John the eschatological atonement takes place through das Kreuzesopfer Jesu (Jesus' sacrifice on the cross) and referred to Knöppler's 2001 work with approval.

16. F. van Segbroeck et al., eds., *The Four Gospels. Festschrift Frans Neirynck.* Leuven: Leueven University Press, 1992.

them "prolepses," 221–22), as do explicit comments like John 2:21:22; 7:39; 11:51–52; 12:33 and implicit ones with 7:33–36 being an example of where the cross is the background against which the conflict with the Jews is played out (223–25). John 12 discusses the soteriological significance of the cross (227), and Zumstein detects an atoning significance of the death of Jesus in the insertion of 19:34b–35 which point to the Eucharist (233). He surveys the Johannine Passion story, bringing out the themes which he believes are there, and, as a result, maintains that a theological circle which does not attribute any significance to the death of its Lord does not work in this way (234). The cross continued to be a controversial theme of reflection in the Johannine circle (234). In his conclusion, Zumstein detects an "ambivalence" in the Johannine interpretation of the cross for all its paradox: it stresses the basic humanity of the Son and yet points in the direction of a docetic theology of glory, which Zumstein sees exemplified in the later approaches of 1 John and the Acts of John respectively (237–39).

U. Wilckens had dealt with the Johannine interpretation of the death of Jesus very briefly in his commentary (338–401), and he took the opportunity in his contribution to *Gemeinschaft am Evangelium*, the Festschrift for W. Popkes (1996), to deal with the theme, under the title: "Christus traditus se ipsum tradens. Zum johanneischenn Verständnis des Kreuzestodes Jesu." This has been reprinted in his *Der Sohn Gottes und seine Gemeinde* (2003). Wilckens argues that Jesus' death on the cross is the goal and climax of the whole book. He then concentrates on John 1:29 (which is probably quoted in 1 John 3:5). Jesus' own sinlessness is of basic significance for the understanding of the atoning effect of Jesus' death on the cross. Believers participate in him through his representation. The saving significance of the cross depends on the relationship of sending between the Father and the Son. John 3:16 includes a reference to the death on the cross, which is the "most external side" of Jesus' giving himself for his own (the "inner side" is the relationship of knowing between Jesus and his own). The man Jesus who suffers is the Son of God who takes on himself the reality of sin and death in order to overcome them for men and women. The atoning power of Jesus' death is equally the power of resurrection which is life-creating and which bestows eternal life. Wilckens believes that John retains the paradox of Jesus' sovereign initiative and his powerlessness in the passion story and also that God's love in Jesus' self-giving in his death is the real scope of the whole "sending" Christology of John's Gospel.

C. Dietzfelbinger wrote on "Sühnetod im Johannesevangelium?" in *Evangelium—Schriftauslegung—Kirche*, the Festschrift for Peter Stuhlmacher (1997). Though brief, the importance of this article for its insights far outweighs its size. Dietzfelbinger sets out first the passages concerning the death of Jesus which, he believes, John took over from his tradition in which either the atoning idea of Jesus' death is present or which are open to such an interpretation, and then passages about the death of Jesus which are characteristic of John's mode of speech. The atonement idea is not found in the latter, but many other ideas (e.g., death as return to the Father; his exaltation and glorification; the completion of God's work in creation; it leads to the coming of the Paraclete; it will mean that eventually believers will be where Jesus is). How is this duality to be explained? Dietzfelbinger believes that John affirmed the tradition which he took over, not as the sole explanation of Jesus' death but as part of and useful for a larger context. John melds the different hermeneutical horizons of pre- and post-Easter. The Jesus who speaks and acts pre-Easter is brought by John already into the horizon of the cross; he speaks and acts as the one who has accomplished his sending in his death.

U. B. Müller continued to deny that John had a theology of the cross in another article, his "Zur Eigentlichkeit des Johannesevangelium: Das Problem des Todes Jesu" (1997). J. Schröter was also one who did not think that it was appropriate to say that John has a "theology of the cross."[17] John's interpretative model was that of a willing surrender of one's life to help save others (ἀποθνῄσκειν ὑπὲρ), which has its closest analogies in pagan Greek thought. John has related the death of Jesus to the upward way of his descent-ascent Christological scheme (unlike Phil 2:6–11). Through his death Jesus will complete the establishment of the fellowship of those who are his, whom he will protect and preserve. Jesus' departure brings about the coming of the Paraclete and his ministry in the post-Easter period. Schröter takes John 1:29 as referring to the

---

17. J. Schröter, "Suhne, Stellvertretung und Opfer. Zur Verwendung analytischen Kategorien zur Deutung des Todes Jesu," 55 n.14. His earlier article, "Sterben für die Freude. Uberlegungen zur Deutung des Todes Jesu im Johannesevangelium," was not available to me. However, from this later article and from remarks by J. Frey in *Theologia crufixi*, the approach of Schröter can be adequately described.

way of Jesus as a whole, by which those who belong to him are separated from the world.[18]

Two essays in the volume *Kreuzestheologie im Neuen Testament*, which appeared in 2002, were devoted to John's understanding of the cross and put forward differing approaches. The first was by J. Frey, "Die 'theologia crucifixi' des Johannes- evangeliums." Frey was critical of the fact that some German scholars decided the theological legitimacy of the Fourth Gospel by its nearness to or distance from Paul's thought. The issue should be whether the cross of Jesus as the crucified one defines John's presentation and whether the cross is of abiding theological significance (180). He also strongly maintained that it was inappropriate to regard tradition as not having any significance for John (183). He maintained that the cross and glory are thought of together in John, not from the perspective of a theology of glory but from the perspective of a theology of the cross (191). Frey devotes a section to the narrative significance of the cross in John (191–200) and then goes on to defend the soteriological meaning of Jesus' death as a representative, atoning event (200–219). Only through the deeper insight mediated by the Paraclete-Spirit can the believer see Jesus' death as lifting up and glorification and victory over the world (227). Frey coins the term "staurocentricity" of John's speaking about "lifting up" (228). The cross has universal and abiding significance and is constitutive for the post-Easter state of salvation (229–30). Jesus in his Easter appearances gives himself to be recognized by the *signa crucifixi* as the Crucified One. Even as the risen one he remains the Crucified One. With the person of the glorified Crucified One, the results of the cross are present (235). In a never obsolete way, it is the Crucified One in whom God gives himself to be recognized in a way that leads to salvation (236).

The second essay was by Esther Straub: "Der Irdische als der Auferstandene: Kritische Theologie bei Johannes ohne ein Wort vom Kreuz." She believes that it is possible that a theology which is not exclusively orientated to the cross can reflect a gospel which is in harmony with that of the justification of the godless (243). From her interpretation of Jesus' conversation with Nicodemus, Straub argues that where humans do not recognize God as their and the world's creator, as long as they presume their earthly origin to be the source of life, then they are in

18. See the summary by Scröter himself in *Deutungen*, 64–65, and compare Frey's criticism in "*Theologia crucifixi*," 203 n.160.

John's theology in an existence dominated by death (246–49, 256). Next, she considers the Cana wedding story, which, she believes, encapsulates John's Easter experience (255). God has freed Jesus from entanglement in his earthly origin and raised him to life; in the story Jesus distances himself from his earthly origin and reveals his close link with his heavenly Father (250, 254–55). Straub emphasizes that the vocabulary used to talk about the cross is either verbs of spatial movement or being glorified/exalted, i.e., the end of his earthly existence means his departure from the world and his return to his heavenly Father (257–58, 261). The humiliation of the cross is not a theme discussed—there is no paradox of the cross (261).

It is, however, not only German scholars who have occupied themselves with this debate. Here we may mention some contributions from outside Germany in the last decade or so. Firstly, John T. Carroll and Joel B. Green jointly wrote *The Death of Jesus in Early Christianity* (1995), of which the fifth chapter was, "'When I am Lifted up from the Earth . . .': The Death of Jesus in the Gospel according to John." The authors begin by showing that conflict between Jesus and his own people permeates the narrative, and that the death of Jesus is its natural and inevitable culmination (88). Through the hour motif, the death of Jesus comes as a surprise neither to Jesus nor to John's reader. Jesus' death is a destiny which he willingly embraces in order to ensure life for those whom he loves (100)—the outflow of blood and water from the crucified Jesus points to the fact that the death of Jesus imparts life to all who receive the beloved disciple's witness (90). Through his death, Jesus (the Son) returns to the Father (101). The cross is the judgment of the world because the repudiation of Jesus expressed there is the epitome of unbelief and the essence of sin is primarily unbelief (103). The writers deny that Jesus removes sin by the sacrificial offering of his life's blood.[19] Jesus' death is paradigmatic for disciples. It is a model of self-giving service that disciples should emulate: they should be willing to surrender life out of love for their friends. In the world, the disciples must continue Jesus' mission and they may face the inevitable hostility of the world secure in the knowledge that the ruler of this world is powerless before the one who reigns from the cross (109).

19. The writers are in agreement with Forestell, *Word of the Cross*, to whom they refer (103 n.65).

Helen C. Orchard, *Courting Betrayal: Jesus as Victim in the Gospel of John* (1998), took issue with the dominant view in Johannine scholarship that John had portrayed Jesus as a majestic figure, in sovereign control of his destiny. She argued to the contrary, that the evidence pointed to Jesus as a victim of violence, sometimes provoking the anger of opponents, at other times colluding with them in the violence. Although the meaning of the death of Jesus is not her specific focus, she does make it clear that she regards his death in the Fourth Gospel as a vicarious, atoning death.

We mention the contribution by Helge K. Nielsen to a volume of the papers delivered at a conference on the Fourth Gospel by Scandinavian scholars. In "John's Understanding of the Death of Jesus," she shows that the Fourth Gospel presents the death of Jesus as both God's will and Jesus' own decision. This death opens up a new fellowship between Jesus and believers, a new life that must unfold itself in the lives of disciples. While Nielsen accepts that there are sayings in which Jesus' death is a death for the sin of humanity, she says that she is "rather cautious" about this aspect—she does not think that the evangelist has made it unequivocally clear (e.g., 243–44, 250, 253). She concludes that the ideas of "*theologia gloriae*" and "*theologia crucis*" should be linked together in interpreting John's Gospel.

Finally, mention should be made of J. A. Dennis, *Jesus' Death and the Gathering of True Israel. The Johannine Appropriation of Restoration Theology in the light of John 11.47–52* (2006). This study aims to show that John has used concepts from Israel's restoration theology (Israel's plight due to sin; dispersion; hope of God's action to gather a renewed Israel and place her in the Land and to worship in a restored/new Temple). Ironically, the Judean leadership's attempts to thwart the ministry of Jesus only result in God's purposes being brought about. Jesus' death effects the gathering of the true Israel into one. Although the study does not explore the meaning of Jesus' death in the Gospel in any detail, Dennis argues that if the true Israel is released from the consequences of its sins, this must indicate that Jesus' death is in fact a vicarious atonement for sins (351–53, esp. 353). John 1:29 should be understood along the lines of atonement theology and as a programmatic statement for all other Johannine texts concerning Jesus' death (352–53).

8. Summary

We may summarize the results of our survey as follows:

Firstly, a large number of scholars maintain that for John salvation comes through revelation. They either argue that the cross is not at the centre of his thinking and has no saving significance (Bultmann, Taylor, Schultz, U. B. Müller, Becker, Ashton, Voulga) or they subsume its meaning for him under the concept of revelation—it reveals the Father's and the Son's love (Dodd, Forestell, Ruckstuhl, Haenchen, Loader, Obermann, Johanna Rahner, Painter).

Some scholars admit that there are some passages which contain the thought of atonement but explain these as either the "relics" of tradition and, therefore, not typical of the evangelist, but only peripheral (e.g., U. B. Müller, Appold, Ashton) or later additions by an ecclesiastical redactor aiming to bring the Gospel more in line with "mainstream" church thought (Bultmann, Becker, Haenchen, Theobald, de Boer).

All would agree in seeing the cross as Jesus' departure from this world, the return "home" and his exaltation, and in seeing the passion as an event over which Jesus exercises sovereign control and in which he is basically the victor (especially Vergote, Käsemann, Appold, Nicholson, Grayston, Carroll and Green, Helge Nielsen, Esther Straub, with Helen Orchard being an exception). This exaltation in and through the cross means that Jesus is able to continue to pour out eternal life on men and women (Vergote, Dodd, Blank, Riedl, Loader, Theobald, Gniesmer, Esther Straub, Painter; cf. Voulga).

Secondly, an equally large number of scholars argue the opposite—that the cross of Jesus is central to the Fourth Gospel and that his death does have atoning power. Several seek to combine the concepts of revelation and atonement in the thought of John (e.g., Müssner, Schürmann, Th. Müller, Thüsing, Cadman, Caird, Blank, Schnackenburg, Wilkens, Riedl, Lindars, Beasley-Murray, Koester, Hofius, Metzner, Wilckens, Dietzfelbinger, Frey, Zumstein). Within this second major group, most treat the Gospel as a unity, planned and written as such, and refuse to separate out a theology of source(s), a theology of the evangelist and a theology of the redactor.

Of those who do postulate a development, Wilkens placed the centrality of the cross in the final stage of the development of the Gospel by the same author, whereas Richter believed that the redemptive significance of the cross was held at a very early stage of Johannine tradition and that, later, a more paraenetic interest developed the idea of imitating Jesus' act of love on the cross. De Boer postulated four stages with an emphasis on the saving quality of Jesus' death only coming in at the final stage.

Thirdly, Thüsing's idea of a two-stage glorification of Jesus (up to and including the cross, and post-cross) has been rejected by a number of scholars (Blank, Käsemann, Riedl, Ashton), though he has continued to maintain it in subsequent editions of his work.

Fourthly, we have seen that many German scholars defended the claim that John had a "theology of the cross"—Hegermann, Luz, Kuhn, Hahn, Lindemann, Thyen, Wengst, Klaiber, Schnelle, Kohler (Swiss), Knöppler, Wilckens, Dietzfelbinger, Frey, Zumstein, plus the Danish scholar, Helge K. Nielsen.

Fifthly, Scröter interprets the death of Jesus in John within the pagan Greek concept of someone voluntarily surrendering their life on behalf of others to save them from some disaster. Through his departure, Jesus enables the coming of the Paraclete and so the insight into the meaning of scripture and Jesus' words.

Finally, it is clear that there is thus no consensus among scholars about the meaning of the death of Jesus in the Fourth Gospel. We may offer the following study in an attempt to see whether there is a way forward.

B. SOME PRELIMINARY QUESTIONS ON METHOD

The first question concerns the way in which many Johannine scholars peel off sources used by the evangelist and differentiate between a theology of his sources and that of the evangelist, relating these differences to different phases in a reconstruction of the history of Johannine Christianity. Alternatively, a *Grundschrift* of the evangelist is said to have been edited by a more ecclesiastically minded redactor or revised at a later stage in the history of Johannine Christianity when docetism was a threat, to make it more serviceable in the crisis: again, different theologies are claimed to be apparent. No longer is there talk about the "seamless robe" of this Gospel! Rather, it is claimed, tensions and clashing viewpoints exist in our present document.

Of the erudition which lies behind these analyses there can be no doubt, but there is a strong case for claiming that the present form of the Fourth Gospel made sense in the eyes of the final author. We have above quoted a sentence from C. H. Dodd written in a work published in 1953 and in reaction to the many theories about rearranging the order of the Fourth Gospel:[20] Dodd stated his aim to try and make sense of the Gospel in its present form. C. K. Barrett, a pupil of Dodd, expressed skepticism about the whole venture of trying to isolate sources.[21]

In recent years many scholars have very forcibly made the point about dealing with the text in front of us. Thüsing, in the second edition of his *Erhöhung* (1970), responded to criticisms made in reviews that he had not sufficiently related his discussion of ὑψωθῆναι and δοξασθῆναι to the different layers in the Gospel. Apart from maintaining the fact that the Fourth Gospel does not lend itself as neatly to the traditio-historical approach as the Synoptic Gospels, Thüsing pointed out that there were communities for whom the Fourth Gospel and the Letters were the sole written witness about Jesus and, therefore, it was legitimate to seek to read the Gospel as the author wished it to have been read. He maintained "This 'chief redactor' is in my opinion identical with the 'evangelist.'"[22]

H. Thyen—who in a series of articles in the 1970s produced monumental surveys of Johannine scholarly literature—believed that the Fourth Gospel had been edited by the addition of 1:1–18, all the passages about the Beloved Disciple, and chapter 21 as a whole, and that this redactor was the evangelist.[23] J. Riedl, in his study, *Die Heilswerk*, asserted that "One cannot reasonably doubt the unity of John's Gospel."[24]

L. Schenke, in his study on John 6, began by setting out his presuppositions. He agreed with Thyen's position and asserted that, "only the text in front of us is to be seen as the 'Gospel' and its author as 'the Evangelist.'"[25] Nicholson asked in what sense an earlier writer could be the evangelist if a redactor has changed his work drastically. Those who divided up the Gospel into the work of the evangelist and the redactor do not take the literary integrity of the final form of the gospel seriously.[26]

20. Dodd, *Interpretation*, 290 (the whole paragraph on 289–90 is worth reading).

21. Barrett, *John*, viii.

22. Thüsing, *Erhöhung*, 297–98.

23. Thyen, *Johannes 13*, 343–56, and *Entwicklungen*, 267.

24. Riedl, *Heilswerk*, 417.

25. Schenke, *Struktur*, 38; see also 21–22.

26. Nicholson, *Departure*, 6.

U. Schnelle also maintained that the exegete must *first* interpret the Gospel in its present shape, which may not correspond to logical demands today imposed on a text. What may be called contradictions in content or of a theological nature all too often depend on the subjective judgment of the exegete. He brings to bear some trenchant criticisms of attempts to reconstruct different theologies from within the Gospel.[27]

In the introductory section of his *Prozetz Jesu vor Pilatus*, Gniesmer surveyed "New Ways in the Ongoing Dispute about Method" and quoted with approval the position of Thyen and Schnelle that it was the end product which should be the subject of investigation.

Also adamant that we should treat the text of the Fourth Gospel as it stands was Wilckens, and he registered his rejection of the approach that saw passages which were claimed to disagree with the viewpoint of the evangelist.[28] Frey also heavily criticized those (e.g., Schultz, U. B. Müller and Becker) who attempt to separate the evangelist from his tradition or the evangelist from a secondary redactor. Only the text of the Gospel as handed-down is to be interpreted, not some text reconstructed by the interpreter (singling out Bultmann's commentary especially). He challenged the reconstructed view of the evangelist as a theological outsider who reinterpreted the traditions of his circle with radical boldness and whose work had to be corrected by his pupils or successors.[29]

Richard Bauckham has also insisted on taking the text as it stands. In the introduction to his collected essays on the Fourth Gospel, he pointed out "The more so-called aporias in the text are seen to fulfill an intelligible function in the structure and meaning of the text as we have it, the less cogent become the old explanations of them as revealing the seams at which preexisting sources have been sewn together by a redactor."[30]

Enough scholars have been quoted[31] (and all these are scholars pursuing what we may call the traditional critical methods, or, pursuing a

27. Schnelle, *Antidocetic Christology*, 7–9, 25.

28. Wilckens, *Johannes*, 8–9.

29. Frey, *Theologia crucifixi*, 180–85.

30. Bauckham, *Testimony*, 30.

31. Among some other scholars to insist on operating with the text in front of us we mention (without aiming to be complete in any way) Teresa Okure, *Mission*, 50, 301; Hengel, *Johannine Question*, 83–94; Knöppler, *Theologia crucis*, 22–24: Mary Coloe, *Temple Symbolism*, 9; Brown, *Introduction*, 6, 44–45, 86; Dennis, *Jesus' Death*, 8–9, 120; Chibici-Revneanu, *Herrlichkeit*, 50.

diachronic examination of the text—it goes almost without needing to be said that "narrative criticism" and scholars who pursue a synchronic study take the text as it stands)[32] to show that the proposal in this book to try and make sense of the totality of the Gospel and its understanding of the cross and the significance of the cross for salvation is no outlandish position. This must not, on the other hand, be taken as in any sense denying that the material in the Gospel as we have it has undergone development and reuse. What it does affirm is that one writer considered that what we call the Fourth Gospel made sense as it stands.[33]

The second major issue on methodology is to endorse the protests made by certain scholars against a too one-sided interpretation of aspects of Johannine thought. Two examples can suffice. There is a widespread assumption that, because there is a tremendous stress on the present experience of salvation and judgment, the writer could not also have held to a future judgment and reception of salvation;[34] and equally the assumption that, because the Fourth Gospel stresses believing on Jesus (and the various parallel expressions like coming to him, seeing him, hearing him, etc.) as necessary for salvation, the author could not have believed that baptism and the Lord's Supper were important (neither being opposed nor indifferent to them).[35]

32. E.g., Culpepper, *Anatomy*, 5, says, "The gospel as it stands rather than its sources, historical background, or themes is the subject of this study." Stibbe, *John as Storyteller*, who seeks in fact to wed the diachronic and synchronic approaches in what he calls his integrative narrative hermeneutic (1) and to set before us "John's narrative Christology," speaks about reclaiming the final form of the text as a narrative unity (29).

33. Thomas, *Footwashing*, 77, puts the matter admirably: "The existence of the text in its final form suggests that it was regarded by author(s) and readers alike as comprehensible and interpretable. In other words, the text as it stands must have made sense to some group at a particular point in history."

34. See the remarks of Wilckens, *Johannes*, 9, where he criticizes such an approach as due "to the incapacity or unwillingness on the part of the interpreter himself, to hold together in theological reflection what is clearly thought-of in a unity in the text of John." He believes that such literary critical carving up of the text does not serve to interpret the text but is a historical retrojection of one's own theological disagreement with definite statements of the text to be interpreted.

35. Cf. Wilckens, *Sohn Gottes*, 53, who protested against the tendency of many scholars to assume that where in an ancient text there are passages which do not fit in with modern logic, the solution lies in accepting the juxtaposition of different voices which have arisen through redactional work; and also the criticism of Becker's polarisation of baptism and coming to faith through the Spirit's activity by Theobald, *Herrenworte*, 91 n.160, and his criticism of Dietzfelbinger's attribution of a disinterest in the sacraments to the evangelist in *Herrenworte*, 163 n.478.

In respect to our theme, this one-sided approach tends to operate as follows: salvation comes through revelation; therefore, any idea that the cross achieves anything must be ruled out; therefore, any text which suggests this is to be dismissed either as a relic of tradition outgrown by the writer or as the work of a later editor.[36]

More room must be left for a "both-and" approach rather than an "either-or" one, quite apart from the fact that a writer could have easily omitted material with which he allegedly disagreed.

C. ASSUMPTIONS

In this study, it is assumed that the tradition of Jesus' words has been reflected upon by the evangelist and has been transposed into a Johannine idiom (though there are occasional instances where sayings have not been subject to this process to any considerable degree: e.g., 2:19; 4:44; 12:25; 13:16, 20; 20:23). There can be no doubt that while the evangelist writes a Gospel about Jesus of Nazareth, he does so from the perspective of after the cross, resurrection, and exaltation. The evangelist would no doubt claim that, under the ministry of the Paraclete-Spirit (16:14–15), he has allowed the glorified Christ to interpret and draw out the full significance of his earthly ministry. The evangelist has selected a limited number of episodes (20:30–31) and so constructed the episodes (story; dialogue; monologue from Jesus) that the truth about Jesus the Incarnate Word is presented.

C. H. Dodd finely represented this: "the Christ of the Book of Signs [i.e., John 2–12] is the Christ who dies and rises again; and this truth about Him is the essential presupposition of the whole picture of His ministry . . . The 'signs' are all true, provided that He who works them is the Son of Man who was exalted and glorified through the cross. In that sense, each several act of Christ contains within it the whole truth of the Gospel, and should disclose this truth if it is sufficiently pondered and probed." "The Book of Signs is so constructed that each episode contains

---

36. Cf. the remark, in criticism of Forestell, by Metzer, *Sünde,* 10: "In John's mind, representation, atonement and the forgiveness of sins on the one hand as well as revelation and the mediation of new life to faith on the other hand are not mutually exclusive, but are complementary factors in the Johannine understanding of salvation."

in itself the whole theme of the Gospel: Christ manifested, crucified, risen, exalted, communicating eternal life to men."[37]

The evangelist's presentation presupposes the completed work of Christ, and each episode is based on the assumption that in it the Christ who has been lifted up speaks to the hearer. This, in our opinion, vitally important, point should be borne in mind when considering the claim that Jesus is the Revealer but only reveals that he is the Revealer (Bultmann)[38] or that he is an enigma (Wayne Meeks).[39] It suggests that the evangelist has insinuated the importance of the death of Jesus in the manner in which the revelation is given.

In chapter 2, after a brief sketch of the background of the Gospel, we shall begin by looking at the basis in the Gospel for the view that John teaches salvation by revelation during the ministry of Jesus. Then we shall examine evidence which suggests *prima facie* that the cross is of paramount significance for him.

---

37. Dodd, *Interpretation*, 383, 386. Compare Culpepper, *Anatomy*, 89 "Each episode has essentially the same plot as the story as a whole"; Loader, *Christology*, 106, from a different perspective: "Jesus' death brings to sharp focus what is already at stake in each encounter with Jesus in his ministry"; Davies, *Rhetoric*, 114 "Every action, dialogue and discourse is therefore a microcosm of the whole." On similar lines, Okure, *Mission*, 299; Lang, *Johannes und Synoptiker*, 311.

38. Bultmann, *Theology*, 2. 66.

39. Meeks, *Man from Heaven*, 151.

2

An Examination of the Case that Salvation in the Fourth Gospel is by Revelation

GENERAL BACKGROUND

RATHER THAN DISCUSS OUR subject in a "vacuum," so to speak, we shall set out briefly[1] the background to the Gospel as the text itself lets us deduce it (we have no other means of reconstructing it). At the same time, we must be aware of the point made by narrative critics that one cannot proceed directly from the world of the narrative to the world of the recipients of a text.[2] This warning heeded, it is still true to say that there is widespread agreement among scholars that the Gospel of John was written in a period when Jewish Christians had left or had been forced out of the synagogue, an experience which was traumatic and which has left its mark on the way the story of Jesus has been told.[3]

1. To attempt a much more detailed presentation would demand far more space than would be appropriate here.

2. As an example we may mention the remarks of D. F. Gniesmer in his fine study *Prozetz*. While accepting that there is no direct route from the reality of the text to the reality of life, he nonetheless asserts that, in order to get at the pragmatic dimension of texts, it remains important to ask under what historical situation, as the horizon of communication, a text with the intention to be found in it appears meaningful (ibid., 30–31).

3. A minority of scholars do not feel that the evangelist and his congregation(s) were in any direct contact with the synagogue—e.g., Kimelman, *Birkat Ha-Minim*, 226–44; Hengel, *Johannine Question*, 114–24; Margaret Davies, *Rhetoric and Reference*, 303–4.

The author states that he has recorded a selection of the signs which Jesus did in order that the addressees might either believe for the first time (πιστεύσητε) or go on believing (πιστεύητε) that Jesus is the Messiah, the Son of God, and that, thus believing, they might have life in the name of Jesus (20:30–31).[4] Belief in the Messiahship of Jesus suggests a Jewish audience, and certainly the Messiahship of Jesus figures prominently in the first part of the Gospel (chapters 1–12). Thus, John the Baptist denies that he is the Messiah (1:20; 3:28), as well as Elijah or the Prophet (i.e., the prophet like Moses based on Deut 18:15–18). This may constitute a denial that John the Baptist would occupy the role of eschatological king, high priest, and prophet: the three offices which a restored Jewish theocracy would require.[5] In the subsequent scenes in chapter 1, there are a series of messianic confessions from the first few disciples who come to Jesus. Andrew declares to his brother, Simon: "We have found the Messiah" (1:41), while Philip announces to Nathaniel "We have found him of whom Moses wrote in the Law, and the prophets—Jesus, the son of Joseph, from Nazareth" (1:43). The at first sceptical Nathaniel eventually acknowledges Jesus: "Rabbi, you are the son of God, the king of Israel" (1:49).

Jesus openly declares to the Samaritan woman, who has said that she knows that the Messiah is coming, that he who speaks to her is he (4:25–26). After the feeding of the five thousand, the people want to make Jesus a king and say, "He is truly the prophet who should come into the world." Either the crowd interpret Deut 18:15–18 messianically, or they are thinking in terms of a Moses-like deliverer figure who will replicate the signs of the first exodus and wilderness period (like those mentioned by Josephus and who figure in the speech of Gamaliel in Acts 5:35–39).[6]

The crowds in chapter 7 discuss whether Jesus could be the Messiah and whether the authorities perhaps really think that he is. Certain crite-

---

4. The textual witnesses are fairly evenly divided over the two readings and it is not easy to decide between them: see Metzger, *Textual Commentary*, 256. Perhaps the fact that chapters 13–17 are very much addressed to the believing community tilts the balance in favour of the present subjunctive active.

5. See Baukham, *Testimony*, 211–12.

6. Bauckham, *Testimony*, 212–25, 238, strongly maintains that John carefully distinguishes between the various expectations in pre-70 Jewish Palestine. He suggests that the prophet like Moses figure was much more popular among common people than in the circles which produced literature.

ria are mentioned to see whether Jesus measures up to them. Three in all are put forward. Firstly, there is the belief that the origins of the Messiah will be unknown (7:27; cf. what John the Baptist said at 1:26, 31, 33). Secondly, the question is asked whether the Messiah will perform more signs than Jesus has done (7:31: here the expectation is of a redeemer figure like Moses on the basis of Deut 18:15). Finally, there is the assertion that the Messiah will be descended from David and come from Bethlehem, David's town (7:41–42). The evangelist comments: "There was, therefore, a division among the crowd because of him" (v. 43).

During the course of the repucussions of the healing of the man born blind, the evangelist says that the reason why the man's parents were indecisive was because the Jews had agreed that if any should confess Jesus as the Messiah, they should be put out of the synagogue (ἀ ποσυνάγωγος 9:22), and later in the story the evangelist states that the authorities cast the healed man out, i.e., from the fellowship of the synagogue (καὶ ἐξέβαλον αὐτὸν ἔξω 9:34). This is the first of three occasions when the evangelist uses ἀποσυνάγωγος. In his summary of the results of Jesus' ministry and his explanation of why people did not believe in him, at the end of the first part of the Gospel, John declares that some of the ruling class did believe but did not confess Jesus for fear of being put out of the synagogue, a lack of boldness which earns his criticism (12:42–43). Finally, in the Farewell Discourse, Jesus warns the disciples that they will be put out of the synagogues and not only will they be hated because of their allegiance to him but that people will try to kill them in the mistaken idea that they are doing God a service thereby (15:18—16:4). At the very least, this prediction in the Farewell Discourse indicates tension and antagonism, and presumably in the locality in which John and his hearers were based.

The issue of Jesus' Messiahship is raised once again by the Jews at the Feast of Dedication in Jerusalem, and they ask him to declare openly whether he thinks that he is or is not the Messiah. The discussion widens onto the question of Jesus' divine Sonship (10:24–38).

All this is a fairly substantial amount of material spread over the "public ministry" part of the story.

Dovetailing into this whole question is the position of Moses vis-à-vis Jesus. The Pharisees, in the story of the healing of the blind man, seek to drive a wedge between Moses and Jesus when they say that the healed man is a disciple of Jesus, whereas they are disciples of Moses. "We know that God has spoken to Moses, but as for this fellow, we do not know where[7] he comes from" (9:29). However, the evangelist calls on Moses to support Jesus. Philip said to Nathaniel, "We have found him of whom Moses wrote in the Law, and the prophets—Jesus of Nazareth, son of Joseph" (1:45). Moses' action of lifting up the serpent in the wilderness for the healing and restoration of the Israelites is a prefigurement of Jesus' being lifted up on the cross and to glory so that believers might have life (3:14–15). At the end of the discussion in Jerusalem between Jesus and the Jews, Jesus said that he would not accuse them to the Father. There was no need for him to do that, because in fact Moses, on whom they had set their hopes, would be their accuser. "For if you believed Moses, you would believe me. For he wrote about me. If you do not believe what he wrote, how can you believe my words?" (5:45–47).[8]

Not only is the toweringly great figure of Moses claimed as supporting Jesus, but the same is true also of the founding father of the nation, Abraham himself. Not only does the Johannine Jesus deny that the Jews are the true children of Abraham (8:37–40)—their deeds belie such a claim, irrespective of their physical descent—but he claims that Abraham rejoiced to see his own day (8:56) (an allusion to an interpretation of Gen 15:12, according to which God granted to Abraham a vision of the age to come).[9] Furthermore, one of Israel's greatest prophets, Isaiah of Jerusalem, is said to have seen the glory of Jesus (12:41).[10]

But, as we might deduce from the statement of purpose in 20:30–31, how one takes Messiahship depends crucially on how the juxtaposed title "Son of God" is to be understood. Thus, for example,

7. Τοῦτον δὲ οὐκ οἴδαμεν πόθεν ἐστίν: the issue of the origin of Jesus is of crucial significance in the Gospel (see 7:27–28; 8:14; 19:9).

8. There is no need to read a pejorative sense into the sentence in the Prologue at 1:17 (in agreement with Schnackenburg John 1:277; Lindars, John, 97–98; Moloney, John, 46; Jeremias, Μωϋσῆς, in TDNT 4. 872–73). Rather, the sentence should be taken as an instance of synthetic parallelism with the climax occurring in the second member. "The Law was given through Moses; grace and truth came through Jesus Christ." Later, in chapter 6, the evangelist seeks to counter Jewish interpretation of the manna as the bread of heaven, based on Ps 78:24; Exod 16:13–14. "It was not Moses who gave you the bread from heaven, but my Father is giving you the true bread from heaven" (6:32). By comparison, the bread that Jesus gives, which is he himself, is vastly superior to the manna (see 6:48–51, 58).

9. See the commentaries for precise details.

10. See below for an interpretation of this saying, the exact reference of "glory" being disputed.

Nathaniel's confession that Jesus is the Son of God, the king of Israel, could be taken in a messianic sense, along the lines of the messianic interpretation of 2 Sam 7:12–16 and Pss 2:7 and 89:26–29.[11] In the Fourth Gospel, however, the titles "Son of God" and "the Son" are used frequently in the sense that its bearer has come from God, from heaven, to earth to carry out a God-given commission (e.g., 8:36, 42; 10:36). In other words, what "Messiah" means for the evangelist is determined by what "Son of God" means.

When challenged because he has healed a man on the Sabbath, Jesus responded: "My Father is working up till now, and I am working" (5:17). At this the Jews sought all the more to kill Jesus, "because he not only broke the Sabbath, but also called God his Father, making himself equal to God" (5:18). Later, in another altercation, Jesus claimed that he and the Father were one, which prompted the Jews to take up stones to stone him. When Jesus asked why they were trying to stone him, they replied, "We are not trying to stone you for a good work, but because of blasphemy,[12] because you, though a man, are making yourself out to be God" (10:33). These two passages take us to the heart of the matter. For the evangelist, Jesus of Nazareth, the son of Joseph, can only be understood if he is seen as the incarnate Word/Son who has come from God and will return to God (e.g., 6:42, 48–50). Pre-existence, incarnation, and return to heaven is the way of the Son of God. But the claims of the Johannine Jesus are unacceptable to members of the Synagogue, for they immediately raise the question of Israel's confession of the one God (Deut 6:4). To the "Jews" in the Fourth Gospel the claims of Jesus to be the Son of God and the Christian confession of this infringe the whole basis of Israel's faith. They infringe the uniqueness of the one transcendent God and appear to postulate a second deity alongside of the one God of Israel. It seems to them to be a case of a mere man, Jesus of Nazareth, the son of Joseph, claiming equality with God and making himself out to be God (see 5:18; 6:42; 10:33–38; 19:7). The response of the fourth evangelist runs along the following lines. While the highest prerogatives are indeed accorded to Jesus (he can give life and he

11. With 4Q246 affording an example of the actual use of "Son of God" for a messianic figure in pre-Christian times; see Collins, *Son of God Text*. Collins concludes that this text illustrates "the usage of the title in the matrix from which Christianity emerged: the eschatologically orientated Judaism of the early Roman empire" (ibid., 82).

12. Taking the intervening καὶ as explanatory, and, therefore, not requiring to be translated here into idiomatic English.

executes judgment, both traditionally attributes of God alone), he has these only insofar as the Father has commissioned him and sent him into the world and has given these prerogatives to him. Thus, there is not the slightest suggestion that Jesus sets himself up as a *rival* to God; on the contrary, he is at all times the obedient Son/agent, who speaks the words given him by God and does the works given to him by the Father to accomplish. There is complete unity of purpose between him and the Father, and Jesus' sole aim in life is to do his Father's will. He and the Father are indeed one.[13]

We may add to this material two further considerations. In the first place, there is the fact that the evangelist is well acquainted with many Jewish traditions and interpretations of biblical passages, opposing to them his own christological interpretation. Some examples of this knowledge are the ladder in Jacob's dream at Bethel (1:51); the interest in the possibility of ascent/journeys to heaven (e.g., 3:13); the serpent lifted up on a pole by Moses (3:14–15); the dispute with the Samaritans over Mount Gerizim (4:20–24); the manna traditions (6:32–35); the water ceremonies at Tabernacles (7:37–38); Abraham's dream vision (8:56–58); Isaiah's vision in the Temple (12:41). Secondly, we must bear in mind the very careful use of the actual OT quotations throughout the Gospel, as Overmann and Menken have convincingly demonstrated.[14] John accepts Scripture as authoritative (10:35). It is a valid word of God which addresses people in the present. He does not quote Scripture atomistically, but knows and respects the original context.[15] The Scriptures bear witness to Jesus (5:39)—they have a christological dimension and reach their purpose to give life only insofar as they are understood as witnessing to Jesus (5:40). At the same time they provide the decisive category for understanding God's saving action in Jesus (e.g., the manna

---

13. This paragraph is based in the main on the argument of 5:19–47, together with 10:32–38. For a fuller look at many of the points made here, see chapter 4. Bauckham, *Testimony*, 252, has aptly described John's Christology as "christological monotheism, a form of monotheism in which the relationship of Jesus the Son to his Father is integral to who the one God is" (the whole chapter entitled "Monotheism and Christology in the Gospel of John" is well worth consulting).

14. See Obermann, *Christologische Erfüllung,*—see below, pp. 96–98; Menken, *OT Quotations.*

15. E.g., Obermann, *Christologische Erfüllung,* 124, 127–28, 149, 166, 202, 213, 270, 296.

as God's saving response to the people's need and Jesus as the true bread of heaven who gives life in John 6).

John stands within the variety of interpreting Scripture in Judaism at the end of the first century AD, but his christological interpretation marks him off from his non-Christian Jewish contemporaries. John's use of Scripture is part of his strategy of helping an embattled Christian community in its faith and life over against members of the Synagogue (16:1–4).

All in all, then, the case for seeing John as in some sort of touch with and still debating with members of the local Jewish Synagogue becomes very strong.[16]

In the eyes of many Jews, the fact that Jesus had been put to death in a shameful way by crucifixion was confirmation that he was not the promised Messiah. God had not stepped in to prevent his ignominious death. That being so, at least one of the issues which would be debated and discussed was whether a crucified person could possibly be the Messiah and a/the Son of God.[17] The early Christians thus faced the task of overcoming this "hurdle" in their attempts to persuade their fellow countrymen and women that Jesus was indeed the Messiah. The cross was a stumbling block to them. We experience something of this in a passage at the end of Jesus' public ministry in the Fourth Gospel. After Jesus had announced that the hour had come for the Son of Man to be glorified (12:23) and for him to be lifted up (12:32) and after the evangelist has pointed out that the term "lifted up" referred to the manner of death he was to suffer (12:33), we read that the crowd said, "We have heard from the Law that the Messiah remains for ever. And yet how can

16. Cf. the remark of Dunn, *Let John be John*, 356–57, "In attempting to set John within its historical context, it is the context of late first century Judaism which must have first claim on our attention . . . somewhere after the destruction of Jerusalem in A.D. 70."

17. Another could be that of Jesus as the true fulfillment of the Temple (in ruins since its destruction by the Romans, a traumatic event for all Jews): this is the argument of Gale Yee, *Jewish Feasts*, 16–27; Motyer, *Your Father*, ("The sin of destroying Jesus is God's means of rebuilding Israel after the disaster. The sin of destroying the Temple *of Jesus' body* anticipated the sin which led to the destruction of Herod's Temple—and provides atonement for it."—140); and Mary Coloe, *Temple Symbolism*, 1–3, 14, 62, 130, 170, 210–12, 214, 219–21), while Dennis, *Jesus' Death*, broadens this suggestion to include the whole of Israel's "Restoration Theology" (God's forgiveness, gathering in of the dispersed of Israel, restored/new Temple, the Land), which, he believes, was very much a live issue after 70 AD.

you say that the Son of Man must be lifted up? Who is this Son of Man?"
(12:34). There is no need here to go into all the exegetical questions raised
by these verses. Suffice to say that the reference to the Law is probably to
Ps 89:37,[18] while the reference by Jesus to lifting up = crucifixion = death
seems to the crowd to conflict with a messianic dogma that the Messiah's
reign would be established forever. They are puzzled by the term "Son
of Man" (used in 12:23), which, they assume, is used as an equivalent to
"Messiah."[19] In this passage, then, we hear echoes of a controversy over
the fact that Jesus had been crucified and that for Judaism this ruled
out Jesus as Messiah.[20] But, for the evangelist, this Scriptural assertion
was fulfilled, for Jesus did "remain for ever"—by being crucified and,
thereby, lifted to the Father to be with him eternally.[21]

OT quotations from John 1:23 up to 12:16 are introduced with some
form of γράφειν/ "it is written." But from then on, i.e., within the Passion
Story, the evangelist changes to using the verb πληροῦν (12:38; 15:23;
19:24, 36), the exception being 19:28 where he uses τελειοῦν (perhaps to
prepare for the famous τετέλεσται of 19:30). This change has the effect
of reminding the hearer/reader that the death of Jesus was foretold in
Scripture and, therefore, corresponded to the will of God. The death on
the cross does not disprove Jesus' Messiahship and Sonship; on the contrary, it reinforces them. Indeed, John sees divine providential overruling
in the very manner of the death of Jesus (12:33), for the "lifting up" on the
cross is also his "lifting up" to the glorification with the Father.

Justin Martyr's *Dialogue with Trypho* is evidence from around the
mid-second century AD that the issue of the death of Jesus continued to
be a matter of disagreement between the two sides.[22]

In other words, in relation to our theme of the cross, it is not a
question of a segment of some theoretical doctrinal scheme worked out

18. See van Unnik, *Quotation*, 174–79.

19. Actually, the messianic interpretation of the one like a son of man in Dan 7 had
been effected by 4 Ezra 13 (a writing which may have been roughly contemporary with
the Fourth Gospel) and by the Similitudes of Enoch (*1 En.* 37–71), the date of which is
a hotly debated issue among scholars. Collins, *Son of God Text*, 81, believes that the author of Q285 himself may have fused the son of man figure of Dan 7 with the traditional
hope for a Davidic Messiah.

20. Barrett, *John*, 428; Brown, *John* 1:479; Schnackenburg, *John* 2:395; Lindars, *John*,
434; Carson, *John*, 445–46; Lincoln, *John*, 353.

21. Cf. Koester, *Symbolism*, 126.

22. See especially *Dialogue with Trypho* 16:4; 89:1–2; 90:1.

without reference to the practicalities of everyday life. On the contrary! Explaining the cross was a vital part of Christian discipleship and witness for the evangelist and his fellow Christians, now no longer part of the synagogue community but engaged in controversy and debate with their former associates.[23]

Whatever the difficulties of relating the passages about being put out of the synagogues to what we know of the historical situation between Jews and Christians in the period after the destruction of Jerusalem[24] and the whole issue of the insertion of a curse on heretics within the Jewish Prayer known as the Eighteen Benedictions,[25] a major feature of the *Sitz im Leben* of the Fourth Gospel, on the basis of internal evidence, seems to be that of Christians forced out of the synagogue and having to defend their views about Jesus, and not least defending those views against the criticism that his death on the cross disproved those views. This is not all that may be said about Johannine church life, but it is sufficient for our purpose in that it demonstrates that the theme of the cross was of crucial importance for Johannine Christians *vis-à-vis* their former associates, quite apart from the development of what we may call "Johannine spirituality" and the place of the cross within that. The two no doubt went hand in hand and mutually interacted.

23. Cf. Dennis, *Jesus' Death*, 323, "Jesus' rejection and death are clearly important christological issues and as such issues in need of legitimation vis-à-vis the likely objections raised by the synagogue." (cf. ibid., 324–31). See also Smith, *Johannine Christianity*, 31–34; Evans, *Word and Glory*, 177–84.

24. As, to mention only one scholar, Gniesmer, *Prozetz*, 408–11 rightly indicates.

25. The link between expulsion of Jewish Christians from the synagogue due to the insertion of the curse on the Minim into the Eighteen Benedictions by the Jewish teachers at Jamnia allegedly sometime in the 80s, as the key to interpreting John's Gospel is particularly associated with Martyn, *History and Theology and Gospel of John*, 90–121; and also Wengst, *Bedrängte Gemeinde*. For doubts raised about who were intended by the 'Minim' and whether the earliest version of the curse can be dated to the 80s, see Kimelman (see note 3); Horbury, *Benediction*, 19–61; Katz, *Issues*, 43–76; Overman, *Matthew's Gospel*, 48–56; Dunn, *Partings of the Ways*, esp. 220–29; Dunn, ed., *Jews and Christians*, 6–11; Lincoln, *Truth*, esp. 263–332; Gniesmer, *Prozetz verwickelt*, 402–11. See the comment of Graham Stanton, *Gospel*, 142: "I believe that the *birkath ha-minim* has been a red herring in Matthean scholarship, just as it has been in discussion about the historical setting of the Fourth Gospel."

SALVATION BY REVELATION IN THE FOURTH GOSPEL

There can be no doubt that in the Fourth Gospel the incarnate Word appears on earth, sent by the Father, as Revealer. This is stated by the Prologue: "No one has ever seen God: the only God, who is in the bosom of the Father, has declared (ἐξηγήσατε) Him." (1:18). The first clause is polemical and denies any validity to claims to have seen God by those within the Jewish tradition (e.g., apocalyptic seers; possibly Jewish mystics) or outside of it, or on behalf of others (e.g., interpretations of Moses' ascent up Sinai by Philo).

The Word—here described, as in 1:1, as Θεὸς—is, even while incarnate[26], said to be "in the bosom of the Father," a picture of intimacy and closeness. (I have retained what might be thought an archaic translation in order to preserve what I believe is an intended allusive parallel in 13:23 where the Beloved Disciple is said to have reclined in the bosom of Jesus). Even while on earth, the incarnate Word is in the closest possible relationship and communion with the Father. Out of that relationship and communion he can reveal the Father to men and women.

What he says is entirely determined by

(a) what he has heard from the Father ("I speak to the world what I have heard from Him" 8:26b; cf. 8:40; 15:15, and 3:32)

(b) what he has been taught by the Father (8:28 "I speak as the Father has taught me").

(c) or, what he has been given by the Father (17:8 "I have given them the words which You gave me").

At 8:31, the word of Jesus conveys the truth, is the truth, and hence has liberating power—presumably to set free from the sphere of sin, falsehood and alienation from God, into the sphere of truth, God's sphere. Alternatively, it may be said that his words convey life-giving Spirit (6:63; cf. verse 68).

In the Farewell Discourse, Jesus says to the disciples "You are already clean because of the word which I have spoken to you" (15:3). To

---

26. Barrett, *John*, 170; Schnackenburg, *John* 1:279–80; Lindars, *John*, 99; Beasley-Murray, *John*, 16; Carson, *John*, 135; Moloney, *John*, 46–47; Wilckens, *Johannes*, 36; Zemke, *Logos-Hymnus*, 64; de la Potterie, *Vérité* 1:238–39; Theobald, *Fleishwerdung*, 208, 260–61, 263; Hüber, EN APXH, 116. Brown, *John* 1:17, says that no conclusive decision seems possible. Bultmann, *John*, 82, asks whether the phrase relates to the pre- or post-existent one, inclining to the latter. Margaret Davies, *Rhetoric*, 124–29, refers it to the post-existence of Jesus.

abide in Jesus and to abide in his words (e.g., 15:7) amounts to the same thing, for the Revealer and his word(s) cannot be separated. The obverse side of the fact that the Revealer's word offers eternal life is that, when refused, it brings condemnation. It will act as a judge of the one who refuses it, at the Last Judgment (12:47–50).

It is clear that the evangelist believes that the words of Jesus continue to be the norm, even after he has left the world. The task of the Paraclete-Spirit is to teach the disciples everything by[27] causing them to remember all that Jesus had said (εἶπον, 14:26): he will take what belongs to Jesus and interpretatively declare (ἀναγγελεῖ[28]) it to the disciples, in this way leading them into all the truth (16:13–15).

Ashton has helpfully pointed out that, since there is no longer any chance of seeing Jesus, the works of Jesus have been transformed into words.[29] So, in the Fourth Gospel, the importance of holding on to or keeping or remaining in Jesus' words is a reiterated theme (e.g., 8:31; 15:7,10; cf. 17:17, 20). In the light of all this, it is small wonder that Ashton wrote, "John's theology is first and foremost a theology of revelation."[30]

There can be no doubt that the idea of revelation is prominent in the Fourth Gospel. Yet does this mean that the cross is no longer of crucial significance for the salvation of women and men?[31] Is it no longer in Johannine thinking central for the relation of human beings and God? Are passages which seem to speak otherwise only of peripheral importance? Are they mere relics of an older tradition which the evangelist has—carelessly or indifferently—allowed to stand, or which time prevented his eliminating in a revision of his material?

---

27. Taking the καὶ as explanatory or epexegetic—so Bultmann, *John*, 626(6); Schnackenburg, *John* 3:83; Brown, *John* 2:650–51; Beasley-Murray, *John*, 261; Moloney, *John*, 413; Olsson, *Structure and Meaning*, 269; de la Potterie, *Vérité* 1:377; Porsch, *Pneuma und Wort*, 265; Franck, *Revelation Taught*, 42; Bennema, *Saving Wisdom*, 229.

28. cf. Bultmann, *John*, 575; Schnackenburg, *John* 3:135; Brown, *John* 2:708; Beasley-Murray, *John*, 283; Carson, *John*, 540–41

29. Ashton, *Understanding*, 522.

30. Ibid., 497; Bultmann, *John*, often refers to saving revelation, e.g., 46, 56, etc, or the saving event enacted in the mission of the revealer, 152; Forestell, *Word of the Cross*, 17, speaks of "Revelation the central theme of the Johannine theology."

31. Bennema, *Saving Wisdom*, 142, comments on the paradox that "eternal life seems to be available only after the cross, whereas, on the other hand, eternal life seems to be available in the person and revelatory teaching of Jesus, and hence already before the cross" (cf. 191–92, 195, 201).

We shall now turn to a consideration of evidence within the Gospel which *prima facie* suggests that in fact the cross is of decisive and crucial and central significance for its author.

WEAKNESS OF THE SALVATION BY REVELATION APPROACH

The first piece of evidence to be considered is the concept of "the hour" in the Fourth Gospel.

1. *The Hour Concept.*

We shall leave out all references to a definite time (1:39; 4:6, 52–53; 19:14, 27) together with 11:9 (twelve hours in the day) and 16:21 (the illustration of the hour of childbirth). The majority of the remaining instances refer to a particular point in Jesus' ministry.[32]

(i) A "Not Yet/Has Come" Contrast

There is a group of hour sayings marked by a *"not yet/has come"* contrast.

These are:

- 2:4 "Madam, what have we to do with each other? My hour has not yet come."

See below, in the excursus, for a detailed argument that the cross is here in mind (certainly, not the hour for performing a miracle).

- 7:30 "Then they sought to arrest him, but no one laid hands on him because his hour had not yet come."

- 8:20 "He said these words while teaching in the Temple treasury, but no one arrested him because his hour had not yet come."

Both 7:30 and 8:20 assert that it was impossible to arrest Jesus before his hour, and the natural assumption is that the passion or death of Jesus is meant by "hour".[33]

- 12:23 "The hour has come for the Son of Man to be glorified."

After 7:30 and 8:20 it is natural to assume that the hour means Jesus' death here. This is confirmed by the parable of the grain of wheat which

---

32. See Brown, *John* 1:517–18, for different analysis from the one that we offer. The article on ὥρα in *TDNT* 9. 677–80, is not very helpful for Johannine usage.

33. Cf. also Thüsing, *Erhöhung,* 75–76.

helps to elucidate 12:23: the grain of wheat needs to die in order to bear much fruit.

The idea of being glorified—in and by his death—will be treated separately, but if 12:23 refers to the cross, then it is natural to take the next verse to be mentioned in a similar way, since the idea of glorification binds the two verses together:

- 17:1 Jesus "lifted his eyes up to heaven and said, 'Father, the hour has come; glorify Your Son.'"

To this group of passages using ὥρα, we may also add a further verse which uses καιρὸς (time) but with the same connotation:

- 7:6 "Then Jesus said to them [his brothers], 'My time has not yet come, but your time is always at hand.'"

The similarity with the conversation between Jesus and his mother at 2:4 is obvious. The brothers wish to compel him to a public and open revelation of himself. He cannot do that. What they wish will indeed happen, though in a manner very different from their assumptions—at the cross.

From a literary point of view, these passages indicate that the climax and culmination of the ministry of Jesus is the cross. The readers' suspense is built up by means of the "not yet" occurrences until at last the announcement comes that the hour has arrived. These hour passages are a crucial indicator of how the ministry is to be viewed by the addressees.

It is possible that we should add in this category 19:25 (excluded above). There the evangelist said that, after Jesus' dying command to him, the Beloved Disciple took Jesus' mother to his home ἀπ᾽ ἐκείνης τῆς ὥρας. At one level this is a purely temporal reference, and, indeed, could be translated generally as "from that moment." The evangelist may have intended a double-entendre here, however. The "hour" is the hour of the cross.[34] At the cross Jesus has begun the process of creating a new "family," of whom Jesus' mother and the Beloved Disciple are the representatives (for this suggestion, see chapter 5, pp. 167, 181–82). Moloney, who has suggested this interpretation of ὥρα, wants to take ἀπό in a

---

34. See Hoskyns, *John*, 530; Schnackenburg, *Johannesevangelium* 3:325; Moloney, *John*, 503, and *Israel*, 357. Barrett, *John*, 552, lists it as a possibility, while Carson, *John*, 617, appears to accept that the reference is to Jesus' death/exaltation.

causal sense—"because of that hour."[35] While that is possible grammatically, it need not be absolutely necessary; the temporal sense could apply and the double nuance still stand. In view of the evangelist's penchant for the double-entendre, this suggestion may well be right. If so, it would fit in with the rest of this category, *viz.* that there comes a point when the hour has come and consequences stem from this fact.

(ii) The Hour "Is Coming, Indeed Has Come"

One passage uses the formula *"is coming, indeed has come."*

- 16:32. At the end of the Farewell Discourse, Jesus says to the disciples: "Look—the hour is coming and has come, when each of you will be scattered, everyone for themselves, and you will leave me alone."

The reference is, again, to the cross when the disciples will abandon Jesus and leave him on his own.

(iii) The Hour "Had Come"

One passage uses the expression that the hour *"had come."*

- 13:1 "Before the Feast of the Passover, Jesus, because he knew that his hour to depart out of this world to the Father had come."

Here the language used (ἵνα μεταβῇ ἐκ τοῦ κόσμου τούτου πρὸς τὸν Πατέρα) emphasizes the impending death as departure out of this world to the Father. The death is a means to an end and results in Jesus' "return home." The difference of terminology may be due to the fact that Jesus is now depicted as concentrating on "his own," whom he is leaving behind in the world when he returns to the Father (the language of coming forth from and going to/departing to God figures prominently in the Farewell Discourse, e.g., 14:28, 16:28, etc.).

Nicholson[36] has argued that 13:1 is the key text for interpreting what "the hour" meant for the evangelist and that it should interpret the other passages rather than vice versa: the hour of Jesus is the movement of Jesus' return above to the Father (in which movement the crucifixion has a part). Nicholson maintains that the Synoptic interpretation of hour as Jesus' death must not be imposed on the Fourth Gospel.

35. Moloney, *John,* 503, and *Israel,* 357.
36. Nicholson, *Departure,* 147–48.

We believe that he is imposing a strait-jacket on the sayings. Thus, 7:30, 8:20 are more likely to indicate that Jesus could not be put to death until the moment appointed by God for his death. These two verses do not preclude that on other occasions the dominant sense might be the return to the Father via the cross as in 13:1 (and 13:3),[37] while what might be meant by the hour of the glorification of the Son of Man could also carry a further nuance.

(iv) The Hour Is Coming and Now Is

There are two sayings which use the formula about the hour—"*is coming and now is.*"

The first instance is at 4:21–23(24). When the Samaritan woman raises the question of worship and its true location, Jesus first responds by referring apparently to the future: "Madam, believe me that the hour is coming when you will worship the Father neither in this mountain nor in Jerusalem," and then goes on to "correct" this future stress: "*The hour is coming, and now is*, when the true worshippers will worship the Father in Spirit and Truth; for the Father seeks such to worship Him. God is Spirit; and they who worship Him must worship Him in Spirit and Truth."

True worship, which will not be linked to any particular geographical location, will come about through the work of the Spirit of Truth, and this Spirit will be given after Jesus' death and return to the Father. This explains the phrase "the hour is coming," but what about "and now is"? Probably the meaning is that the true worship is a present possibility because Jesus, the incarnate Word, whom to have seen is to have seen the Father, and who is the way to the Father (14:6, 9), is present in the world.[38]

Thus, even in this passage, the hour has a reference to the cross implied within it.

There is another possible interpretation, however: *viz.* that "the hour is coming" refers to the cross with the gift of the Spirit dependent

---

37. Knöppler, *Theologia Crucis*, 228–31, maintains that John uses ὑπάγειν to describe Jesus' death, resurrection and his departure from the earthly scene and that in 13:3 it is set in the context of the Passion informed by a theology of the cross.

38. Bultmann, *John*, 190; Barrett, *John*, 237; Schnackenburg, *John* 1:435–36; Brown, *John* 1:172; Lindars, *John*, 189; Becker, *Johannesevangelium* 1:178; Carson, *John*, 224; Moloney, *John*, 128; Blank, *Krisis*, 135; Olsson, *Structure and Meaning*, 196; de la Potterie, *Vérité* 1:683; Burge, *Anointed Community*, 192–94.

upon it, while "and now is" refers to the time of the evangelist who witnesses to the fulfillment of the promise.[39]

While in one sense the whole of the Fourth Gospel is written from the standpoint of the evangelist's time, it is open to question whether the evangelist operates in the way envisaged on this view. For example, he does add explanatory notes (e.g., 2:21–22; 4:9; 7:39; 12:16, 33, etc.) in other contexts. The fact that he chose a gospel form is an indication of the importance which he attached to the ministry as well as the passion of Jesus.

Actually, whichever of the two options is found the more convincing, the case being argued here would not in fact be affected, for both interpretations accept a reference to the cross in the first phrase "the hour is coming."

The second instance occurs at 5:25, when Jesus says: "Truly, truly, I say to you, *the hour is coming and now is* when the dead shall hear the voice of the Son of God and those who hear shall live."

In the light of the preceding verse 24, when the promise was made "the one who hears my word and believes my Sender has eternal life and will not come into judgment but has passed from death to life," it seems unlikely that a literal raising from death is in mind. The word, the message, the preaching of Jesus is life-giving (cf. 6:63b) and that word is going forth in the present.[40]

But, in the future, it will be the task of the Spirit to take what Jesus has said and re-proclaim it in an interpreted manner (16:14–15) so that people may hear and understand and respond. Since the Spirit comes after Jesus' death and departure, the hour here in 5:25 too has some reference to the cross.

(v) The Hour Is Coming

Sayings which use the phrase "*is coming*" only.

- 16:25 "I have said these things to you figuratively; *the hour is coming* when I will no longer use figurative language with you but will speak openly to you about the Father."

---

39. Thüsing, *Erhöhung*, 98, 151–52, 281; Riedl, *Heilswerk*, 21. Cf. Haenchen, *John* 1:222. This, too is the logic of Cullmann's position, as outlined in *Early Christian Worship*, 37–38, though Cullmann does not in fact exegete 4:21, 24.

40. Thüsing, *Erhöhung*, 98, agrees on this. Riedl, *Heilswerk*, 21, takes "and now is" of the time of the church.

The "open" speaking about the Father can only refer to the idea that when Jesus has returned to the Father, he will speak through the Spirit[41] (cf. 16:12–15). That being so, there is still a link with the cross, within this idea of the hour that is coming in 16:25.

In this category, we might also mention 16:1–4: "I have spoken these things to you in order that you may not be caused to stumble. Men will put you out of the synagogues. In fact,[42] the hour is coming when everyone who kills you will think that he is offering service to God. And they will do these things because they have known neither the Father nor me. But I have spoken these things to you that when their[43] hour comes you will remember that I spoke them to you."

We are justified in linking this with Jesus' death. The hatred and persecution of the world will, after Jesus' physical departure out of this world, be drawn on to the disciples as his representatives in the world (cf. 15:18–21; 17:9–19).

There remains 5:28–29, which seems clearly to refer to the Last Times, the Resurrection of the Dead and the Last Judgment. As an hour passage, therefore, it stands on its own (though there are other references to the time of the End in the Fourth Gospel—6:39–40, 44, 54; 12:48; 14:1–3). Some attribute it to a later redactor,[44] while others see it as a piece of old tradition which, while the evangelist does not reject it, he does "modify" by including the material vv. 19–27 prior to it.[45]

Given the views on methodology already expressed, the latter view is the more acceptable, though it is not beyond the bounds of possibility that the evangelist interpreted the material in the light of 5:24 and took "those in the tombs" to refer to mankind in the sphere

41. See also Barrett, *John*, 495; Brown, *John* 2:724, 735; Schnackenburg, *John* 3:161; Beasley-Murray, *John*, 287; Lincoln, *John*, 426. Thüsing, *Erhöhung*, 97, 150, 212–13; Porsch, *Pneuma und Wort*, 291; Burge, *Anointed Community*, 214. Moloney, *John*, 453, refers it "to Jesus' public revelation of the Father on the cross," but even this would need the illuminating work of the Spirit.

42. Ἀλλά may be used to introduce an additional point, meaning in fact—BDF, para. 448 (6).

43. Αὐτῶν has the support of P66 (it seems), A B Θ, etc. The MSS that have only one αὐτῶν in v. 4 have probably dropped the other one, perhaps to conform to Johannine usage of the "hour."

44. e.g., Bultmann, *John*, 261; Schnackenburg, *John* 2:166; Becker, *Johannesevangelium* 1:243; Haenchen, *John* 1:253.

45. E.g., Barrett, *John*, 68, 263; Lindars, *John*, 226.

of death or darkness: to hear the voice of the Son of Man demands a response which will lead either to life or judgment.[46]

If this were so, then some link with the cross and the gift of the Spirit would be possible; if this is deemed too daring, then 5:28b in pointing to the hour of the End is unique in the Fourth Gospel. It would, however, be an indication that the evangelist found the "hour" idea in the tradition and re-interpreted it, bringing it from the future into the present of Jesus and the church.

(vi) "This hour" (12:27–28a)

I have deliberately left this passage to the last, for it is of crucial significance in assessing the theme of the hour.

Jesus, after referring to the fact that the hour has come for the Son of Man to be glorified (12:23), says, "Now I[47] am troubled. And what shall I say? Father, save me from this hour? But for this reason I have come to this hour. Father, glorify your name."

It is usual to assume, rightly we believe, that Jesus is referring to himself as being "troubled"[48] and to see the verse as a reflection of the Gethsemane tradition, though more recently Nicholson has suggested that Jesus is troubled for his disciples.[49] His view should be rejected. Its weaknesses are:

(a) Would Jesus pray "Save me" if the disciples were his real concern?

(b) This Gospel stresses the necessity for his going.

(c) The fact that this going is advantageous for the disciples is emphasized in 16:7.

(d) The prayer of chapter 17 displays no such trouble but confident assurance that the Father will keep the disciples.

Jesus asks whether he should pray to be saved from this hour, i.e., the hour of the cross. But this hour represents his destiny, the very rea-

---

46. Dodd, *Interpretation*, 364–66, is prepared to accept something like this. According to U. Schnelle, *Trinitarisches Denken*, 376 (note 53), J.-C. Kammler, *Christologie und Eschatologie*, 224–25, understands 5:28–29 in terms of present eschatology.

47. Literally, ἡ ψυχή .

48. Thüsing, *Erhöhung*, 79, believes that John intended to suggest the fulfillment of Scripture (Ps 42:6–7) rather than some psychological state of Jesus.

49. Nicholson, *Departure*, 128.

son why he has come into this world, the purpose of his ministry. To try and avoid the hour would be to deny both the reason for his coming into the world and the goal of his ministry. He must embrace what is involved in this hour. Submissive as always to the Father's will, he can only pray "Father, glorify your name."

SUMMARY

We have now surveyed the texts and can draw together some conclusions. We might say that what Passion Predictions are to Mark's Gospel (8:31, 9:12, 31, 10:33–34, 45), the hour texts are to the Fourth Gospel.[50] They form a key structural element, pointing to the cross as a climax of the ministry.[51]

The verses surveyed in categories (i), (ii), and (vi) reveal this. There is a period when the hour has not yet come; then, at last, it has come and it proves to be the crucial event to which the ministry has been heading. Considerable consequences stem from this hour because the gift of the Spirit ensues from Jesus' death and because the disciples or believers become the agents or representatives of Jesus in the world after he has returned to the Father. Verses included in categories (iv) and (v) attribute true worship; life from death; clearer understanding of revelation; and persecution, to the effects of the hour. In category (iii), 13:1 uses the language of departure to the Father.

Our analysis has shown that the hour concept has a certain elasticity about it in this Gospel. Its meaning can expand from a reference to the actual event of the cross, to include the return to the Father via the cross, and the consequences or results which stem from the cross and the return to the Father. The context pulls it along to have a wider connotation.[52]

50. In contrast to Lincoln, *Truth on Trial*, 69, who compares the three Johannine lifting up passages to the three Marcan Passion Predictions.

51. Buhler, *Kreuzestheologe?* 194, in stressing the importance of the narrative form of the Fourth Gospel, asked whether the cross has a decisive role in "the narrative-pragmatic strategy" of the Fourth Gospel or not? The hour texts demand a strongly affirmative answer to Buhler's question. Olsson, *Structure and Meaning*, 93, rightly asserted that, "the 'hour' of Jesus and its consequences are the reality from which all the material is presented."

52. Cf. the use of the phrase "tensive symbol" in relation to the kingdom of God by Norman Perrin, *Jesus and the Language of the Kingdom*, 29–32, a phrase drawn

What we may confidently say is that any view that minimizes the importance of the cross in the Fourth Gospel may be ruled out of serious consideration on the basis of the hour concept.[53] The hour concept of itself suggests that John has a *theologia crucis*. What that "theology of the cross" is remains to be seen. The hour passages encourage us in our quest for it.

Excursus: Interpretation of 2:4 (7:6)

Above, I assumed that at 2:4 "hour" referred to the cross. It seems self evident that it does not refer to the time of changing water in wine (or the commencement of performing his signs, with the translation "Has not my hour come?").[54] But how can a reference to the cross be a suitable response to Mary's statement that the hosts had run out of wine (2:3)?[55]

It seems to me that we can get a coherent flow of thought if we assume that the evangelist is using Mary's statement as an implied hint or request to usher in the messianic era, for abundance of wine is precisely one of those recurring features in various Old Testament and Jewish texts which look forward to an era of blessedness (e.g., Amos 9:13–14; Hos. 2:2, 14:7; Joel 2:19, 24; 3:18; Jer 31:12; Isa 25:6; *1 En.* 10:19; *2 Bar.* 29:5).[56]

The reply of 2:4 would then comprise two elements. Firstly, a distancing of himself by Jesus from his mother. He is not under her direction but under his heavenly Father.[57] Secondly, the hour for what she seeks is not yet here, but will come in the future—no doubt in a form

---

from the work of Philip Wheelwright, *Metaphor and Reality.* Bloomington: Indiana University Press, 1962.

53. As held by Bultmann and those scholars who have basically followed his approach (see, 4–7 above).

54. As maintained by Boismard, *Baptême,* 155–56; cf. de la Potterie, *Hour,* 22.

55. Charlier, *Signe,* 60–61, rightly in my opinion, suggests that we start from Jesus' reply and work back to Mary's suggestion: how can Mary's words merit "My hour has not yet come" as a response? Cf. the discussion in Carson, *John,* 171–73.

56. Charlier, *Signe,* 61–62; Schnackenburg, *John* 1:338; Wilckens, *Johannes,* 59; Carson, *John,* 172; Knöppler, *Theologia Crucis,* 105.

57. Schnackenburg, *John* 1:330; Beasley-Murray, *John,* 35; Becker, *Johannesevangelium* 1:108; Haenchen, *John* 1:173; Carson, *John,* 171; Moloney, *John,* 67; Wilckens, *Johannes,* 56; Lincoln, *John,* 128; Charlier, *Signe,* 47-51, 62; Esther Straub, *Der Irdische,* 254.

different from Jewish expectations, as is hinted at in the changing of the water, which was put into pots for Jewish purificatory rites, into wine.[58]

We shall return later to the revelation of Jesus' glory in such an event as the sign at Cana (2:11) and the glorification which takes place in the cross (12:23, 17:1) and how his glory can be revealed at Cana and yet his hour had not yet come.

What we have proposed is similar to the way in which we would wish to interpret 7:6.[59] His brothers want him to reveal himself to the world (v. 4). But he is not under their direction either, and the revelation to the world will take place supremely through the cross and what stems from it, as the evangelist makes clear in 12:20–36; also 10:16; 11:49–52.

Thus, right at the beginning of his narrative, the evangelist has set the ministry of Jesus under the sign of the cross.[60]

2: The Glory and the Glorification of Jesus

In our study of "the hour" concept in the Fourth Gospel, we saw that according to 12:23 the hour was an hour of glorification. Since in the Prologue the evangelist said that "the Word became flesh and dwelt among us and we beheld his glory, glory as befits the Father's Only Son, full of grace and truth" (1:14),[61] we need to ask, What is the relationship between these two assertions? Does the hour of the cross reveal the glory already manifested in the ministry, or is there a sense in which the evangelist sees "extra" glory as accruing to Jesus through the cross and which can be called his glorification?

(i) Glory in the Ministry of the Incarnate Word

We shall firstly consider *the glory visible in the incarnate Word's ministry,* the historical Jesus of Nazareth.

---

58. The interpretation offered here meets the objection raised by Esther Straub, *Der Irdische,* 254, that a reference to the cross cannot explain Jesus' repudiation of his mother and his performance of the miracle.

59. Cf. too Wilckens, *Johannes,* 56; Charlier, *Signe,* 63.

60. Cf. now Zumstein, *Relecture,* 271, who says that 2:4 "perceives Jesus' first act of revelation from the perspective of the cross and consequently places the whole of the ensuing narrative within the horizon of the coming hour."

61. Cf. the statement by Käsemann, *NT Questions,* 159, 164, that the weight of the evangelist's propositions in the prologue falls on "and we beheld his glory"; cf. *Testament,* 6–7.

We have quoted 1:14 above and this is clearly programmatic (whether or not Käsemann's precise interpretation is accepted).[62] We note that the evangelist uses the noun δόξα here (as he does three times elsewhere of this glory visible in the ministry). The believing community claims and confesses to have seen the glory of the incarnate Word. This glory befits one who also may be described as the Father's only (or beloved) Son (or as the Only or Beloved Son who came from the Father—no great difference of sense results). It will be left to the evangelist's presentation to disclose how this glory was perceived by believers.

At the conclusion of the first sign, at Cana in Galilee, the evangelist wrote:

"Jesus performed this first of his signs at Cana in Galilee and revealed his glory and his disciples believed in him" (2:11). In what sense did this sign reveal Jesus' glory? In some way for the evangelist, Jesus' power which turned water into wine revealed that God's power,[63] ultimately to give life and execute judgment, had been bestowed upon his only Son (cf. 5:19–27, and also 3:35 "The Father loves the Son and has given all things into his possession"). The water was put into jars for Jewish purification rites; the wine drawn out represented the new life brought by the incarnate Word.[64]

The concept of glory also appears in the raising of Lazarus, on two occasions. At 11:4, when told of Lazarus' illness, Jesus said "This illness is not unto death, but for (ὑπέρ) the glory of God," i.e., so that God's life-giving power vested in Jesus might be revealed.[65]

The same meaning as this ὑπέρ phrase applies to 11:40 where Jesus said, in response to Martha's protest that her brother had been in the

---

62. For a review and criticism, see Kohler, *Kreuz*, 45–63; Marianne Thompson, *Humanity*, 88.

63. Thüsing, *Erhöhung*, 244 ("the power which comes from the unity with the Father"); Wilkens, *Zeichen*, 32 (Jesus has a share in God's creative power); Knöppler, *Theologia Crucis*, 53 ("God's presence in Christ").

64. We see no reason to assume that the primary reference is to the Eucharist (as does, e.g., Wilckens, *Johannes*, 59). Brown, *John* 1:109, rightly comments that "if there is eucharistic symbolism, it is incidental and should not be exaggerated"; cf. too the remarks of Schnackenburg, *John* 1:337–40, that the main interest of the evangelist is concentrated on the messianic and christological self-revelation of Jesus.

65. For ὑπέρ meaning purpose, see *BAG*, 846, under 1.b of ὑπέρ, where John 11:4 is classified.

grave for four days and his corpse would smell: "Did I not tell you[66] that if you believe, you will see the glory of God?" In raising Lazarus, Jesus will reveal the life-giving power of God vested in himself. As the one who faithfully fulfils his Sender's commission, Jesus can only let the glory *of God* become visible.

To these four instances, we ought also to add 12:41. In an assessment of the ministry of the incarnate Word, the evangelist quotes Scripture to explain why, although Jesus performed many signs in the presence of the Jews, they did not believe. First, he quotes Isa 53:1 "Lord, who has believed our report? And to whom has the arm of the Lord been revealed?" as an indicator that Scripture foresaw the lack of response to Jesus. The lack of faith in Jesus does not disprove his claim to be sent by God; on the contrary, it confirms that he is the one promised in Scripture. The evangelist then takes a further step and adds that the Jews could not believe because they were predestined not to do so, and, in support, quotes Isa 6:10 (oft quoted in the early church to explain Jewish unbelief): "He blinded their eyes and hardened their hearts lest they should see with their eyes and understand with their hearts, and repent and I will restore them."

The evangelist then comments: "Isaiah said these things because he saw his glory and spoke about him." Despite numerous scholars' assessment to the contrary, the context surely demands that "glory" here refers to the ministry of Jesus, the incarnate Word.[67]

---

66. Nicole Chibici-Revneanu, *Herrlichkeit,* 151, suggests that 11:4 was spoken to the messenger to pass on to Martha and Mary, and this explains the reference to σοι in 11:40. Whether the evangelist was concerned about such consistency is open to question.

67. In favor of this are Hoskyns, *John,* 428; Moloney, *John,* 364; Dupont, *Essais,* 269–73; Dodd, *Interpretation,*207; Freed, *OT Quotations,* 84; and Borgen, *Bread,* 152 (note 1). Dahl, *Johannine Church,* 132, combines ministry and cross: he believes that Isaiah saw "the glory of Christ incarnate and crucified . . . he had in his vision seen the glory of the crucified Son of God." Brown, *John* 1:487, and Carson, *John,* 449–50, both list it as one of two possible interpretations, the pre-existent Christ or the life of Jesus. Schnackenburg, *John* 2:417, seems to favor a reference to the pre-existent Word, yet comes close to the other interpretation ("Isaiah did not have a direct vision of the σημεῖα in Jesus' earthly life, but of the pre-existent Christ in his glory, though of him as destined for his work on earth. This last aspect is probably what the evangelist is thinking of in the second illustrative clause: he spoke of Jesus and his work of 'healing'." In 4:151, he says that the pre-existent one spoke these words to the prophet Isaiah and argues that only in this way can we explain "I will heal them"). Whitacre, *Johannine Polemic,* 82, wishes to combine the historical and pre-existence aspects, as does Bühner,

Isaiah predicted the divine hardening leading to a lack of response because (reading ὅτι rather than ὅτε) he, like Abraham (8:56–58), had a vision of the glory of the incarnate Word's ministry, and also foresaw the failure of the Jewish people to believe. Thus, the Old Testament predicted the events of the ministry of Jesus. If, then, the two quotations refer to the fact that the Jewish people did not respond to Jesus, how can it be said that it fits *that* context to say that Isaiah saw the glory of the pre-existent Christ? The evangelist is surely saying that what Isaiah said has now had its final fulfillment in the ministry of Jesus the incarnate Word.

In all these instances which appertain to the earthly ministry, John has employed the noun δόξα.

(ii) "To Glorify"

We shall next consider the use of the verb *"to glorify"* in the Fourth Gospel. We begin with 12:23. Informed that some Greeks wish to see him, Jesus says, "The hour has come for the Son of Man to be glorified" (ἵνα δοξασθῇ). That the cross is being referred to may be maintained on the following grounds:

(a) Verse 24 serves to elucidate v. 23, and this verse speaks of a grain of wheat which dies, though in dying it bears much fruit.

(b) The hour idea is repeated in v. 27 where initially Jesus asks whether he should pray to be saved from this hour. Such a prayer is meaningful in relation to death, but not otherwise.

(c) The double νῦν of v. 31 draws vv. 31–33 into consideration, and v. 33 points us firmly to Jesus' death.

So, then, we may confidently assume that the cross is in mind at 12:23.[68] Jesus' death is going to be a moment of glorification.

Der Gesandte, 355, and Nicole Chibici-Revneanu, Herrlichkeit, 195. Pamment, Meaning, 13, believes that John is thinking of the Cross = glorification when he said that Isaiah foretold his glory: this is preferable to taking δόξα of the pre-existent Word, but it is probably due to Pamment's not distinguishing between δόξα and δοξασθῆναι. Morris, John, 605, believes that both the ministry and the cross are in mind, but, as this passage is in a review of the past ministry, the latter idea is unlikely at this stage.

68. Bultmann, John, 424; Barrett, John, 422; Brown, John 1:470; Schnackenburg, John 2:382; Morris, John, 593; Beasley-Murray, John, 211; Carson, John, 437; Moloney, John, 352 (and earlier, Johannine Son of Man [hereafter JSM] 176–81); Blank, Krisis, 267–69; Dauer, Passionsgeschichte, 237; Riedl, Heilswerk, 119; de Boer, Johannine Perspectives, 188–89; Nichole Chiibici-Revneanu, Herrlichkeit, 180; also Thüsing, Erhöhung, 75–76,

Secondly, when Judas passes out into the night to betray Jesus—
and so the crucifixion has as good as taken place—Jesus said (13:31):
"Now the Son of Man has been glorified (νῦν ἐδοξάσθη) and God has
been glorified in him."[69]

Because Jesus is dedicated to doing the Father's will, any glorification of him cannot be independent of the glorification of the Father,
but is indissolubly linked to it. Their union with one another will mean
mutual glorification. *Both have been glorified in the cross.*[70] (At this stage
in our enquiry we merely note the assertion and will seek an explanation
later)

Verse 32 builds on this with the renewed assertion: "If God has
been glorified in him" (i.e., in union with him).[71] If this phrase were not
original (it is lacking in P66 א* BD, but this could be due to *homoioteleu-
ton*), no great difference would be made to our argument. Verse 32 goes
on to make two further statements. The first is: God will glorify δοξάσει
αὐτὸν ἐν αὐτῷ. One or other of these occurrences of αὐτός must be
the abbreviation for the reflexive pronoun: ἑαυτὸν or ἑαυτῷ.[72] Either
God will glorify himself in union with him (Christ) or God will glorify
him (Christ) in union with himself. In the former case, the meaning
would be that the Father will be glorified as more disciples are won by
the followers of Jesus who live in union with him (cf. 15:8). In the latter

---

101, yet, since v. 24 clarifies v. 23 and since Thüsing believes that the accent in v. 24 lies
on fruit bearing, he believes that what he deems the second stage of the work is to be
understood in v. 23,—see 106, 122, 242.

69. Caird, *Glory*, esp. 271, believes that ἐδοξάσθη should be taken as an intransitive
passive, and translates "God has revealed his glory in him."

70. Dauer, *Passionsgeschichte*, 239; Carson, *John*, 482; Moloney, *John*, 385; Lincoln,
John, 386–87; against Weidemann, *Tod Jesu*, 110, 119–20, who takes both occurrences
of ἐδοξάσθη in 13:31 to refer to the departure of Judas and, therefore, the cleansing of
the circle of the disciples from the power of the devil and the gathering together of the
true children of God announced in 11:52. Weidemann's interpretation is an attempt to
do justice to the change in tense from aorist indicative passive in 13:31 and the future
in 13:32 together with the different temporal phrases νῦν in v. 31 and εὐθὺς in v. 32.
But, in response, it may be argued that 12:23 has already announced the coming of the
hour of the cross, while 12:31 has twice used νῦν of the cross. Weidemann seems to
underestimate the way in which in the Farewell Discourse the evangelist can switch the
time referents within a comparatively short space (see footnote 80 below and especially
Culpepper's comments quoted there).

71. Assuming ἐν αὐτῷ carries the same sense as in v. 31b (against Thüsing,
Erhöhung, 236).

72. In fact, many mss (including Sinaiticus, A D Q) have the reflexive.

case, the sense would be that the Father glorifies Jesus as, in continuing union with the Father, the Son sends the Paraclete-Spirit and the Son's work is extended (cf. 17:5, 21).[73]

Arguably, both ideas are Johannine, but perhaps the final clause in v. 32 favors the latter, and to that clause, as the second statement contained in these verses, we now turn: "and God will glorify him immediately."[74] The εὐθὺς could refer either to the gift of the Paraclete-Spirit or the mission of the church, or both since the two are closely bound together. This final clause serves to emphasize the immediacy of the glorification promised in the previous clause.[75]

We thus meet in 13:31–32 a double glorification: one that is asserted to have happened, i.e., the cross, and one that follows this and flows from it. There is a distinction and yet also a close connection.

Thirdly, Jesus prayed at 17:1 "Father, the hour has come: glorify your Son that the Son may glorify you." The statement of 12:23 is now put in terms of a prayer. Like 13:31, this prayer shows that the glorification of the Son involves that of the Father—there is a mutual glorification in the hour of the cross.[76] Jesus' prayer is that despite his impending death on the cross the Father will recognize him as his Son and vindicate him (cf. 16:10). If the disciples abandon Jesus in this hour, God does not and the prayer asks that the Father will in fact vindicate his Son and accredited envoy's surrender of his life in the service of his Father.[77] As the continuation of the sentence in v. 2 (a καθὼς clause) shows, this glorification has saving consequences for all humanity in terms of the gift of eternal life.

Fourthly, in the High Priestly prayer, at 17:4, Jesus says, "I have glorified you on earth, having accomplished the work which you gave me to do." The assertion that he has accomplished the work entrusted to him

---

73. Thüsing, *Erhöhung*, 236, sees the Johannine idea of mutual glorification as support for this interpretation. He sees ἐν αὐτῷ here as equivalent to παρὰ of 17:5 (as does Riedl, *Heilswerk*, 121).

74. Cf. Thüsing, *Erhöhung*, 237.

75. Chibici-Revneanu, *Herrlichkeit*, 213, suggests that from the narrative standpoint there is a glorification still to come.

76. There is no need to project this glorification into the future after the cross, as Thüsing, *Erhöhung*, 191, does (in his second stage). Dauer, *Passionsgeschichte*, 239, sees the Passion and Resurrection referred to, but also a pointer to the future.

77. Chibici-Revneanu, *Herrlichkeit*, 255, has helpfully pointed to the paradox that though Jesus will be abandoned by his disciples, he will nonetheless be glorified.

"looks back" at the cross (cf. 19:30 "It is finished"). This helps to focus the ἐδόξασα on the cross also,[78] rather than taking it as a complexive (or constative or summary) aorist and as applicable to the entire ministry.[79] Coming so soon after the prayer of 17:1, this may surprise the reader/ hearer. But once we recognize that the evangelist oscillates between a Supper standpoint and the post-cross situation of the church,[80] the juxtaposition of prayer and assertion in vv. 1 and 4 becomes intelligible.

The phrase "on earth" is conditioned by the fact that so much of the prayer is spoken from the standpoint of the exaltation to heaven. From the "standpoint" of heaven, the cross is "on earth;" from the standpoint of earth, the cross involves a being lifted up from earth.

Fifthly, we turn to a comment made by the evangelist on the invitation to come to Jesus and on the attached promise of receiving streams of living water (7:37–38): "He said this about the Spirit, whom believers in him were to receive; for the Spirit was not yet [given], because Jesus had not yet been glorified" (v. 39). The Spirit is not given during Jesus' earthly ministry but only after Jesus has returned to the Father (cf. 16:7), which he does at and through his death. His being glorified is associated with his death.

Sixthly, in a similar note at 12:16, the evangelist comments on the triumphal entry and the quotation of Zech 9:9: "His disciples did not understand these things at first, but when Jesus had been glorified, then they remembered that these things had been written about him and people had done these things to him." Jesus had to die and return to the Father before the coming of the Spirit, one of whose tasks is to

---

78. Strathmann, *Johannes,*232; Brown, *John* 2:242 (apparently); Carson, *John,* 557; Lincoln, *John,* 435; Knöppler, *Theologia Crucis,* 113, 181–82; Chibici-Revneau, *Herrlichkeit,* 258. Moloney, *John,* 461, sees ministry and cross involved.

79. Against Barrett, *John,* 504; Schnackenburg, *John* 3:168; Beasley-Murray, *John,* 297; Thüsing, *Erhöhung,* 73–74; Blank, *Krisis,* 273; Riedl, *Heilswerk,* 111; Ferreira, *Johannine Ecclesiology,* 92. Lindars, *John,* 520, seems on his own in applying ἐδόξασα solely to the ministry and then taking v. 5 to refer to the cross (he compares this with 12:28).

80. Brown, *John* 2:742; Schnackenburg, *John* 3:174,201; Lincoln, *John,* 386–87, 433; Thüsing, *Erhöhung,* 73. See also Onuki, *Gemeinde,* 165–66, 169 (Onuki constantly throughout his work speaks of a melding of past and present horizons). Culpepper, *Anatomy,* 91, comments that the temporal perspectives of the Farewell Discourse "are notoriously difficult to sort out." Zumstein, *Kreative Erinnerung,* 213–17, has a brief but helpful analysis of the aorist, perfect and future tenses in John 17 in his essay "Die verklärte Vergangheit. Geschichte *sub specie aeternitatis* nach Johannes 17:2"

make the disciples remember what Jesus had said and done, with deeper understanding (14:26; 16:14–15),[81] together with imparting a deeper understanding of Scripture.

It is well at this stage for us to recall that a not dissimilar remark about an initial lack of understanding by the disciples followed by a later remembering occurred earlier at 2:22. There, however, the evangelist did not mention Jesus' glorification but rather "When he was raised from the dead." This phrase points us to the post-Easter period, the time of the Paraclete-Spirit, the time of the church. It suggests that the resurrection would not be absent from the evangelist's mind when he spoke about a glorification in the cross and a return to the Father.[82]

The seventh passage to be mentioned is 11:4, to which we return after our previous consideration of part of it in the section on the δόξα visible in Jesus' ministry. In full, it runs: "This illness is not unto death but for the glory of God in order that through it the Son of God might be glorified."

There are many exegetes who assume without discussion that the meaning is that Jesus the Son of God will be honored because of the miracle which he has performed.[83] But there is another possibility, viz.: the raising of Lazarus will lead to the crucifixion and it is that event which brings about the glorification of Jesus. The phrase "through it" (δι' αὐτῆς) points us forward to vv. 45–53, where the different reactions to the sign are recorded: many believed (v. 45), but some went to the Pharisees and informed them (v. 46). Therefore (probably οὖν has its full inferential force here), the chief priests and Pharisees summoned the Sanhedrin (v. 47), and it was at that meeting that a decision was taken to put Jesus to death (v. 53). Thus, as is universally agreed, it is the raising of Lazarus which in the Fourth Gospel leads to the death of Jesus. In the light of the evangelist's usage, the second view of 11:4b is to be preferred: the evangelist describes the death of Jesus as his glorification yet again.[84]

81. Pamment, *Doxa*, 12–13, says that 7:39 and 12:16 "expect a specific event in Jesus' life which is his glorification and this glorification refers to Jesus' death."

82. Thüsing, *Erhöhung*, 279–80, where he regards the "second stage" as beginning with the Resurrection.

83. So Barrett, *John*, 390; Lindars, *John*, 387; Carson, *John*, 406.

84. So Strathmann, *Johannes*, 174; Bultmann, *John*, 397–98; Brown, *John* 1:431; Schnackenburg, *John* 2:323 (holds to both meanings); Morris, *John*, 539; Becker, *Johannesevangelium* 2:356; Beasley-Murray, *John*, 187; Moloney, *John*, 325, 336 (earlier, JSM, 210); Lincoln, *John*, 319; Thüsing, *Erhöhung*, 229–30; Betz, *Paraklet*, 202; Koester,

Eighthly, in dispute with the Jews, Jesus asserts "I honor (τιμῶ) my Father . . . I do not seek my own glory (τὴν δόξαν μου)" (8:49–50; cf. 5:41). Jesus is thus acting as an agent should, *viz.* to seek his sender's glory (cf. 7:18), whereas his opponents basically seek glory from one another (5:44; cf. 12:43).[85] Indeed, were he to seek to glorify himself, such glory (δόξα) would count for nothing (v. 54). Jesus has, in reality, no need to seek his own glory, for "it is my Father ὁ δοξάζων με" (8:54). How and when does the Father glorify Jesus? There seem to be three possibilities:

(a) in his public ministry through his signs and his revelation;[86]

(b) in his death;[87]

(c) through the work of the Spirit, cf. 16:14–15.[88]

To take ὁ δοξάζων με of the cross would fit admirably into the evangelist's linguistic usage as revealed thus far. If this is acceptable, it would be a case of the full meaning only becoming apparent at a "second reading"[89] (δοξάζειν has only occurred at 7:39 previous to this passage)—that is, for a new reader. Johannine Christians, "in the know" as far as Johannine language is concerned, would be aware of

---

Symbolism, 117; Nicole Chibici-Revneanu, *Herrlichkeit*, 143, 148, 154–55.

85. Chibici-Revneanu, *Herrlichkeit*, often stresses the conflict in John of two glory systems—the one in which God's glory is all that matters, and the other in which humans seek recognition from one another (see, e.g., 92–105, 108–9, 114, 125–41, 198–204, 214, 330, 516, 583–90, 618, 624).

86. Wikenhauser, *Johannes*.184; Bultmann, *John*, 301; Schnackenburg, *John* 2:220–21; Blank, *Krisis*, 272.

87. Marsh, *Saint John*, 369–70; Beasley-Murray, *John*, 137–38; Carson, *John*, 356; Moloney, *John*, 286; Wilckens, *Johannes*, 152 (apparently, for while not saying so expressly, he refers to 12:28; 17:1); Chibici-Revneanu, *Herrlichkeit*, 131 (but she raises the question whether the present participle suggests a process rather than a particular event. She also maintains that ὁ κρίνων suggests that in the hour of his glorification judgment will be given for Jesus, referring to 12:31; 16:11). Strathmann, *Johannes*, 153, combines (a) and (b).

88. Thüsing, *Erhöhung*, 198–99.

89. Interestingly, Onuki, *Gemeinde*, 208, makes the observation that one needs to read John's Gospel at least twice—the story of Jesus Christ diachronically, to understand his person, but then the story is only truly understood when one has first understood the person of Jesus Christ, while Culpepper, *Anatomy*, 179, says that the work gains from repeated readings. Carson, *John*, 171, states that, "the book becomes deeper and more complex when it is read the second, third and subsequent times." Cf. also Bauckham, *Testimony*, 245.

the nuances. In all honesty, it cannot but be admitted that meaning (a) would fit the context, but it does have overall Johannine usage against it. Meaning (c) is also possible and fits Johannine theology (see below), but the glorification of Jesus by the Paraclete-Spirit still flows from what happens in the cross.

Ninthly, we turn to 12:28, which follows the announcement that the hour has come for the Son of Man to be glorified (v. 23). Jesus sets aside the possibility of asking to be saved from the hour. He prays, "Father, glorify your name." In response a voice from heaven says: "I both have glorified it and will glorify it again."

One possible explanation is that the aorist indicative active ἐδό ξασα looks back over the earthly ministry as a completed event[90]—it has been used by the Father to glorify himself,—while the future indicative active δοξάσω looks forward to the cross.[91] On this view, the Father affirms as his aim in the cross what the Son asserts to be his aim in his prayer of 17:1 ("Father, the hour has come: glorify your Son that the Son may glorify you").

There is, however, an alternative explanation which is attractive, viz. to take the ἐδόξασα as either including the cross[92] or as a specific reference to the cross[93] and the δοξάσω as referring to the period after the exaltation when the Paraclete-Spirit works[94] or the fate of the disciples after Easter.[95]

Once we recognize the way the evangelist's thought may anticipate the cross, there is a case for taking ἐδόξασα as referring solely to the cross, and this interpretation receives support from the perfect indicative active ἐλήλυθεν in 12:23 and the two-fold νῦν of 12:31 (cf. 13:31

90. The so-called Complexive or Constative Aorist.

91. E.g., Carson, *John*, 441; Lincoln, *John*, 352. Weidemann, *Tod Jesu,* 119, takes ἐδό ξασα to refer to the raising of Lazarus and the future δοξάσω to refer to the death of Jesus, but this is based on his interpretation of 11:4 where he takes the verb to refer to the ensuing event of the raising of Lazarus—an interpretation which we have rejected above.

92. So Thüsing, *Erhöhung*, 195–96; de Boer, *Perspectives*, 197. Brown, *John* 1:476, sees this as "plausible."

93. Morris, *John*, 596; Pamment, *Doxa*, 13; Chibici-Revneanu, *Herrlichkeit*, 187.

94. Thüsing, *Erhöhung*, 195; Riedl, *Heilswerk,* 122.

95. Pamment, *Doxa*, 13; de Boer, *Perspectives*, 197 (specifically, the martyrdoms of Johannine Christians, by which God is glorified—John 12:25–26). Chibici-Revneanu, *Herrlichkeit*, 187, maintains that the πάλιν δοξάσω shows that Jesus' glorification does not disappear into the past, but is an abiding reality after the hour.

The Son of Man ἐδοξάσθη). While absolute certainty is impossible, this interpretation deserves serious consideration.[96]

Thus far, building on the solid ground provided by texts like 12:23; 13:31; 17:1, 4; 7:39; 12:16, we have argued that the evangelist sees the cross as the glorification of Jesus by the Father. Into this interpretation 11:4 fits nicely. Two further texts (8:54; 12:28c) would also fit in with this line of interpretation, but this meaning is less certain in their case. On the other hand, if 8:54; 12:28c were taken to be referring to the cross, a uniformity of linguistic usage would result: by this we mean that the evangelist would be using δοξασθῆναι of the cross and not the earthly ministry, whereas the noun δόξα at 1:14; 2:11; 11:4, 40 unquestionably refers to the ministry.

We continue our survey: there is a glorification of Jesus in the period *after the cross/return to the Father*. In the first place, it is said of the Paraclete-Spirit that he will glorify Jesus because he will take from what belongs to Jesus and interpretatively proclaim it to the disciples (16:14). More will be said on this verse later: here it is sufficient for us to point out that since the Paraclete-Spirit comes after Jesus' glorification (7:39), and since the death of Jesus must be included in what can be classified as part of what belongs to Jesus, then there is a link between the glorification on the cross and the future that flows from it.[97] They are separable and yet inseparable. By recalling to mind and interpreting what Jesus said and did (cf. 12:16; 14:26), the Paraclete-Spirit glorifies Jesus.

Secondly, in the High Priestly prayer, Jesus declared that he was praying for those whom the Father gave him (17:9ab). They belonged to the Father (v. 9c), but, since the Father has given everything to the Son (3:35), Jesus can say: "All that is mine is Yours and Yours is mine, and I have been glorified (δεδόξασμαι) in them" (v. 10). As so often in this prayer, we are in the situation after Easter.[98] It is believers who have recognized that the Son came from the Father and that he was sent by the

---

96. Chibici-Revneanu, *Herrlichkeit*, 187, prefers the continuity of one glorification through time on the basis of πάλιν (following Moloney, *John*, 360).

97. This is what Riedl, *Heilswerk*, 170, 181, 183–86, describes as the extension of the Son's work or its becoming fruitful. Chibici-Revneanu, *Herrlichkeit*, e.g., 229, 617, 628, also asserts that the basic glorification in Jesus' death continues in the ongoing glorification in the community assembled by Jesus.

98. Bultmann, *John*, 501; Brown, *John*, 2:758, 763; Lindars, *John*, 523; Moloney, *John*, 461; Thüsing, *Erhöhung*, 174–76, 179. Barrett, *John*, 507, includes both the earthly and post-Easter periods.

Father, who has bestowed everything on the Son, and they have received the words of the Father from Jesus (17:6–8). Thus, the very existence of believers is a sign of the victoriously completed work of the Son.[99] In addition, in the light of 14:12, we may think of the fact that in union with Jesus, the disciples are doing greater works than he (14:12) and so they have glorified their Lord and Master and that has ongoing effects (hence the perfect tense δεδόξασμαι).[100]

But, if there is a glorification of Jesus after the cross according to 16:14; 17:10, the Son's work of glorifying the Father will be continued by his agents, his disciples (17:18; 20:21), when they "bear fruit" by abiding in the true vine and by engaging in prayer in union with him. At 14:13 Jesus promises: "I will do whatever you ask in my name in order that the Father might be glorified in the Son." The petitionary prayer of disciples who are united with Jesus will promote the glory of the Father who is himself in union with the Son. The Son will act through his disciples— greater works—and, as in his earthly life and death, so he seeks the glory of the Father after the cross

At 15:8, Jesus says: "My Father will be glorified[101] by this, that you bear much fruit and so prove yourselves to be my disciples." Whether fruit-bearing refers to ethical conduct or engaging in missionary work will be discussed later. Here all that needs to be said is that in union with Christ, lifted up on a cross and to the Father, the disciples will bear fruit and this will glorify the Father.

A specific example is also given in the supplementary chapter 21: Peter will glorify God by the manner of his death (v. 19).

Thus, our survey of δοξασθῆναι has shown four aspects:

(a) Jesus is glorified *in* the cross

(b) Jesus is glorified *after* the cross

(c) Jesus glorifies *the Father in the cross*

---

99. As Chibici-Revneanu, *Herrlichkeit*, 282, rightly maintains. She also adds the fact of love between the disciples that is a sign that they are his disciples (13:35).

100. Against Lincoln, *John*, 436, who takes the glorification of Jesus to be displayed in the response of the disciples in the earthly ministry.

101. The aorist indicative passive (ἐδοξάσθη) has been taken as a timeless aorist (Barrett, *John*, 474) or gnomic aorist (Brown, *John* 2:662). However, where the subordinate clause is referring to the future as in 15:8, the main verb must also refer to the future: what is indicated is deemed as certain to occur (cf. *BD*, para. 333 (2), where it is called a "futuristic aorist"; Brooks and Winberry, *Syntax*, 94).

(d) Jesus glorifies *the Father after the cross*

(iii) Glory Before and After Jesus' Incarnate Ministry

There is a δόξα of *the pre-existent and post-earthly state*. In 17:5 Jesus asks for the glory which he had with his Father before the creation of the world and presumably did not have during his earthly life or else he would not ask for it.[102] "And now, Father, glorify me with your own self with the glory which I had with you before the world was." The glory is presumably being with the Father.[103] The prayer is a prayer, uttered on the threshold of the cross (καὶ νῦν), to return home (cf. the statement about returning to the Father in 13:1; and also 6:62).

At the end of the prayer, Jesus prays that those whom the Father has given him might be where he is, "that they might see my glory which you have given me, because you loved me before the foundation of the world" (v. 24). The perfect indicative active (δέδωκας) in v. 24d indicates that this particular wish is uttered from the standpoint of after the cross-exaltation.[104] But Jesus' obtaining the pre-existent glory also has the disciples in mind—it is not something that just concerns him alone. They are to see this glory. One day, the disciples will see the full glory of Christ, when they are reunited with Christ where he is, in the Father's home (cf. 14:1–3),[105] and perfected into one (17:23).

This "seeing" is something different from the "seeing" mentioned in 1:14 of the glory visible in the incarnate Logos' ministry—it is what the

---

102. Thüsing, *Erhöhung*, 206, 222; Haenchen, *John* 2:502; Carson, *John*, 557. Even Chibici-Revneanu, *Herrlichkeit*, 266, who is keen to deny that there is a distinction of δόξαι in John, says that Jesus did not have δόξα in the same way as he had it when he returned again completely into the unity with the Father (Rather than speaking of different δόξαι, she prefers to speak of one δόξα in relation to different places—see 265–66, 275). Käsemann has vehemently opposed this interpretation (e.g., *Testament*, 12: "He does not really change himself, but only his place" in the incarnation, and on 18–19 he argues that "the glory of Jesus is not the result of his obedience . . . On the contrary, obedience is the result of Jesus' glory and the attestation of his glory in the situation of the earthly conflict"), but he does not discuss 17:5.

103. Thüsing, *Erhöhung*, 206–7 stresses this forcibly.

104. Barrett, *John*, 513–14; Brown, *John* 2:771; Sanders, *John*, 378. Cf. the comment of Meeks, *Man from Heaven*, 159, on chapter 17 as a whole—"the summary de-briefing of the messenger" (quoted with approval by Ashton, *Understanding*, 497).

105. Bultmann, *John*, 519; Lindars, John, 532; Chibici-Renveanu, *Herrlichkeit*, 300–301, 310–11, although not ruling out some present eschatological sense, uses the phrase that this seeing takes place "outside of the world."

author of the first epistle meant when he wrote "We shall see him as he is" (1 John 3:2).[106]

The two petitions of vv. 5 and 24 form a kind of inclusion[107] insofar as both speak of the glory with the Father: v. 5 speaks of being with the Father, v. 24 of the love between Father and Son.

In a similar way to 17:24, the tenses of 17:22 point to the time after Jesus' exaltation and to the standpoint of the time in which the writer was living. Jesus has just asked that the unity of his disciples may reflect the unity between him and the Father (vv. 20–21). He then says at v. 22: "I have given them the glory which you gave me, that they may be one even as we are one." We note firstly that the Father has given glory to Jesus (τὴν δόξαν ἣν δέδωκας). This assertion points to the fulfillment of the request of v. 5[108] where Jesus prayed for the δόξα enjoyed with the Father before the foundation of the world. This assumption, plus the purpose clause of v. 22b "that they may be one even as we are one," surely indicates that we should take "glory" here to mean that perfect fellowship of love between the Father and the Son.[109]

Secondly, Jesus has passed this on (δέδωκα) to the disciples. Already the disciples share in this glory (of fellowship with the Father) because they are already united with him—Jesus is in them and they in him. That being taken up into the unity of the Father and the Son

---

106. Bultmann, *John*, 519; Schnackenburg, *John* 3:223; Beasley-Murray, *John*, 304; Carson, *John*, 569; Lincoln, *John*, 440, refer to 1 John 3:2, though differing in whether they think that John has in mind the eschatological consummation or the individual believer's death. Chibici-Revneanu, *Herrlichkeit*, 301, points out that John has used the verb θεωρεῖν here (differently at 2:11—probably she meant 1:14; 11:40; and 12:41). She sees the new element at 17:24 as the new type of seeing (301, 326).

107. Cf. Thüsing, *Erhöhung*, 220. Carson, *John*, 569, also sees an unambiguous reference to v. 5.

108. Barrett, *John*, 513; Brown, *John* 2:771; Schnackenburg, *John* 3:218; Thüsing, *Erhöhung*, 178, 181–82, 184.

109. Thüsing, *Erhöhung*, 182, and Moloney, *John*, 474, take this glory as the loving union between the Father and the Son. See Beasley-Murray, *John*, 302, for a discussion of the interpretations of glory in this verse. Carson, *John*, 568–69, sees Jesus speaking proleptically about the completion of his revelatory work in manifesting God's character. Bultmann, *John*, 515, takes the "glory" of Jesus to consist in his being the revealer and being believed to be such, with his community receiving a share in his work of revelation. Chibici-Revneanu, *Herrlichkeit*, 286–99, interprets the glory to be that of the envoys of the Envoy of the Father ("Gesandte des Gesandten"). Christ, now in perfected unity with the Father who sent him, himself becomes the sender. The disciples are incorporated into the glory and the sending-commission of the God who gives.

has a missionary aim: twice it is said that the unity which should exist between disciples should have belief-arousing potential. It should lead the world to believe that the Father has sent the Son (v. 21), and this thought is repeated in v. 23, this time "that the world may known that you have sent me and that you have loved them as you have loved me." The exclusion of the world from the prayer at v. 9 is, thus, more apparent than real. The unity of believers, grounded in the unity of the Father and the Son, has, therefore, a certain revelatory quality.[110]

(iv) The Relation between 17:1 and 17:5

What is the relation between the prayers of 17:1 and 17:5? *Prima facie*, there is a difference and yet there is an overlap. In 17:1, the prayer for glorification is linked with the hour which is the hour of the cross. The prayer of 17:5 looks to the resumption of fellowship with the Father in the Father's house. Insofar as the cross is the means by which he leaves this world and goes on his way home, there is an overlap and a link. There is to Western minds, trained to express themselves in neat, progressively unfolding logic, a rather bewildering and disconcerting sequence in 17:1–5:

(a) Verse 1 is a prayer for the Son's glorification that the Son may glorify the Father

(b) Verse 4 is a statement that he has completed the task (which must, at least, include the cross) entrusted to him, and thereby he has glorified the Father

(c) Verse 5 is a prayer for a resumption of his glory, the glory of fellowship with the Father, when he returns from his task.

It is, however, imperative that we let John speak for himself and not try and impose Western logic on him!

There are two considerations on which we can reflect. Firstly, at this point John may let his use of δοξασθῆναι become more flexible, so that he uses it both of the cross (v. 1) and of the return home (v. 5). There is here no rigid separation between what takes place on the cross and what follows.

Secondly, the prayer for his glorification on the cross that he in turn may glorify the Father (v. 1) is in some way linked with vv. 2–3 as the καθὼς (v. 2) shows. The theme of vv. 2–3 is eternal life of which

110. Chibici-Revneanu, *Herrlichkeit*, 296, 299.

the Father has made the Son the mediator and dispenser. The Father has given the Son universal authority (v. 2a) in order that he in turn might give eternal life to those whom the Father gave him (we note, but do not pursue at this stage, the predestinarian coloring of this phrase). What sense has καθώς, then, and how are vv. 1 and 2 linked? The prayer for glorification in the cross (v. 1) will in fact be the realization of the Father's purpose to give eternal life ("even as you gave him authority . . . to give eternal life to all those whom you gave him"). By conferring eternal life on those who belong to the Father and whom the Father gave him, he will both glorify the Father and be glorified! At what point did this power which the Father gave him become effective? We may be reasonably confident in saying—at the cross![111]

This is an important clue. As Lindars aptly says, "It is not just Jesus' own position which is at stake. It is the salvation of all men, whose eternal destiny has been committed to his charge."[112] The cross is vital for the salvation of humanity, for eternal life.

(v) A Two-stage Glorification?

We are now ready to address the issue at stake between Thüsing[113] and his critics. As we mentioned before, Thüsing maintained that there were two stages in Jesus' glorification (up to and including the cross and post-cross. It should be mentioned that Thüsing pointed out that he did not intend the idea of "stages" to be taken in a Lucan sense[114]). We begin by setting out the evidence afresh in summary form:

> i. There is a glory of the Word's pre-existent state—17:5. The evangelist uses δόξα for this.
>
> ii. There is a glory revealed in the incarnate ministry, for which again the evangelist uses δόξα (1:14; 11:4, 40).
>
> iii. There is a glory of the cross: here the evangelist uses the verb

111. Cf. Schnackenburg, *John* 3:171. Thüsing, *Erhöhung*, 231, sees the bestowal as pre-temporal, but its realisation as happening through the lifting up or going to the Father (cf. 191, 225)—cf. Brown, *John* 2:740; Carson, *John*, 555.

112. Lindars, *John*, 518; cf. Strathmann, *Johannes*, 232: "In this first section [i.e., 1–5] it is only apparently a question of a prayer of Jesus for himself. Not for his own sake but for the sake of this goal [*viz.* achieving God's saving will]. For the sake of God's glory through the saving of people, Jesus prays for his exaltation to his heavenly place of honour." See also Thüsing, *Erhöhung*, 220.

113. Moloney, *JSM*, 196, has endorsed Thüsing's position.

114. Thüsing, *Erhöhung*, 311.

δοξάζειν. The Father glorifies the Son in and through the cross (accordingly, both active and passive forms of the verb may be used: 7:39; 8:54; 11:4; 12:16, 23, 28a; 13:31; 17:1). The Son's glorification involves a glorification of the Father, 13:31; 17:1, 4.

iv. There is a glorification of the Son in his post-earthly state, by the Paraclete-Spirit and by his disciples (16:14; 17:10), for which the verb is also used. The Son continues to glorify the Father through his disciples (14:13; 15:8—the verb is used in both these instances also).

v. The Son returns home to the Father and this state is described as one of glory (δόξα at 17:5, 22, and 24, with the verb δοξασθῆναι being used once, in conjunction with δόξα, at 17:5).

It may be puzzling at first sight that the evangelist can speak of (a) a manifestation of Jesus' glory in his incarnate ministry and a glorification of Jesus on the cross,[115] *and* (b) the glorification of Jesus in the cross and a further glorification in the post-cross era. Yet that is exactly what he does do! Actually, both Blank and Riedl do in fact speak in terms of some sort of development, while formally denying it on the grounds that from John's standpoint it is the glorified Christ who speaks. Thus Blank speaks of both the glory of the ministry, which has a symbolic and preliminary character ("zeichenhafter und . . . vorläufigen Charakter"), and a specific glorification which marks the beginning of the definitive state of glory ("der definitive Herrlichkeitstand").[116] Riedl sees in the Fourth Gospel the pre-existent glory of Christ; an earthly glory; and a glory after death (in which what was done in the ministry, and especially the cross, becomes permanently present)[117]—since death is the means by which Jesus returns to his pre-temporal glory, he may be said to be glorified.[118]

One is left wondering whether what we have is a difference of emphasis rather than an unbridgeable gulf, especially as Thüsing would now stress the relation between the concepts of being lifted up and glorified more closely and would link more strongly together the lifting up and its effect.[119]

115. As mentioned earlier, Kasemann, *Testament*, 7, calls it "astonishing,"

116. Blank, *Krisis*, 272.

117. Riedl, *Heilswerk*, 78, 129, 169.

118. Ibid., 132.

119. Thüsing, *Erhöhung*, 305. Note too how on 46 Thüsing had written that John

Thüsing is, of course, perfectly well aware of John's mode of presentation—that he lets the glorified Christ speak to the reader,[120] but
claims that John does differentiate between a "being glorified" and "not
yet being glorified" (7:39; 12:23 etc.),[121] and he is surely right here. We
may also raise the question whether Riedl has ended up by downplay-
ing John's choice of a Gospel-form. Thus, e.g., he can say that the future
tenses are used at 13:32 only from a literary point of view: they are determined by the Gattung of a Gospel.[122] This undermines his criticism that
Thüsing has failed to maintain consistently the post-Easter standpoint
from which the evangelist wrote the Gospel.[123]

We are left wondering why John chose a Gospel form and not
a meditation like the Gospel of Truth. The more one stresses John's
creative genius, the less likely is it that he would have felt bound by
Christian "precedent" (irrespective of the issue whether he knew any of
the Synoptic Gospels in their present form). John wrote a Gospel, a form
which enabled him to say something about both the earthly Jesus and
the exalted Lord; or, to put it another way, to let the exalted Lord interpret his earthly life and work (the agents of that interpretation being the
Paraclete-Spirit and the evangelist).

Neither Blank[124] nor Riedl[125] explore any possible distinction between the noun δόξα and the verb δοξασθῆναι, yet our study has revealed that the evangelist does appear to have made a careful distinction
between them in his use of them.

In the end, while not accepting all of Thüsing's exegetical positions—we see the cross specifically referred to in more glorification texts
than Thüsing who apportions them to his second stage—we think that
he is more correct than his critics in discerning that the evangelist has
wanted to indicate a "fresh access"[126] of glory to Jesus (and to his Father)

---

attaches importance both to setting the glorification, which lies in the past from the
standpoint of "the hour," over against the future glorification which derives from "the
hour," and combining the two (The relevant sentence is in italics in the original).

120. Ibid., e.g., 73, 164, 177–78.

121. Ibid., 311–12.

122. Ibid., 20–21.

123. Ibid., 30.

124. Blank, *Krisis*, 244, 264, 272, 277.

125. Riedl, *Heilswerk*, 75–81, 118–30, 417.

126. I draw the phrase from Caird, *Glory*, 269: "On the cross Jesus is to be invested with a new access of divine glory." Language is rather inadequate at this point.

in the cross and a further enhancement of that glory in the post-cross era. Provided we do not stratify in rigid sections this "development," we can accept that John has sought to indicate that something decisive and important occurs in the cross which marks the cross off from the ministry and which flows over into the post-cross era as the results of what happened in the cross are actualized. We may happily accept the terminology of Blank and Riedl that the cross is the point of intersection or transition, a radical turning,[127] to indicate the connection between the cross and what happens afterwards.

This lengthy survey of the themes of glory and glorification in the Fourth Gospel has served to confirm the conclusion from the survey of the hour texts—that John does have a theology of the cross. Something so decisive happens that the cross may be described as the glorification of the Son—and indeed of the Father, for it is vital for the salvation of the human race. One may feel even from this survey that more is being said about the cross than that through it Jesus is established permanently as the giver of life.[128]

We turn now to consider passages that speak of the lifting up of the Son of Man.[129]

Technically, Riedl (*Heilswerk*, 153, 170, 173) may be right in objecting to the idea of growth in glory for the Father and the Son, but perhaps, on the other hand, this is Western logic, not John's. Interestingly, Wilckens, *Johannes*, 262, wrote on 17:5 that Jesus' "reunion with God in the glory of the beginning before the creation of the world contains also *a decisively new aspect* [ein entscheidend neues Moment] beyond the beginning: that believers are incorporated into this unity of the Father and the Son." (My italics.) Kollmann, *Kreuzigung*, 177, also maintains that we should distinguish the glory (Herrlichkeit) of the incarnate Logos during his earthly life and the glorification (Verherrlichung) in the hour of the Passion. In being prepared to talk of a fresh access of glory to Jesus, we are in disagreement with the latest treatment of the theme of the glory/glorification in the Fourth Gospel by Chibici-Rivneanu, *Herrlichkeit*, already referred-to on several occasions. As already mentioned (note 102), she is adamant that there are not several δόξαι in John's treatment, and prefers to speak of one δόξα in relation to different places or the one glorification in relation to different times (see her discussion on 265–66).

127. E.g., Blank, *Krisis*, 273, and Riedl, *Heilswerk*, 103, 150, 156–57. Thüsing himself often uses a phrase like 'derived from' (ausgehend) the cross to indicate the connection.

128. As maintained by scholars like Vergote, Dodd, Blank, Riedl and others, mentioned above on pp. 10–13.

129. At this point, we may mention a remark by Zumstein, *Kreative Erinnerung*, 163, fn. 11: "While in other early Christian writings ὑψόω and δοξάζω are theologumena which belong to the story of Easter or have been identified with the resurrection,

3. The Lifting Up

As we turn to study John's use of ὑψοῦν, it is worth bearing in mind two facts:

(a) in literature before and around the New Testament era, this verb is used mainly in a metaphorical rather than a literal sense.[130]

(b) the propensity of the evangelist to use words and concepts with a double-meaning.

There are three occasions when the verb is used in the Fourth Gospel: Firstly, "And as Moses lifted up the serpent in the desert, so the Son of Man must be lifted up in order that everyone who believes may have eternal life in him" (3:14–15). The parallel with the action of Moses (Num 21:9) demands that in the first place the reference in the οὕτως clause must be to the lifting up on the cross, to the death of Jesus by crucifixion.[131] The cross is declared to be within the divine plan as the δεῖ shows (cf. 12:34; and also Mark 8:31; Luke 17:25; 24:26). God wills this event. The purpose of this being lifted up is to bring eternal life to everyone who believes, i.e., in Jesus the Son of Man. In union with Christ, the believer receives eternal life.[132]

In context, the statements in 3:14–15 and 16 offer the objective basis for the subjective experience mentioned earlier in the conversation with Nicodemus in connection with the work of the Spirit—birth from above.[133] Furthermore, if 3:13 has a purely christological stress and

---

these two concepts are in John linked to the cross."

130. The statistics are as follows: LXX has 184 occurrences, of which 145 are metaphorical and thirty-nine literal in meaning; Philo uses the word twice, both metaphorical, while Josephus' usage is the reverse—the five instances are all literal. Denis and Janssens, *Concordance grecque*, list nineteen instances, of which certainly twelve are metaphorical, four are probably literal and three could be either, but tending to the metaphorical. All fifteen cases in the NT outside John's Gospel and the four in the Apostolic Fathers are to be classified as metaphorical. (The neologism ὑπερυψοῦν is used metaphorically at Phil 2:9). Thus, in total, in Jewish and Christian literature, there are 229 occurrences of ὑψοῦν of which 181 are metaphorical and only forty-eight literal, i.e., 79% or roughly 4/5ths are metaphorical instances.

131. Morris, *John*, 224–25; Barrett, *John*, 214; Brown, *John* 1:145; Schnackenburg, *John* 1:394–97; Lindars, *John*, 157; Beasley-Murray, *John*, 50; Carson, *John*, 201; Lincoln, *John*, 153; Thüsing, *Erhöhung*, 4, 7–8; Moloney, *JSM*, 60–61 and *John*, 95,101; Bertram, ὕψος κτλ, *TDNT* 8. 610; Frey, *Schlange*, 182–83; Knöppler, *Theologia Crucis*, 157; Weidemann, *Tod Jesu*, 105.

132. Thüsing, *Erhöhung*, 14–15; Hofius, *Johannesstudien*, 64 (note 138).

133. E.g., Beasley-Murray, *Baptism*, 230–31, and Beasley-Murray, *John*, 54–55;

thereby provides a basis for what is said in vv. 14–15, the emphasis in 3:14–15 is a soteriological one:[134] the Son of Man obtains eternal life for the believer through his death on the cross. Theobald has pointed out that the comment in 12:34 really points back to 3:14–15: they both stress the divine necessity of the lifting up on the cross.[135] The evangelist has thus provided a kind of inclusio between the beginning and the end of the public ministry.

Secondly, "Then Jesus said to them, When you lift up the Son of Man, then you will know that ἐγώ εἰμι" (8:28). Since the Jews are responsible for lifting Jesus up, his death on the cross is certainly in mind. This fits in with the context where Jesus has spoken of his going away (vv. 21 [twice], 22). The crucifixion will have revelatory significance—people may know that, because of his union with the Father, he is the mediator of the divine presence on earth—hence the application of ἐγώ εἰμι to him.[136] (We shall discuss this passage at greater length in chapter 5).

Finally, "And if I be lifted up from the earth, I will draw all to myself." (Now he said this to signify by what kind of death he was going to die.) Then the crowd answered him, 'We have heard from the law that the Messiah remains forever. So how can you say that the Son of Man must be lifted up? Who is this Son of Man?'" (12:32–34).

12:33 is crucial and makes clear that the evangelist wants the reader to think of Jesus' death on the cross.[137] We believe that Nicholson is incorrect to let 13:1 dominate the discussion of the lifting up and that his claim that 12:33 raises the issue of what kind of death talk of "lifting up" allows for[138] can be countered by the need to remind readers of the literal

---

Dunn, *Baptism*, 192–93; Frey, *Schlange*, 179; Hofius, *Johannesstudien*, 59, 74, 78.

134. See Theobald, *Herrenworte*, 205, 214.

135. Theobald, *Herrenworte*, 36, 201.

136. See my *Cross*, 219–26; Moloney, *John*, 271, 274; Lincoln, *Truth*, 89, "The cross will be the means by which the divine identity and glory of Jesus . . . will be revealed" (repeated in Lincoln, *John*, 269).

137. Cf. Thüsing, *Erhöhung*, 3–4, 24 (curiously, apart from here, Thusing does not utilise 12:33); Brown, *John* 1:468; Schnackenburg, *John* 2:394; Morris, *John*, 599; Lindars, *John*, 434; Beasley-Murray, *John*, 215; Becker, *Johannesevangelium*, 2:397; Moloney, *JSM*, 262, 173–74, 182, and esp. 206, and *John*, 355, 360–61; Carson, *John*, 444; Lincoln, *John*, 352–53; de Boer, *Perspectives*, 170.

138. *Departure*, 137 [See above, p. 14–15]. Nicholson's other arguments are that (i) the theme of the Ascension occurs in the wider context (3:13; 8:21–22)—but, while true, this cannot weaken what the verses within themselves say; (ii) the lifting up must be interpreted within the overall descent-ascent schema, which is the structural frame-

sense, when in common usage the verb was employed predominantly in a metaphorical sense. Furthermore, the bewilderment of the crowd fits the idea of crucifixion, for the idea of such an ignominious death contradicts traditional Jewish ideas of the Messiah (cf. 1 Cor 1:22–23). Accordingly, we reject Nicholson's attempt to place most of the weight on ascension (accomplished through Jesus' death).

The question "How is it that you say that the Son of Man must be lifted up?" (formally this has not actually been said) contains the word δεῖ and points to the divinely-willed nature of the event (as at 3:14–15).[139] The lifting up will result in the drawing of all men and women to Jesus, the meaning of which will be discussed later in chapter 5.

Of course, for the evangelist, there would be no clash of meaning between what Scripture said and what Jesus had said. Through the literal lifting up on the cross Jesus will in fact be exalted to the Father, and will, therefore, abide forever.[140]

It will be noticed that in all three passages the lifting up is connected with the title Son of Man, though we cannot pursue that theme in this study.

Our survey, then, has revealed that ὑψοῦν refers in the first place to the cross. But is crucifixion only in mind? This is the position of Thüsing.[141] Here we believe that he does not make enough allowance for John's technique of double-entendre. Thüsing is probably afraid of weakening his theory of a two-stage glorification, by accepting that in the ὑψωθῆναι texts John might envisage a both/and: *both* the death on the cross *and* an exaltation back to the Father. In actual fact, Thüsing's discussion of the lifting up as enthronement is instructive:[142] Jesus enters

work for the Gospel, but it is still possible to do this without insisting that the major weight in ὑψωθῆναι must be on the ascension; (iii) the setting of John's approach is discussion and controversy about interpreting Jesus' death, with John seeing the cross as not an ignominious death, but a return to glory, an ascent. Controversy could well be in the background, but, again, this does not demand Nicholson's emphasis. We believe that Nicholson has not made sufficient allowance for John's penchant for double-entendre. Moloney, *John*, 361, calls Nicholson's view "unacceptable."

139. Frey, *Schlange*, 185, believes that 3:14b clearly stands in the background of John 12, as does Theobald, *Herrenworte*, 36, 201 (see note 135).

140. Cf. Scholtissek, *Geschrieben*, 218.

141. Thüsing, *Erhöhung*, 3–4, though he does maintain that ὑψωθῆναι is not simply a synonym for σταυρωθῆναι (12). See also Hofius, *Johannesstudien*, 62.

142. Thüsing, *Erhöhung*, 33–34.

on his lordship through the cross, but this throne is always still the cross insofar as Jesus rules in this way. The lifting up of Jesus is to the throne of his cross; it is his enthronement and is revelatory of salvation. Thüsing expressly says that the lifting up is not from an earthly to a heavenly world but to a throne.[143] The crucified is seen as the King dispensing life. This seems to me to be a rather too subtle interpretation. I can understand what he means when he says that Jesus' lordship is defined by his death on the cross ("denn auch das Herrschen ist ja noch von ihm bestimmt"),[144] but I am puzzled by his attempt to distinguish enthronement and entry into heaven.[145]

Thus, we feel that neither Nicholson nor Thüsing are to be followed in their differing one-sided interpretations. We would wish to put the primary emphasis on the cross, but the cross interpreted also as an exaltation. What the evangelist has done is to draw the theme of exaltation on to the cross[146] rather than to envisage two separate "moments"—the nadir of humiliation and degradation (cross) and the exaltation (whether this be seen in terms of resurrection, e.g., Paul in Rom 14:9, or ascension/session at God's right hand, e.g., Hebrews, or even resurrection-ascension-session at God's right hand, e.g., Luke-Acts). John interprets the cross as exaltation. It is as if he says to the readers: "This is how I see the cross. Come and see it from my perspective and share my vision." Or, perhaps, this ought to be rephrased: "This is how we see the cross. In a hostile world which sees things differently, do not let go of this vision of what the cross means, given us by the Paraclete-Spirit."

Has this re-interpretation of the cross been carried through because death was seen as departure—through death Jesus passes back to the Father and returns home? Of course, 13:1 is an indication that that is one aspect of the evangelist's thinking ("because Jesus knew that his hour to depart out of this world to the Father had come"). But, true as this is, is it *all*? Is it *merely* the return to the Father that secures eternal life? How are women and men drawn to Jesus? *Does something occur which justifies the*

---

143. Ibid., 34.

144. Ibid., 32.

145. Loader, *Christology,* 111, firmly rejects Thüsing's notion.

146. Cf. a similar approach too in Carson, *John,* 201; Lincoln, *John,* 153, 269, 353; Moloney, *JSM,* 63; de Boer, *Perspectives,* 170.

use of language like "If I be lifted up from the earth, I will draw all people to myself"' concerning the cross?[147]

At this stage we mention one other point concerning the three passages. Why did the evangelist leave it till 12:33 to make such a comment as he does there? The same might be said of the comment at 7:39—why not earlier at 4:14? It is certainly characteristic of his technique that the reader/hearer might not fully grasp the deepest significance of what has been said or done until he/she has read/heard much more of the story. Other examples would be 2:22 and 12:16: would these be fully intelligible until 14:26 had been read? Perhaps the evangelist left it till 12:33 because at this stage in the narrative the Passion was actually imminent. It is interesting to observe that Mark who from 8:30 onwards stresses the Passion leaves it till 10:45 before giving us a saying which explains something of the meaning of Jesus' death.

In summary, we may say that the lifting-up of Jesus in the Fourth Gospel contains a double meaning—literally, on a cross, and metaphorically, to the Father. Part of the divine purpose, it has revelatory significance and becomes the means of bestowing eternal life because in the lifting-up Jesus draws all people to himself. The relation between the revelation and being drawn into unity with Jesus will need to be explored.

Thus, it is certainly true that one aspect of the cross in John is that it is the means of the return of Jesus to the Father. We may concur with scholars[148] who stress this without however accepting that this is the only emphasis in John's thinking.

4. The Role of 1:29 in the Introduction[149]

There would be a general consensus that the section 1:19–51 has been shaped by the evangelist for theological purposes, specifically to point

---

147. We are not concerned with how or why the evangelist chose ὑψοῦν/ὑψωθῆναι. The verb does not occur in the LXX narrative in Num 21:8–9, where Moses is told to put the serpent on a pole: θὲς αὐτόν. It may well be that the evangelist was influenced by Isa 52:13 LXX (so Thüsing, *Erhöhung*, 36 (apparently); Moloney, *JSM*, 63, 180; Pamment, *Doxa*, 15–16; Kammler, *Johannesstudien*, 133; whereas Schnackenburg, *John* 2:407, says that this view is "not certain"). Hollis, *Johannine Pun*, 475–78, sees the influence of ns' used at Gen 40:13, 19, 20–22 (to lift up the head in the sense of restore to office of the cup-bearer and to lift the head off, meaning beheading and hanging on a tree in respect of the chief baker) and Isa 52:13

148. See pp. 13–15 for the views of Käsemann, Appold, Nicholson, and Ashton.

149. Traditionally, "Prologue" covers 1:1–18, and so I have opted for "Introduction"

further to the person of Jesus, already set forth as the Word Incarnate in 1:1–18. Negatively, John the Baptist bears witness to the fact that he himself is unimportant—he is neither the Messiah nor Elijah nor the prophet (like Moses). Positively, he bears witness to Jesus as the Lamb of God, the One who baptizes with the Holy Spirit and either the Elect One or the Son of God (whichever reading is adopted).[150]

There then follows a series of confessions by disciples—Messiah v. 41; the One of whom Moses and the prophets wrote v. 45; Son of God, King of Israel v. 49, culminating in Jesus' use of Son of Man v. 51. The entire section vv. 19–51 is concerned to set forth the significance of Jesus by means of these various descriptions and titles. It is as if the evangelist "lays his cards on the table": "This is the One about whom I am going to write. What I will have to say subsequently about him will substantiate that he is what he is here declared to be."[151]

Embedded among these titles and descriptions which focus on the person of Jesus we find one verse which concentrates on his function or work. The Prologue had emphasized his revelatory role in making known the otherwise un-seeable God (v. 18) and also his ability to enable believers to become children of God (v. 12); 1:29 centers attention on another function: "Look—the Lamb of God who takes away the sin of the world."

While a lot of ink has been expended on the search for a traditio-historical background to explain the juxtaposition of the title and the function, but without success,[152] there is a fair degree of unanimity that

---

to cover 1:1–51 rather than "proem" used by Dodd, *Interpretation*, x, 292. Theobald, *Fleishwerdung*, constantly speaks of the whole of chapter one as "the opening section of the Gospel" (die Evangeliumeroffnung), e.g., 169–71, and he refers to vv. 1–18 and 19–51 as "the opening diptych" (ibid., 171).

150. At v. 34, ὁ ἐκλεκτός is the harder reading, and it is easier to envisage its being altered to υἱὸς than vice versa. On the other hand, ὁ υἱὸς is better attested—by early witnesses like P66 and P74; by A and B, plus some Old Latin mss; and by Origen. If it was altered to υἱὸς, it was probably done fairly early—before P66 and P74. Schnackenburg, *John* 1:305; Brown, *John* 1:57; Becker, *Johannesevangelium* 1:97; and Carson, *John*, 152, accept it, while Barrett, *John*, 178, and Lindars, *John*, 112–13 incline to it. For a defense of υἱὸς τοῦ θεοῦ, see Wilckens, *Johannes*, 43.

151. Cf. Koester, *Symbolism*, 177, "The repeated reference 'the Lamb of God' in 1:36 indicates that Jesus' sacrificial death is basic to his identity."

152. See, e.g., the detailed discussion in Dodd, *Interpretation*, 230–38, and Brown, *John* 1:58–63, and more recently, Hasitschka, *Befreiung*, 15–173, and Knöppler, *Theologia Crucis*, 81–91.

an expiatory sense is to be understood for the phrase "who takes away the sin of the world."[153] This view involves the conviction that Jesus is the spotless lamb of God. His sinlessness (cf. 8:46), or, to put the matter positively, his perfect obedience (cf. 8:29), is presupposed: that alone guarantees that the "sacrifice" is acceptable. As the Lamb of God, he is spotless before his Father.

Granted this conceptual background to the phrase, many, however, then go on to deny that this is significant and allege that John has merely taken over traditional material from his community and this does not really accord with his own theology. Bultmann may be cited as a representative of this approach: on 1:29 he writes, "The death of Jesus is only rarely seen by him from the point of view of sacrifice, and in any case he nowhere else attaches the gift of forgiveness of sins specifically to Jesus' death, but understands it as the effect of his word (8:31f). The title must come from the Jewish Christian tradition, perhaps from its liturgical vocabulary."[154]

To which it has to be said—Then why did the evangelist include the phrase "who takes away the sin of the world" if it was at such odds with his own viewpoint? Why didn't he just have "The Lamb of God" (as at v. 36)? There is something inherently unsatisfactory about an approach that accords tremendous creativity and mastery over the material to a writer and then attributes the incorporation of material, alleged to be alien to his own viewpoint, to his tradition.[155]

It is unsatisfactory when a concept is held to be the dominant and controlling theme in a work (in this instance, salvation by revelation), and then, when other ideas appear allegedly in tension or conflict with or alongside of this concept, they are dismissed as church tradition and, therefore, lacking in significance.

---

153. So Bultmann, *John*, 96; Barrett, *John*, 176–77; Schnackenburg, *John* 1:298; Lindars, *John*, 109; Morris, *John*, 148; Becker, *Johannesevangelium* 1:97; Beasley-Murray, *John*, 25; Carson, *John*, 150; Lincoln, *John*, 113; Mussner, *Leben*, 101–2; Müller, *Heilsgeschehen*, 45; Wilckens, *Zeichen*, 76; Reidl, *Heilswerk*, 100; Lindemann, *Gemeinde*, 142 (note 60); Kohler, *Kreuz*, 199. Exceptions are Dodd, *Interpretation*, 237–38; Forestell, *Cross*, 157–66; Moloney, *John*, 59; and also Grayston, *Dying, We live*, 287 (the practice of sinning).

154. Bultmann, *John*, 96–97.

155. Metzen, *Sünde*, 23, is one of the latest scholars to voice this viewpoint: in criticism of Haenchen's dismissal of 1:29, he said that the question must be asked "why John has then taken up this source if it contradicted his intention?"

Alternatively, the phrase "who takes away the sin of the world" is attributed to a redactor who aimed to bring the original writing into line with church tradition/the theology of the First Epistle.[156] Again, is there not something unsatisfactory in this procedure, when evidence is eliminated because it does not fit a theory? And are we not dealing with a new author—the evangelist—if alleged changes of this nature are introduced?

We have pointed out the importance of the section 1:19–51. It is really Part Two of the Introduction.[157] May there not be a case for saying that the evangelist *deliberately* included 1:29 because he wanted to get the ideas contained in it across to the readers early on?[158] For the evangelist there may not have been an irreconcilable tension between salvation by revelation and through the cross.

It is also worth pointing out that here at the beginning of the Gospel there is a reference to the removal of sin and also at what may have been the original ending of the Gospel, and even in the Gospel's present shape is near the end, *viz.* 20:23. The disciples are commissioned to continue the ministry of Jesus (20:21b); Jesus breathes the Holy Spirit on them (20:22); and then he promises them, "Whose sins you forgive, they have been forgiven (ἀφέωνται); whose sins you retain, they have been retained (κεκράτηνται)" (20:23). Though the two halves of this saying are perfectly balanced, we may confidently assert that for John the emphasis falls on the first half[159]—after all, the Father's intention in sending the Son into the world is for the world to be saved (3:17) and the mission of

156. E.g., Becker, *Johannesevangelium*, 1:92; Ashton, *Understanding*, 491

157. Dodd, *Interpretation*, 292, said that "Chapter i forms a proem to the whole gospel. It falls into two parts: 1–18 commonly designated the Prologue, and 19–51, which we may, from the nature of its contents, conveniently call the Testimony."

158. The idea that 1:29 makes "a programmatic main thesis of the evangelist's Christology" is asserted by Metzner, *Sünde,*137 (which Knöppler, *Sühne,* 242, quotes with approval); also 112 (note 209), while 115–58 discuss 1:29, 36 under the heading "The confrontation of God and sin through the Lamb of God." Knöppler, *Theologia Crucis,* 91–92, also believes that "the exposed position" of 1:29 shows that it is a "key text of the Gospel." Schmid, *Gegner im 1. Johannesbrief?* 259, wrote "In 1:29 Jesus appears for the first time, which bestows on this verse special importance." See also Müller, *Heilsgeschehen,* 45; Turner, *Atonement,* 121; Hasitschka, *Befreiung,* 108; Frey, *Theologia Crufixi,* 213, and *Probleme,* 40; Dennis, *Jesus' Death,* 352.

159. With Schnackenburg, *John* 3:389; Heckel, *Hirtenamt,* 25. Theobald, *Herrenworte,* 194, believes that the positive member comes first because of the mission context of John 20:23, which, he argues, is more original than the ecclesiological one of Matthew 18:18 (16:19).

the disciples as presented in the High Priestly prayer is directed towards bringing the world to believe and so to be saved (17:18; 20–21, 23b). Without going into all the issues involved in this verse, we note that the verbs in the main clauses are both in the perfect passive indicative (divine passive construction). Either we take these verbs as "prophetic perfects"[160] or there may well be within the tense a picking up of the fact that the Lamb of God has in his death on the cross already taken away the sin of the world and so sins have already in one sense been forgiven. The mission of the church will actualize that forgiveness in the experience of those who respond positively in faith to the message about Jesus the Messiah, the Son of God.

The occurrence of the Lamb of God statement near the beginning of the Gospel and a reference to the forgiveness of sins after the cross should be borne in mind as probably another indicator of the importance of the cross in the thought of the evangelist.[161]

Another point to be borne in mind is that we have been assured that John the Baptist was a man sent from God with the express purpose of bearing witness to the light, to the Word (1:6–8; cf. 1:15) and this is the first statement by John the Baptist after he has actually seen Jesus in the story.[162] From the point of view of the flow of the narrative, therefore, 1:29 surely must have considerable significance. Furthermore, this stress on John the Baptist as a witness is maintained in further passages about him (3:27–30; 5:33–35; 10:40–42), so that at a second reading of the Gospel, the importance of what he had said at 1:29 would be even more realized by the reader.

5. The Cleansing of the Temple (John 2:13–22)

The evangelist has for thematic reasons moved the story of the cleansing of the temple from its original position close to the passion story.[163] The

160. See Robertson, *Grammar,* 898, where he refers to the "futuristic present perfect" as sometimes called "prophetico-perfect."

161. Those who see an overarching connection between John 1:29 and the promise of the forgiveness of sins in 20:23 include include Schnackenburg, *John* 3:388–89; Ruiz, *Missionsgedanke,* 274–75, quoted by Heckel, *Hirtenamt,* 25; Hasitschka, *Befreiung,* 144, 421; Metzner, *Sünde,* 12, 25, 27, 29–30, 271, 274, and 291; and Heckel, *Hirtenamt,* 25.

162. Wilckens, *Johannes,* 41. Helge K. Nielsen, *John's Understanding,* 253, stresses that John the Baptist is presented as such a powerful witness to Jesus.

163. In all probability, v. 17 betrays the original connection with the passion story, in the quotation from Ps 69:9, a psalm of the Righteous Sufferer, alluding to what will

Johannine story consists of a "diptych" of Temple Action (vv. 14–17) and Temple Word (vv. 18–22).[164] Both parts of the "diptych" contribute to the theme we are pursuing.

In the Temple Action, Jesus made a whip, drove out the animals and the doves on sale for sacrifice and their sellers and overturned the tables of the money changers (vv. 14–16), with the words, "Take these things from here. Stop making my Father's house a trading place" (v. 16b). The evangelist then commented that his disciples remembered that it had been written, "The zeal for your house will consume me." This is a quotation from Ps 69:9 (LXX 68:10), where the speaker laments that his loyalty to God and his zeal for God's house and its services have drawn upon him derisory taunts of godless enemies and placed his life in jeopardy. John altered the aorist indicative of the LXX (κατέφαγέν) into the future indicative καταφάγεταί and thus made the sentence into a prediction that Jesus' zeal for God's house would bring about his death ("consume" in the sense of "destroy").[165]

Thus, early on, we have a passion prediction. It is an early indication that Jesus' life is set under the sign of his death. The clash with the authorities (v. 18) indicates what will be the outcome of Jesus' life.[166]

At the heart of the second half of the "diptych" is the so-called Temple Logion (v. 19). Unlike the Synoptics, John records this saying in the discussion which follows Jesus' action in the temple. The Jews demanded a legitimating sign from Jesus to authenticate why he had dared to act as he had done within the temple. They are the custodians of the Temple and responsible for what transpires within it. "What sign do you

bring about the death of Jesus. Morris, *John*, 188–91, and Carson, *John*, 177–78, both defend a double cleansing of the Temple.

164. So the analysis of Johanna Rahner, *Tempel seines Leibes*, 256–330.

165. See Lindars, *John*, 140 (he has a lengthier discussion of the issues concerning the use of Ps 69:9 in *NT Apologetic*, 104–8. For taking consume in the sense of destroy, see also Schlatter, *Johannes*, 77–78; Bultmann, *John*, 124; Brown, *John* 1:124; Schnackenburg, *John* 1:347; Dodd, *Interpretation*, 301, and *Historical Tradition*, 158; Menken, *OT Quotations*, 40–44. In its present setting, it may also carry the connotation of "use up the energies of," "fire up for action," "consuming zeal" (so Barrett, *John*, 199), but if so, it would be another case of the evangelist's use of double-entendre.

166. I shall not go into the suggestion made by Schlatter, *Johannes*, 77–78; Barrett, *John*, 198; Schnackenburg, *John* 1:347; Menken, *OT Quotations*, 42, and Johanna Rahner, *Tempel seines Leibes*, 266, 277–78, that the disciples' remembering is an *immediate* reaction to Jesus' action and is not, as in the case of v. 22, to be set in the post-Easter era. This suggestion does not affect the point that we are pursuing.

show us [to justify the fact] that you are doing these things?" (v. 18). Jesus replied: "Destroy this temple and I will raise it in three days" (v. 19).[167]

The Jews pick up the phrase "this temple" and assume that the reference is to the Herodian temple (v. 20)[168] John used what for him was a misunderstanding, playing on the ambiguity contained in ὁ ναός and deliberately corrected it when he wrote: "But he was speaking about the temple of his body" (v. 21). So, *for the evangelist,* v. 19 meant "If you destroy *my body*, I will raise it in three days."

There is here a clear illusion to the resurrection in the use of ἐγείρειν (perhaps instead of οἰκοδομεῖν as in Mark 14:58) and "in three days."[169] Thus, as Brown remarks, "the interpretation of the cleansing in reference to the death of Jesus prepares for the interpretation of the saying about the Temple in reference to his resurrection."[170] The saying about the temple, interpreted by the evangelist of the raising of Jesus' body, thus itself contains a response to the demand by the Jews for a sign to justify his actions (v. 18). *The sign will be that when his body has been killed, he will raise it in three days.*[171]

The importance of the death and the resurrection to the evangelist is clearly seen. He goes on to say: "When, then, he had been raised [or had risen] from the dead, his disciples remembered . . ." Later on at 12:16, he will use the phrase "When Jesus had been glorified, then they [his disciples] remembered . . ." (cf. 7:39). The parallelism of 2:22 and 12:16 shows that the resurrection belongs within the glorification of Jesus.[172] Later on, Jesus will refer to the authority vested in him by the Father in terms which cover both his death and resurrection: "For this reason the Father loves me because I lay down my life, that I might take it again. No one takes it from me but I lay it down of my own accord. I

167. Arguably, a more original form than Mark 14:58, except for the use of ἐγείρειν.

168. That would indeed be the inference from Mark 14:58.

169. Johanna Rahner, *Tempel seines Leibes*, 307–9, points out that "in three days" is unusual in John's Gospel, but too much stress ought not to be placed on this, since nowhere else in his Gospel does John refer to a prediction of the resurrection "on the third day" or "after three days." Some have seen an allusion to the resurrection at 2:1, where the evangelist said that there was a wedding in Cana on the third day.

170. *Brown,* John 1:124.

171. Compare the independent Matthean treatment of the sign of Jonah (Matt 12:38–40).

172. Cf. Thüsing. *Erhöhung,* 279.

have authority to lay it down and I have authority to take it again. I have received this command from my Father." (10:17–18)

We come back to the question why the evangelist moved the cleansing from its position within the larger passion story and placed it at the beginning of his Gospel. We must not assume *a priori* that only one reason necessarily moved him to take this step. Thus, clearly, the cleansing of the temple raises the question of Jesus' relation to the old order, especially to Judaism, and the theme of worship. As such, it fits in with the preceding Cana miracle, for the water turned into wine is drawn from jars for Jewish rites of purification (2:1–11), and with the succeeding story of Nicodemus, a member of the Jewish authorities, a representative of Judaism, so to speak (3:1–2). The theme of worship (temple) further links it with the themes of living water (in Ezek 47:1 water flows from the temple) and localities of worship (Jerusalem and Gerizim), in the conversation with the Samaritan woman (4:7–26).[173]

However, in a more overt way than the Cana miracle at first reading (2:4), the cleansing of the temple episode sets the ensuing story of the ministry under the over-arching prospect of Jesus' death and resurrection: the temple of his body will be destroyed but it will be raised again after three days. The importance of 2:17–22 *for the story still to come* is plain. The ministry of Jesus is heading for death and resurrection[174] (cf. the hour texts reviewed earlier).

6. The Appearance of the Risen Jesus to His Disciples and Thomas[175]

After Jesus appeared to Mary Magdalene near the empty tomb (20:11–18), he then appeared to the disciples as a whole (less Thomas, vv. 19–23, 24). He greets them with "Peace be to you" (v. 19), arguably in this con-

---

173. Cf Johanna Rahner, *Tempel seines Leibes*, 335–39. Rahner strongly emphasizes that John's message is that Jesus himself is the new Temple, the new place of God's presence (e.g., 309–11, 332, 336–39).

174. Cf. Schnelle, *Antidocetic Christology*, 170–71: The fourth evangelist "has placed the cleansing of the Temple . . . at the beginning of his Gospel (John 2:14–22), thereby lending a central importance to the theologia crucis and to the miracle stories as stages on the way to the cross"; also Becker, *Johannesevangelium* 1:127: "for the evangelist, the theme of Jesus' death is present from the beginning . . . John also—formally analogous to Mark—is a passion story with an extended introduction." This is being increasingly recognised—see Wilckens, *Johannes*, 60; Margaret Davies, *Rhetoric*, 233; Knöppler, *Theologia Crucis*, 123–32; Johanna Rahner, *Tempel seines Leibes*, 305, 333–34; Gniesmer, *Prozetzt*, 184; Weidemann, *Tod Jesu*, 403, 423. Cf. too Painter, *Quest*, 158.

175. See Kohler, *Kreuz*, 159–91, for a very full discussion of these pericopes.

text more than the traditional greeting and rather a word of forgiveness after their abandonment of him (16:32), a word which also fulfils
his promise of peace and joy in the Farewell Discourse (14:27; 16:22,
32–33). Then come vv. 20–21: "When he had said this, *he showed them
his hands and his side.* Then the disciples were glad when they saw the
Lord." The Lord is the Crucified One, recognizable because of his hands
and his side: the former pierced by the nails, the latter by the spear thrust
(19:34a, 37). His resurrection does not (as it were) obliterate the marks
of his crucifixion.

This stress on the marks of the crucifixion borne by the Risen One
continues in the next scene, referred to as the "Thomas Episode." Thomas
insists on seeing in Jesus' hands the mark of the nails and placing his fin-
ger in those marks and putting his hand in the side pierced by the spear
(v. 25). He is in fact invited to do so by the Risen Jesus (v. 27),[176] with
the command to cease being faithless and to believe. *It is the Risen One
bearing the marks of crucifixion that Thomas adores* and confesses "My
Lord and my God" (v. 28). In this way the evangelist has ensured that
the reader understands the importance of the cross even in the Easter
situation. The cross is not left behind and obliterated by Easter glory. It
follows that if the first disciples could recognize the Risen Jesus only as
the crucified one, later generations can only recognize him (spiritually)
in the same way. Subsequent believers have to believe without seeing as
Thomas did, but *they must still believe that the Jesus who appeared is the
One who was lifted up on a cross and crucified.*

In their own way, then, the episodes in 20:19–29 within the Easter
story make their own contribution to underlining the *permanent* significance of the cross in the Johannine understanding of Jesus and his work.

7. The Difference in the Use of Scripture Before and During the Passion

The comprehensive study by A. Obermann of what he calls "the christological appropriation" of the Old Testament in the Fourth Gospel[177] has

---

176. Kohler, *Kreuz*, 177: "The Risen One wishes to be identified as the Crucified
One"; Moloney, *John*, 531, 537; Lincoln, *John*, 497; Klauck, *Erste Johannesbriefe*,
110; cf. Riedl, *Heilswerk*, 145; Hofius, *Johannesstudien*, 63 (note 135); Kammler,
Johannesstudien, 209; Hasitschka, *Beifreiung*, 415, 417; Metzner, *Sünde*, 111 (note
208); Knöppler, *Theologia Crucis*, 266–68; Frey, *Theologia crucifixi*, 231–36; Zumstein,
Kreative Errinerung, 232, note 33.

177. Obermann, *Christologische Erfüllung*.

drawn attention to the different way in which the Old Testament is used (i) up to and including the triumphal entry (i.e., basically the period of Jesus' public ministry: 1:23; 2:17; 6:31, 45; 10:34; 12. 13, 15) and then (ii) from 12:36b onwards (i.e., from the point where the story reaches the threshold of the passion story and on to the cross: 12:38–40; 13:18; 15:25; 17:12; 19:24, 28, 36–37) respectively.

In the former, the Old Testament quotations are basically organic elements of the narrative.[178] They are embedded in the context of the event and they provide the explanatory background of the narrative. They interpret and illuminate the work and way of Jesus.[179] There is a mutual interplay and influence between the Old Testament text and the event. The latter is explained by the former; the former receives a new concretization by the latter. Forms of γράφειν are used in the formulae employed with the quotations in five out of the seven. The exceptions are 1:23, where John the Baptist "says" and Isa 40:3 is quoted, followed by "as Isaiah the prophet said," and 12:13, where the crowd kept on shouting "Hosanna. Blessed is he who comes in the name of the Lord, even the King of Israel."[180] However, from 12:38 on, the introductory formula uses πληροῦν in eight out of the nine cases, the exception being the use of τελειοῦν at 19:28.

Obermann argues that it is the end of Jesus' activity in public which conditions the change in the manner in which Scripture is appropriated and used.[181] Now, in the cross, the narrative thrust finds its climax.[182] The revelation of God in definitive form takes place there.[183] In the cross, Jesus completes the work given to him by the Father. This is the explanation as to why the evangelist now uses Scripture in the form of an explicit fulfillment of OT quotations.[184] This change is the deliberate intention of the evangelist.[185]

178. Ibid., 345.

179. Ibid., 215–17. Obermann draws the use of "way" into relation to Jesus from the quotation from Isaiah 40:3 in John 1:23: "Make straight the *way* of the Lord."

180. Here Obermann believes that John has used MT Ps 118:22 and LXX Ps 117:22, since "Hosanna" is not in the LXX (ibid., 186).

181. Ibid., 337.

182. E.g., ibid., 343, 363.

183. Ibid., 343.

184. The quotations from 1:23 to 12:15 are *implicit* fulfillment quotations (ibid., 348–50).

185. Ibid., 347–48.

For Obermann, John 19:28–30 forms the theological climax of Jesus' story,[186] for the cross is the goal of Jesus' way; it is his lifting up.[187] Obermann believes that the unique use of τελειοῦν in 19:28 is due to the fact that for the evangelist Scripture as a whole has come to its goal.[188]

Obermann's meticulous study has drawn attention to another significant piece of evidence which indicates that the cross is *central* in the fourth evangelist's thinking. It is the direction, climax, and goal of his story.

8. Other Evidence which Could Point to Something Significant Happening in the Cross

(a) Jesus' Mission as Work to be Done

Jesus speaks of his mission in terms of a *work to be done or accomplished.* Twice in the course of the Gospel he refers in the singular to the work given him by God:

- 4:34: "My food is to do the will of my Sender and to accomplish his work."
- 17:4: "I have glorified you on earth, because I have accomplished the work which you gave me to do" (attributing a causal sense to τελειώσας).[189]

This work must be differentiated from the works (τὰ ἔργα), the signs or miracles which the Father has given Jesus to perform (e.g., 5:36b), including the reference in 7:21 to one work which links back to the miracle of Jesus in 5:1–9.

Then, on the cross, just before he breathes his last breath, Jesus says "It is finished" (19:30). What in the prayer of 17:4 was conceived of as having already taken place has now been accomplished. The cross is the goal and climax of the ministry of Jesus; with it, he has completed his task, the work entrusted to him by his Father.

---

186. Ibid., 354, 364.

187. Ibid., 354.

188. Ibid., 355–56, 363.

189. Riedl, *Heilswerk*, 69, sees these two verses as offering a framework for the Gospel.

Bultmann takes the work which Jesus accomplishes as the task of revealing the Father.[190] His death on the cross is Jesus' release from this task. But this understanding is bound up with his view that Jesus' death has minimal significance in the Gospel. If this latter view is called in question, then this must affect our understanding of the work given Jesus to do by the Father.

Here we might also mention the verse in the arrest scene when Jesus rebukes Peter for attacking the high priest's servant: "Sheathe your sword; shall I not drink the cup which the Father has given me?" (18:11). In all probability, this was part of the tradition of the passion story as it came to the evangelist (cf. Mark 14:36, Matt 26:52),[191] but that he allowed it to stand was not due to carelessness or inertia, but to the fact that it was another way of saying that the cross was a task, imposed on Jesus by the Father and one which he embraced. It agrees with the concept of the work of 4:34 and 17:4.[192]

It will be convenient to discuss here the passage 19:28–30 as a whole. "After this [the entrusting of his mother and the Beloved Disciple to each other] Jesus, knowing ὅτι ἤδη πάντα τετέλεσται ἵνα τελει– ωθῇ ἡ γρααφή, said, 'I thirst.' A jar full of sour vinegar was standing (there). Therefore, some filled a sponge with the sour vinegar, put it on hyssop and put it to his mouth. When, therefore, Jesus had received the sour vinegar, he said, 'τετέλεσται,' bowed his head and gave up (his) spirit." The Greek words have been, for the moment, left unpunctuated and untranslated.

Jesus' knowledge that by then all things had been completed (ὅτι ἤδη πάντα τετέλεσται) is reminiscent of the evangelist's statements both at 13:1 that Jesus *knew* that his hour had come and that the Father had given *all things* into his hands, and at 18:4 that Jesus *knew all things* that were going to happen to him. Here at 19:28 the evangelist says that all things had been completed, i.e., the work which the Father had laid upon him and sent him to accomplish was now completed (cf. 17:4). He had done that for which he had come. This is confirmed by the cry of triumph, τετέλεσται, at 19:30. Thus, τετέλεσται forms a kind of inclusio in this small unit (vv. 28–30), and this verb thus "frames" the reference to the fulfillment of Scripture and the event of Jesus' being

---

190. Bultmann, *John*, 194 (note 3); cf. *Theology* 2:52.

191. See Dodd, *Historical Tradition*, 68–69, 78–79.

192. Cf. Riedl, *Heilswerk*, 100–3, esp. 102.

given sour vinegar to drink.[193] The evangelist has *by this linguistic device indicated that his story has reached its climax.*[194]

As earlier observed, the evangelist has used the verb τελειοῦν with reference to the fulfillment of Scripture here, whereas since 12:38 he has employed πληροῦν (12:38–40; 13:18; 15:25; 17:12; 19:24, 36–37). This linguistic switch is a marker or indicator to the reader: Scripture has come to its goal and fulfillment and completion *in the cross,* just as Jesus' own way and work has reached its climax in the cross. The two go together, for Scripture is the revelation of God's will and Jesus in all matters seeks to do the will of God.

But how are the εἰδὼς (knowing) clause and the ἵνα (in order that) clause related to one another and to the main verb, "He said, 'I thirst'"? Should we translate as either "Knowing that now all things had been completed in order that Scripture might be fulfilled, Jesus said, 'I thirst'"; or as, "Knowing that now all things had been completed, Jesus said, 'I thirst,' in order that Scripture might be fulfilled"? On a grammatical-syntactical point, while ἵνα clauses might normally be expected to follow the main clause, they can on occasions occur in the pre-position.[195] Thus, the issue cannot be decided on grammatical-syntactical reasons alone.

Some scholars think that the evangelist has added the εἰδὼς clause to a pre-Johannine source,[196] and this could well be correct, but it still leaves us with the question why did the evangelist add the clause to the existing account? What sense did he intend?

The first translation fits in with the Johannine picture of Jesus as in control of events in the Passion, but then seems to detach the "I thirst" from this thought, though it would be no more abrupt than, say, John 13:4 after vv. 1-3, where the solemn opening verses are followed by the reference to Jesus rising from supper and girding himself with a towel. On the second translation, there is a certain dislocation between the "knowing" clause and the rest of the sentence. *If all things had been com-*

193. Schnackenburg, *John* 3:329; Obermann, *Christologische Erfüllung*, 355–56.

194. Schnackenburg, *John* 3:329; Obermann, *Christologische Erfüllung*, 350–64.

195. In fact, *BDF*, para. 478, list John 19:28 as an example of this. Dauer, *Passionsgeschichte*, 201 (note 232), gives ten such examples for the NT, including John 1:31 (?); 14:31; 19:31. Those who advocate this suggest that the ἵνα clause is in the pre-position here for emphasis, e.g., Schnackenburg, *John* 3:330; G. Delling, τέλος κτλ, *TWNT* 8:82.

196. Dauer, *Passionsgeschichte*, 201–02; Fortna, *Gospel of Signs*, 130, 185, and 244.

pleted, why is there still need for another action in order to complete the fulfillment of Scripture?

In other words, did the evangelist intend one major thought, namely that Jesus knew that all things necessary for the fulfillment of Scripture had now been completed in his death on the cross, or was John trying to get across two thoughts, namely that Jesus was fully aware that his mission was now completed and that one further action (thirsting) was necessary to complete Scripture? As already stated, the latter drives a wedge between the will of God determining the mission of Jesus and Scripture which equally contains the will of God. Furthermore, would not the εἰδώς clause fit better after the reference to Jesus' receiving the drink of sour vinegar if the evangelist wished to get across the two thoughts mentioned above? Another occurrence of τετέλεσται so close in v. 30 would be no counter argument, since in v. 28 as it now stands we have τετέλεσται and τελειωθῇ in close proximity. The evangelist appears not to have had any objections to the piling up of the τελ- group of words so close to one another.

Accordingly, we prefer the translation "knowing that already all things had been completed in order that Scripture might be fulfilled."[197] We see in this a further confirmation of the vital importance of the cross to the evangelist. It is indeed the climax of Jesus' ministry and the evangelist's story. (It must be admitted that those who prefer the second translation would also accept that considerable weight is being attached to the specific event at the end of Jesus' earthly life and the cross in general by vv. 28–30.)

(b) The Gift of the Spirit

There is no disagreement that the sending or gift of the Spirit is consequent upon the death of Jesus in the Fourth Gospel (7:39 and the

---

197. Obermann, *Christologische Erfüllung*, 350–64, sees in the episode of Jesus' saying "I thirst" and being given a drink of sour vinegar on hyssop a reference to *both* Ps 69:21 and, therefore, the idea of Jesus in his suffering and isolation, *and* Exod 12:22, with its allusion to God's saving action of the Hebrews in their distress in Egypt. The possibility that the hyssop does refer typologically to the Exodus story, and, therefore, hints at God's saving act through Jesus lifted up on the cross, is accepted by Hoskyns, *John*, 531; Sanders, *John*, 409; Brown, *John* 2:910, 930; Lincoln, *John*, 478; and regarded as possible by Lindars, *John*, 582, and Moloney, *John*, 504; whereas those who are skeptical include Bultmann, *John*, 674; Schnackenburg, *John* 3:331; Beasley-Murray, *John*, 352; Carson, *John*, 620; Dodd, *Historical Tradition*, 123–24; Dauer, *Passionsgeschichte*, 208.

Paraclete Sayings in the Farewell Discourse). Within this total idea, there is one Paraclete Saying which postulates a different relationship before and after the cross, *viz.* 14:17[198] where Jesus says: "The world cannot receive [him] [the Spirit of Truth] because it does not see him nor does it know him; you know him, because he abides alongside of you and will be in you."

There is a two-fold contrast here—the tenses of the verbs (present μένει and future ἔσται)[199] and the prepositions used (παρά and ἐν). In the pre-cross era, the Spirit's relationship to the disciples is an external one—he is alongside of (παρά) them. After the cross he will be within (ἐν) them. At the moment Jesus, who has been given the Spirit in fullest measure (3:34; cf. 1:32–33), is with them and so the Spirit impinges on the disciples' lives. After the cross, he will reside within them.

How and why can this happen? Defenders of the salvation by revelation view never really explain this satisfactorily.[200] They may explore comparative religious analogies to the idea of one figure leaving and another coming to take his place, but I do not think that they have sought to probe whether the evangelist saw a theological explanation of why once Jesus has been glorified on the cross, the Spirit comes. The question must arise whether there is a connection for the evangelist between the work accomplished by Jesus and the gift of the Spirit.

(c) Discipleship Before and After the Cross

The next point is closely bound up with the last one: *discipleship before and after the cross.* The Farewell Discourse makes it clear that there is a difference in the quality of discipleship between the present (i.e., pre-cross period) and afterwards (i.e., post-cross).[201]

i. *Understanding.* Peter does not understand what is happening

198. See my *John 14:17b*, 93–96; Moloney, *John*, 406–7.

199. Accepting ἔσται as the true reading and ἐστι as a dogmatically inspired correction.

200. E.g., Bultmann, *John*, 558, is not clear.

201. Weidemann, *Tod Jesu*, 139, summarizing what 13:31–38 contributes to his theme, comments, "Jesus' death will be understood in the proem of the farewell speech [13:31—14:31] as the decisive event . . . *after* which the situation of the disciples will be basically different" (eine grundlegend andere). Indeed, he speaks of the impossibility of pre-Easter discipleship (266–67, 305). Zumstein, *Kreative Erinnerung*, 73–75, commented on the qualitative difference between following Jesus after Easter and before Easter (see especially the remark on 75, note 29).

now in the foot washing, but afterwards he will understand (ἄρτι . . . μετὰ ταῦτα, 13:7). Akin to this is 16:25, where there is a contrast between the way in which Jesus speaks figuratively now (ἐν παροιμίαις) and how he will speak plainly in the future (παρρησίᾳ) about the Father.

ii. *Deeds.* As a result of Jesus' departure via the cross to the Father (13:1), the disciples are promised that they will do even greater works than those that Jesus has done (14:12).

iii. *Prayer.* In the future the disciples will enjoy bold access to God in prayer and the confidence that their prayers will be answered (16:23–24, 26–27; also 14:13–14; 15:16).

iv. *Union with the Father and Christ in this life.* After the cross they will not only know concerning the mutual abiding of Father and Son but they will also know the abiding of Christ in them and they in him (14:20) and will experience the coming of the Father and Son to dwell in them (14:23; cf. 17:20–23).

v. *Enjoyment of the heavenly Father's home.* At the beginning of the Farewell Discourse, Jesus announced that he would be with the disciples for only a little while longer. They will seek him, but he repeats what he had said earlier to the Jews, they will not be able to follow where he is going (ὅπου ἐγὼ ὑπάγω, 13:33). When Simon Peter enquired where Jesus was going, he was told that he (Simon) could not now follow Jesus where he was going but afterwards he would follow ((νῦν . . . ὕστερον, 13:36). Jesus first has to return via the cross to the Father and prepare a place for his disciples in his Father's home before they can go there (14:1–3).

This is, in fact, the third time that the evangelist has used the idea of Jesus' being with people for a little while and then he would go away (ὑπάγειν).[202] The first occasion was in Jerusalem at the Feast of Tabernacles at 7:33–34. The audience is mentioned after the saying as being "the Jews" (v. 35), and they could be some of the people of Jerusalem (mentioned in v. 25) or the officers sent by the Chief Priests and Pharisees to arrest Jesus (v. 32) or both. Jesus said, "I will be with you for a little time yet and

202. See Theobald, *Herrenworte*, 424–55, for a detailed examination of this saying and its occurrences in John, which he classifies as one of a few "Wisdom Words" to be found in the Fourth Gospel.

then I will go to the One who sent me. You will seek me but you will not find me, and where I will be you cannot come." This reference to a journey puzzles the Jews, who speculate whether Jesus will go to the Diaspora and teach the Greeks (vv. 35–36). This "going away" is a veiled reference to his death seen as a departure from this world back to the Father who sent him. A Johannine Christian would know this; someone reading the Gospel for the first time might be puzzled, but would understand either in retrospect or at a second reading/hearing, because of what he or she would read/hear later about Jesus' going away.

The second occurrence of this motif also takes place at the Festival of Tabernacles at Jerusalem a little later (8:20–21). Jesus repeated his statement "I am going away and you will seek me, and you will die in your sins. Where I am going you cannot come." (v. 21). This time the Jews wonder whether this means that he will commit suicide (a piece of Johannine irony, because it will be "the Jews" who will secure the condemnation and death of Jesus). On this occasion, the evangelist has not included the phrase "You will seek me but you will not find me." Theobald believes that the evangelist has interpreted this phrase theologically—to fail to find Jesus means death in one's sins.[203]

On the narrative level, the evangelist helps the reader at the beginning of the new section beginning at 13:1. Here he states that Jesus knew that his hour to depart (μεταβῇ) out of this world and go to the Father had come (v. 1) and then repeats the idea at v. 3: "he knew that the Father had given all things into his hands and that he had come forth from God and was going to God (πρὸς τὸν Θεὸν ὑπάγει)." This is, so to speak, a vital clue to the reader. Jesus departs from this world, but it will be a return to the Father from whom he came.[204]

Not surprisingly, when Jesus speaks to the disciples in the Farewell Discourse at 13:33, there will be no mention of "not finding" because after his glorification they will do so. He goes on to say that he is going ahead to prepare a place for them in his Father's home and will come again to take them to himself so that where he is, there they may be also (14:2–3, 28; cf. 17:24).

203. Theobald, *Herrenworte*, 426.

204. Cf. 8:14d, where Jesus claims knowledge of whither he is going.

(From another angle, Jesus will "find" the disciples after his "lifting up," and he will come to them, 14:18, 28; he and the Father will come to them, 14:23; or the Paraclete-Spirit will come to them, 14:17).[205]

Why, then, this emphasis on the necessity of Jesus' departure? Why is his death needful? Only Jesus can achieve the going to the Father, the preparation of a place in the Father's home and the reunion with the disciples. The disciples are not able to achieve this.[206] This is grace (cf. 1:17)![207] This is why the disciples should have rejoiced when he told them that he was going to the Father (14:28).

vi. *The disciples* become "friends" of Jesus. After the second occurrence of the "love command" and its grounding in the general truth that there is no greater love that some can show than to give their life for their friends, with its implied specific application to Jesus' own giving of his life for them (15:12–13), Jesus goes on to say "You are my friends if you do what I command you. I will no longer call you servants, because the servant does not know what his master is doing. But I have called you friends, because I have made known to you all that I have heard from my Father" (15:14–15). Once again, we see how the Farewell Discourse is spoken from the standpoint that the cross-glorification has already taken place (cf. 13:31–32). There is a difference before and after the cross-glorification. It has transformed the position of the disciples from servants into friends.[208] This transformed

205. The evangelist expatiates on the theme of a journey or way after the promise that Jesus is going to the Father to prepare a place for them. From Jesus' conversation with Thomas (14:4–6), the readers learn that in fact the way is not something separate from Jesus; rather, Jesus is himself the way (14:6).

206. Cf. Theobald, *Herrenworte*, 453, who stresses that the first Farewell Discourse aims to deal with the question why the agonizing separation of Jesus from the disciples through his death is necessary. The separation cannot be overcome from the side of the disciples; only Jesus as the one exalted to the Father can do that. Later, Theobald, in discussing 13:33 specifically, stresses that this verse indicates the saving necessity of Jesus' death (516–20, esp. 517).

207. See Ashton, *Understanding*, 448–52; Knoppler, *Theologia Crucis*, 228–31, for brief but helpful comments on John's association of ὑπάγειν with death and the completion of mission.

208. See Josephine Ford, *Redeemer*, 108–201, who explores friendship and motherhood themes from a feminist perspective, with a tendency to read into the text some of

situation receives another grounding in the revelatory work of Jesus—he has passed on to them all that he has heard from his Father. (Full understanding of this only comes after the cross and when the Paraclete-Spirit comes, as 14:26 and 16:13–15 make clear). We note that this new standing as friends does not obviate the need for these "friends" to obey the commands of Jesus.

As mentioned, this sub-section is linked with the previous one, since many of the themes can be traced to the Spirit who guides into all the truth, expounds what Jesus has said, empowers the disciples for mission and so on. However, we still need to ask whether the change in quality of discipleship after the cross is due to something decisive happening on the cross and so enabling the change to take place?

(d) The Inadequacy of Faith before the Cross

We have agreed above that Jesus appears and summons people to believe in him in order to receive eternal life. When, however, the Gospel is carefully examined, it becomes clear that before the cross all human faith is inadequate.[209]

The evangelist announces that many in Jerusalem believed on Jesus as they saw the signs which he did (2:23). Yet it is evident that there is something unsatisfactory about this faith, for it is said that Jesus did not entrust himself to them, because he knew all people and did not need to be told about people, for he knew their inner thoughts and motives (vv. 24–25). One such specific example is immediately given: Nicodemus acknowledges that God must have sent Jesus and must be with him, because of the signs which Jesus was doing, but is bluntly told that he must be born from above (3:1–12).

In the episode concerning the Capernaum nobleman, Jesus says (the verbs are actually in the plural): "Unless you see signs and wonders, you will not believe" (4:48). The nobleman repeats his request without

---

the latter ideas; Sharon Ringe, *Wisdom's Friends*, esp. 64–83, for an exploration of the theme of friendship in the Fourth Gospel, though not all her arguments are persuasive. See also Bennema, *Saving Wisdom*, esp. 223–25. Both link the theme of friendship with the Wisdom themes in Judaism and the Fourth Gospel.

209. Culpepper, *Anatomy*, 91, goes so far as to say that whatever conflict there is with the disciples "follows in part from the necessity that their faith be incomplete until after the completion of Jesus' work at his death"—cf. "The necessity of Jesus' death is established by the disciples' faithlessness" (ibid., 95). Painter, *Quest*, 332, 334, 345–46, maintains that authentic faith was not a reality during Jesus' ministry.

reference to this word of Jesus and is told to go home as his son lives. We are told, "The man believed the word which Jesus had spoken to him and went" (v. 50). A little later the man learns that his boy recovered at precisely the moment when Jesus uttered the words "Your son lives," and "he and his whole household believed" (v. 53). Apart from the theme of the life-giving word of Jesus, the evangelist seems to be concerned also with the theme of faith. There is an inadequate type of faith (v. 48). True faith believes the word of Jesus and acts upon it (v. 50). A miracle can be a sign that evokes or confirms belief (v. 53). The inadequate type of faith seems to be highlighted again in chapter 6. At v. 2, we read that "a large crowd followed him because they saw the signs which he was doing on the sick." After they had been fed and later found Jesus, he challenges their motive: "In truth, in very truth, I tell you, you are not searching for me because you saw signs, but because you ate of the loaves and were satisfied" (v. 26). Mere satisfaction of physical hunger has motivated their search, not because they had a true spiritual insight into the meaning of Jesus' signs.

A continual sifting seems to go on through the ministry. People can observe a miracle and yet not "see" it (i.e., its true meaning). At the end of the Bread Discourse, which has been punctuated by expressions of unbelief (vv. 41, 52), many of his disciples said "This is a hard saying; who can hear it?" (v. 60). Jesus "knew that not everyone truly believed" (vv. 64–65). "Many of his disciples . . . turned back and no longer accompanied him" (v. 66). Though called "disciples," they clearly do not really belong to those whom the Father had given to Jesus (v. 65) or drawn to him (v. 44).

We might formulate the matter thus: while signs ought to produce true faith (20:30–31),[210] they can produce an inadequate type of faith which needs to progress to true faith (like the Capernaum nobleman) or it will regress into outright opposition. An example of the latter would be 8:31–58, where Jesus addressed those Jews who had believed in him.[211] There develops an exchange characterized by extreme abuse and invective, and those who have apparently believed end up by accusing Jesus of

210. See the careful study of Bittner, *Jesu Zeichen*, for a rejection of the view that the evangelist sought to correct a view, present in his source(s)—often regarded as a Signs Source—that signs lead to faith.

211. There is no justification for excising πεπιστευκότας αὐτῷ in 8:31 as a gloss (against Lindars, *John*, 323). Such a procedure is purely arbitrary. The phrase makes perfectly good sense on the interpretation that we are suggesting.

being a Samaritan and having a demon (v. 48) and wishing in the end to stone him (v. 59).[212] On the narrative level, one might say that there is a sieving process still continuing.[213]

The evangelist's summary at the end of the public ministry is extremely pessimistic. "Though he had done so many signs in their presence, they did not believe in him" and he quotes two passages from Isaiah to provide scriptural explanation for this. He also adds that though many of the synagogue rulers believed in him, they did not confess him for fear lest the Pharisees would excommunicate them from the synagogue (12:37–43).

Then the evangelist has Jesus concentrating on "his own." Before long, however, we learn that one will betray his master (13:2, 18, 21–30); another will deny him (13:36–38), while there are ominous signs of lack of understanding exhibited (13:6–11; 14:5, 8–11, 28b). Significantly, at 14:29 (which may have been near the end of the original Farewell Discourse, concluding with the summons to leave the room and be on their way at 14:31b), Jesus said, "And now I have told you (these things) before they occur, in order that when they happen you might believe." The object of what Jesus has told them, which we have supplied in the translation, refers to all that has been said previously, specifically to his departure back to the Father and his return. The verb "to believe" is used absolutely: what sort of object/predicate is implied? The choice seems to be either "that my word is true" or that the absolute use implies belief in Jesus himself. A similar type of statement at 13:19 favors the latter. At 13:19, in an allusion to the fact that Judas will betray him, as predicted in Scripture, Jesus said, "I am telling you now before it happens, in order that, when it does happen, you may believe that ἐγώ εἰμι." The echoes of Yahweh's declarations in Second Isaiah seem unmistakable (Isa 41:21–23; 43:10–13; 44:8; 45:21; 48:3–6). Since betrayal leads to the death of Jesus on the cross, and since the cross is a moment of revelation that Jesus is ἐγώ εἰμι (8:28), once more the readers/hearers are pointed to the importance of the cross. To return to 14:29: the read-

212. Wilkens, *Zeichen*, 55–59 (which are headed "Man in the Crisis of Faith") discusses helpfully how the sign stories illustrate all possible variations between confession and repudiation.

213. The debate as to whether these Jews who believe represent some opponents of the evangelist's own day continues. See for a recent discussion Theobald, *Abraham*, 172–83, esp. 176–82.

ers/hearers could not fail to recall 13:19 when they heard 14:29.[214] What 14:29 implies is, therefore, that until later—i.e., after the cross, resurrection, return to the Father, the gift of the Paraclete-Spirit—the disciples will not have come to full faith.[215]

At the end of the entire discourse in its current shape, the disciples assert "Now we know that you know all things and that you have no need of anyone to put a question to you. We believe by this that you have come forth from God" (16:31). They receive the following reply from Jesus: "Do you now believe? Look—the hour is coming and has come when each of you will be scattered, every man for himself, and you will leave me alone" (v. 32).[216] Even "his own" will abandon him and leave him in the lurch. Jesus will be on his own at the cross. Human "faith" has proved inadequate.[217] This is where the narrative sequence of the Gospel seems to leave us as we come to the passion story and the cross.[218]

---

214. Weidemann, *Tod Jesu*, 36–37, 60, 61–63, lays great stress on 14:29 as an indicator that 13:31—14:31 is intended as a commentary on, or advance instructions to the readers on how to interpret, the passion story and Easter account.

215. Cf. Brown, *John* 2. 555, 655 (on 13:19 and 14:29 resp.).

216. Surely the Johannine equivalent of sayings like Mark 14:27, 50.

217. Caird, *Will of God*, 116–17, wrote "We find a large group of initial believers which gradually melts away and finally disappears, leaving Jesus alone (6:66–68; 16:31–32) . . . incipient faith . . . (is) not robust enough to survive the arrest of Jesus." Thüsing, *Erhöhung*, 226(16) maintains that there is only faith in the full sense after Jesus' exaltation (cf. 228); similarly, Wilkens, *Zeichen*, 65; Riedl, *Heilswerk*, 255, 275, 281, 314; Porsh, *Pneuma und Wort*, 279; Lindars, *Word*, 57; Whitacre, *Johannine Polemic*, 113; Segovia, *John* 13:1–20, 45; Onuki, *Gemeinde*, 193–94 (Compare 66–69, 86—true following is only possible after Easter); Kammler, *Johannesstudien*, 127; Hasitschka, *Befreiung*, 47, 197; Kostenberger, *Missions of Jesus*, 168, 177, 180. Wilckens, *Sohn Gottes*, 73, after noting the tension between complete faith (6:69) and faithlessness at decisive moments in the story, goes on to comment on "the far-reaching difference between pre-Easter and post-Easter discipleship" (cf. also 157, where he says that only Easter faith is the true and perfect faith). Weidemann, *Tod Jesu*, 266–67, 305, 310, argues that the evangelist has made a theme (thematisiert) of the impossibility of pre–Easter discipleship in 13. 33 (36–38) and 18:1–11, together with the story of Peter's denial (18:15–18, 25–27), and maintains that Jesus does not reply to Annas' question about his disciples (18:19) because at that point he has no disciples (296–98). On the other hand, Bennema, *Saving Wisdom*, 144, 211, 243, argues that the disciples did have an adequate belief before the cross and were in a life-giving relationship with Jesus. Teresa Okure, *Mission*, 217, takes a middle position, and says that the disciples "are still very much half-convinced believers" (commenting on 16:29–33).

218. Weidemann, *Tod Jesu*, 287, believes that on the narrative level the remark that Peter, after his first denial, "was standing with them [the servants and officers of the high priest] and warming himself" (John 18:18c) is an indication that he is standing

Diagrams using the old type of egg-timers to illustrate a reduction of Israel to the remnant and finally to Jesus himself at the cross could be used of the Fourth Gospel: the top half of the egg-timer would represent the time of the ministry of Jesus during which believers are gathered and sifted; the nodal point of the two halves would represent the cross at which Jesus is on his own (16:32); and the bottom half of the egg-timer would represent the post-cross era during which the work of Christ produces much fruit (12:24) and the Paraclete-Spirit is at work in the disciples of Jesus, guiding them into the truth and empowering them in mission. This post-cross era culminates when Jesus takes his own to the Father's home and they see his glory (14–1–3; 17:24).

It might be argued that there is a significant exception, indeed significant exceptions, to the picture which we have been presenting, namely the Beloved Disciple who was present at the cross (19:26) and testified to its life-giving significance (19:35); and the group of women followers at the cross[219] (19:25–27), who may have been chosen to represent believers[220] as a contrast to the unbelieving soldiers, in a kind of diptych.

It would be outside the immediate aim of this study to discuss whether the Beloved Disciple was an historical or ideal figure or both; whether the Beloved Disciple passages represent a late literary stratum or an integral part of the work; whether the Beloved Disciple has been retrojected in to the ministry of Jesus; or whether he was a southern disciple of Jesus. We can, however, state that we seem to be faced with some sort of tension in the material between 16:32 (all the disciples will be scattered) and 19:25–27 (a group including the Beloved Disciple at the foot of the cross). It may be that, in fact, the evangelist was trying to say two things—*both* the failure of all human faith before the cross, or at any rate that it was inadequate, *and* the Beloved Disciple and the women

---

with the opponents of Jesus and that, therefore, "Jesus has no disciples."

219. In the Synoptics they stand at a distance. Presumably, the evangelist himself has adapted the tradition at this point—so Bultmann, *John*, 671; Barrett, *John*, 551; Schnackenburg, *John* 3:275–76; Lincoln, *John*, 476. But Dauer, *Passionsgeschichte*, 194, attributes this alteration to John's source. Brown, *John* 2:992, does not decide the matter. Becker, *Johannesevangelium* 2:583, attributes 19:26–27 to the redactor, as apparently does Haenchen, *John* 2:193.

220. Cf. Hoskyns, *John*, 530; Dauer, *Passionsgeschichte*, 316–18.

represent a continuity between the period of the incarnate ministry and that of the exalted Christ.[221]

If we have correctly discerned an important strand in the evangelist's picture—the inadequacy of faith before the cross, then what, we have to ask, does this do to the salvation-by-revelation view? This salvation-by-revelation view does not, in fact, take into full consideration the Johannine picture. If all human faith has failed or is inadequate before the cross, does this mean that Jesus has to accomplish something in the cross to reverse the situation?

SUMMARY

We have seen that by means of the hour passages the fourth evangelist has indicated that the cross is the climax of the ministry. It is a lifting up in both senses of the word—literally, on a cross, and, metaphorically, an exaltation, including a return to the Father who sent Jesus. It is also a glorification, and we claimed that this is to be distinguished from the glory which the Word had with the Father before the world was, to which the incarnate Word is returning, and the glory which was visible in the ministry. Why is the cross the climax of his ministry and why is it the glorification of Jesus?

An examination of two pericopes, both edited by the evangelist in varying ways, the cleansing of the Temple and the encounter of the risen Jesus with his disciples, showed that both asserted the importance of the death of Jesus. In the first of these, the cleansing of the Temple (moved deliberately by the evangelist to the beginning of the story), the ministry is set under the sign of his death and resurrection. In the other, it is clear that the risen Jesus is only knowable as the One who was crucified—the crucifixion retains its importance after Easter.

The death of Jesus seemed to mark a watershed in other respects—the quality of discipleship differs before and after it; the coming of the Spirit depends on it; human faith is inadequate before the cross.

Language about the work to be accomplished and which is accomplished further raises the question that has become pressingly in-

221. Barrett, *John*, 497–98, expresses the matter succinctly: "It is difficult to avoid the conclusion that John is trying to represent two things at the same time: on the one hand, the isolation of Jesus and the complete failure of the Twelve . . . and on the other, the continuity between Jesus and the church."

sistent—does something decisive happen in the cross which alters the situation?

We also raised the question of the inclusion of 1:29 in the Introduction of the Gospel, occurring as it does amidst a series of important titles and descriptions of Jesus.

The evidence thus far surveyed seems to call in question the view which sees the cross as *merely* the means by which Jesus returns to the Father, as if this were the really Johannine way of looking at the death of Jesus. The evidence surveyed is Johannine too (even if our claim about 1:29 were discounted)!

We must press on further, then, in a quest to discover the meaning of the cross in the Fourth Gospel. But, first, we must ask the question why do men and women need salvation? Why do they need to be saved? What is it that stands in the way of their relationship with the God who has created them? This question demands an answer and we shall address it accordingly in the next chapter.

3

The Johannine Doctrine of Sin

BEFORE WE CONSIDER THE Johannine understanding of the cross, it is necessary first to consider the Johannine concept of sin.[1] We begin with the observation that the fourth evangelist thinks in terms of spheres or areas of power.[2] Human beings are either in one sphere or another. God and the devil exercise power in these opposite spheres. John has a series of antithetical pairs by which to describe these spheres ruled over by God and the devil: light/darkness; truth/falsehood; Spirit/ flesh; above/below; and not of the world or the earth/of the world or of the earth. Though there is no speculation about the origin of evil, the evangelist accepts the existence of an evil power hostile to God and uses four phrases by which to describe this power:

(1) THE DEVIL (8:44; 13:2; CF. 6:70–71)

In chapter 8, Jesus accuses the Jews of having the devil as their father, v. 44 (and not God or Abraham as they claim, vv. 39, 41). The devil is described as the father of lies, who has never adhered to the truth because

1. There is a thorough study of this theme now by Metzner, *Sünde*. See also Hasitschka, *Befreiung*; Zumstein, *Kreative Relecture*, 83–103 [= Sünde in der Verkündigung des historischen Jesu und im Johannesevangelium].

2. Cf. Schnackenburg, *John* 2.197–99; Blank, *Krisis*, 132; Riedl, *Heilswerk*, 220, 299; Hasitschka, *Befreiung*, 174, 201–2, 223, 231, 239–40, 243, 249, 278–81, 306, 346, 408, 423.

he is alien to it and loves falsehood. He is also described as a murderer from the beginning, v. 44. These two fundamental characteristics—of being false and a murderer—probably rest on the account of the Fall in Gen 3,[3] when the serpent is described as subtly misrepresenting God and attributing God's prohibition of eating the fruit from the tree of the knowledge of good and evil to jealousy and fear on his part, lest the human pair become like Him (Gen 3:4). Thus, the serpent has sown in Eve's mind the idea that God's command is not really for their benefit: it is worthwhile for them to transgress this command, for to transgress it will lead to a fuller life and greater opportunities, in short, to be better off. The resultant transgression of Adam and Eve leads to the punishment of death, and so the serpent/the devil can be branded as in fact a murderer.[4] "Death and the devil belong together and are set in radical opposition to the world of God."[5]

The devil may use individuals for his purposes to spoil God's plan and Judas is one such instrument (13:2). Indeed, Judas is described as a devil (6:70–71).

(2) SATAN (13:27)

Little needs to be added here, for the sole occurrence in 13:27 parallels 13:2—Satan enters Judas to use him. We note that Satan is now a personal name, not the designation of an office (as in Job 1–2), and Satan takes hold of people for his evil ends (and is not just a recording angel making note of the misdeeds of men and women). Weidemann would go even further than this reference to Judas. He believes that when Jesus defined his kingship as the witness to the truth and asserted that every one who is of the truth listens to him, Pilate's response—"What is truth?" (18:38a)—is an indication that he does not belong to the truth and that

---

3. Cf. Barrett, *John*, 349; Schnackenburg, *John* 2.213; Beasley-Murray, *John*, 135; Carson, *John*, 353; Maloney, *John*, 280; Metzner, *Sünde*, 183 (note 106); and against attempts to link it with Cain's murder of Abel in Gen 4, as maintained by Dahl, *Der erstgeborene Satans*, 70–84.

4. Cf. Wis. 2:23–24: "God created humans for immortality, and made them the image of his own eternal self, but it was the envy of the devil that brought death into the world."

5. Weidemann, *Tod Jesu*, 261

behind Pilate stands the devil who has never stood in the truth (8:44).[6] He and the Jews at the end of the trial are lined up together as part of the devil's sphere of power.[7]

(3) THE EVIL ONE (17:15)

This designation only occurs in the High Priestly prayer where Jesus prays that his disciples might be kept in the world from the Evil One (17:15).[8] The clear implication is that the evil one attacks people and seeks to undermine their loyalty to God and to Jesus and his word.

(4) THE RULER OR PRINCE OF THIS (THE) WORLD (12:31; 14:30; 16:11)

The note of conflict again emerges: the ruler of this world is coming, clearly with no good purpose, but he has no hold or claim on Jesus (14:30). The cross is, in fact, his downfall, for at the cross he is judged and cast out (12:31; 16:11). We shall look at 12:31 (cf. 16:11) and 14:30 in more detail later, to ascertain whether the conflict is primarily legal or military.

Meager as the evidence is, it is sufficient to confirm the statement made earlier of spheres of power. That Jesus prays in chapter 17 for the safety of his followers is an indication of the power of the adversary. It is also an indication that these spheres are not rigidly determined—one can pass from one to the other:[9] here the implication is that without divine aid the disciples might pass under the power of the evil one and into his sphere of influence (as Judas did).

It is consonant with this overall idea of a sphere of power that the sinner is described as a slave to sin: "Every one who does sin is the slave of sin" (8:34). There is need to be delivered or set free from such slavery,

---

6. Ibid., 335, 356, 365.

7. Weidemann, *Tod Jesu*, 365; cf. how the same is said about the Jews on 352–53, 366.

8. This interpretation is better than taking the phrase to be "evil" in the abstract.

9. Barrett, *Essays*, 106, speaks of a "dualism in motion." When people believe and accept the light, they "become what they were not before, and possess what they did not previously have" (ibid., 107).

and the only possibility of this lies in the Son of God (8:36) and his word which is truth (8:32).[10]

Sin is not just something that concerns the individual: it has a corporate aspect or dimension. This emerges in the Johannine idea of the world. Though created by God through the Word (1:3, 10), the world is in opposition to God and has developed its own lifestyle, mores, mindset, etc. It has its own fellowship—it loves its own (15:19); it offers a sort of peace (unlike that which Jesus gives, 14:27); and it has its own joy (16:20) that may take the form of delight at the discomfiture of Jesus' disciples. Strong language is used, typical of the Semitic mind: the world not only does not know God (15:21; 17:25) nor the Spirit (14:17), but actually hates God (15:23–24), God's Son (7:7; 15:18) and Jesus' followers (15:19; 17:14) (hate = anything less than total love and may include a range of attitudes). In accordance with the idea of spheres, it can be said that those who are evil prefer the darkness to the light and will not come to the light, for this would expose the fact that their deeds are in fact evil and not done with God's help (3:19–20).

Because the world has created its own lifestyle and attitudes, it may be said that those who belong to it seek praise and reputation (δό ξα) from one another, not from God (5:44). Or, it may be said that it is possible to seek one's own glory or reputation (7:18) rather than God's glory. An example of such is given right at the end of chapter 12 in the evangelist's summary of the ministry. Some even of the Jewish rulers secretly believed, but refused to confess this openly for fear of being excommunicated from the synagogue, "for they loved the praise (δόξα) of people rather than the praise of God." (12:42–43)

So, men and women may feel too comfortable within this fellowship of the world, the sphere of darkness, and refuse to respond when the light (i.e., God's Son and Agent, Jesus) comes. The essence of sin is thus focused on the issue of faith or unbelief towards Jesus, and in the post-cross era, it will be the Paraclete-Spirit's task to convince the world of sin either because or in that "they do not believe in me" (16:9).[11]

---

10. Cf. 17:17, where the truth has consecrating power, i.e., it sets the disciples apart for the service of God and of His Son. Carson, *John,* 350, rightly says that we are set free not to do anything we please, but what we ought. Esther Straub, *Der Irdische,* 256, comments that "believers allow themselves to be set free by the word of the revealer."

11. So, e.g., Kammer, *Johannesstudien,* 130, "The essence of sin is here defined as unbelief over against the incarnate Son of God, Jesus Christ"; cf. Moloney, *John,* 440.

Though Jesus has come in the Father's name, people do not "receive" him nor will they "come to" him to receive eternal life (5:39, 43). His coming in effect has a judgment side to it. Though the primary purpose is to save the world, the obverse side of this is that refusal to believe him incurs judgment—and judgment already now in the present: "The person who believes in him is not judged, but the person who does not believe has been judged already because they have not believed in the name of the only Son of God. This is the judgment that light has come into the world and people loved darkness more than the light" (3:18–19).

What takes place at the Last Judgment will only reveal what has already happened: i.e., Jesus' word becomes the judge of men and women (12:48). Many scenes in the Fourth Gospel illustrate this fact. One example is the Pharisees who in chapter 9 refuse belief in Jesus and so incur judgment. Thus, at the end of chapter 9, Jesus can say: "I have come into this world for the purpose of judgment so that those who do not see may see and that those who [think that they] see may become blind" (9:39). The Pharisees retort "Are we also blind?" [The Greek construction expects the answer "No"]. Jesus' answer is: "If you were blind [i.e., acknowledged your blindness], you would not have sin. But now you say 'We see'; your sin remains" (9:41). Another example is Pilate who refused to act in accordance with what he knows is right and true, and condemned an innocent man (18:38; 19:4, 6), and so ended up by judging himself.

The expression "to have sin" recurs in 15:22, 24 where, following comments on the hatred of the world, Jesus says: "If I had not come and spoken to them, they would not have sin;[12] but now they have no excuse for their sin . . . If I had not done among them the works which no one else has done, they would not have sin; but now they have both seen and hated me and my Father." People like the Pharisees in particular (chapter 9) and the world in general (15:18–25) believe that they possess the light and know what is right and presume to judge others. They are satisfied with their criteria, but fail to recognize the true light when it shines and so fail to respond to the living God when he confronts them in Jesus.

To "have" sin suggests an ongoing state, a continuing refusal to recognize the truth/the light, a refusal to believe in God and his Son. This

---

12. Εἴχοσαν is an example of how an aorist ending has been tacked on to an imperfect stem—see *BDF* para. 84; Robertson, *Grammar*, 335–36.

persistence means, "your sin remains" (9:41). It is being locked into the sphere of unbelief where the ruler of this world holds sway. This persistence can be called by implication ἀδικία in 7:18, where the context is a discussion of Jesus' teaching and whether it comes from God or whether Jesus speaks on his own authority. The issue is one of the legitimacy of the agent: Jesus claims to be the agent of God and faithfully and honestly to pass on his Sender's message. He seeks only the glory of his Sender and this is really a guarantee that he is true and that there is no dishonesty in him.[13]

Since he charges his hearers in chapter 5 with seeking their own glory (5:44), anyone like them is by implication guilty of ἀδικία. They are not acting in accordance with the truth.

This leads us on to make a refinement of what we said earlier about the essence of sin as refusal to believe: *viz.* a peculiar Johannine contribution to the understanding of sin is that it is branded as *falsehood*. Sin is contrasted with truth.[14]

We have seen earlier that the devil is the father of lies and he speaks what is τὸ ψεῦδος. He has persuaded the world to believe that it is better off disobeying God or to accept a "counterfeit" religion, so that one believes that one has the correct criteria by which to measure everything, and hence know what is God's activity and what is not (see, e.g., the debates in 7:25–43 or the Pharisees' approach in chapter 9 or what is said in 16:2-3—"The hour is coming when every one who kills you will think that they are offering service to God. And they will do these things because they have not known the Father nor me." The sincerity of such people is not in doubt; it is not a matter of hypocrisy). Such persons are in the grip of what is false and do not respond to what is true. "How can you, who seek praise from one another and do not seek the praise which comes from the only God, believe?" (5:44). They search for life in the Scriptures—and that is right; but they are searching in the wrong/false way, because in fact the Scriptures, and Moses in particular, witness

13. So Brown, *John* 1:312; Lindars, *John,* 289; Beasley-Murray, *John,* 108. Others like Schnackenburg, *John* 2:133 and Haenchen, *John* 2:14, take ἀδικία to mean wickedness in general and to be a virtual synonym for ἁμαρτία, while Barrett, *John,* 318, interprets it as unreliable; Moloney, *John,* 245, and Lincoln, *John,* 249, as falsehood; while Bultmann, *John,* 276, combines deceit and wrongdoing.

14. Cf. Conzelmann, ψεῦδος, in *TWNT,* 9:602: "the lie is not just error but an active contesting of the truth, i.e., unbelief."

about Jesus (5:39, 46–47), and so they fail to respond to Jesus (5:40) who not only brings the truth (e.g. 8:40) but is the truth (14:6).

Judgment is already a present actuality, just as life is a present experience. A good summary occurs in 3:36: "The person who believes in the Son has eternal life; but the one who disobeys the Son will not see life, but God's wrath remains on them."[15] (None of these clauses excludes the possibility of a future aspect.)

The link between sin and death comes out clearly in 8:21–24. Jesus tells his hearers: "I am going away, and you will seek me, and you will die in your sin" (v. 21). This remark is misunderstood (v. 22) and this leads to a reiteration of it: it was because his hearers belong to the sphere "below" or "this world" that Jesus said, "You will die in your sins. For, if you do not believe ἐγώ εἰμι, you will die in your sins" (v. 24). The only way out of this nexus of sin-death is to believe in Jesus as God's Son and agent who perfectly represents him and to whom, therefore, it is appropriate to apply the self-proclamatory formula of God in the Old Testament ("I AM"). To refuse to believe means that one is and will continue to be in that realm, one of whose characteristics is death.[16]

The singular ἁμαρτία of v. 21 denotes the sin of unbelief, from which particular sins (ἁμαρτίαι, v. 24) as expressions of the fundamental sin of unbelief may stem, as the γὰρ clause in v. 24b shows. There is basically no difference between the singular and plural in vv. 21 and 24.[17]

Although it is clear that in John's Gospel the cross falls within the purpose of God who has revealed this purpose within Scripture, that does not absolve the responsibility of those who bring about the event of the crucifixion. During the trial before Pilate, at one point the Roman

15. See Fey, *Schlange*, 196–97, for the suggestion that John 3:36c shows acquaintance with Wis 16:5 (cf. 18:20), though John is not interested in the interpretative scheme of the sapiential synkrisis of God's action towards the righteous and the godless, but in the Christ event which dominates everything.

16. Schnackenburg, *John* 2:197, "The non-believer faces death in all its annihilating power"; Kammler, *Johannesstudien*, 130, "The fourth evangelist understands sin (just like Paul) as a deadly power, which radically defines and enslaves human beings in their being and nature" (cf. also ibid., 175). Just as life in the Fourth Gospel is both present and future, so also is death—as is revealed by the assertion that the believer "has passed (μεταβέβηκεν !) from death to life" (5:24).

17. Metzner, *Sünde*, 162–64, sees the plural as "the comprehensive sphere of activity of the one sin (8:21; 8:34) which proves itself as unbelief over against the revealer (8:24; 16:9)."

governor challenges Jesus' silence and refusal to answer his question about Jesus' origin, by reminding Jesus of his authority to release or crucify him (19:9–10). This does elicit a reply from Jesus to the effect that Pilate would have no power were it not for the fact that the present situation confronting Pilate as representative of Roman authority has been brought about "from above."[18]

However, "the one who handed me over to you has the greater sin" (19:11b). Although the verb παραδιδόναι is used nine times of Judas' betrayal, it is also used twice by the Jewish authorities themselves to describe their action in delivering Jesus to Pilate (18:30, 35). In addition, Judas is not mentioned after the arrest scene (18:1–10), and it is the Sanhedrin members who take Jesus to Pilate (18:28). Not many scholars, therefore, think that Judas is in mind.[19] The vast majority opt for either Caiaphas—often referring to him as representative of the Jews or Jewish authorities (influenced by the singular and the fact that Caiaphas was the leading figure in the decision to get Jesus put to death, 11:49–53)[20]—or the Jews[21] (taking the singular as a generic singular[22]). While there is no complete exoneration of Pilate (he still has some responsibility for what he eventually decides), the greater sin lies with those who took the initiative and handed over Jesus to him. Thus, in 19:11, human responsibility and divine sovereignty lie juxtaposed side by side, without any attempt to resolve the riddle of where one ends and the other begins (in typical Hebraic style). Sin, then, consists in being confronted with the revelation of God through his agent and refusing that revelation; or, put in another way, of being confronted by the truth and turning one's

18. This somewhat vague phrase is an attempt to do justice to ἦν δεδομένον σοι ἄνωθεν in 19:11a, which, as Carson, *John*, 601–2, rightly points out, is neuter, whereas ἐξουσία is feminine. He takes the phrase to be referring to the entire turn of events, or, more precisely, the event of the betrayal. Barrett, *John*, 543, suggests that the sense is "unless it had been granted you to have authority."

19. Bauer, *Johannesevangelium*, 213; Barrett, *John*, 543.

20. Westcott, *John*, 271; Strathmann, *Johannes*, 246; Brown, *John* 2. 879; Morris, *John*, 797; Beasley-Murray, *John*, 340, Carson, *John*, 601; Moloney, *John*, 500; Dauer, *Passionsgeschichte*, 310. Weidemann, *Tod Jesu*, 345, sees here a reference back to 18:35 with its statement that "your nation and the chief priests have handed you over to me."

21. Wikenhauser, *Johannes*, 328; Hoskyns, *John*, 524; Bultmann, *John*, 662–63 (note 6); Brown, *John* 2:879 and *Death* 1:842; Lindars, *John*, 569; Schnackenburg, *John* 3:302; Lincoln, *Truth*, 133, 196; Griesmer, *Prozetz*, 314.; cf. Schlatter, *Johannes*, 345.

22. BDF, para. 139, though not instancing John 19:11, say that the generic singular "appears several times in the NT with persons, " and quote Rom 3:1 as an example.

back on it and refusing to allow that truth to determine one's actions. In varying degrees, Caiaphas/the Jews and Pilate both bear responsibility for their decision and what they do on the basis of that decision.[23]

Finally, we turn to three statements made to the disciples, to see whether they have implications for our present theme. The first occurs after the foot washing and is made to Peter: "The person who has bathed does not need to wash but is wholly clean; and you are clean (καθαροί) but not all" (13:10). The second is near the beginning of the Vine Discourse: "Already you are clean (καθαροί) because of the word which I have spoken to you" (15:3). Do these statements imply that sin has a defiling, tainting effect, from which people need to be washed clean? This has been disputed for 15:3 in view of the play on words in vv. 2 and 3—καθαί ρει . . . καθαροί—and some have preferred the meaning clean from all that prevents fruit bearing: "clean" means capable of bearing fruit.[24]

We would do well to heed Dodd's point, made in a discussion on "Symbolism in the Fourth Gospel, " and specifically in connection with the Vine Discourse: "The language indeed changes to and fro between the literal and the metaphorical in a way which would be bewildering, if the reader were not conscious all through that all the statements made really refer to Christ and his disciples, under the symbol of a vine and its branches, rather than to any earthly vine."[25] Accordingly, it is probably unwise to press an either/or approach and to try and exclude the idea of cleansing or forgiveness from sin.[26] We are probably entitled to say that the sense can embrace the initial cleansing *and* the ongoing cleansing: *both* are necessary for abiding in the vine and being fruitful branches. Thus, the idea of cleansing may not be a frequent one in the Fourth Gospel, but at least it does occur.

At the end of the scene in which the risen Jesus appears to the (ten) disciples in the evening of Easter Day, he said to them after having breathed on them "Receive the Holy Spirit." He then continued: "Whose sins you forgive, they have been forgiven to them; whose sins you re-

23. The view of Cordula Langner, "Was für ein Konig ist Jesus?" 260, that God is the one intended in ὁ παραδούς μέ, seems very strange.

24. So Borig, *Weinstock*, 42, and Brown, *John* 2:676–77.

25. Dodd, *Interpretation*, 136.

26. Hoskyns, *John*, 475, speaks of the moral purification of the disciples, while Bultmann, *John*, 534 (note 3), says that this word "includes the forgiveness of sins, but does not refer specifically to it."

tain, they have been retained" (20:23). We may rule out the interpretation that relates this to what came later to be known as the institution
of penance (the formal forgiveness of post-baptismal sins) as anach-
ronistic. The saying asserts that there will be divine ratification of the
forgiveness or retention of sins on earth.[27] Where the followers of Jesus
continue his mission and as men and women respond to their word
with faith (17:20), these new believers there and then receive forgiveness and are drawn into union with the crucified and exalted Jesus. This
act is indicated in the punctiliar nuance of the aorist subjective active
ἀφῆτε in 20:23a. Where men and women refuse to respond in faith,
they remain in the sphere of the Evil One (indicated by the nuance of
the present subjunctive active, κρατῆτε, indicating a state).[28] Thus, this
saying[29] fits in with the Johannine concept of spheres of power dominated by God and his Son and by Satan respectively.[30]

SUMMARY

The statement that the Father sent the Son into the world to save it is no
bland assertion. Human beings need to be saved, for they are otherwise
within that sphere—variously described as darkness, falsehood, below,
this world, etc.—which is ruled over by the devil, and are enslaved by
him in sin and falsehood and darkness. The world has developed its own
outlook, approach, and lifestyle, and resents any disturbance of these,
any pointing out of its wrongness and falsity. The ultimate outcome of
belonging to this sphere is death—indeed, death could be one of the

27. The passive voice of the verbs ἀφέωνται and κεκράτηνται are the "divine
passives."

28. This interpretation follows the helpful exposition of Weidemann, *Tod Jesu*,
475–77, though his claim that both these verbs are legal technical terms is not borne
out with regard to κρατεῖν by the reference quoted by him in *TWNT* 3: 910, nor by *LSJ*.
The legal use of ἀφιέναι is attested in the papyri (ἀφίημι, κτλ, in *TWNT* 1:509–12).

29. Probably a saying drawn from the pool of tradition in his community by
the evangelist. It has a parallel in Matt 16:19; 18:18, but the differences between the
Johannine and Matthean versions suggests that they are based on a common original
which has been altered in the course of transmission. See the discussion in Brown,
John 2 1023–24, 1039–45; Dodd, *Historical Tradition*, 347–49: Theobald, *Herrenworte*,
174–96.

30. Cf. Weidemann, *Tod Jesu*, 486, who says that the fourth evangelist understands
forgiveness as a being drawn out of the sphere of sin and death.

descriptions of this sphere. God's wrath already rests on those who do not believe and they will not see life.

For the evangelist there is, as Schnackenburg puts it, "an unbreakable link between human sinfulness and unbelief . . . It is a vicious circle . . . which man, through faith, not only must break out of, but can break out of."[31]

There is need of a birth from above, from God (1:12–13; 3:3–8), in order to break out of this sphere into that sphere where God rules, which is salvation and eternal life. This birth from above, as we have mentioned earlier,[32] has its objective basis in the lifting up of Jesus on a cross and to glory.

A further enquiry is necessary before we move to a consideration of passages to do directly with the cross. Precisely in order to shed light on what the cross achieves, we need to consider the way the evangelist depicts the ministry of Jesus up to the cross and its purpose in the divine plan. In this way, in the end, we shall gain an added dimension by which to look at the work of Jesus in the cross.

31. Schnackenburg, *John* 2.198; cf. Bultmann, *John*, 348, in a similar vein.
32. See p. 84. n. 133.

4

Jesus' Ministry up to the Cross in the Fourth Gospel

W E SHALL EXAMINE THE ministry of Jesus up to the cross under two main headings—the mutual companionship between Jesus and the Father and the shared purpose that exists between them. We shall see that it is God's purpose that what the Son enjoys uniquely with him should be extended to others.

(1) MUTUAL COMPANIONSHIP BETWEEN THE FATHER AND JESUS

The Prologue begins by describing how the Eternal Word existed with God (ἦν πρὸς τὸν Θεόν) (1:1–2). The Word is distinguished from God but not in such a way as to suggest separation, since everything that can be said about God can be said about the Word. In chapters 2–17, Jesus frequently refers to having come forth from God, while in the High Priestly prayer he asks for the glory which he had with the Father before the world existed (17:5) and refers to the fact that the Father had loved him before the foundation of the world (17:24).

The evangelist stresses in a variety of ways that *that fellowship continued through the incarnate ministry of the Word*. "The Word became flesh and dwelt among us . . . No one has ever seen God: the only God who is in the bosom of the Father has declared Him" (1:14, 18). As argued earlier,[1] verse 18 refers to the incarnate ministry. The incarnate Word, here described as ὁ ὢν εἰς τὸν κόλπον τοῦ Πατρός (cf. 1:1 and

1. See p. 54.

124

14), continues to enjoy the closest fellowship with the Father. He knows and experiences the love of the Father. This assertion in the Prologue fits in with the claim enunciated by Jesus that he is never alone but that the Father is always with him.[2]

In dispute with the Pharisees he claims that his judgment is true and reliable "because I am not alone, but I and the Father who sent me [are constantly together]"[3] (8:16). A little later, he makes the same claim, "He who sent me is with me; he has not left me alone because I always do what pleases him." (8:29). Here the companionship is grounded on Jesus the Son's obedience to his Father's pleasure[4] (cf. 16:32 spoken on the eve of the cross, which will be discussed later).

There are many passages which indicate that *Jesus is in constant touch with his Father.* They speak of Jesus' listening to his Father or being taught by his Father or observing his Father and learning from Him. A classic illustration of this is 5:19–20: "Truly, truly I say to you, the Son can do nothing on his own authority, except what he sees the Father doing. For what he does, the Son also does in a similar way. For the Father loves the Son and shows all that he is doing to him." Clearly, an ongoing relationship is here being described as is further evidenced by the statement in 5:30: "I can do nothing on my own authority; as I hear, I judge." The ἀκούω can only refer to the Son's constant listening to the Father in the present, i.e., the incarnate ministry.

Sometimes the tense used is that of the aorist indicative as, e.g., in 8:26, 28:

Verse 26: "My Sender is true and I say to the world what I have heard from him."

Verse 28: "I speak as the Father has taught me" (cf. 12:49, "The Father who sent me has given a command what I should speak and say," where the perfect is used ἐντολὴν δέδωκεν).

---

2. Thüsing, *Erhöhung*, 207–9, says that it is never (niemals) said of the earthly Jesus that he is with the Father (datz er "beim Vater" sei); on earth he has unsurpassable unity with the Father, but "in spite of this, he is not 'with the Father.'" (ibid., 208). Technically, this may be correct, but the evangelist does say that the Father is with Jesus.

3. Brown, *John* 1:339, translates "I have at my side the One who sent me"; JB—"the one who sent me is with me"; NIV—"I stand with the Father, who sent me."

4. Though Riedl, *Heilswerk*, 142, believes that the unity of will is a reflection of the unity of being (Wesens-Einheit) and that this can be heard from 8:29 (heraushoren kann), he does agree that on the whole John's stress is on the practical rather than the metaphysical side (202; cf. 110 discussing 10.17–18).

Consider also 10:18 and 15:15:

10:18, "I have received this command from my Father."

15:15, "I have revealed to you all things that I have heard from my Father."

Here the references could be to his pre-existent state, or they could be to past points of his earthly life, i.e., they could be instructions given as the agent sets off or they could be instructions given while he is on his mission but "in touch with base HQ." The latter cannot be excluded, both on specific and general grounds.[5]

The mutual companionship theme receives striking linguistic formulation in the idea of *the Father's being in the Son and vice versa*. This first appears in 10:38: "but if I do do [the works of my Father], even if you do not believe me, believe the works that you may come to know and continue to know that the Father [is] in me and I [am] in the Father." It recurs at 14:10–11 (where it is also said that it is the Father abiding in Jesus who does His works); 14:20; and 17:21–23.

Whatever difficulties the idea may pose to our twenty-first-century Western minds,[6] it is meant to express the closest possible bond of union between the Father and the incarnate Son, Jesus of Nazareth: the Father is in Jesus and Jesus is in the Father. In the light of these statements, we cannot rule out the possibility that the aorist indicatives (and perfect), just looked at in 8:26, 28; 10:18; 12:49; 15:15, still refer to the incarnate ministry.

As we might expect, the relationship between Father and Son is described in terms of *mutual love*. The love that existed before the foundation of the world (17:24) continues during the incarnate ministry. Thus, the evangelist can state that "the Father loves the Son and has given all things into his hand" (3:35) or shows the Son all that He is doing (5:20). Equally, it can be said that the Father loves the Son because he is willing, in obedience to his Father's command, to lay down his life for the sheep (10:17–18) (for the link between obedience and the love between Father and Son, cf. 15:9–10). The obedience of Jesus to the Father is a constant theme in the Gospel and this leads us on to our next section.

5. See Bühner, *Der Gesandte*, for a full discussion of the role of a messenger. While it would not be possible for an ancient messenger to "keep in touch with base HQ," nevertheless the Johannine picture of Jesus enjoying unbroken fellowship with the Father could modify the basic messenger concept at this point! Cadman, *Open Heaven*, 1–6, strongly defends a reference to the earthly ministry in these verses.

6. See the discussion in Dodd, *Interpretation*, 249, and Moule, *Christology*, 48–54.

(2) SHARED PURPOSE BETWEEN THE FATHER AND JESUS

This may be stated as follows: the Father has willed the incarnation of the Eternal Word;[7] what the Eternal Word had with the Father, the man Jesus of Nazareth enjoys on earth; the Father wills that what the incarnate Word enjoys should be extended to men and women who respond in faith in Jesus. This is confirmed when a number of Johannine concepts are examined.

(i) Life

The Prologue celebrates the life-giving activity of the Word. "In him was life" (vv. 3–4). The whole world was made through him (vv. 3, 10b). The descent to earth has a purpose to impart life: "I have come that people should have life and have it abundantly" (10:10), for "as the Father has life in himself, so also he has given the Son to have life in himself" (5:26; cf. 17:2). This is conveyed pictorially: the hungry may come to Jesus for the bread of life (6:32–35), the thirsty for the living waters (4:13–14; 7:37–38), the benighted for the light of life (8:12; 9:5), etc. Those who respond in faith to him receive eternal life (17:3; 20:31; 3:16).

We have already seen that this life comes through believing in Jesus (e.g. 6:47) and the Father who sent him (e.g. 5:24), yet also the death of Jesus is necessary before this life is really available (3:14-15; 6:51-58).

(ii) Light

The Prologue passes from life to light, "the life was the light of men and women" (v. 4). Indeed, the Word, the true light, enlightened everyone, for he was always coming into the world (v. 9). The incarnate Word, Jesus, is the light of the world (8:12; 9:5) and his capacity to give light to men and women is illustrated by the restoration of the sight of the man born blind (chapter 9). The public ministry closes with the appeal: "The light is still among you for a little while. Walk while you have the light lest the darkness overtake you. The person who walks in the dark does not know where they are going. While you have the light, believe in the light in order that you may become children of the light" (12:35–36).

---

7. If we link the ἦλθεν of 1:11 with the designation of the Father as ὁ πέμψας με (e.g. in 6:38), this is a legitimate assertion.

(iii) Truth

While the Prologue does not expressly link truth and the pre-existent Word, the evangelist sees the Father, with whom the Word dwells, as true (8:26; 17:3; cf. 3:33) and his word as truth (17:17). He also associates truth with the Son who abides in the house and whose word conveys the truth and sets men and women free (8:31–36). Jesus is himself the truth and, therefore, can act as the way to the Father[8] (14:6).

If law came by Moses, grace and truth came through Jesus (1:17; cf. 1:14). His purpose in coming into the world is to bear witness to the truth, and it is said that everyone who belongs to the truth hears his voice (18:37). To describe people in a sense as already ἐκ τῆς ἀληθείας is yet another example of Johannine predestinarian language and must not be so pressed as to minimise the importance of faith.

Truth is not a series of abstract propositions but Jesus himself and what is bound up in his mission. It is not just that "God is love" or that "Jesus is the Revealer," but rather that God wills in love to draw men and women into a union with Jesus the incarnate Word and, hence, into union with himself, so that they may enjoy what he wills to give them.[9]

(iv) With God

The Prologue says that the Word was with God (πρὸς τὸν Θεόν). Though that exact phrase is not actually used of the incarnate Word, other phrases convey the closeness and intimacy of the fellowship of Jesus and the Father:[10] he is in the Father; he is in the Father's bosom

---

8. I here assume that the primary image is "way" and coming to the Father by that way, which is Jesus: cf. Bultmann, *John*, 604–7; Barrett, *John*, 458; Brown, *John* 2:621; Schnackenburg, *John* 3:64; Lindars, *John*, 472–73; Haenchen, *John* 1:124; Beasley-Murray, *John*, 252; Moloney, *John*, 395, 398; Lincoln, *John*, 390; de la Potterie, *Vérité*, 1.241–78; Theobald, *Herrenworte*, 305–22 . (Less emphatically, Carson, *John*, 491.)

9. Cf. Cadman, *Open Heaven*, 14; Caird, *NT Theology*, 51, 302. Lincoln, *Truth*, 230, correctly says that in John truth is "soteriological. Truth is the divine reality as it comes to expression in the whole of Jesus' mission, including his death, and it is the establishment of the divine verdict of life through that death." Compare the comment of Margaret Davies, *Rhetoric*, 101, on knowledge in John—"that God loves the world and *acts to save humanity*" (italics mine). Wilckens, *Johannes*, 147, has expressed the matter in this way in a comment on 8:32: "Truth is much more the continual faithfulness of God to Himself . . . God is true when He realises His promises of salvation for His elect in His deeds towards them; for therein He corresponds to His own Name (Ex. 34:6)."

10. See p. 125, note 2, for Thüsing's comment on being "with the Father" and our criticism.

(1:18); he is not alone but the Father is with him (μετ'ἐμοῦ in 8:29; 16.32; cf. 8.16); he and the Father are one (10:30); and they abide in each other (14:9–10, etc.)

Jesus promises believers that he is going home, to his Father's house, in order to prepare a place for them. There are many rooms in his Father's house. The result will be that they will be where he is—in the Father's home and presence (14.1–3; cf. 12.26; 17.24).

(v) Glory

The pre-existent Son enjoyed δόξα with the Father before the world began (17:5). On earth he reveals his glory (1:14; 2:11; 11:4a, 40) and is glorified on the cross (12:23; 13:31; 17:1). In return, he has sought to enable his disciples to share in his glory: "And I have given to them the glory which you gave to me, that they might be one as we are one" (17:22). That this giving by Jesus refers to a time after and dependent upon his own glorification (17:1) is likely,[11] but is not important at this stage in our enquiry. Jesus' wish expressed in 17:24 shows that the glorification of the disciples awaits fulfilment in the future, for his desire is that those whom the Father has given him may be with him where he is, so that they might see the glory that the Father has given him. (This glory is totally distinct from the δόξα which humans give each other—5:41, 44; 12:43.)

(vi) Spirit

Although not expressly said, presumably in the evangelist's thinking the Paraclete-Spirit is also with the Father and the Word in eternity. During the incarnate ministry, Jesus enjoys the presence and power of the Spirit in fullest measure: "For he whom God sent speaks the words of God, for he [i.e., God[12]] does not give the Spirit by measure. The Father loves the

---

11. See our earlier discussion on p. 78.

12. Taking the subject of δίδωσιν as God and not Jesus himself for two reasons. Firstly, this grounds v. 34a much better than if Jesus were the subject, even though it involves a change of subject within v. 34. Secondly, it accords better with v. 35, which also speaks of the Father's giving to the Son. Thus, we agree with Bultmann, *John,* 164; Barrett, *John,* 226; Schnackenburg, *John* 1:386; Lindars, *John,* 170–71; Beasley-Murray, *John,* 53–54; Carson, *John,* 213; Moloney, *John,* 111–12 (though conceding that both are possible); Lincoln, *John,* 162; Burge, *Anointed Community,* 83–84. Against Brown, *John* 1:158; Thüsing, *Erhöhung,* 154–55; Dodd, *Interpretation,* 311–12, 410; Porsch, *Pneuma und Wort,* 101–5; Kammler, *Johannesstudien,* 171–73. Dunn, *Baptism,* 20, 32, thinks a

Son and has given all things into his hand." (3:34–35; cf.1:32–33, where John the Baptist testifies that he saw the Spirit descend on Jesus and remain on him). In turn, Jesus promises that the Paraclete-Spirit will reside in the disciples after he has returned to the Father and asked the Father to send the Paraclete-Spirit (14:16–17).

(vii) Love

In the High Priestly prayer, Jesus mentions that the Father "loved me before the foundation of the world" (17:24). He, the incarnate Word, continues to enjoy that love during his ministry on earth (3:35; 5:20; cf. 15:10). The Father wills to extend that love to others, and his sending of the Son is a sign of that intention (3:16). Jesus assures his disciples that the Father loves them because they have loved Jesus and believed that he came forth from the Father (16:27).

That is couched as a prayer in the High Priestly prayer: "Righteous Father . . . I have made known to them your Name and will make it known so that the love with which you have loved me might be in them and I in them." (17:25, 26). God's love is in the end the presence of Jesus with his own ("I in them"). Love is a person, so to speak.

SUMMARY

In this chapter we have explored the mutual companionship which existed between the Father and the incarnate Word, Jesus of Nazareth, and the various ways in which this is set forth (e.g., mutual abiding, mutual love, the Son's not being alone). The Son's obedience is a sign of his love for the Father, and this led on to a consideration of the purpose shared between Father and Son, *viz.* to extend the companionship to include those who believe in Jesus. A range of concepts were looked at which suggested that what the Word/Son enjoyed in eternity continues to be enjoyed by the Word/Son Incarnate, Jesus of Nazareth, on earth and it is the Father's intention through Jesus to draw men and women into a participation in the same blessings, above all the divine life existing between Father and Son.

As we shall see, the results of this chapter will provide an illuminating background against which to set the enquiry of the next chapter

---

double reference is possible, as does Morris, *John*, 247.

about the meaning of the cross, especially when we bear in mind the argument earlier (pp. 106-11) that human faith before the cross is inadequate, with the result that the divine purpose remains unfulfilled and the inevitable question arises whether something more is needed to achieve this purpose.

5

The Cross in the
Fourth Gospel

"$\mathbf{F}$OR GOD DID NOT send his Son into the world to condemn the world but that the world might be saved through him" (3:17). How is that salvation achieved? Does the cross contribute to that purpose? We shall explore whether that is so in this chapter.

(1) NECESSITY OF THE CROSS FOR ETERNAL LIFE (3:14–15; 6:51–58)

That the cross is a necessary, essential, divinely-willed part of the process of "salvation" is stated in no uncertain terms in 3:14–15: "As Moses lifted up the serpent in the desert, so the Son of Man must be lifted up in order that every believer might have eternal life in him."[1] The δεῖ denotes divine purpose: the lifting up is part of God's purpose, and that purpose is to offer eternal life through the Son of Man to all who believe (clearly in him). If we are right in seeing a reference to the cross behind ὑψωθῆναι,[2] then this verse asserts that the gift of eternal life depends on the cross. (Those who want to emphasize the ascension as the primary reference of "lifted up," interpret the phrase as meaning that the Son of

---

1. Grammatically, the phrase ἐν αὐτῷ must go with ἔχῃ, since πιστεύειν takes the dative or εἰς or ἐπί, but not ἐν. Some scribes have altered ἐν into either ἐπ' or εἰς to secure the sense "believe in him."

2. See the discussion on 84–88. Becker, *Johannesevangelium* 1:143–44, is surely wrong to see no reference to the cross at all.

The Cross in the Fourth Gospel

Man is released from earthly conditions by the ascension to pour out the eternal life given him by the Father on all.)

Unfortunately, our verse does not elaborate on *how* the cross and the gift of eternal life are linked. We shall have to turn elsewhere in the hope of learning something of the evangelist's mind.

The same message that the cross is necessary for eternal life emerges also from 6:51–58. Discussion over this passage of the Gospel has raged for some time. The arguments are well known and need not be discussed in detail yet again:

(a) From the point of view of *style and vocabulary*, vv. 51–58 are of a piece with the rest of the Gospel. However, it has to be admitted that an editor could imitate Johannine style and vocabulary—indeed the editor might not need consciously to imitate, for Johannine style and vocabulary might be his as well.[3]

(b) The issue of the *structure* of the discourse came to the fore with particular sharpness when Borgen put forward his thesis that the discourse was based on an exposition of Exod 16:15, quoted in v. 31, with Isa 54:13 as a supportive text: vv. 32–51 takes up the theme of "bread" (ἄρτος) from Exod 16:15, while vv. 52–58 picks up "eat" (φαγεῖν).[4]

The rejoinder has been that Borgen's pattern covers vv. 32–51b better than vv. 32–58.[5] The term "bread" certainly occurs eleven times in the first half of the discourse, but its distribution is not even and it occurs in clusters in vv. 32–35, 41, 48–51. In vv. 36–47 there is another theme that occupies centre-stage—faith/ coming to Jesus (raised by v. 35, and previously by vv. 29–30), and believers as those drawn by the Father.[6]

The term "to eat" (φαγεῖν) occurs three times in vv. 52–58 (and its synonym, τρώγειν four times), while it occurs three times

---

3. For the most thorough defence of 6:53–58 as Johannine from a literary angle, see Ruckstuhl, *Einheit*, 220–71. See also Jeremias, *Joh. 6:51c–58*, 256–57. On the other side, G. Richter, *Einheit von Joh 6:31–58*, 21–55, esp. 39–40, sought to demonstrate the differences between verses 31–51a and 51b–58.

4. Borgen, *Bread; Midrashic Character*, 232–40.

5. Richter, *Einheit*, esp. 21–31.

6. Barrett, *Flesh*, 39–40, maintains that the discourse as a whole is not midrashic, and he goes on to point out that the midrashic form "not . . . but . . ." (used at 6:32) does not continue throughout.

in vv. 49–51. The Exodus quotation will not explain the use of πί
νειν three times in vv. 53–58: it is probable that the unexpected
occurrence of "will never thirst again" at v. 35 helps to prepare for
the "drinking" theme in vv. 53–8.

Borgen's claims do need some modification to allow for the
significance of v. 35 in the discourse and the way in which that too
has exercised a controlling effect on the flow of thought.[7] Dorothy
Lee has also argued that Borgen underestimates the significance
of the actual feeding of the five thousand, the "sign" from which
the movement of the whole chapter sets off and which provides
it with its central symbolism. She argues that although there may
have been a complicated pre-history to the material of John 6, in
its present form it is a unified whole, in which sign, image and
feast are combined and tightly interwoven.[8] Borgen has also not
taken sufficient account of the dialogue element in the text—see
vv. 34, 41, and 52.

There is much to be said for the way Zumstein has put the
matter: John 6 "is a christological reflexion in the form of a dialogue, which derives its support from the witness of scripture and
its midrashic explanation."[9]

(c) From a literary angle, *the crucial importance of v. 51c as a turning point in the flow of the discourse has been emphasized.*[10] This
verse is one of those twists given to the progression of thought,
which moves spirally rather than logically from A to Z. (Clearly if
vv. 53–58 were to be deleted, then vv. 51c–52 would have to go as
well.) Again, it has to be admitted that there is some plausibility
in the claim that v. 51ab could provide a suitable conclusion to

7. Lindars, *John*, 253, makes the pertinent comment that there is a tendency to
expect John to be too closely bound by the rules of Jewish homiletic. He claims that
what we have in John 6 is "not then the homily as John preached it in the eucharistic as-
sembly, but as he has adapted it for his book." Zumstein, *Kreative Erinnerung*, 136, says
(rightly in our opinion) that "the word 'Ego Eimi' in v. 35 forms the central statement
dominating the structure of the text." See now Theobald, *Herrenworte*, 48, for a similar
stress on the centrality of 6:35.

8. Dorothy Lee, *Symbolic Narratives*, 127–28, 130–31. Cf. the same criticism of
Borgen made by Obermann, *Christologische Erfüllung*, 142–50, and also a defence of
the unity of the whole chapter (13–50).

9. Zumstein, *Kreative Erinnerung*, 136.

10. See especially Schurmann, *Joh 6:51c*, 244–62; also Schweizer, *Zeugnis*, 359.

the discourse; it would provide something of an inclusio with v. 35, with the themes of the bread of life or the living bread; never hungering or thirsting again; and living forever.[11]

(d) The *relation of 6:63 to vv. 51c–58* has been much discussed. While some feel that 6:63 fits on to vv. 31–51ab but not on to vv. 51c–58,[12] a strong case can be made out that 6:63 would read oddly as the conclusion to a discourse which lacked vv. 51c–58[13] and that the stress on the Spirit is akin to a similar emphasis in 3:6–11 after 3:5.

(e) As to *theological ideas*, it has been argued that vv. 53–8 are alien to the rest of the discourse and the Gospel as a whole. These scholars assume that the original evangelist operated with a "Word theology" to which faith is the required response and that he was either anti-sacramental or indifferent to the sacraments. Since vv. 53–58 are assumed to be about the Lord's Supper, they are ascribed to a later redactor who has thereby introduced a radically new note into the original work. Such an approach may, however, be criticized as too one-sided:[14] why is the response of faith to the Word regarded as incompatible with an emphasis on the sacraments? (Paul could hold the two together.) Several scholars have argued that faith has primacy in the sacramental theology of the Fourth Gospel.[15]

While the arguments are finely poised, and one suspects that pre-suppositions govern decisions allegedly reached on exegetical grounds, I am not persuaded that the case for deleting vv. 51c/53–58 has been made

---

11. Richter, *Einheit*, 21–31, has argued this point strongly.

12. So very forcefully Bornkamm, *Eucharistische Rede*, 164–68; see too Richter, *Einheit*, 50–53.

13. Dunn, *John VI*, 332. Cosgrove, *Place*, 534, also challenges the view that vv. 60–71 link on better to vv. 41–51b than on to vv. 51c–58. Barrett, *Flesh*, 40–42, points out that it is a characteristic of John to break up discourses by means of objections, so that actually a new unit begins with v. 52, not with v. 51c.

14. Wilckens, *Eucharistische Abschnitt*, 233, maintains that there is no sound ground for denying any interest in the sacraments to the evangelist.

15. E.g., Mussner, *Leben*, 138–39; Schürmann, *Joh 6:51c*, 258; Wilkens, *Abendmahlzeugnis*, 360–62, 370; cf. too Schnackenburg, *John* 2:59; Wilckens, *Eucharistische Abschnitt*, 231.

out,[16] nor am I convinced that it is necessary to argue that the evangelist himself later expanded the discourse to include vv. 51c/53–8.[17]

We are taking the Gospel as it stands, to see if sense can be made of it, [18] and only if we cannot do that, do we think that it would be permissible to resort to surgery and to excise vv. 51c/53–58.

Up to v. 51b the theme has in the main been about bread and eating (the idea of thirst in v. 35c is unexpected and is not immediately developed). Jesus has identified himself as the bread of life/true bread from heaven/bread of God (vv. 32–35, 48–51b). Clearly, if bread is the dominant image, then eating will be one of the primary modes of appropriation and will be a synonym in context for faith in Jesus[19] (πιστεύ ειν is used at vv. 35c, 40, 47), as are "coming to him" (ἔρχεσθαι, vv. 35b, 37 bis, 44, 45) or "seeing him" (v. 40 θεωρεῖν), with "eating" used again at vv. 50–51 (φαγεῖν). In contrast to the manna given in the desert to the fathers (which may not properly be called bread from heaven, vv. 32–33), the bread, which Jesus gives, which is he himself, confers eternal life vv. 49–51b; this is pictorially expressed in v. 35 as never hungering. It is entirely natural and appropriate that the theme of faith should be explored in this discourse, the first to contain an "I AM" saying.

But then, v. 51c introduces a new thought.[20] That "bread" can only be given to men and women if Jesus dies: "The bread which I shall give

16. As so many German scholars do (e.g., Bultmann, Becker, and Haenchen in their commentaries, and also E. Lohse, *Wort und Sakrament*, 117–20; Bornkamm, *Eucharistische Rede*, 163–64; 168–69; Richter, *Einheit*, 35–47).

17. Jeremias, *Joh. 6:51c–58*, 256–57; Brown, *John* 1:285–87; Wilckens, *Eucharistische Abschnitt*, hold this view.

18. Among those who uphold the unity of the discourse are Barrett, *John*, 283–85; Lindars, *John,* 50, 234; Beasley-Murray, *John*, 86–87; Carson, *John*, 276–77; Lincoln, *John*, 223–25; Borgen, *Bread*; Schürmann, *Joh 6:51c*, esp. 262; Schweizer, *Zeugnis*, 353 (with some hesitation); Schneider, *Himmelsbrotrede*, 131–42; Dodd, *Interpretation*, 333–40; Leon-Dufour, *Mystere*, 481–523, esp. 486–89; Leenhardt, *Structure*, 1–13; Wilkens, *Abendmahlszeugnis*, 354, 370; Feuillet, *Johannine Studies*, 118; Dunn, *John VI*, 328–38, esp. 329–30; Wilckens, *Eucharistische Abschnitt*, 226, 247; Barrett, *Flesh*, 40–42; Schenke, *Joh 6, 26–58*, 21–41; Culpepper, *Anatomy*, 197; Regensberger, *Overcoming the World*, 71–77; Knöppler, *Theologia Crucis*, 41–42; Lee, *Symbolic Narratives*, 130–31.

19. So very emphatically, Koester, *Symbolism*, 99–104, 302–9. Eating is a vivid way to speak of believing in the incarnate and crucified Christ. See also note 22 below.

20. Schurmann's thesis (*Joh 6:51c*, 244–62) is crucial. Others who accept that v. 51c refers to the death of Jesus are Bultmann, *John*, 235; Barrett, *John*, 298; Schnackenburg, *John* 2:55; Brown, *John* 1:291; Lindars, *John*, 267; Haenchen, *John* 1:294, 299; Beasley-Murray, *John*, 94; Carson, *John*, 295; Moloney, *John*, 219–20 (and earlier *JSM*, 115);

is my flesh for the life of the world." There is here a clear allusion to the
death of Jesus and its necessity. The bread of life only becomes available
when Jesus gives himself up to death that the world may have life. (It is
quite possible that there is here an allusion to or use of the formula of
the Last Supper over the bread. If the Hebrew *basar* or the Aramaic *bisra'*
were originally used by Jesus at the Last Supper, then the Johannine tradition of σάρξ could have preserved this just as much as the Synoptic
and Pauline accounts with σῶμα.)[21]

v. 51c provokes the retort, "How can this man give us his flesh to
eat?" (v. 52), i.e., how can men and women appropriate the life-giving
power which Jesus has to offer? The answer comes in vv. 53–58—by appropriating his death, and this is described in terms of eating his flesh
and drinking his blood. A spiritual feeding, a spiritual drinking of Christ,
is primarily in mind. Once flesh was substituted for bread in v. 51c, the
retention of "eating" from the previous part of the discourse would make
the point about spiritual appropriation in a striking and arresting, and,
indeed, potentially offensive, manner.[22]

"Flesh and blood" is a natural Semitic idiom for a human person
(cf. Matt 16:17; Gal 1:16; Eph 6:12) and, as we have mentioned, the introduction of thirst in v. 35c prepared the way for the introduction of
blood and drink in vv. 53–58.

The theme of vv. 53–58 is not primarily the Lord's Supper, but appropriating Christ lifted up on the cross for the life of the world ("Christ
crucified" to use Pauline language). We believe that 20:30–31 is warrant
for seeking first and foremost the christological interpretation of any

---

Schweizer, *Zeugnis*, 359; Marianne Thompson, *Humanity*, 45–46; Painter, *Quest*, 238–
39; Menken, *John 6:51c-58*, 1–26, esp. 9–12, 13, 16; Knöppler, *Theologia Crucis*, 47 and
Sühne, 245–47, 249–52; Dorothy Lee, *Symbolic Narratives*, 149–50; Koester, *Symbolism*,
102.

21. See the discussion in Jeremias, *Eucharistic Words*, 117–18, 198–201.

22. Cf. Marianne Thompson, *Humanity*, 47: "a metaphor for appropriating the benefits of Jesus' death by faith"; Painter, *Quest*, 239: "Eating and drinking are symbols for
coming and believing, not now simply in the person of Jesus . . . but belief in the efficacy
of his death"; Knöppler, *Theologia Crucis*, 43 (with note 92)—"Eating and drinking are
pictures for faith against the background of v. 35b and in looking back to v. 47"; Lee,
Symbolic Narratives, 151, "Thus φαγεῖν is an image of relationship with God through
Jesus, in which God nourishes the life of believers and the believing community."
Carson, *John*, 297, says that v. 54 is a metaphorical way of referring to what is expressed
in v. 40 (looking to the Son and believing on him).

passage in the Fourth Gospel; only secondarily ought the exegete to raise the question of other levels of interpretation (e.g., the sacramental).[23]

Keeping at the metaphorical or spiritual level fits in nicely with vv. 60–63. Some of Jesus' followers describe "this"—in context, vv. 53–58—as a hard saying, difficult to accept (v. 60). There is evidence enough for the scandalous nature of the idea of a crucified Messiah for Jews—Paul indicated this in 1 Cor 1:23, while Mark 8:31–33 and Luke 24:21, 25–26 would be corroborative evidence from within the Synoptic tradition, plus John 12:34 from the Fourth Gospel itself. Jesus' reply is to point to the ascension (v. 62), which the Johannine Christian knows full well is the necessary prelude to the coming of the Paraclete-Spirit who will take the things of Jesus and declare them interpretatively to the disciples (16:7, 12–15). The person reading/hearing the Gospel for the first time might not fully understand all this—it is part of the "in" language of the Johannine communities.[24]

The realm of flesh is powerless to confer life.[25] Only the Spirit can bestow life. It is the role of the Spirit to take the words of Jesus and make them life-giving to the hearers of this Gospel (v. 63). In the words of

23. So emphatically Dunn, *John VI*, 333 ("Jesus is the focus of the whole speech . . . Jesus himself is central; throughout—not his revelation (as distinct from himself) and not the sacramental elements"), 337–38 ("the primary emphasis in John 6 is on Jesus himself—not the Incarnate Jesus only but as given up to death"). Cf. Carson, *John*, 295, 297–98. Dorothy Lee, *Symbolic Narratives*, 152, agrees that the christological focus is primary, though she believes that the sacramental meaning is consonant with John's symbolic worldview (the Eucharist as a symbol disclosing Jesus as the true bread of heaven). Koester, *Symbolism*, 308–9, also insists that the christological reference must be primary (cf. 13 for Johannine symbolism in general), while Helen Orchard, *Courting Betrayal*, 123–26, also argues that the primary message is concerned with Jesus' suffering and death and that eucharistic significance is secondary, submerged some way beneath the surface layer of the text. Cf. too the remark of Burridge, *People*, 124, about the material in the Gospels in general: "We need to ask what this story or incident is designed to tell us about the author's understanding of Jesus."

24. Cf. the oft quoted phrase of Leroy, *Rätsel*—"Sondersprache," the special or private language of the community. See Meeks, *Man from Heaven*, 152, 163–64, on "in" language, and Nicholson, *Departure*, 29–41, for a useful discussion of the author and his readers. I do not wish to suggest, however, that this language is necessarily completely opaque to "outsiders." See now Bauckham's criticism of an exaggerated emphasis on "in" language, in *Testimony*, 21, 119–22. Koester, *Symbolism*, 18, and Nicole Chibici-Revneanu, *Herrlichkeit*, 54, also believe that Johannine language was accessible to the uninitiated.

25. Lee, *Symbolic Narratives*, 155, comments that here σάρξ represents "a closed materialistic worldview," that which "claims for itself independence of the Creator."

Jesus, now written down in the Gospel, the hearer is confronted with the possibility of receiving life, provided that he or she will accept this life from the Christ, the Son of Man, who gave his flesh for the life of the world, who was lifted up on the cross for the world. Only by directing faith to this Jesus can a person receive life.

We have maintained that the primary level of interpretation ought to be—What does the passage tell us about Jesus? This does not exclude the possibility of a secondary level of interpretation. Here I would wish to acknowledge the strength of the position of those who advocate a reference to the Lord's Supper in vv. 53–58. The language does seem to point in that direction, and we might well ask whether any Christian at the end of the first century could hear 6:53–58 without being reminded of the Supper? A way forward is possible, *viz.* that the evangelist may have used language from the Lord's Supper in order to refer to the spiritual feeding on the crucified Christ available to the believer in all the circumstances of daily life.

Thus, many scholars, as already mentioned, believe that v. 51c reflects at least part of words of explanation over the bread in the Lord's Supper in Johannine churches. Wilckens has also suggested that v. 54 contains traditional Lord's Supper material, with vv. 55–57 as the evangelist's interpretation and expansion of it.[26] Of course, Wilckens believes that 51c–58 is about the Lord's Supper and deals with how believers participate in Jesus—through the Eucharist meal, an essential bond with the Person of Jesus is effected and the communicant experiences what Jesus gives. His suggestion about v. 54 could still be accepted, even if we do not follow the view that the Eucharist or Lord's Supper is being specifically dealt with.

The suggestion that Lord's Supper language is being used but that the Supper itself is not the theme, is not new, and a number of scholars past and present have espoused it.[27] An analogy to this—albeit from

---

26. Wilckens, *Eucharistische Abschnitte*, 239–43.

27. See Schnackenburg, *John* 2:65–66; Lindars, *John*, 253; Odeburg, *Fourth Gospel*, 239; Borgen, *Bread from Heaven*, 186; Cadman, *Open Heaven*, 87, 89 (partially); Dunn, *John VI*, 334 ("John uses eucharistic terminology with a metaphorical sense, namely, to describe not the effects of the sacrament as such, but the union of the ascended Jesus with his believing followers through the Spirit"); Moloney, *JSM*, 104–5, and *John*, 223–24; Caird, *Language*, 55; Marianne Thompson, *Humanity*, 47; Painter, *Quest*, 238; Menken, *John 6:51c–58*, 8, 15, 24; Lincoln, *Truth*, 216, and *John*, 232–335. Carson, *John*, 277–80, 296–98, accepts allusions to the Lord's Supper. Barrett, *Flesh*, 42, 44, while

another author, though one who may have had some links with the
Johannine circle—would be the way in which Lord's Supper language
is used in Revelation 3:20 (the Risen Lord comes and "'sups" with the
believer)[28] in order to refer to the possibility of the individual believer's
encountering the Lord Jesus in the various situations of his/her life.

Whether such a procedure contained a protest against a tendency
to narrow too much the idea of encountering Christ to specific church
services like the Lord's Supper would be open to discussion. Such an
eventuality could be possible, though it is only an inference, and the
evidence is not watertight by any means.[29]

Even if the metaphorical interpretation is rejected and vv. 53–58
held to refer directly to the Lord's Supper, the main argument which
I am putting forward would not, in fact, be invalidated because v. 51c
refers quite clearly to the death of Jesus. Without that death, the bread
of life, which is Jesus himself, cannot be appropriated by the believer.
The death of Jesus is essential in order for the believer to have life.[30] The
appropriation of this death is the basis of union between Christ and the
believer. And that offer of life is available to all, to the world.

We have thus run up against an issue which cannot be evaded: in
this Gospel, statements occur which on the one hand offer life to those
who respond to the word of Jesus in faith and which on the other hand
make that life dependent on the death of Jesus. Into the latter category

believing that the Eucharist is in mind in vv. 53–58, asserts that the whole discourse is
about the kind of relation between the believer and Jesus, a relation parallel to that of
Christ and the Father (*viz.* obedience and faith, cf. 4:34). De Boer, *Perspectives*, 226–28,
accepts that eating the flesh and drinking the blood are meant metaphorically at his
Stage II, but then argues that at Stage III they mean to be subject to the murderous
hostility of the Jews and the risk of martyrdom (ibid., 228–36). He has introduced a
very sharp change of thought here and there is a risk of a "catch all" approach, quite
apart from the fact that the evangelist deals with the idea of martyrdom in the Farewell
Discourse at 15:18—16:4.

28. In agreement with Preston and Hanson, *Revelation*, 68; Caird, *Revelation*, 58;
Roloff, *Revelation*, 65; Böcher, *Kirche*, 51 (note 147); Karrer, *Johannesoffenbarung*,
215–16, 254; mentioned without comment by Hemer, *Letters*, 206.

29. See Brown, *NT Essays*, 51–95, and Dunn, *Unity*, 168–71, for useful discussions
of Johannine sacramentalism or anti-sacramentalism; see also Barrett, *Church*, 74–75.

30. See Knöppler, *Theologia Crucis*, 202–3, for a discussion of how 6:51c points
to the death of Jesus as an atoning sacrifice: the death of Jesus is representative (ein
Geschehen suhnender Stellvertretung). Knöppler believes that this clear emphasis may
mean that in other texts the same idea may be implicit, even if not explicit.

fall 3:14–15 and 6:51c–58. How is this to be resolved? Neither of the two passages resolve it for us and we shall have to press on in our study.

(2) THE CROSS AS REVELATION

(a) *The Person of Jesus (8:28–29; 16:31–2)*

Jesus said to them (the Jews as 8:22 shows): "When you lift up the Son of Man, then you will know that ἐγώ εἰμι, and I do nothing on my own authority, but I speak as the Father has taught me. My Sender is with me; he has not left me alone, because I always do what pleases him. And I do nothing on my own authority, but I speak as the Father has taught me" (8:28–29). Of the Johannine character of these verses there can be no doubt.[31]

That the "lifting up" refers primarily to the cross is confirmed here because the Jews were active in securing the condemnation and crucifixion of Jesus (though it is improbable that 19:16 should be pressed to indicate that the evangelist thought that they actually carried out the crucifixion). They could hardly be said to have effected the ascension/exaltation.

The event of the cross, then, has revelatory significance and power—"then you will know that . . ." The evangelist knew that not all Jews had believed but some had, and the possibility was always open to them to recognise the truth being revealed (through the ministry of witnessing by the Paraclete and the church, e.g., 15:26–27).[32]

What is the content of the revelation? Is the ἐγώ εἰμι being used absolutely[33] or does it need a predicate to be supplied? Thus Bultmann, Lindars and Haenchen supply "the Son of Man"; Nicholson, "the One sent by the Father"; and Loader, "who I claim to be."[34] To add "Son of Man" seems almost tautologous and destroys the parallelism with 8:24 where Son of Man could hardly be added. The absolute use of ἐγώ εἰμι is

31. So, e.g., Bultmann, *John*, 353–54; Schnackenburg, *John* 2:196; Becker, *Johannesevangelium* 1:292–96.

32. Cf. the discussion of "you will know" in Moloney, *JSM*, 137–38.

33. So Barrett, *John*, 342–43; Brown, *John*, 1:348; Schnackenburg, *John* 2:202; Beasley-Murray, *John*, 140; Schultz, *Untersuchungen*, 118; Moloney, *JSM*, 138, and *John*, 271–72; cf. too Bauckham, *Testimony*, 245.

34. Bultmann, *John*, 349; Lindars, *John*, 322; Haenchen, *John* 2:28; Nicholson, *Departure*, 121; Loader, *Christology*, 48.

attested elsewhere in John and makes good sense elsewhere. Nicholson's suggestion is based on the phrase ὁ πέμψας με in 8:26 and he also wants to add to the "I am" of 8:24 "from above." Though we do not see the need for a predicate, Nicholson's suggestion would not totally destroy our suggestion, since the sending formula as used by John does envisage the divine origin of the Father's agent—he is sent from heaven, nor would Loader's, for Jesus claims to be sent by the Father from heaven.

What we would suggest is that the lifting up on the cross will disclose the divine nature of Jesus the Son of Man: it has revelatory power. Why is that? The subsequent part of the verse goes on to stress Jesus' dependence on the Father, and his lack of independence and self-assertiveness. This also seems to be part of what will be revealed by the lifting up on the cross, the καὶ co-ordinating the two halves. In other words, it is precisely in his dependence on the Father that his own person is most revealed, "and I do nothing on my own authority but I speak as the Father has taught me."[35]

In word and deed, action and speech, he follows what his Father has laid down and that includes being lifted up on a cross to glory. There is a constant fellowship and communion between himself and the Father—he is thus never on his own—and this rests on his obedience ("I always do what pleases him").[36]

There is a verse at the end of the Farewell Discourse which dovetails into 8:28–29 and affords a vital clue as to the evangelist's thinking on the cross as revelation. I refer to 16:32. Jesus has just dismissed his disciples' declaration of faith that he has come from God: "Look, the hour is coming and has come, when each of you will be scattered, every man for himself, and you will leave me alone; *and yet I am not on my own, because the Father is with me.*"

The failure of the disciples to stand by Jesus, their being "scattered,"[37] will only serve to offset what has always been true

35. Cf. Thüsing, *Erhöhung*, 18: "The ἐγώ εἰμι is still more defined, however, by the statement about the dependence on the Father which stands parallel to it in v. 28 and is linked immediately to it."

36. Hanson, *Prophetic Gospel*, 122–23, believes that Wis 9:9–10 has influenced John in his composition of 8:29.

37. John uses σκορπισθῆτε; compare διασκορπισθήσονται in Mark 14:27/Matt 26:31, quoting Zech 13:7 LXX(A) (where LXX (B) has ἐκσπάσατε). Zech 9–14 was an area of the OT used from a very early time to illustrate the Gospel story (See Dodd, *Scriptures*, 64–67) and John need not be dependent on Mark at this point (conceded by

throughout the ministry—that the Father is with him. Human deser-tion acts as a foil that heightens the oneness of the Father and Son. The failure of the disciples to be one with Jesus in the crucial hour only lets the unity of Father and Son stand forth more clearly. The cross becomes revelatory! The fact that he is not on his own but still enjoys the Father's presence and companionship justifies the absolute use of ἐγώ εἰμι at 8:28. The cross reveals that Jesus is the One to whom, by reason of his union with the Father, the divine self-revelatory formula ἐγώ εἰμι at 8:28 may legitimately be applied. The cross then discloses the identity of Jesus the Son of Man in the fullest sense of his oneness with the Father.[38]

(b) Of the Love of the Son and the Father (13:1; 15:13; 3:16)

The evangelist commences the new section of his Gospel with the sono-rous and weighty sentence: "Before the feast of the Passover, Jesus, be-cause he knew that his hour to depart out of this world to the Father had come, having loved his own who were in the world, he loved them εἰς τέλος" (13:1). The untranslated phrase is probably yet another instance of Johannine double-entendre: εἰς τέλος may mean "completely, fully, " or "to the end." On either sense, a suitable meaning ensues: either Jesus, who had throughout his ministry loved his disciples, now demonstrated that love completely and fully by his death (cf. how the good shepherd gives his life for the sheep 10:11, 15—it is a sign of his goodness as a shepherd and springs from his intimate knowledge of them); or Jesus, who had throughout his ministry loved his disciples, now demonstrated that love to the end of his life—he carried on loving them right to the end, in his death.

On either or both senses, the cross becomes a revelation of the love of Jesus for his own.[39] (This is picked up in the first occurrence of the love command at 13:34, in the phrase "as I have loved you.")

Barrett, *John*, 497). It is just possible that John also wished to evoke the Shepherd dis-course (10:12—so Schnackenburg, *John* 3:186). Brown, *John* 2:737, goes too far when he says "On the level of meaning intended by the Johannine writer, the passage lost its reference to the disciples in Gethsemane and became a prediction of the suffering to be endured by the Christians scattered in a hostile world."

38. Cf. my *Cross*, 219–26.

39. Thüsing, *Erhöhung*, 70; Forestell, *Word*, 76, 88; Riedl, *Heilswerk*, 147.

This idea also emerges very clearly in 15:13, following on a repetition of his command to love one another as he has loved them[40] (15:12 cf. 13:34–35):[41] "No one displays greater love than this, that someone lays down their life for their friends." This may have been a popular proverb in circulation, [42] but in its present context in the Farewell Discourse it is a commentary on Jesus' death and is a supporting basis for Jesus' command. His death is proof of the unsurpassable nature of his love for his "friends." Thyen has rightly claimed that the theme of giving one's life for one's friends is not merely an accidental thought on the fringe (so to speak) but is "a central motif and structural principle of the Johannine Passion story and Christology" and he points especially to 18:8 as an illustration ("If then you seek me, let these men go"—Jesus' intercession for the disciples at the time of the arrest).[43]

No doubt the idea of dying for one's friends is conditioned by the context of the Farewell Discourse addressed to the disciples on the eve of his death/departure, and must not be taken to imply a limitation on the scope of his death.

Again, an assertion is made rather than an explanation offered: Jesus displays his love for his friends in giving his life for them. It is not explained *how* this death benefits them, how it is "for them." He goes on to say that he will no longer call them slaves but they are his friends, though friendship with him does not eliminate obedience, vv. 14–15.

Thus far, on the basis of 13:1 and 15:13, we can say that the cross reveals the love of Jesus. Since he is of one mind and purpose with the Father, we could infer that his love is also an expression of the Father's love.[44]

---

40. In the light of 13:1, 34, we may see a reference to the death of Jesus in the phrase "as I have loved you" in 15:12; cf. Onuki, *Gemeinde*, 123.

41. Several scholars see chapters 15–16 as an insertion by a later redactor, Schnackenburg, *John* 3:89–90; Brown, *John* 2:586 (though genuinely Johannine); Wilckens, *Johannes*, 234–35, and *Sohn Gottes*, 59; Becker, *Abschiedsreden*, 215–46 (a position maintained in his Commentary); Borig, *wahre Weinstock*, 21; Segovia, *John 15:1–17*, 115–28, esp. 125–28. For powerful protests against such a view see Thyen, *Grossere Liebe*, 467–81, esp. 471–72, 478–79; Schnelle, *Abschiedsrede*, 64–79.

42. So Dibelius, *Joh 15:13*, 168–86 (204–20); Hengel, *Atonement*, 6–15, esp. 13.

43. Thyen, *Grossere Liebe*, 476, 480–81. On 477, he says that 15:9–16 takes the position in John which the Passion predictions have in the Synoptics, but it would be better to say that of the hour texts.

44. Cf. Painter, *Quest*, 411.

However, 3:16 offers itself as a basis for making more than an inference: "God so loved the world that he gave his only Son that whoever believes in him might not perish but have everlasting life." We note here that the evangelist uses ἔδωκεν, where Johannine usage might have led us to expect the use of πέμπειν or ἀποστέλλειν. The most likely explanation is that John chose διδόναι in order to get a double reference—both to the incarnation and to the cross. God gave his Son both in the sense of sending him and giving him up to the cross. An impressive list of scholars indicates the extent of support for this interpretation.[45] Both the incarnation and cross are a proof of God's love for the world. The cross has revelatory significance as well as the incarnation.

It should be noted that the function of 3:16 in its present context is to offer support for 3:14–15 which has spoken of the necessity for the Son of Man to be lifted up. The γάρ of 3:16 offers the foundation on which the assertion of 3:14–15 has been made. The lifting up is grounded in the expression of God's love. The function, then, of 3:16 confirms the probability of a double meaning to "gave" in the verse.

The cross, then, is revelatory of the Father's love for the world; the world which has turned from him and which without his saving intervention in his Son would be lost. 3:16 fits in with, while being expressed differently from, 13:1 and 15:13. The cross shows both the Father's love and that of Jesus.

(3) THE CROSS AS JUDGEMENT AND DRAWING INTO UNION WITH CHRIST (12:20–34)

This section of the Gospel is crucial for the evangelist's understanding of the cross.[46] Some Greeks approach Philip with the request to see Jesus

45. Bultmann, *John*, 153 (note 3); Brown *John* 1:134; Schnackenburg, *John* 1:399; Morris, *John*, 229; Lindars, *John*, 159; Becker, *Johannesevangelium* 1:145; Haenchen, *John* 1:205; Beasley-Murray, *John*, 51; Carson, *John*, 206; Wilckens, *Johannes*, 71 and *Sohn Gottes*, 40; Lincoln, *John*, 154; Thüsing, *Erhöhung*, 9–10; Kuhl, *Sendung Jesu*, 119; Riedl, *Heilswerk*, 145; Ruckstuhl, *Abstieg*, 336; Bühler, *Der Gesandte*, 410; Kohler, *Kreuz*, 255–57; Menken, *John 6*, 13; Knöppler, *Theologia Crucis*, 95–96 and *Sühne*, 244–45. Wilckens, *Christus traditus*, 40, 46; Nissen, *Community*, 201–2. Indeed, Hofius, *Johannesstudien*, 64–65, refers it exclusively to the cross, as, it would appear, does Dennis, *Jesus' Death*, 198.

46. Most scholars treat this passage as a composition of the evangelist, however diverse his material may have been. In contrast to this, Bultmann, *John*, 354, severs 12:34

(vv. 20–22). We are never told whether the request was granted, and this is no doubt deliberate on the part of the evangelist who knew that the non-Jewish mission got underway after the cross. The evangelist uses the occasion to reveal something of the meaning of the cross.

Jesus announces that the hour has come for the Son of Man to be glorified (v. 23). Earlier we raised the question whether the evangelist intended this to be understood in the sense of an "extra access" of glory to Jesus. The answer to that question comes in the next verse: "Truly, truly I say to you, unless a grain of wheat falls into the ground and dies, it remains alone (μόνος); but if it dies, it bears much fruit (πολὺν καρπὸν)" (v. 24). This small parable[47] illustrates why the cross is the glorification of Jesus.

We have seen that, humanly speaking, Jesus is on his own just before the cross—the disciples leave him μόνος (16:32).[48] He is, therefore, like the grain of wheat (v. 24a). But in the parable this grain of wheat bears much fruit. In between the two states—being on its own and bearing much fruit—lies death. The death is necessary in order to bear much fruit. So also the inference is that Jesus has to die in order to bear "much fruit."[49] The one produces the many.

What does "much fruit" mean? Three factors suggest that it means a harvest of disciples. The first is the content of the parable. The contrast between one and many supports the idea that converts are in mind, i.e., the church. There is an organic link between his death and the participation of others in his life, between his death and the creation of the church.

---

and makes it follow 8:21–29. Becker, *Johannesevangelium* 1:382, attributes vv. 24–25 to a redactor and Theobald, *Herrenworte*, 102–3, 129, believes that originally v. 23 was followed by v. 27 and that a redactor added vv. 24–26.

47. Theobald, *Herrenworte*, 119–20, believes that originally this was a generally valid law of nature, but which was open to a christological application in the light of v. 23.

48. Weidemann, *Tod Jesu*, 310, also speaks of Jesus' being *alone*, when he interprets Jesus' silence to Annas' question about his disciples (18:19). "Jesus in this phase of his work is *alone* [italics original] . . . he [the evangelist] makes it clear to his readers that this circle [of disciples] in the narrower sense still does not exist." (Perhaps surprisingly, Weidemann makes no reference to 16:32.) Weidemann, as already mentioned, links this aloneness with the impossibility of true pre-Easter discipleship.

49. Onuki, *Gemeinde*, 61, speaks of the soteriological necessity of the death of Jesus for the founding of the church, in his comment on 12:24 and 32 (a conviction alien to Gnosticism).

The second is that of Johannine usage. Whatever may be the correct interpretation of 4:34–36 as a whole (e.g., questions like who are the "others" of v. 38 and when did Jesus send the disciples to reap a harvest?), it is clear that the passage refers to missionary endeavor. "The fields white to harvest" are people ready to be evangelised. Those who reap (i.e., those who engage in missionary activity) will gather fruit (i.e., converts) for eternal life (v. 36). In fact, many Samaritans believe in Jesus and confess him to be the Savior of the world (vv. 39–42).

The phrase also occurs in chapter 15 in the Vine Discourse. Here the picture is of growth: every branch which bears fruit is pruned in order that it might bear more fruit (15:2); the disciple who abides in Jesus and Jesus in the disciple bears much fruit (v. 5). Disciples win more disciples.[50]

A third factor to be taken into consideration is the context of 12:20–34. Some Greeks approach Philip and want to see Jesus, while at v. 32 Jesus says that when he would be lifted up, he would draw all to himself, which indicates the universal effect of his death on the cross.

In view of these three factors, we are surely right in seeing 12:24 as interpreting the cross in terms of winning disciples. The cross achieves what the ministry has failed to do (12:37–43)—it achieves a harvest of converts. This is a most important insight into the Johannine under-

---

50. So also Schlatter, *Johannes*, 305; Hoskyns, *John*, 476; Brown, *John* 2:662, 676; Lindars, *John*, 489; Thüsing, *Erhöhung*, 107, 113, cf. 213 [In the second edition, Thüsing combined the missionary and religious-ethical interpretation, seeing brotherly love as missionary and pointing to 17:21, 23 and 13:35]; Lazure, *Valeurs Morales*, 36–37; Kuhl, *Sendung*, 201–9; Cadman, *Open Heaven*, 135; Olsson, *Structure and Meaning*, 247–48; Teresa Okure, *Johannine Approach*, 164, 197, 201, 211–12, 231. Ferreira, *Johannine Ecclesiology*, 68, rightly commented in a footnote: "in John καρπός is defined in terms of harvest, i.e., salvation of people for eternal life." (See also his comments on fruit bearing on 160.) Barrett, *John*, 474, prefers "living the life of a Christian disciple." Schnackenburg, *John* 3:100; Becker, *Johannesevangelium* 2:483–83; Moloney, *John*, 420–21; Wilckens, *Sohn Gottes*, 65; Lincoln, *John*, 407; and Theobald, *Herrenworte*, 168, refer to brotherly love. Borig, *Wahre Weinstock*, 237–46, favors keeping Christ's commands, especially that of brotherly love. Ford, *Redeemer*, 163, prefers "the moral-religious caliber" of the disciples rather than their mission. Onuki, *Gemeinde*, 125, takes it as a reference to church life as a whole. Beasley-Murray, *John*, 273, combines every demonstration of the vitality of faith, especially Christian love, with the idea of effective mission (cf. Carson, *John*, 517). Nissen, *Mission*, 218, says, "For John that Jesus 'bears fruit' is mission."

standing of the cross. Even Bultmann describes the glorification of Jesus as an event of salvation history—the gathering of his community.[51]

The evangelist then proceeds to clarify the thought thus far with sayings from the tradition. "The person who loves their life will lose it; and the one who hates their life in this world shall keep it to eternal life" (v. 25). This verse has parallels in the Synoptic Gospels (Mark 8:35/Matt. 16:25/Luke 9:24; Q Matt. 10:39/Luke 17:33) and refers there to a law of discipleship. In one sense it is also true of Jesus—by giving up his life, in a deeper sense, he "keeps" it, for he will become the source of life, eternal life, to others. What 12:25 asserts is, in the first place, true of the Master, and then becomes the law of discipleship for those in union with Christ. The believer must be prepared to lose his/her life, which is bound up with this world, and only so can he or she receive eternal life. The believer must follow their Lord who dies and so gives life.[52] The reward is to be where Jesus is: "Where I am, my servant shall be there also. If anyone serves me, the Father will honour them." (v. 26)

We have previously discussed vv. 27–28, which return to Jesus. The hour of the cross is the hour for which his ministry has been destined (v. 27). He receives the assurance that the Father will be glorified in the cross (v. 28). The gaining of converts will glorify the Father also!

Then come key verses for an understanding of John's theology of the cross (12:31–33):

> Now is the judgment of this world;
> now the prince of this world will be thrown out;
> and when I am lifted up from the earth, I will draw all people to myself.
> He said this to signify by what kind of death he was going to die.

It must be said at the outset of our discussion that in practice there seems to be (at worst) a widespread ignoring of or (at best) underestimating of the double νῦν which must be held to control v. 32 as well as v. 31.[53] The twofold "now" occurs in an emphatic position at the beginning of the two clauses in v. 31. "Now": that is to say, in the cross; "now, " not later

---

51. Bultmann, *John*, 325. Nicole Chibici-Rivneanu, *Herrlichkeit*, 173, 176, 181, 287, also sees the saving significance of Jesus' death to be this gathering of his commuity.

52. Onuki, *Gemeinde*, 67, sees following as belonging to the rich fruit of Jesus' death—it first becomes possible after Jesus' death and exaltation.

53. Among exceptions we may note Schnackenburg, *John* 2:392; especially Beasley-Murray, *John*, 213; Thüsing, *Erhöhung*, 22; Dennis, *Jesus' Death*, 205; and Chibici-Revneanu, *Herrlichkeit*, 544.

in the future. The exegete has, therefore, it seems to me, to ask how are the three statements true of the moment of the cross, not of what might happen subsequently, after the cross.

We, therefore, ask firstly how is the cross the moment of the judgment of the world? The majority answer runs—the cross exposes the unbelief of the world and, therefore, brings condemnation and judgment for the world. The world refuses to believe that Jesus is sent from God, and the cross is the supreme moment of that refusal to believe. Not to acknowledge that Jesus is the agent and Son of God is to incur the judgment of God. Thus, on this view,[54] the cross is both an outcropping of sinful refusal to accept God's activity (this time in his Son) and unveils that sin of the world and reveals its basic nature as revolt against God.

What, then, is the difference between this moment and, let us say, the attitude of the Pharisees in chapter 9? Theirs is clearly one of refusal to believe that Jesus is the Christ, the Son of God. They ask, in a question expecting the answer "No": "Are we also blind?" to which Jesus replies: "If you were blind, you would have no sin; but now you say, 'We see', your sin remains" (vv. 40–41). They become illustrations of the fact that Jesus' ministry has its "dark" side, as he himself said: "I have come into this world for judgment, in order that those who do not see may see and those who see may become blind." (v. 39)

The Pharisees are typical of those who think that they see and confidently dismiss Jesus as a law-breaker who cannot possibly be sent by God (e.g., vv. 24, 29). What was said at 3:18b–19 may be quoted: "The person who does not believe has been condemned already, because they have not believed in the name of God's only Son. Now this is the judgment, that light has come into the world, but people loved the darkness more than the light, for their deeds were evil."

Clearly, the truth enunciated in general at 3:18–19 and with reference to particular people in 9:39–41 did not come true first at the cross—it was already true of the ministry of the incarnate Word. Jesus' coming provoked crisis and demanded decision from the start: the pro-

---

54. Basically to be found in Strathmann, *Johannes*, 190; Bultmann, *John*, 431; Schnackenburg, *John* 2:390–91; and Sanders, *John*, 296. Wilkenhauser, *Johannes*, 234; Brown, *John* 1:477; Lindars, *John*, 433; Becker, *Johannesevangelium* 1:392; and Moloney, *John*, 354, tend to fuse comment on judgment on this world with judgment on the prince of this world.

cess of receiving salvation or judgment, of obtaining life or incurring God's wrath, was present from the start.

What, then, is the difference between what was already happening during the ministry and what happened on the cross? The view mentioned above does not seem to draw any distinction at all, and must therefore be held to ignore or underestimate the significance of νῦν.[55] Dissatisfaction with this leads, therefore, to the search for a better explanation and one which will ensure, in addition, that the cross will also be the casting out of Satan and the drawing of all human beings into unity with Jesus.

Another interpretation does suggest itself, *viz.* that in his death on the cross Jesus identifies himself with the human race in the sphere of judgment and death (8:21, 24). He who was alone (μόνος), a solitary figure both as life incarnate and in his obedience to God, becomes at the cross a representative figure. He who had himself been entrusted with judgment identifies with his fellow human beings bound in the sin-judgment-death nexus. He who was set over against men and women in respect of judgment, now shares with them in receiving judgment. In the hour of the cross, the world—and Jesus identified with the world—is judged. Here, human beings in the person of Jesus are judged.[56] On

55. E.g. Loader, *Christology*, 106, maintains that Jesus' death "brings to sharp focus what is already at stake in each encounter with Jesus in his ministry . . . It brings to a climax the issues of Jesus' life." But is this really satisfactory?

56. Schlatter, *Johannes*, 270–71, said, "This world, humanity as it is, is set under God's judgment through the fact that Christ is repudiated and killed. But this brings not death but forgiveness because Christ died for it." Caird, *Judgment and Salvation*, 234–35, maintained that it was in the cross that Jesus was united with mankind, identifying himself with them in their sin and accepting for himself their condemnation and death. Because he so identified himself with the accused, the cross became the defeat of Satan and the point where all men were drawn into unity with Jesus and therefore with the Father. Blank, *Krisis*, 282, argued that the judgment in 12:31 is to be "understood completely objectively"; "it is not merely the exposure of the sins of the world but a punitive judgment [Strafgericht] . . . through which 'this world' . . . really ceases to exist, comes to an end, and indeed, which is absolutely decisive, in Jesus Christ Himself . . . He the crucified and risen Christ is in his person . . . the end of the old world, fallen into death's sway [todverfallen], and the beginning of God's new world of life. In himself that turn which deals the death blow to this world takes place . . . in him the transformation . . . which changes death into life itself results." Beasley-Murray, *John 12:31-4*, 74: "We must understand that the sentence of judment passed on 'this world' is endured by the One whom this world murders—the Son of Man"; repeated in *John*, 213. Kammler, *Johannesstudien*, 134, can also say on 16:11, which looks back to 12:31, that "the judgment on the world and its lord has taken place in the cross once for all," though he

the cross, under the judgment of God, he who was μόνος, becomes the inclusive representative of humankind. Here, on the cross, the One represents the many.

Before we consider possible objections to this interpretation, it will be best to consider the second half of v. 31 plus v. 32 to see whether this interpretation can cohere with a satisfactory explanation of vv. 31b and 32. Verse 31b runs: "Now the prince of this world will be thrown out." The interpretation of v. 31a that we have suggested above does justice to both parts of v. 31. If the cross is taken as judgment in the sense of revealing sin, no adequate explanation can be given of why the prince of this world will be cast out. If the interpretation sketched above is followed, we can understand why at one and the same time the judgment takes place and the prince of this world will be cast out.

The picture is still a judicial one. With this in mind,[57] we can fill out the brevity of John 12:31b. The prince of this world, who lords it over sinful men and women and claims them in death (cf. 8:21, 24), enters the court to claim his victim. But Jesus is in fact the Righteous One (cf. 8:46), who has perfectly obeyed the Father at all times. The prince of this world has, therefore, no claim on him (cf. 14:31), for Jesus' life has been lived on principles diametrically opposed to the evil one. Jesus belongs to God. The prince of this world's case falls to the ground[58]—he is, therefore, cast out of the heavenly court.[59] His domination over the cosmos has been broken, because the one man, Jesus, has been perfectly obedi-

---

does not explore the implications of that remark. Finally, we mention Lincoln, *Truth*, 203, who speaks of the judge being judged on behalf of, indeed instead of, those who deserved this judgment, and on 215 states that Jesus' death is "God's judgment of both him and the world."

57. This metaphor, or possibly remnant of a "myth" (see appendix 2 at the end of this chapter) can also help in illuminating 1 John 2:1–2: now, in place of the accuser, we have an advocate, Jesus Christ the righteous (cf. Betz, *Paraklet*, 204)—see chapter 9 below.

58. What Schnackenburg, *John* 3:131–32, says on 16:11 is helpful too for 12:31: "The judgment has taken place and, as 12:31–32 shows clearly, at the very 'hour' when Jesus was 'exalted.'"

59. Weidemann, *Tod Jesu*, 423–50, esp. 447–50, denies that Satan is cast out of heaven. He argues that the blood of Jesus the true Passover lamb has power to ward off Satan and thus create a Satan-free sphere on earth. There is no reason, however, why John could not envisage the expulsion of Satan from the heavenly court and the creation of a new power sphere on earth where the new life of Jesus is operative and which is protected by the power of God vested in Jesus from Satan's attacks (cf. 17:2, 15).

ent, and he has identified himself with human beings under judgment. In accordance with Johannine thinking in terms of spheres and power related to those spheres, we could say that the power of the prince of this world has been broken. Potentially, therefore, freedom from his power is available. The transfer from his sphere of domination becomes available at and through the cross, through the Jesus who is lifted up.

If v. 31 gives us a negative side of the cross, v. 32 gives us a positive side: "and when[60] I am lifted up from the earth, I will draw all people to myself." Invariably this has been applied to the future mission of the church, to the preaching of the cross and its "attractive" power. The cross will be like a magnet drawing men and women to Jesus.[61]

This interpretation leaves one with a sense of dissatisfaction for three reasons. In the first place, it ignores the fact (as stated above) that the double "now" of v. 31 controls v. 32 also.[62] Secondly, it tends to emphasize the response of men and women more than the text itself suggests. The text says that *Jesus* will draw all to himself, not that men and women will respond and let themselves be drawn to him. There is a strong probability that the language used here is indebted to LXX Jer 38:3: (MT 31:3).[63] This appears in a passage in which God assures Israel, in exile as a result of the Assyrian conquest, that he has loved her with an everlasting love and he promises to restore Israel. "For this reason I have drawn (εἵλκυσα σε)[64] you in compassion." Israel will enjoy the restoration of its life in the land and there will be a reunion of Israel and

60. For ἐάν meaning "when," see *BAG* 210, who lists John 12:32 under this category; see JB, GN, NIV, REB and NRSV translations.

61. E.g., Wilkens, *Zeichen*, 104, says that 12:32 includes the work of the Paraclete by whom Jesus will draw all to himself; cf. Riedl, *Heilswerk*, 424. When Theobald, *Herrenworte*, 401, says that, "This takes place first after Easter in the mission of the church," he appears to mean that it is first actualised in the mission of the church, given his statement later in the book referred to in note 62 below.

62. Cf. Thüsing, *Erhöhung*, 22, who says that 12:31 and 32 do not refer to temporally successive events, while Theobald, *Herrenworte*, 521, says that "it is important that in 12:32 the ἑλκύειν of the apodosis is linked immediately with the event of 'lifting up' articulated in the protasis conditional clause, so that one must say that the 'drawing to himself' is the *immediate* soteriological consequence of the event of lifting up" (my italics).

63. Another possibility is the Hebrew of Hos 11:4: "I led them with cords of human kindness, with bands of love." The LXX has translated this as ἐν διαφθορᾷ ἀνθρώπων ἐξέτεινα αὐτοὺς ἐν δεσμοῖς ἀγαπήσεώς μου.

64. The Hebrew has "I have continued to deal with you in loving kindness."

Judah in Zion (LXX 38:1–6). Thus, what we probably have in John 12:32 is a case of language used of God being transferred to Jesus.[65] In the third place, it overpresses the future indicative ἑλκύσω in the main clause. Grammatically an ἐάν clause is normally[66] followed in the main clause by a future indicative, but it does not demand that the action of the verb in the main clause be separated from the time of the action expressed in the condition laid down in the ἐάν clause.[67]

What, then, is the alternative? The alternative is to take the text as it stands and at face value, and accept what it says—Jesus, lifted up on the cross (and to glory) does *ipso facto* draw men and women into a unity with himself (πρὸς ἐμαυτόν).[68] If Jesus has identified himself with humanity under judgment at the cross, he has also drawn that same humanity in union with himself representatively into the Father's presence.[69]

65. Those who accept that language of LXX Jer 38:3 is being used include Brown, *John* 1:468; Wilckens, *Johannes*, 103–4; Thüsing, *Erhöhung*, 26; Kollmann, *Kreuzigung*, 171; Dennis, *Jesus' Death*, 204, 330; Painter, *Sacrifice*, 309. Schnackenburg, *John* 2:50, mentions LXX Jer 38:3 (and Hos 11:4) when commenting on John 6:44. The idea of a possible allusion to LXX Jer 38:3 is more convincing than the suggestion that John has in mind the Heb of Job 21:33b made by Hanson, *Living Utterances*, 128–29, because of the context of the Jeremiah passage.

66. I am aware that John himself affords an exception to this at 15:16!

67. Schnackenburg, *John* 2:392 rightly says "The point of the future in 12:32 is also not so much to announce a process which begins with the lifting up of Jesus, whereby the exalted One draws all to himself, *as to state the immediate fact and certainty*" (italics mine).

68. Painter, *Quest*, 323, correctly states "But it is 12:32 that tells us that *in this event* Jesus will draw all men to himself" (my italics). Hofius, *Johannesstudien*, 63, has also written "In the hour of his dying . . . the one handed over to death binds those separated from God with himself and even thereby with the Father (12:24, 32; 17:19)," though Hofius then limits the "all" of 12:32 to those elected to believe (see the next footnote). Okure, *Mission*, 163, referred to the glorification of Jesus as "the definitive act whereby the work is completed once for all, *the drawing/gathering activity is programmatically achieved* (12:32; 10:16; 11:52)" (italics mine); see also 202, 208. Theobald, *Fleischwerdung*, who is not concerned primarily with working out John's understanding of the death of Jesus, believes that only through participation in the destiny (Geschick) of the Son of Man is the new being grounded in the Spirit obtainable: on 383 (note 47) he writes "The Son of Man *through his lifting up has become the representative of those who believe in him* and the giver of life for them" (my italics) and believes that this is what the speech about the glorification of the Son of Man says (12:23; 13:31–32), but Theobald thinks that Jesus draws believers not to himself on the cross but to the Father's home (12:32; 14:2). We believe that he has missed the emphasis on the "now" of the cross in 12:31–32.

69. Haenchen, *John* 2:98, has no right to say of the "all" that "the word 'all' is here in

Of late, there have been some severe criticisms of the use of "corporate personality," as set out by Wheeler Robinson, Aubrey Johnson, and others in Old Testament scholarship and its use by New Testament scholars, especially with reference to Paul and his idea of Jesus as the second Adam.[70] It has been suggested that we should think more modestly of corporate representation. Actually, as we have pointed out, legal ideas permeate John 12:31, so that in a sense there would be no difficulty in seeing corporate representation in v. 32. We would then have in v. 32 salvation stated as an accomplished fact in the lifting up, whereas in 17:24 we would have this expressed in terms of a prayer: "Father, I wish that where I am, those[71] whom you have given me might be with me, that they might see my glory which you gave me, because you loved me before the foundation of the world."

Is it satisfactory to describe the union between Jesus and his disciples as legal representation? Certainly, the Vine Discourse in chapter 15 in particular has been the basis for talking about Johannine mysticism. Mysticism is a notoriously slippery word, and certainly must not be taken as some absorption of the disciple into Christ or the deification of the disciple.[72]

The idea of mutual abiding of Christ and disciples in John 15 and of the mutual abiding of Father and Son and disciples through the mediation of the Son in John 17 seems to take us beyond the idea of legal representation. Several years ago, Theo Preiss[73] coined the phrase "juridical mysticism" to describe Johannine thought, and it may be that we could

---

error" [sic]. More correct is Riedl, *Heilswerk*, 414, "But since the Word of God does not return 'empty' to the Father, he certainly takes in and through his dying the total believing world back with himself into preexistent glory." But why limit this to believers? The same criticism should be levelled at Knöppler, *Theologia Crucis*, 163, and at Hofius, *Johannesstudien*, 66, both of whom interpret "all" as all elected to believe, while Dennis, *Jesus' Death*, 202–5, appears to limit the "all" to Israel (in accordance with his emphasis on the place of the theology of Israel's restoration on John).

70. See J. R. Porter, *Legal Aspects*, 379–80; Rogerson, *Hebrew Conception*, 1–16; S. E. Porter, *Two Myths*, 289–307 (he prefers corporate representation). But see the remark of Wright, *Climax*, 46 (note 17), that, though to be used carefully, the theme "corporate personality" should not be abandoned altogether.

71. Interpreting the collective singular as a plural *ad sensum*.

72. See Barrett, *John*, 85–87, for a judicious and balanced assessment of mysticism and the Fourth Gospel.

73. Preiss, *Life in Christ*, 25. Barrett, *Essays*, 114, commented on Preiss' statement: "the phrase as a whole is not far from the mark."

use this phrase with profit for what we seem to be meeting in 12:31–32. Firstly, at the cross Jesus establishes juridical representation between himself and the world; then, secondly, when (as we shall see later) men and women actually respond to what has been done on their behalf and become Jesus' own (οἱ ἴδιοι), then a union between him and them ensues, to which we may apply in some sense, hesitations notwithstanding, the label mystical union.

Jesus has been lifted up on the cross and to glory, back to the Father's presence (though in another sense he has never been away from the Father—see 1:18; 8:29; 16:32, etc.), where he was before (6:62). He draws men and women into that communion with the Father that he himself enjoys.[74] He can mediate to others that communion with the Father which he alone previously enjoyed (e.g., 6:46; 14:6). Where he is, others can also be (12:26). To put it another way, there is a new power-sphere established: that of being in Christ, where his power and life are operative. As life-giving sap flows from the vine to its branches, so life and power flow from Christ to disciples united to him.

This interpretation reinforces the point made by the grain of wheat analogy in 12:24. The grain of wheat dies and bears much fruit: on the cross Jesus drew all men and women to himself. This interpretation, furthermore, coheres with what the foot washing and other passages to be discussed below teach.

Our argument has been that something objective happened at the cross, in the thinking of the evangelist: Jesus identifies himself with the world under judgment, but, because he is the Obedient One, the prince of this world loses his case and is ejected from the heavenly court (by implication, Jesus takes his place as our Paraclete/Advocate), while Jesus draws men and women into union with himself, into the Father's presence. He has indeed become the Saviour of the world (4:42).[75]

Before we continue our study, it will take up the point about meeting a potential objection to the interpretation just suggested, [76] *viz.* that

74. Cadman, *Open Heaven*, 33–34: 'the sense of "unto myself" is no less than "into my own union with the Father."'

75. de la Potterie, *Vérité*, 1:108–10, maintains that the Son of Man became fully king and savior at Calvary. Lincoln, *Truth*, 218, makes the comment that "As the divine life absorbs the sentence of death on humanity in Jesus' death and embodies the verdict of life in his resurrection, this opens the way for humans, through believing, to be united with that life that overcomes death" (cf. 228).

76. See p. 151.

we have overstressed the "corporate" aspect of John's thought and that we have been in danger of importing Pauline ideas and terms into the Johannine presentation. There has been a good deal of stress on the "individualism" of Johannine thought and it has been pointed out that where John uses imagery for the church, these images (the Shepherd and his flock and the Vine and its branches) relate the individual Christian to Jesus, rather than Christians to each other.[77] Without wishing to deny this individualism, it must be also said that it is possible so to overstress it that we do not do justice precisely to the corporate aspects present in the Fourth Gospel.[78] There is, after all, such a thing as 'the fellowship of the individualists'![79] The following passages point to the corporate aspect:

i. Believers are to be gathered into one by Jesus' death (11:50–52; cf. the "one flock" of 10:16).

ii. Believers are to love one another (13:34–35; 15:12), which implies fellowship.

iii. Believers are to be one, reflecting the unity of the Father and Son (17:20–26).

iv. John's dualistic language, his way of thinking in terms of spheres, would reinforce the community's sense of cohesion and separateness from the world (I here assume the conclusions drawn from the application of sociological modes of study to the New

77. See, e.g., the important article by Moule, *Individualism*, 171–90, together with his comments on the difference between Pauline and Johannine Christology in *Christology*, 50–51, 65–66, 102–3. (Of course, Bultmann's existentialist approach to expounding the Gospel encouraged an individualistic approach to its message). Moule's article was less than a decade after Dodd, *Interpretation*, 244, had argued that as Son of Man Jesus was "in some sort the inclusive representative of ideal or redeemed humanity." Dodd has recently been followed by Wink, *Son of Man*, 117–24. I have reached my conclusions by a very different route than either of these two scholars.

78. Even in 1967, Kuhl, *Sendung*, 157, had protested against the tendency to overstress the individualism of the Fourth Gospel. See also Onuki, *Gemeinde*, for a study which reveals a strong sense of community behind the Fourth Gospel (though it is not his aim to engage in the individualism versus corporate debate); Regensberger, *Overcoming*, esp. 80–81, 113–14, 127–30, for a stress on the solidarity of the Johannine community; and Margaret Davies, *Rhetoric*, 187–88, for a criticism of the stress on the individualism of the Gospel. Likewise, Lincoln, *Truth*, 245–46, stresses the importance of a loving community in relation to the credibility of witness in the world.

79. I heard the late Dr. Gunter Wagner use this phrase concerning the Fourth Gospel in a New Testament seminar during the 1978 Conference of European Baptist Theological Teachers at Hamburg.

Testament).[80]

A strong individualism and a strong sense of fellowship are by no means mutually contradictory or impossible.[81] Accordingly, after careful thought, I am prepared to adhere to the interpretation of John 12:20–34 offered here. The thought of the fourth evangelist is both individualistic and corporate: the former may be slightly the more dominant, but the latter is by no means weak. [82]

(4) THE FOOTWASHING AS A SYMBOL OF CHRIST'S DEATH (13:1–11)

Clearly, the section 13:12–17(20) concentrates on the ethical implications of the foot washing. Jesus becomes a model for his disciples to imitate—he has given them an example that they should follow. Washing the feet of others becomes a symbol of loving service to fellow-believers. The later new commandment to love one another as Jesus has loved us (vv. 34–35) fits nicely into this lesson. (Scholarly opinion divides on whether vv. 12–20 come from (i) a pre-Johannine source, with vv. 6–11 as the work of the evangelist, [83] or (ii) the evangelist, with 1–11 as tradi-

80. E.g., Meeks, *Man from Heaven*, 44–72; and see in general, Onuki, *Gemeinde*.

81. My own branch of the Christian Church, the Baptists, it could be argued, exhibit precisely these two features in our congregations (indeed the "classic" Baptist position has stressed both the independence of the local congregation and its inter-dependence with other congregations). Recent Johannine scholarship, epitomised by Brown, *Community*, has emphasised the strong sense of community as well as the individualistic ethos in the Johannine congregations.

82. Preiss, *Life in Christ*, 26–27, 30, saw Paul and John close together in terms of juridical mysticism, and he protested against the tendency to exaggerate unduly the difference between them (ibid., 14).

83. E.g., Bauer, *Johannesevangelium*. 166; Bultmann, *John*, 462; Haenchen, *John*, 2:107; Dodd, *Historical Tradition*, 60; Boismard, Lavement, 5–24, esp. 21–24; Fortna, *Gospel of Signs*, 155–57. Zumstein, *Kreative Erinnerung*, 168–74, believes that vv. 12–17 represent the first interpretation (of the oldest tradition which probably consisted of vv. 4–5, 16) from the Johannine school, with vv. 6–11 as the work of the evangelist.

tion, [84] or (iii) a later redaction; [85] while others defend the unity of vv. 1–20 from the evangelist[86]).

The foot washing itself, i.e., judged by what is said within vv. 1–11, points in another direction, however. We have already mentioned the distinction between ignorance now and future knowledge of what has taken place (13:7). The present ignorance will be dissolved by the ministry of the Paraclete-Spirit: this is not, however, referring to the meditation of vv. 12–20 (however much this also may be prompted by the Paraclete-Spirit!). A hint of what is meant in 13:7 is afforded by what follows in v. 8. When Peter refuses to allow Jesus to wash his feet, Jesus says to him: "Unless I wash you, you have no part with me." Here the foot washing is viewed as something of crucial and decisive significance which Jesus must do for the disciple (who equally must allow it to take place upon or for him/her). Without it Peter has no part with or share in Jesus. The phrase used is ἔχειν μέρος. *BAG* translates as "to have a place with someone."[87] In the LXX, μέρος is nearly a synonym for κλῆρος (inheritance), and perhaps the phrase in 13:8 could be taken eschatologically and refer to a place in the Father's home (14:1–3), [88] though then we might have expected τόπος. However, μέρος can mean "share" and in that sense what qualifies the preposition would be vital and decisive. What can having a share in a person mean? It is presumably this that leads so many scholars in their exposition of 13:8 to speak of *fellowship with Jesus*,[89] with some then specifying life/salvation[90] or sonship[91] as the more precise underlying thought.

84. Beasley-Murray, *John,* 231.

85. Brown, *John* 2:562; Schnackenburg. *John* 3:10–15; Becker, *Johannesevangelium,* 2:420; Richter, *Fusswaschung,* 309–20; Thyen, *Johannes 13,* 343–56; Segovia, *Footwashing,* 31–51, esp. 37 (Segovia sees parts of vv. 1–3 as coming from the same hand as vv. 12–20).

86. E.g., Wilckens, *Johannes,* 210 and *Christus traditus,* 43; Lincoln, *John,* 374–76.

87. *BAG* 507.

88. Schnackenburg, *John* 3:19 (being where Jesus is); Carson, *John,* 464; Cadman, *Open Heaven,* 134, 145, 159; Hultgren, *Johannine Footwashing,* 542, 544.

89. Schlatter, *Johannes,* 282; Bultmann, *John,* 468; Lindars, *John,* 450; Haenchen, *John* 2:107; Lincoln, John, 368; Schneider, μέρος *TWNT,* 4. 597; Michl, *Fusswaschung,* 701–2; Zumstein, *Kreative Erinnerung,* 173, 176.

90. Becker, *Johannesevangelium* 2:423.

91. Richter, *Fusswaschung,* 291.

With John's capacity for realized eschatology, one is inclined to see the primary reference as fellowship with Jesus (i.e., bordering on that incorporation which we have suggested takes place at the cross), while allowing that, ultimately, sharing in Jesus will involve seeing his glory with the Father (17:24).

What can the foot washing signify if it conveys such a decisive benefit? What does it mean if it mediates such an important blessing? Jesus has performed the slave's task; he has humbled himself to serve them (though the roles ought to have been reversed, for he is their Lord and Master/Teacher). If it conveys a share in Jesus—and 12:32 has indicated that Jesus draws people into unity with himself at the cross—then we have to say that the foot washing is like an act of prophetic symbolism, conveying what it symbolises, enacting proleptically Jesus' service in death. Jesus enacts his death under the symbolism of washing his disciples' feet:[92] he who humbled himself to perform lowly service will humble himself in death for men and women. Jesus initiates his disciples into the mystery of the hour and prepares them for fellowship with himself in and through his lifting up on the cross. This is his gift—he incorporates them into union with himself. This is their sharing in his death and exaltation to the Father.

The story of the foot washing continues with Peter's misunderstanding—he asks that not just his feet but also his hands and head will be washed. Jesus' reply is, unfortunately, complicated by textual variants. The "shorter reading" runs: "The one who has been bathed[93] [or

---

92. There is widespread agreement that this is the Johannine interpretation of the foot washing—see Bultmann, *John*, 469–70; Barrett, *John*, 442; Brown, *John* 2:568; Schnackenburg, *John*, 3:16, 19, 21–22; Lindars, *John*, 447, 452; Becker, *Johannesevangelium* 2:423; Haenchen, *John* 2:108; Beasley-Murray, *John*, 234–35; Carson, *John*, 459–66; Richter, *Fusswaschung*, 288–95; Michl, *Fusswaschung*, 701–2 (includes the death but not restricted to it); Thüsing, *Erhöhung*, 133; Cadman, *Open Heaven*, 133–35; Robinson, *Significance*, 144–47; Dunn, *Washing*, 248–49, 252; Segovia, *Footwashing*, 32, 43; Culpepper, *Anatomy*, 95; Onuki, *Gemeinde*, 61; Hultgren, *Footwashing*, 541; Schnelle, *Christology*, 85, 170–72; Marianne Thompson, *Humanity*, 97–102; Knöppler, *Theologia Crucis*, 105; Lincoln, *Truth*, 449; Zumstein, *Kreative Erinnerung*, 173–74 (the footwashing as a metaphor for the cross); Kollmann, *Kreuzigung*, 151–52, 155; Bauckham, *Testimony*, 194. On the other hand, Thomas, *Footwashing*, argues for a practice of footwashing as a religious rite, preceding the Lord's Supper and signifying the cleansing from post-conversion sin, in the Johannine communities.

93. Assuming perfect participle passive (so, e.g., Barrett, *John*, 441).

has bathed[94]] does not need to wash [again] but is completely clean." ὁ
λελουμένος οὐκ ἔχει χρείαν νίψασθαι (Aleph and Origen ensure that
this is not just a Western reading, supported as it is by some Old Latin
mss—aur. and c—and Tertullian). On this reading, the perfect participle passive (or middle) λελουμένος and the aorist infinitive middle νί
ψασθαι act as synonyms. The meaning is, then, that what is conveyed by
the foot washing is complete in itself and does not need to be repeated
or supplemented by further washings. A new idea is introduced by the
words καθαρὸς ὅλος, "completely clean." The foot washing mediates
cleansing—clearly from anything that defiles, stains or pollutes, and
thus hinders fellowship and union with what is pure, with God.[95] This
reading, then, contains the idea of the sole sufficiency of what the cross
achieves—there is no need to be "washed" again.[96]

The "longer reading" runs: "The one who has been bathed does
not have any need except to wash their feet but is completely clean." ὁ
λελουμένος οὐκ ἔχει χρείαν εἰ μὴ τοὺς πόδας νίψασθαι (so BC*;
most of the Old Latin mss (except aur.c), Origen, Augustine). (Perhaps
here we may point out that while the shorter reading would read better if
it had a πάλιν with νίψασθαι, so the longer reading would flow better
if it had a μόνος, as perceived by some scribes who have added it).

The weakness of most interpretations which uphold the longer
reading is that they end up by making the foot washing into a subordinate action—which it cannot be in the light of 13:8. There are those who
refer λελουμένος to baptism and τοὺς πόδας νίψασθαι to the Lord's
Supper.[97] Bultmann rightly brands this as grotesque[98]—there would be
no congruence whatever between the sign and what is signified.

94. Assuming perfect participle middle (so, e.g., Brown, *John* 2:548).

95. Zumstein, *Kreative Erinnerung*, 173, in discussing the foot washing as a metaphor for the cross, rightly speaks of "the productive character of Jesus' death which
alone can create a positive relationship with God."

96. Dunn, *Washing*, 252, writes that John "concentrates on the sufficiency and the
once-for-allness of the cleansing effected by Jesus uplifted on the cross…No one can
claim a fuller cleansing or a more complete salvation than that wrought by Jesus in his
uplifting and glorification."

97. E.g., Cullmann, *Early Christian Worship*, 105–10.

98. Bultmann, *John*, 469 (note 2). The same would apply to Correll, *Consummatum
Est.*, 72, who interprets the foot washing of "the sacrament of penance," and de Boer,
Perspectives, 289, who argues that the water symbolises the blood which Jesus will
shortly shed in his sacrificial death.

Most recently, F. Segovia[99] has defended the longer reading by sug-gesting that ὁ λελουμένος refers to partially correct belief on the part of the disciples during the ministry, but the disciples need what Jesus will accomplish in the cross, symbolized by the foot washing, to which Peter must submit. This avoids the weakness of other defences of the longer reading just referred to, but it may be asked whether λελουμέ νος naturally refers to partially correct belief on the part of the disciples during the ministry, prior to the moment of the foot washing? True, 15:3 says, "You are already clean because of the word which I have spoken to you" (though Segovia believes that 15–17 together with 13:12–20 were added as part of a larger revision of an earlier edition of the Gospel in a situation like that of 1 John). I agree with Segovia that perfect faith is impossible before the hour of the cross, but I am not persuaded that the imperfect faith of the disciples is being referred to in λελουμένος .

In his discussion of the foot washing (actually within a section on the betrayer), Knöppler distinguishes between a partial cleansing and a basic cleansing. He refers the former to νίψασθαι and the latter to λελουμένος, basing this presumably on a preference for the longer reading without actually stating this, and interpreting it as the gift of perseverance (donum perseverantiae).[100] But this seems to be import-ing a concern for post-conversion/baptism sins into a passage which is concerned with setting forth the soteriological benefits of Christ's death on the cross, as Knöppler himself stresses.

Lincoln sees the foot washing as symbolises the death of Jesus, but as illustrating how the divine master has humbled himself to the point of death, thus subverting the normal notions of social hierarchy, a lesson Peter needs to take on board if he is to continue in fellowship with Jesus. Lincoln supports the longer reading and assumes a distinction between "bathing" (the disciples are already Jesus' own through believing on Jesus) and "washing" (the recognition of the reversal of values which Jesus has demonstrated in the foot washing). There is some similarity with Segovia's position, both defending the longer reading. As to the argument that the disciples are Jesus' own and, therefore, not in need of cleansing, we may point to how insecure the position of the disciples is. The following passages show that the disciples are far from secure

99. Segovia, *Footwashing*, 31–51; it is defended also by Carson, *John*, 465–66; Thomas, *Footwashing*, 19–25; and de Boer, *Perspectives*, 286.

100. Knöppler, *Theologia Crucis*, 221.

in their belonging to Jesus—13:36–38; 14:8–9, 22; 16:29–32; and cf. 18:15–18, 25–27. And all these references occur despite 15:3!

The shorter reading has the merit from the angle of textual criticism of being preferable as a general rule, and the longer reading could be explained either by the influence of the custom for guests to have a bath at home and have their feet washed on arrival at their hosts' home[101] or by the suggestion that a scribe did not recognise that ὁ λελουμένος referred to the foot washing and so inserted εἰ μὴ τοὺς πόδας.[102]

In conclusion, we hold to the view that the foot washing in 13:1–11 points to the need for disciples to receive what the death of Jesus effects in order to have a share in him and receive cleansing.[103]

Jesus' death is a service to the disciples. Once again, we have found evidence for the crucial importance that the death of Jesus has in Johannine theology. Jesus' death ensures union with him and cleansing from sin, for those who allow him to impart those benefits to them.

(5) THE ΥΠΕΡ TEXTS
(6:51; 10:11, 15; 11:51–52; 15:13; 17:19)

The use of ὑπέρ in connection with the death of Jesus in various passages calls for separate comment, especially in view of the fact that phrases linked with ὑπέρ occur in early Christian material of a traditional nature: 1 Cor 15:3 ("Christ died for our sins"); 11:24 ("This is my body which is [or, is broken] for you; " cf. Luke 22:19, "This is my body which is given for you"); Luke 22:20 ("This cup is the new covenant in my blood, which is shed for you"); and possibly 1 Pet 3:18 ("Christ died for (περὶ) sins, the righteous for (ὑπέρ) the unrighteous.")

The Fourth Gospel uses ὑπέρ in connection with Jesus' death several times:

101. So Barrett, *John*, 441; Lindars, *John*, 451.

102. So Brown, *John* 2:568; Beasley-Murray, *John*, 229.

103. Cf. Barrett, *John*, 442; Brown, *John* 2:563, 566, 568; Schnackenburg, *John* 3:19, 21–22; Thüsing, *Erhöhung*, 133; Robinson, *Significance*, 147; Lindars, *Passion*, 73; Marianne Thompson, *Humanity*, 100–103. There is no need to postulate a veiled reference to baptism, as does Moloney, *John*, 375, while de Boer, *Perspectives*, has a complicated theory that the shorter reading expressed the view that cleansing was mediated through baptism, but that the author of stage iv added the excepting clause, directed at the secessionists, to stress the need really and genuinely to have been cleansed by the death of Jesus.

- 6:51 "The bread which I shall give is my flesh for the life of the world."

- 10:11, 15 "The Good Shepherd lays down his life for the sheep."

- 11:51–52 "Jesus was to die not only for the nation but . . ." (cf. 18:14)

- 15:13 "A person lays down their life for their friends."

- 17:19 "Jesus consecrates himself for his disciples."

When the evangelist uses these ὑπέρ phrases at various points, is he evoking an atoning view of Jesus' death? Schnackenburg believes that this is so: "Although the idea of Jesus' reconciliatory death does not emerge very prominently in the Johannine soteriology, it is retained from the common early Christian tradition."[104] Such a position would be espoused by many other scholars.[105] Frey suggests that these texts must be seen against the background of 1:29 and 6:51c and the traditional church formula attested in 1 John (1:7; 2:2; 3:16; 4:9–10) which would be known to the readers, and, therefore, he too sees atoning significance in them ("a dense tissue of statements on the soteriological meaning of the death of Jesus"[106]).

We would suggest that these phrases need to be interpreted in the light of the passage 12:20–34. The ὑπέρ idea certainly has its roots in

104. Schnackenburg, *John* 3:187 (specifically on 17:19, but with other ὑπέρ texts in mind); cf. Loader, *Christology*, 94–101.

105. E.g., Mussner, *Leben*, 101–11; Müller, *Heilsgeschehen*, 56–57, 59, 63–64, 114, 139; Wilkens, *Zeichen*, 72; Lindars, *Passion*, 73; Haacker, *Stiftung*, 168–73; Marianne Thompson, *Humanity*, 92. Knöppler, *Sühne*, 249–52, accepts that the atonement theme is present in 6:51c and 17:19, while 10:11, 15; 11:50–52; 18:14 speak of an action of Jesus for his own which averts disaster (Unheil), and, therefore, he believes that basically an atonement statement lies before us in these texts. Carson, *John,* 295, 386–87, 422, 567, takes these texts as referring to Jesus' sacrificial death, while Lincoln, *John*, 297 accepts this for 6:51; 10:16; and 11:50–52. At the end of his study, Dennis, *Jesus' Death*, 351–53, says that the findings of his work "point in the direction of the 'vicarious aatonement' (*stellvertretende Sühne*) interpretation of Jesus' death in the FG and particularly of the Johannine *hyper* texts." On the other hand, Forestell, *Word*, 75–76, 80–81, 193–94, denies that 6:51; 10:15; 11:51–52; 15:13; 17:19 are in any way expiatory or sacrificial, while Theobald, *Herrenworte*, 389, also denies any atoning concept in 10:11, 14. U. B. Müller, *Bedeutung*, 63, accepts that 1:29 and 10:11, 15 refer to the saving effects of Jesus' death, but dismisses them as tradition and not specifically Johannine.

106. Frey, "*Theologia crucifixi*," 213 ("ein dichtes Gewebe"). In *Probleme*, 39, he speaks of "a semantic network," in which the individual statements mutually interpret one another; it is this network "which in its totality first permits an adequate understanding" of the death of Jesus (*Probleme*, 41).

early Christian tradition, but John has given it his distinctive impress
by how he has interpreted the cross in 12:20–34. By identifying himself with men and women under judgment and by drawing them into
union with himself, Jesus has acted on behalf of men and women[107] and
done something for them which they could not effect for themselves and
which brings about their salvation.

(6) THE CROSS AND THE ONENESS OF GOD'S PEOPLE (11:49–52; 10:15B–16)

At the meeting of the Sanhedrin, summoned after the raising of Lazarus,
Caiaphas offers the advice: "It is expedient that one man should die for
the people and that the whole nation should not perish" (11:50). The
evangelist interprets this as a prophecy that "Jesus was going to die for
the nation, but not only for the nation but that he might gather into one
the children of God scattered abroad" (vv. 51–52).

The purpose of Jesus' death is here said to be not only for the Jewish
nation[108] but also to draw into a unity those whom God foreknew as his
children, who at the time of the ministry of Jesus were "scattered about."
In the light of our discussion of 12:32, we believe that it is right to assume that John is here thinking of an objective fact—something was accomplished at the cross. If Jesus, lifted up on the cross and to glory, drew
all people to himself, then he ipso facto drew into one God's scattered
children. The oneness is a "given," though it has to be also actualized
through the future mission.

What, in describing the children of God as scattered about
(διεσκορπισμένα), did the evangelist have in mind? There are two
possibilities:

Firstly, there is a possible background in the Old Testament and
Jewish idea that God will summon back the scattered tribes of Israel (see
Jer 23:2–3; Ezek 34:12; 37:21; Isa 43:5; 49:12; *Ps. Sol.* 8:34; 4 Ezra 13:47,
etc.). John would have taken this idea up and transmuted it to embrace

---

107. Although Frey does not discuss 12:31–32 at any length, he does believe that
John does not separate atonement (taking this in its widest sense of saving from death
due to our sins and the opening up of the possibility of new life) and representation
("Stellvertretung")—*Theologia crucifixi*, 214

108. Lincoln, *John*, 330, rightly points to the significance of the fact that Jesus' death
will benefit the Jewish nation, in view of John's alleged anti-Judaism.

non-Jews.[109] His description of the people in mind as "children of God" reflects the predestinarian strand in his thinking (e.g., 6:44; and statements that the disciples are given to Jesus by the Father 6:37; 17:2, 7, 24; and also the reference to my sheep in 10:26, 29).

Secondly, the Gnostic idea of the scattered spiritual seed which needs to be awakened by the Revealer to their true nature and destiny.[110] Despite Appold's advocacy of a Gnostic background to the idea, the continuing lack of first century documentation for the kind of Gnosticism that flourished in the second century remains a fatal Achilles' heel to this theory. The borrowing could have gone the other way, i.e., by Gnostics from John.

John uses the simple verb for what the wolf does to the flock, once the hireling has fled (10:12). This may suggest that in the evangelist's thinking the prince of this world had attacked men and women and "scattered" them from God's presence. The purpose of Jesus' death is to effect the reversal of that—he dies to gather into one family God's children. In the very act of dying he effects the gathering-into-one of God's scattered children. What the church does in its missionary activity is to realise what has already been accomplished at the cross. The church itself does not by its labors effect the unity of God's children: that has already been achieved by Jesus in his cross. Thus, 11:49–53 agrees with 12:32.

For the fourth evangelist Jesus is the Savior of the world, and his death will benefit men and women from all parts of the world. They too are destined to be part of God's family, and the cross has brought that about. The "how" of this is not stated here—merely the fact of it. It receives clarification at 12:20–34. Thus, we may say that the evangelist has

109. Barrett, *John*, 407–8; Brown, *John* 1:442–43; Lindars, *John*, 407 (who draws attention to Zech 13:7 also); Beasley-Murray, *John*, 198; Carson, *John*, 422–23; Lincoln, *John*, 330; Knöppler, *Theologia Crucis*, 204; Kollmann, *Kreuzigung*, 188–89; and also Becker, *Johannesevangelium* 2:369–70, who, however, attributes the verses to the church redactor. Moloney, *Israel*, 357, rightly says that once 11:48–52 is read synchronically, in the light of the whole Gospel, the former λαός τοῦ Θεοῦ receives a universal sense. Dennis, *Jesus' Death*, 247–318, denies that Gentiles are in mind. He accepts that John has reinterpreted Israel's restoration theology, but in the sense that Jesus now is the "place" where Israel is gathered (as opposed to a literal land or a restored/new temple).

110. Appold, *Oneness*, 243–44 (denied, however, even by Bultmann, *John*, 384 (note 2) for 10:16, but he hardly comments on 11:52, referring back to his remarks on 384 (note 2)). See Dennis, *Jesus' Death*, 263–68 for further criticisms.

taken up a theme from Israel's eschatological hope—the gathering-in of the dispersed tribes of Israel—and universalized it

Much the same can be said about what is spoken in the Shepherd Discourse. To lay down his life for the sheep is a sign of Jesus' goodness as a Shepherd (10:11). Of course, this assertion breaks the mould of the analogy, for in real life, if the shepherd was killed, his flock was even more exposed to danger from wild beasts. The second reference to Jesus' laying down his life for the sheep (v. 15) follows a second assertion that he is the Good Shepherd (who knows his sheep and they know him, v. 14) and is itself followed by 10:16: "and I have other sheep which do not belong to this fold; I must bring them also, and they will hear my voice, and there will be one shepherd, one flock." The sequence—reference to Jesus' death and then to one flock to which other sheep will belong under the one shepherd, Jesus—fits in with what has emerged from our study of 11:50–52 and 12:24, 31–32. The death of Jesus brings about the unity of believers under his leadership.

It is usual to take the "other sheep" of 10:16 as non-Jews (and "this fold" to refer to Judaism).[111] Appold, however, has challenged this:[112] he thinks that future believers are in mind (cf. 17:20). But his assertion that John has no concept of salvation history ignores 4:22 and the fact that the evangelist seems to have an interest in portraying Jesus as the fulfillment of what the Jewish festivals foreshadowed; and he ignores the clear signs of a break with and continuing debate with the synagogue. Despite a recent further challenge from Dennis,[113] we believe that the traditional interpretation still deserves to be retained.

The other sheep will hear his voice through the ministry and witness of the Paraclete-Spirit and the disciples (15:26–27; 16:7–11). Again, we may say that the missionary endeavour of the church depends on the fact that Jesus has given his life for men and women.

---

111. Bultmann, *John*, 383 (though attributing it to the ecclesiastical redactor); Barrett, *John*, 376; Brown, *John* 1:387, 396; Schnackenburg, *John* 2:299–300, 350; Lindars, *John*, 363; Becker, *Johannesevangelium* 1:332–33 (though attributing 10:1–18 to a redactor, 328); Beasley-Murray, *John*, 171; Carson, *John*, 388; Lincoln, *John*, 298; Theobald, *Herrenworte*, 382. Robinson, *Twelve NT Studies*, 120–21, dissented and believed that 10:16 referrred to the Jews of the Diaspora.

112. Appold, *Oneness*, 258.

113. Dennis, *Jesus' Death*, 293–302, argues (like Robinson) that Jews of the Diaspora are in mind.

It is interesting to note that Hahn believed that the *ego eimi* word in 10:14a and its explanation in v. 14b–15 constituted the core logion of the discourse, and claimed that nowhere else in the Gospel was the theme of the cross so emphatically worked out as in this discourse.[114]

Finally, we may mention 10:17–18 which emphasizes, firstly, that the power both to lay down his life and to take it again has been vested in Jesus by his Father. Death and resurrection go together. His death is no accident brought about by human machinations but rests on the divine will, purpose, and command. He can go to death, knowing that it is not the end. Secondly, these two verses stress that the surrender of his life calls forth the Father's love. Elsewhere it is said that in love he obeys the Father's command to go to the cross (14:31); here, the other side of the coin is stressed—he "wins" the love of the Father because of that obedience, or, better, continues in the Father's love (15:10) given him from eternity (17:24).

A number of scholars[115] have suggested that John has placed the women followers plus the Beloved Disciple at the foot of the cross in 19:25–26 to indicate that through the cross Jesus creates his community. Akin to this is the view that at the cross Jesus "adopts" the Beloved Disciple and thus creates a new, spiritual family, based on his work completed in the cross and on the human response of faith to Jesus, to take the place of natural kinship.[116] Knöppler also points to the fact that the disciples have become "brothers" of Jesus at 20:17 through the cross, resurrection, and ascension which have saving significance.[117]

Thus, we may say that what is said about the consequences of Jesus' death in 11:49–52 and 10:15–16 (and also 19:26–27) dovetails into what emerged from our study of 12:20–34, thereby confirming that study. Jesus' death effects the creation of the one family of God.

---

114. Hahn, *Hirtenrede*, 191, 199–200, though Theobald, *Herrenworte*, 382–83, is not convinced that this is a correct analysis.

115. E.g., Hoskyns, *John*, 530; Barrett, *John*, 552 ("an allusion to the new family, the church, and of the sovereign power of Jesus"); Moloney, *John*, 504; Wilckens, *Johannesevangelium*, 296–97; Lincoln, *John*, 477; Knöppler, *Theologica Crucis*, 247, and also 115; Zumstein, *Kreative Erinnerung*, 232, 262, 269, 273–74; Kollmann, *Kreuzigung*, 189. Weidemann, *Tod Jesu*, 240, also thinks of the constitution of a new family, but attributes the reference to the Beloved Disciple to the redactor.

116. Advocated by, e.g., Stibbe, *Storyteller*, 152–66.

117. Knöppler, *Theologia Crucis*, 236–37; Cf. Carson, *John*, 645.

(7) THE CROSS AND THE CONFLICT WITH AND VICTORY OVER EVIL (16:11, 33; 14:30–31)

Earlier we have reviewed the evidence for the conflict between the two spheres of power in the Fourth Gospel. As we have discussed 12:31 earlier in our exegesis of the section 12:20–34, there is no need to repeat that discussion. It is to 12:31 that 16:8–11 harks back when the evangelist says of the Paraclete-Spirit that he will convince[118] the world concerning sin, righteousness, and judgment. Of the last item, 16:11 runs "concerning judgment ὅτι the prince of this world has been judged" (κέκριται): either the Paraclete-Spirit's case can be made because the prince of this world has been judged at the cross—in which case, the "brief" of the Paraclete-Spirit is to show that the world is wrong in continuing to give its allegiance to the prince of this world and is itself under judgment; or the "brief" of the Paraclete-Spirit is precisely the fact that the prince of this world has been judged at the cross—with the same corollary as in the alternative.

In opting for "convince concerning or about" as a translation for ἐλέγχειν περί, one perhaps gets over the either/or approach and is able to accept both/and.[119] In the end, however, both possibilities refer to the fact that at the cross the prince of this world lost his case and had sentence passed against him, and the world shares in that judgment.

The remaining reference to the prince of this world comes at 14:30–31, at the close of what was either the first edition of the Farewell Discourse or what was one of a number of Farewell Discourses in the Johannine circle. "I will no longer speak much with you, for the prince of this world is coming, but he has nothing on me (καὶ ἐν ἐμοὶ οὐκ ἔ

118. Those favoring "convince" or an equivalent like "prove wrong" or "expose" include Bultmann, *John*, 561; Brown, *John* 2:703, 705; Schnackenburg, *John* 3:128–29; Becker, *Johannesevangelium* 2:495–96; Beasley-Murray, *John*, 267, 280; Moloney, *John*, 438, 440; E. Schweizer, πνεῦμα, *TWNT* 6. 443; Snaith, *Meaning*, 50 (he translates "convincer"); Betz, *Paraklet*, 198–99, 203–4, 208; Trites, *Witness*, 118–19; Porsch, *Pneuma und Wort*, 285; Frank, *Revelation Taught*, 65 (takes the verb to mean correcting and criticising in order to effect a reconsideration on the part of those who receive it); Burge, *Anointed Community*, 210. Some scholars oscillate between retaining convict but using convince or a similar phrase in their comment—Dodd, *Interpretation*, 414; Barrett, *John*, 486–88; Johnston, *Spirit-Paraclete*, 35. Bornkamm, *Paraklet*, 18, 26–27, 51, and U. B. Muller, *Parakletenvorstellung*, 69, use the notion of judge in connection with the Paraclete—this, I believe, introduces an incorrect idea into the picture.

119. Schnackenburg, *John* 3:129, comes near to accepting a both/and approach, but in the end takes the clause as explanatory.

χει οὐδέν), but, in order that the world may come to know that I love the Father and I do entirely as the Father has commanded me, rise, let us go from here." [An alternative translation for v. 31 would be "But this is happening (supplying τοῦτο γέγονεν) in order that the world may come to know that I love the Father; and I do entirely as the Father has commanded me. Rise, let us go from here."]

The phrase ἐν ἐμοὶ ἔχει οὐδέν may be paraphrased as—to have a case against someone, to have a claim against someone, or to have power over someone. Thus far, we have discovered a good deal of legal material in the verses that we have studied. Bearing this in mind, we consider that this is the major reference here. In the cosmic legal battle going on, the prince of this world is coming, confident of his victory, but in fact he has no case against Jesus, for Jesus, out of love for the Father, [120] does what the Father commanded him. He is fully obedient to his Father's orders and the approaching Passion is part of the Father's will. Jesus expresses the hope that the unbelieving world may come to know that his going to the cross, far from a defeat, only demonstrates his love for the Father.

John 14:30 is phrased from the standpoint of what is to happen, whereas 12:31 (to which 16:11 refers) is spoken as if it had happened. This kind of "switch" can be bewildering, but it is Johannine (cf. the statement of 12:23 and the prayer of 17:1).

Within this section also, we believe that it is necessary to discuss 16:33: "I have spoken these things to you, in order that you might have peace in (or through) me; you will have tribulation in the world, but cheer up, I have overcome the world (ἐγώ νενίκα)." Here the cross is in mind and it is viewed from the standpoint of its having already taken place (hence the perfect indicative active tense). In what sense can Jesus be said to have overcome the world? The reason is as follows: The world represents all that is hostile to God. It is in revolt against God and refuses to submit to God or to hear him. It has developed its own life, mores, and outlook. Jesus, by contrast, has always done what pleases God (e.g., 8:29) and has always exercised the power given him by God in dependence on God. He has resisted the world's gravitational pull to draw him into its orbit and has remained faithful to his Sender.

---

120. For the hope that the world may come to saving knowledge as a result of the cross, see 8:28; compare 17:23 (as a result of the union of Jesus' disciples with one another and with him).

The cross is the climax and seal of his obedience and dedication to the Father. Accordingly, Jesus can claim to have overcome or conquered the world. The cross is victory, not defeat. As a result of this, the disciples may be encouraged. This verse is, then, a word of comfort and peace in a threatening world.

(8) THE CROSS AND THE CONSECRATION OF JESUS (17:19)

After praying for the consecration of the disciples in God's truth—for Jesus has sent (aorist indicative active!) them into the world—Jesus then prays: "and I consecrate myself for their sake, that they also may be consecrated in the truth."[121] (17:19)

Clearly, the disciples' consecration rests on the prior consecration of Jesus. A number of scholars have claimed to see more in the use of ἁγιάζειν here than just dedication, important as that might be. They rest their case on the fact that in the LXX this word is used for the preparation of a priest and of a sacrifice:[122] thus, the suggestion is that the cross is being viewed as a sacrifice to which Jesus consecrates himself.[123]

The suggestion is to be endorsed, but it cannot be said that the idea is particularly stressed and it certainly is not developed. Barrett makes the point that it is the context that makes a reference to the death of Jesus necessary, not ἁγιάζειν per se, but he goes on to state that the language

121. There is no need to see here any tension with 10:36, as Knöppler, *Theologia Crucis*, 211, does, if, as we have argued, there is an "extra" glorification in the cross. Nor do we need to translate ἁγιάζειν as "make holy" (so Moloney, *John*, 469, 471), which does not seem appropriate of the Johannine Jesus (see, e.g., 8:29, 46), whereas the idea of a re-consecration to his commission as its climax approaches does seem apt for 17:19. Bauckham, *Testimony*, 263–64, drawing on the position of 10:36 within the Feast of Hanukkah, maintains that this means that God has already consecrated Jesus to be the place of sacrifice, but that obviously the sacrifice has not yet been offered.

122. Though not of the actual act of sacrifice itself—see de la Potterie, *Vérité*, 2:761–62, "by itself ἁγιάζειν never signifies 'to sacrifice' in the external and ritual sense of the term."

123. See Taylor, *Atonement*, 138, 148, 159, and *Jesus*, 234, 237, 242, 244. Cf. Hoskyns, *John*, 502–4; Wikenhauser, *Johannesevangelium*, 307; Bultmann, *John*, 510 (note 5), who accepts a sacrificial allusion, but denies any priestly idea; Brown, *John* 2:766–67 ("plausible that . . . we are to think of him . . . as a priest offering himself as a victim for those whom God has given him"); Lindars, *John*, 529; Becker, *Johannesevangelium* 2:526 (attributes all chapter 17 to the redactor); Haenchen, *John* 2:155; Beasley-Murray, *John*, 301; Carson, *John*, 567; Thüsing, *Erhöhung*, 187; Müller, *Heilsgeschechen*, 62–65, 73; Ashton, *Understanding*, 195 (but belonging to the second edition of the Gospel).

is doubly appropriate to Christ whose task was to die for his friends.[124] Grayston is probably right in describing it as a "covert reference" to the death of Jesus.[125] So, the context demands a reference to the death of Jesus, and the associations of ἁγιάζειν suggest in an allusive manner the idea of sacrifice. Schnackenburg's cautious summary seems to hit just the right note: "It is not possible to exclude the idea of sacrifice from John 17:19."[126]

Jesus, then, consecrates himself to the task ahead of him of dying sacrificially for men and women that they might share in the life of God through him. Specifically, the purpose clause runs "that they also may be consecrated in the truth." Truth in the Fourth Gospel is not an abstract set of propositions, nor is it the truth that God is love. Rather, truth has a saving quality about it: the truth is not only that God is love but that he gave—in the sense both of sending and giving up to death—his Son to save the world (3:16–17). God willed to save the world and draw it back into a unity with himself, through his Son, at the cross.[127]

The truth is, therefore, that he has done this in the cross and that this fellowship with himself is available for men and women. This is the truth that sets people free (8:32)—free from the world and for God.[128] This is the truth that can consecrate the disciples for their mission to the world.

(9) MISCELLANEOUS PASSAGES OF POSSIBLE RELEVANCE

The unprepossessing nature of this heading is due to the fact that here I want to consider some passages that, in the light of what we have discovered so far, may offer further help in considering the meaning of the

124. Barrett, *John*, 511; cf. Morris, *John*, 731.

125. Grayston, *Dying We Live*, 317.

126. Schnackenburg, *John* 3:187.

127. This "theological" way of expressing matters does not conflict with the more "christocentric." phraseology used by de la Potterie, *Vérité*, 1:464–65, in a comment on what is the entire truth into which the Paraclete-Spirit leads believers (16:13): truth is the work and person of Jesus, his message of revelation and his work of salvation, in the end Jesus himself as Son of God.

128. Cf. Bultmann, *John*, 511 "The purpose of Jesus' sacrifice is fulfilled in the existence of a fellowship of his own grounded in him and raised out of the world," though it appears that he has rather a "static" view of the Johannine church's sense of mission (see 510).

cross in John's Gospel. I do so, however, in no dogmatic spirit, and the word "possible" is genuinely meant.

At 1:51, Jesus said to him (Nathaniel), "Truly, truly I say to you (plural) you will see (ὄψεσθε) heaven opened and the angels of God ascending and descending upon the Son of Man." I shall assume that John is a witness here to a rabbinic tradition (only attested from a literary angle in the post-Johannine period), which argued that the ascent and descent of the angels took place on Jacob (Israel), not the ladder. John would, in effect, be saying that it is Jesus of Nazareth, the Word Incarnate, who is the meeting place of heaven and earth, eternity and time. He is the mediator of intercourse between God and human beings (not Jacob—Israel).

What interests us now is the time reference in "you will see." Probably it is assumed by most exegetes that the reference is to the public ministry,[129] with the Cana miracle affording a specific illustration, for Jesus there revealed his glory *viz.* that God had vested in him his own powers and that the Father dwelling in him was doing his work, (3:35a; 14:10c).

Given, however, that Jesus draws men and women into a unity with himself when he is lifted up on the cross and to glory, can we exclude the possibility that John would wish the reader eventually to think not just of the ministry but also of the cross? The cross is the moment when in reality Jesus establishes intercourse between heaven and earth. One often gets the impression with this Gospel that the evangelist intended multilayers of meaning and that re-readings of this Gospel would alone make these clearer.[130] I think that it is possible that 1:51 may be such an instance and that the evangelist intended some allusion to the cross.[131]

129. Bultmann, *John,* 106 (miracles); Barrett, *John,* 187 (incarnation); Brown, *John* 1:91 (immediate future of the ministry); Schnackenburg, *John* 1:321 (all Jesus' work); Lindars, *John,* 122; Becker, *Johannesevangelium* 1:104; Beasley-Murray, *John,* 28; Wilckens, *Johannes,* 54; Schulz, *Untersuchungen,* 102–3; Thüsing, *Erhöhung,* 228.

130. Culpepper, *Anatomy,* 200 "Every re-reading provides additional insights into how various features of the text fit together and affords new glimpses of the mystery to which it points."

131. Among those who see a reference to the cross are Hoskyns, *John,* 183; Dodd, *Interpretation,* 294; Cadman, *Open Heaven,* 28; Moloney, *JSM,* 38–40 ("a valuable suggestion"); Lindars, *Jesus Son of Man,* 148 (changing his position over against his commentary and his article *Son of Man,* 46, where he referred to Jesus' baptismal experience and the passion); Painter, *Quest,* 153, 323, 345 (note 52); and Metzner, *Sünde,* 123, while Forestell, *Word of the Cross,* 67, sees a reference to both the ministry and the cross, as do

At 6:27, Jesus says to the Galileans who have tracked him down: "Do not work for the food which perishes but for the food which lasts unto eternal life, which the Son of Man will give (δώσει) you; for God, the Father, has sealed him." Again, we are particularly interested in the time reference of δώσει: is it what might be called a "logical" future or does it refer to the actual future? In the light of 6:51c, it could be legitimately argued that this food only becomes available after the cross, after the Son of Man has been lifted up.[132] The case is clearer here than in 1:51 and, if accepted, probably carries with it also the gift of living water promised in 4:14 (ἐγὼ δώσω), and this is confirmed by the next passage to be considered.

Finally, in this section, we consider 7:39. The evangelist's comment[133] concerning the promise of living water to anyone who, thirsty, believes in Jesus or comes to Jesus, runs: "Now he said this about the Spirit, whom believers in him were to receive, for the Spirit was not yet (given), because Jesus had not yet been glorified." According to the narrative, the offer (vv. 37–38) is made to those assembled at the Feast of Tabernacles. Yet the comment made in v. 39 clearly indicates that the fulfilment of the promise only comes after the cross when Jesus is glorified. Something happens at the cross that enables the release of the Spirit to take place. The living water is available after the cross, but not before. In fact, in the Fourth Gospel, the gift of the Spirit is accordingly narrated

Carson, *John*, 164, and Lincoln, *John*, 123, while Olsson, *Structure and Meaning*, 276, refers to the time both before and after Jesus' Hour. Higgins, *Jesus*, 159, argues that 1:51 refers to Jesus' exaltation.

132. Hoskyns, *John*, 293; Barrett, *John*, 287; Schnackenburg, *John* 2:36; Moloney, *JSM*, 112–13 and *John*, 209; Lindars, *John*, 152; Riedl, *Heilswerk*, 313, 316; Meneken, *Jüdischen Feste*, 278; and Dennis, *Jesus' Death*, 196; cf. Carson, *John*, 284 ("after Jesus' glorification"). Bultmann, *John*, 225 (note 1) refers the giving to the exalted Lord, but attributes the clause to the redactor, as do Becker, *Johannesevangelium* 1:204, and Haenchen, *John* 1:290, who explain v. 27 sacramentally. Higgins, *Jesus*, 173–76, and Schulz, *Untersuchungen*, 116–17, both attribute v. 27 to a preJohannine eucharistic discourse. Maddox, Function, 196, refers v. 27 to the eucharistic worship of the church; cf. Wilckens, *Johannes*, 100. Brown, *John* 1:264, is rather on his own: "realised in the ministry of Jesus," as is Lincoln, *Truth*, 217, who takes the "sealing" by God as a proleptic confirmation of the verdict yet to be given in the cross and resurrection.

133. So even Bultmann, *John*, 303 (5), who refuses to attribute it to the ecclesiastical redactor. See now Theobald, *Herrenworte*, 455–77, for a detailed traditio-historical discussion.

by means of the "insufflation" when the Risen Jesus meets his disciples (20:22).[134]

I would assume that 7:37–39 reflects a development within the Johannine tradition. Verses 37–38 were originally a product of reflection on the person of Jesus as the bestower of life (possibly using imagery from the Wisdom literature,[135] though there are other Old Testament passages which could have been influential).[136] This underwent a "pneumatological" reinterpretation as the evangelist sees the gift of the Spirit as the fulfilment for contemporary believers of the promise of living water.[137] The evangelist will have taken the future indicative active ῥεύσουσιν within the mixed quotation of v. 38 as pointing to the death of Jesus,[138] while the reference to the glorification of Jesus also points us to this event.

These three passages (1:51; 6:27; and 7:39) can be claimed with justification as containing allusions to the cross.

(10) THE PASSION STORY

Since the cross is for the fourth evangelist an hour of glorification and lifting up, he could not tell the passion story in the same way as Mark does. Mark's passion story could be characterised as a passion story for martyrs and the persecuted—it is grim in its horror and awfulness. The gloom is unrelieved virtually from start to finish, with its surprising denouement at the end when the centurion makes his confession and penetrates the secret of Jesus. John looks at the passion story from a different angle and sees the cross suffused with glory. The difference between John and Mark may be seen in both what John leaves out and what he includes, as well as in the particular emphases which emerge. It

---

134. But see the discussion on the outflow of blood and *water* in 19:34b, below on pp. 176–79.

135. So especially Brown, *John* 1:328; also 178–79; cf. Theobald, *Herrenworte*, 470–71, 476–77.

136. Ps 78:15–16, 20; Zech 14.8; Ezek 47:12; Isa 12:3.

137. Against Brown, *John* 1:327–28, who seems to take vv. 37–38 to be a word of the historical Jesus. Theobald, *Herrenworte*, 458–66, sees v. 37 as Johannine community tradition worked over by the evangelist, to whom he also attributes both the Scriptural quotation of v. 38 and the commentary of v. 39.

138. So also Theobald, *Herrenworte*, 458.

is as if he says to the reader: "This is how I see the cross. Come and stand with me and look at it from my perspective and see if you can share my vision." Or, perhaps, "This is how we see the cross. Let us hold fast to this vision of it in the midst of a world which looks at it so differently."

John edits out[139] the three hour darkness; the mockery of the by-passers, members of the Sanhedrin and those crucified with him; and the cry of dereliction. In his Gospel, Jesus carries the cross, not Simon Cyrene. The women followers, including his mother, are at the foot of the cross, not at a distance. John concentrates on the Roman trial (he may have utilised material from the Jewish trial in a scene like 10:22–38).[140]

There are points in the story where the material has undergone Johannine interpretative handling.

(a) In the arrest scene, Jesus is portrayed as aware of what was to happen and asking the arresting party "Whom do you seek?" When they respond "Jesus of Nazareth," they receive the reply ἐγώ εἰμι and collapse to the ground (18:5–6). They are powerless before Jesus. Eventually he says, "If, therefore you seek me, let these men go." (18:8). Given John's penchant for double entendre, I am persuaded that in these words there are two levels: the straightforward meaning "I'm your man. So let these others go free" and the below-the-surface meaning—he dies for others, for the sheep, for his own, for the world; he dies to take away the sin of the world.[141]

139. I assume that John knew a tradition parallel to, but independent of Mark, a tradition which had some contact with the tradition available to Luke. See the studies of Dodd, *Historical Tradition*; Mohr, *Markus- und Johannespassion*, 1982. Cf. Bultmann, *John*, 635; Brown, *John* 2:791; Schnackenburg, *John* 3:219; Lindars, *John*, 534. Dauer, *Passionsgeschichte*, 226–27, accepts a preJohannine passion story influenced by synoptic traditions, whether written or oral, and his view finds sympathy with Beasley-Murray, *John*, 311.

140. Brown, *NT Essays*, 192–213, esp. 198–203, looks at "four scenes presented as units in the Synoptics but whose members are seemingly scattered in John," including the trial before the Sanhedrin. Zumstein, *Kreatuive Errinerung*, 230–31, goes so far as to describe the trial before Pilate as the point of culmination of the Johannine passion story.

141. Brown, *John* 2:818; Schnackenburg, *John* 3:225 (who alludes to 10:11, 15, 28); Lindars, *John*, 542; Beasley-Murray, *John*, 323; Carson, *John*, 579; Becker, *Johannesevangelium* 2:541, 544, who attributes v. 9 to the redactor; Knöppler, *Theologia Crucis*, 215; Lang, *Johannes und die Synoptiker*, 75 ("Christology proves itself in soteriology"). (Bultmann, *John*, 640, denies any below-the-surface meaning and sees it as the work of the redactor).

(b) In the way John tells the story, characters and events become unconscious witnesses to deep spiritual realities, e.g., the mockery scene, now the centre of the tableaux[142] within the Roman trial, witnesses to Jesus' Kingship (19:1–3); Pilate's words "Behold the Man" (19:5) and "Behold your King" (19:14) fall into the same category; the inscription over the cross is written in Hebrew, Latin and Greek—a kind of witness to the world concerning Jesus (19:20), as if his universal significance is being acknowledged.[143]

(c) Again, in the way John tells the story, characters who in theory are in control, with Jesus on trial, become the ones on trial and they are judged. This is so pre-eminently of Pilate, but also of Annas to a lesser degree (18:19–24).

(d) Jesus' last word from the cross is no cry of dereliction but a cry of triumph and victory—"It is finished" (19:30), consonant with one who has already announced that he has overcome the world (16:33) and already accomplished the task given to him by the Father (17:4).[144]

(e) Only John records the episode of the soldiers' hastening the death of those crucified with Jesus by breaking their legs. But they did not do so in the case of Jesus as he was already dead; instead, one of them pierced his side with a spear (19:31–34a). Two scripture quotations indicate that these events fell within God's providential plan—Ps 34:20 or Exod 12:46 and Zech 12:10, quoted in 19:36–37.

In between these events and the Scriptural quotations occurs another event and a comment on it: "and immediately blood and water flowed out, and he who has seen [this] has borne witness and his witness is true and he knows that he is speaking the truth [or, truly] in order that you also may believe" (vv. 34b–35). Verses 34b–35 break up the connec-

---

142. See the masterly analysis by Brown, *John* 2:857–59. Cf. Zumstein, *Kreative Errinerung*, 230 (note 26); also *Gniesmer, Prozetz*, 173, who comments that the scourging and mockery scene "is not only to be understood as a first climax, but as *the decisive centre* of the whole trial narrative" (He has a slightly different division of the sub-sections of the trial narrative than Brown—see 174–75).

143. Kollmann, *Kreuzigung*, 333–36, 338, 360, believes that John has made Pilate into an instrument of God to proclaim the kingship of Jesus, an involuntary witness to the kingship of Jesus and the saving death of Jesus.

144. Thüsing, *Erhöhung*, 67. In John, Jesus' dying shout becomes a message of salvation for believers; cf. Riedl, *Heilswerk*, 39, 98.

tion between vv. 34a and 36–37, so that it may be reasonably concluded that we have here a growth and development of the Johannine tradition: vv. 34b–35 are a kind of Johannine midrash.[145]

What did the evangelist intend by mentioning an outflow of blood and water, which clearly in the light of v. 35 had belief-arousing potential? We review the suggested interpretations of the outflow of blood and water.

> i. Did he intend to stress the reality of the death of Jesus—it was a real death of a real person? An anti-docetic motive might underlie this stress.[146]
>
> Possibly, but the mention of blood alone could have sufficed;[147] it is the outflow of blood and water which causes the problem, though, quite apart from the fact that some modern medical experts have claimed that such is physiologically possible, there is evidence that in antiquity, both in Jewish and Hellenistic cultures, there was a view that a person consisted of blood and (colorless blood-) water (ἰχώρ).[148]
>
> ii. Did he intend an allusion to the two sacraments, as if suggesting that they are founded on the death of Jesus?[149] This does not really carry conviction for three reasons. In the first place, the order blood and water is strange if this were so. Secondly, while water could stand for baptism, blood by itself is an odd term for the Lord's Supper. Thirdly, as a general principle, we should first ask what an episode teaches about Jesus rather than the place of the sacraments in the life of the church.
>
> iii. Did he mean to suggest "that from the Crucified there proceed those living streams by which men are quickened and the church

---

145. So Bultmann, *John*, 677 (note 6), 678 (attributing it to the ecclesiastical redactor, however). That only v. 35 was an addition is held by Brown, *John* 2:945; Schnackenburg, *John* 3:286–87; Lindars, *John*, 589; Becker, *Johannesevangelium* 2:599; Beasley-Murray, *John*, 354; Lincoln, *John*, 479.

146. See esp Richter, *Blut und Wasser*, 1–21 = *Studien*, 120–42. Cf. Carson, *John*, 623.

147. So Bultmann, *John*, 666 (note 7).

148. See the evidence cited by Schnackenburg, *Johannes* 3. 339 and Beasley-Murray, *John*, 357 (both dependant on Schweizer, *Herrenmahl*, 382); Weidemann, *Tod Jesu*, 393–94.

149. Bultmann, *John*, 666–67; Haenchen, *John* 2:195; Moloney, *John*, 505–6, 509; Böcher, *Kirche*, 162; Zumstein, *Kreative Erinnerung*, 233, 269.

178   **PART I:** The Gospel of John

lives"?[150] On this view, water points to the living water (3:5; 4:14;
7:37–38; 13:5) and Christ's blood is true drink (6:54–58). This
view has the merit of interpreting John by John and interpreting
blood and water by their prior occurrences in the Gospel. But,
given 3:5 and 7:39, would not a more specific reference to the
Spirit be more appropriate as in view iv and v?

iv. Did the evangelist want to suggest that, now that Jesus has died
(blood), the Spirit (water) can be given?[151] However, like is not
being compared with like. Blood is being referred to an event
that had already happened, as a result of which the Spirit comes.

v. Did the writer wish to say that the atoning death of Jesus leads
to the forgiveness of and cleansing from sin ("blood") and the
gift of the Spirit ("water")?[152] The weakness of this view—if it is
a weakness—is that it does rely on the Epistle (1:7; 3:5 plus 2:2;
4:10) for interpreting "blood," and it is precisely in this area of
atonement that some have alleged differences between the Gospel and First Epistle, which, plus other differences, have led to the
widespread view that we are dealing with different authors, albeit
from the same "school" or standing within the same Johannine
stream of tradition (cf. Conzelmann's dictum that the Johannine
epistles are to the Gospel of John what the Pastoral Epistles are to
the genuine Paulines[153]).

150. Barrett, *John*, 557; Morris, *John*, 820; Schnackenburg, *John* 3:294; Lincoln,
John, 479; cf. Thüsing, *Erhöhung*, 161 ("Life which depends indeed on the Spirit in the
closest fashion flows from the body of the One lifted up"); also Dodd, *Interpretation*,
428, and *Historical Tradition*, 133–35; Hasitschka, *Befreiung*, 64; Thomas, *Footwashing*,
101 (who refers to "the life-giving and cleansing qualities of Jesus' death.")

151. Brown, *John* 2:950.

152. Lindars, *John*, 587; Beasley-Murray, *John*, 358; Carson, *John*, 624 (secondary
symbolism); Thüsing, *Erhöhung*, 168, 171–73; Marianne Thompson, *Humanity*, 110
and *1–3 John*, 134; Hofius, *Johannesstudien*, 49 (note 73) and Kammler, *Johannesstudien*,
206–7; de Boer, *Perspectives*, 297; Klauck, *Erste Johannesbrief*, 295–97; Margaret Davies,
Rhetoric, 235. Brown, *John* 2:950–51, comes near and Schnackenburg, *John* 3:294, concedes that it is a possibility. Onuki, *Gemeinde*, 59, 87, 202, takes the water to indicate
the Spirit (he does not discuss the blood). Knöppler, *Theologia Crucis*, 97, 221(note 20),
has a variation on this approach: he seems to take the blood and water as signifying
complete cleansing and atonement (vollkonnene Reinigung und Sühne), presumably
attributing atoning significance to the death of Jesus, as a result of which cleansing
from sin results.

153. Conzelmann, *von Anfang*, 201.

We think that the third, fourth, and fifth suggestions have much in common and are nearest to the truth of what John intended. Common to all three is basically that "water" stands for the gift of life/Spirit. "Blood" presumably points to some blessing, other than the gift of the Spirit, consequent on the death of Jesus rather than the death itself. We have seen via 12:20–34 how Jesus' death is both judgment and a drawing into union with Jesus who is life. This broadens the way in which we would wish to interpret "blood" over against the third and fourth views. We conclude that the evangelist here narrates—or tells a story of the outflow of blood and water—what he states propositionally at 3:15 (the Son of Man must be lifted up on the cross in order that the believer might have eternal life in him) or what he formulates as a startling invitation—the need to drink Christ's blood at 6:53–58.

It would take us far beyond the limits of this investigation to discuss exactly who was the one who saw and the nature of the seeing. I can only here baldly state that I take the seeing to be *spiritual* (i.e., believing) seeing:[154] i.e., the witness of v. 35 is one who has spiritually discerned what he believes is the truth of the cross which he has narratively portrayed in v. 34b, and he has done so in the hope that others may share his "vision" and come to believe in Jesus, the life-giving Messiah and Son of God, who was lifted up on the cross and to glory. Whether this interpretation of seeing is accepted or not, the importance of the cross as a reason for writing the Gospel is quite clear:[155] the one who saw has borne witness in order to evoke that belief which leads to life, and the writer of the Gospel passes on his witness in writing.

(f) There are a number of motifs which can be picked up during the passion story and which may be briefly mentioned:

154. In a similar way, the evangelist himself speaks of seeing the Father in the Son at 14:7, 9; or the author of 1 John speaks at 4:14 about seeing that the Father sent the Son, or in his prologue of having touched the word of life (1:1); cf. Mussner, *Historical Jesus*, 18–23; de Boer, *Perspectives*, 295 (comparing John the Baptist's seeing at 1:34). Margaret Davies, *Rhetoric*, 64, wrote that the unnamed witness "need not have been an eyewitness of Jesus' crucifixion, but a believer for whom Jesus' death had brought the promised new life."

155. Rightly stressed by Knöppler, *Theologia Crucis*, 257–58, who sees 19:35 as comparable to 20:31 and 21:24. Also Lincoln, *Truth*, 388: "What is claimed as true is the beloved disciple's witness to his belief about the significance of Jesus' death . . . Blood and water are the narrative means for conveying this significance." This is repeated in *John*, 481.

i. Jesus appears in control throughout—he lets himself be arrested (18:4–9); he seems to control the discussion with Pilate; he makes arrangements for his mother (19:26–27); and he fulfils Scripture (19:28). We are reminded of how previously in the Shepherd Discourse at 10:17–18, Jesus claimed that he had authority to lay down his life and to take it again.

ii. His own words are shown to be fulfilled (18:9, 32)

iii. as are those of the Old Testament (19:24, 28, 36–37; cf. 13:18, 15:25—probably the evangelist inherited these as part of the passion story which he drew on).

iv. It is possible, though much debated,[156] that Jesus is portrayed as the true Passover Lamb (18:28; 19:36). Much depends here on whether we accept the Synoptic or the Johannine dating of the Last Supper. The pre-Johannine passion story might have seen Jesus as fulfilling the Psalms of the Suffering Righteous One and took 19:36 as a quotation from Ps 34:20, with Zech 12:10 in 19:37 referring also to a Suffering Righteous One, but the evangelist took 19:36 as referring to the Passover Lamb instructions in Exod 12:46 and Num 9:12.[157]

Some scholars see in the reference to hyssop, on which some (the soldiers?) offered the wine-vinegar to Jesus, an allusion to the event of the Exodus.[158] According to Exod 12:22, the Hebrews smeared blood of the Passover lamb on the doors of their houses.

v. The obedience of Jesus is a constant theme in the earlier part

156. That the evangelist sees Jesus as the Passover Lamb from 1:29 right through his gospel, is strongly maintained in the recent works of Knöppler, *Theologia Crucis*, 81–88, 116–21; Metzner, *Sünde*, 143–56; Frey, *Theologia crucifixi*, 196–97, 209–12; Zumstein, *Kreative Erinerung*, 220–21; 231, 247, 267, 269; Christine Schlund, *Kein Knochen*, 119–81 (though she is critical of Knöppler's claim that the Passover had atoning significance by the first century AD); Weidemann, *Tod Jesu*, 416, 445–50. Cf. Lincoln, *John*, 482. That John wished to portray Jesus as the true Passover Lamb is denied strongly by Gniesmer, *Prozetz*, 183–94, 349 (note 1051); while Dauer, *Passionsgeschichte*, 137–43, is reluctant to endorse the suggestion, though not ruling it out completely, and Menken, *OT Quotations*, 158, is cautious, allowing the possibility but insisting that it is unobtrusive.

157. Zumstein, *Kreative Erinnerung*, 233, takes this approach.

158. So, e.g., Obermann, *Christologische Erfüllung*, 359–60; Zumstein, *Kreative Erinnerung*, 267; Weidemann, *Tod Jesu*, 386–87, 397, 416, 447, 449.

of the Gospel and finds explicit reference in the passion story under the metaphor of drinking the cup given him by the Father (18:11).

vi. It is possible, though not certain, that John intended to hint—at a secondary level—at the gift of the Spirit when he records that Jesus bowed his head and παρέδωκεν τὸ πνεῦμα.[159] Perhaps this is less likely in view of 20:22.[160]

vii. The same sort of double reference may be present at 19:13 if a transitive[161] rather than intransitive sense is assumed—Pilate made Jesus sit on the judgment seat in mockery but thereby unconsciously witnessed to Jesus as the Judge of all.

viii. Through the "adoption" of the Beloved Disciple and the committing of him and Mary to each other, the evangelist may be wanting to suggest the creation of a new spiritual family,[162] to take the place of old Israel which has through its leaders forfeited its former position as God's people when the chief priests

159. Hoskyns, *John*, 532; Brown, *John* 2:931 ("a symbolic reference," "evocative and proleptic"); Moloney, *John*, 504–5, 509; Lincoln, *John*, 478 (a possibility); Porsch, *Pneuma und Wort*, 330–31; Burge, *Anointed Community*, 135 (given "in a symbolic, proleptic way"); Ford, *Redeemer*, 195; Frey, *Theologia crucifixi*, 221 (note 235); Zumstein, *Kreative Erinnerung*, 232–33.

160. This is decisive for Barrett, *John*, 554; Schnackenburg, *John* 3:333; Sanders, *John*, 410; Lindars, *John*, 582; Beasley-Murray, *John*, 353; Carson, *John*, 621; Johnston, *Spirit-Paraclete*, 12. Weidemann, *Tod Jesu*, 387–90, firmly rejects the view that John intends a reference to the Holy Spirit, but he does see a reference to the Spirit in the mention of the outflow of water at 19:34b.

161. De la Potterie, *Jesus roi*, 217–47 and *Hour*, 163–65; Meeks, *Prophet-King*, 73–76; Hanson, *Prophetic Gospel*, 206; Lincoln, *Truth*, 134–35 and *John*, 458, 469–70; Ford, *Redeemer*, 185; Dunn, *The Christ & The Spirit*.1, 26. Dodd, *Interpretation*, 428, did not feel able to decide. Barrett, *John*, 544, and Zumstein, Kreative *Erinnerung*, 251, see a double reference, while Chibici-Revneanu, *Herrlichkeit*, 544, believes that the evangelist has deliberately left the issue open. The transitive view is rejected by Carson, *John*, 607–8, and also by Gniesmer, *Prozetz*, 337–47, in a very detailed and thorough discussion.

162. Compare notes 115 and 116 on p. 167. See Wilckens, *Sohn Gottes*, 147–66, for a lengthy discussion of the roles of Mary and the Beloved Disciple. He sees the Beloved Disciple as representing post-Easter believers and as one who "remains" in the figure of every teacher who interprets the Gospel in the same Spirit in which it was written and Mary as both the mother of believers whose role is in the church and also whose role as mother is over against the church (to be a guarantor that the glorified Son of God in whom the church believes had become flesh as her physical son, Jesus of Nazareth). To discuss this interpretation would take us far beyond the bounds of this study.

said "We have no king but Caesar" at 19:15.

ix. It is just possible that in the burial story John might be wanting
to suggest that the cross is already beginning to draw people to
Jesus, as Joseph of Arimathea and Nicodemus, secret disciples,
now come out into the open[163] and show respect for Jesus by giving him an honourable burial.[164]

SUMMARY

I

A wealth of concepts is employed by the fourth evangelist to state or hint
at the meaning of the death of Jesus. He usually asserts or hints without
attempting explanations.

John clearly saw the death of Jesus as necessary (i.e., willed by God)
in order that people might be able to receive eternal life (3:14–15). Jesus
has to yield up his life (flesh) to procure eternal life for the world (6:51–
58). It is as the one lifted up on a cross and to glory that he can confer
eternal life (6:27). So, a series of ὑπέρ passages remind us that Jesus has
accomplished something for others that they were powerless to achieve
for themselves (6:51; 10:11, 15; 11:51–52; 15:13; 17:19). From his death
on the cross stem forgiveness, cleansing, and the gift of the Spirit (7:39;
13:10; 19:34b).

The nearest John seems to come to offering a rationale of this is in
12:20–34, when he states that Jesus vicariously identified himself with
the world under judgment and so can also draw people into that unity
with the Father which he enjoys (12:31–32). Pictorially put, he becomes
a ladder on which the angels of God descend and ascend—the point of
intercourse between God and humankind (1:51). This is also symbol-
ised in the foot washing, for, without "receiving" his death, the disciples
have no share or fellowship in him (13:7). As a result, the evangelist can
speak of Jesus' death procuring the oneness of God's people (11:49–52;
cf. 10:15b–16).

163. Hoskyns, *John,* 536; Schnackenburg, *John* 3:346; Brown, *John* 2:959–60;
Lindars, *John,* 592; Carson, *John,* 629; Moloney, *John,* 510; Lincoln, *John,* 487.

164. This interpretation is rejected by Greissmer, *Prozrtz,* 391, while Weidemann,
in *Tod Jesu,* 401, is doubtful.

Victory over the power of evil is another facet of the cross for the evangelist (12:31 [16:11]; 14:31; 16:33). The prince of this world cannot corrupt the obedience of the one whose meat it is to do the Father's will. His death is a reflection of his dedication to God, and small wonder that the evangelist depicts Jesus as consecrating himself for the impending sacrifice of himself (17:19) and drinking the cup given him by the Father (18:10).

For John, it is inevitable that the cross will be revelatory. It reveals supremely who Jesus is in his oneness with the Father (8:28–29; 16:31–32). It reveals his love for those he came to save (13:1; 15:13) and is, therefore, also a mirror to the love of the Father for the world (3:16).

This wealth of ideas cannot be dismissed lightly as unimportant and without significance. If this is correct, then immediately we face the question what is the relation between this evidence and that which we have characterised as "salvation by revelation through the Incarnate Ministry"? Could the same author hold the two views together? We shall now address that issue.

We believe that John saw the cross as vitally important for the salvation of men and women and, in that, was one with principal Christian thinkers who preceded him (like Paul and the authors of Hebrews, Mark's Gospel, and Ephesians) and those who may have been roughly contemporary (like the authors of 1 Peter and Matthew's Gospel, and John of Patmos). At the same time, John saw the importance too of the earthly ministry of Jesus (as did Mark): it was no mere preliminary to the cross. From his vantage point after the coming of the Paraclete-Spirit, John saw the ministry of Jesus as the revelation of God's eternal Word, given in word and deed. At the same time, it was clear that, historically speaking, human faith before the cross was weak and ineffective and floundered on that "rock of offence," and was restored in the post-cross era by the risen Jesus' appearances and the coming of the Spirit.

Accordingly, we believe that as a theologian John had to do justice to the importance of four factors:

(a) the ministry of Jesus

(b) the fallibility of faith in the pre-cross era

(c) the death of Jesus

(d) the ministry of the Paraclete-Spirit in helping the church to understand both (a) and (c).

By choosing to follow the literary genre of "Gospel," John could do precisely that justice. By integrating sign and discourse and letting this unity be seen in the light of the hour of the cross, he was able to draw out the significance of Jesus as the incarnate Word and enable an encounter to take place, through the written record, between the hearer/reader and Jesus the Word Incarnate who was lifted up on the cross and to glory. The revelation given in the ministry is not divorced from the cross, as if it were independent, but needs the cross to be fully understandable; just as the action of the cross is only fully understandable when integrated with the ministry.

The mingling of the different horizons of time and fact, pre and post the cross, the interpenetration of the historical and glorified Jesus, exclude both the errors of an approach which holds only to the divinity of the Word and those of an approach which would see in Jesus only the son of Joseph.

II

We believe that the interpretations of the cross surveyed in chapter 5 make it intelligible why the evangelist should see the cross as the climax to which the ministry was heading and which he expressed by means of the hour concept. If Jesus becomes the Savior at the cross, then equally we can see why there is a "fresh access" (so to speak) of glory in the cross: Jesus is glorified—his status is enhanced—because what he did has decisive results for the salvation of men and women. What he did in the cross goes beyond what was done during the ministry. The inadequacy of human faith before the cross, the failure to respond to the revelation in a proper manner, means that revelation by itself is not enough—a further step is needed, and this takes place in the cross.

If salvation is in the end linked with the cross, which can, therefore, be interpreted as glorification, it is not surprising that it should also be seen as "lifting up"—literally, on a wooden structure called a cross, and as exaltation. Whether it was Isa 52:13 which suggested the term to the evangelist or not is of no great moment to us; suffice to say that the possible double reference of ὑψωθῆναι enabled the evangelist to suggest forcibly that the cross is not a moment of deepest woe, but one to be rejoiced in. The saving act is also his return to the Father, to glory.

In the light of this way of regarding the cross, John 1:29 is no carelessly left "splinter" of tradition, but a confession deliberately and impressively included and making a vital point in John's opening section. Both Jesus' words at 2:4 and the cleansing of the Temple at the beginning of the Gospel set the impending narrative under the cross, just as the Thomas episode sets the future under the leadership of the Crucified One.

Having thus accomplished the work set him by the Father—that is, the salvation of men and women, Jesus returns to the Father and can ask the Father to send the Paraclete-Spirit to actualise and universalise his work. Without his having brought about the unity of humankind with God through the cross, it would not have been possible to "release" the Spirit. The Spirit dwells in the disciples and both teaches them and enables them to witness to the world.

Accordingly, we reject completely that position which sees no significance of the cross in John, other than the completion of his commission. We believe that the view that sees the cross as itself revelatory is true, but does not do justice to the whole of John's thought on the subject. The view which sees the cross as elevating Jesus to glory and, therefore, able to continue to dispense his saving work is true in what it affirms but not in what it fails to affirm. Those scholars who affirm that in John salvation is by both revelation and redemption are in substance right, and we hope that this study has helped to put that position on an even firmer basis.

Our task is still not complete. We need now to address ourselves to the question of how men and women embrace what has been done on their behalf at the cross.

EXCURSUS 1: INFLUENCE OF EXODUS 17:1–7 IN JOHN'S GOSPEL?

In his book, *Truth on Trial*, Andrew Lincoln expresses the belief that the incident described in Exodus17:1–7 at Meribah is part of the OT background which feeds into the lawsuit motif in the Fourth Gospel and, in particular, is behind the passages in John 7:37–39 where Jesus offers living water to the thirsty who will come to him and 19:34b where blood and water flow from the side of Jesus when pierced by the spear of the soldier.[165]

---

165. The relevant pages are 51–54, with further references at 192, 255, 411, and 424.

His argument runs as follows. Firstly, the use of the Hebrew *rib* in Exod 17:2 shows that it is a case of a lawsuit, not merely against Moses but also really against Yahweh. Secondly, Moses is to go ahead of the people and take the rod with which he struck the Nile. Lincoln interprets this rod as also the rod of judgment (invoking Exod 18:13, which, while it mentions Moses' role as a judge, does not in fact mention the rod). Thirdly, Yahweh promises to stand before Moses on the rock at Horeb, and orders Moses to strike the rock, as a result of which water will gush forth. At this point, Lincoln claims that Yahweh becomes identified with the rock and that He receives the sentence of judgment. "When the true judge takes the penalty the rebellious people deserve, provision is made for them and a stream of life-giving water gushes out from the rock" (52). This provides what we may call a typological parallel (though Lincoln himself does not use this phrase) to Jesus on the cross, "when the true judge accepts the verdict of condemnation at the hands of those who deserve this verdict" (52); "The Fourth Gospel depicts, in the person of the incarnate Logos, this God [*viz.* of the Exodus story] taking the final consequences of being willing to be tried and judged" (411). Fourthly, later Jewish traditions about the Meribah rock hold that first blood and then water came from the rock (*Tg. Ps.-J.* on Num 20:11; *Ex. Rab.* 3:13 on Exod 4:9)[166] (54).

As Lincoln's first point is not of immediate concern to us, we shall not discuss it here. As for his second and third arguments, they do seem a strained interpretation of the Exodus narrative. Moses' rod does not seem to have anything to do with judgment, but is the instrument of the miracles in Egypt and so is appropriately used here in what is a demonstration of Yahweh's power and ability to provide for his people, even though they do not deserve it. This is the point of the story—"Is the LORD among us or not?" (Exod 17:7), with the implication whether or not he can provide for the people. Furthermore, there is not the slightest indication in the text that Yahweh stands on the rock to receive sentence against himself. It is more natural to assume that he stood on the rock so that Moses would know which one to strike.

While I am very sympathetic to the view that Jesus representatively underwent judgment at the cross, I do not believe that Lincoln has strengthened the case for this view by the unconvincing way in which he interprets Exodus 17:1–7.

---

166. Brown, *John* 2:949 mentions the latter.

As to the final point, I am aware that in the end it is not what was the original intention of the final writer of Exod 17:1–7 that counts, but how the text was taken in the evangelist's day or by him personally. It is just possible that the fourth evangelist knew of the tradition about blood and water coming out of the rock (though in this exegetical tradition these do not flow out simultaneously but following two separate strikes on the rock), but we may be sure that he read his own interpretation into the significance of the event described in 19:34b.

EXCURSUS 2: REVELATION 12 AND ITS POSSIBLE LINKS WITH JOHANNINE TRADITION

In exploring the contents of Rev 12:7–11, we are not making any assumptions about authorship. What we are interested in finding out is whether something like the "myth" contained especially in Rev 12:7–12 might be known by the congregation(s) for which the fourth evangelist wrote.[167] Or, to put the matter in another way, is John 12:31 a fragment of a larger myth, a fuller form of which appears in Rev 12:7–11?

John of Patmos' vision in Rev 12 is of crucial significance. It could be said to "rival" chapter 5 in its importance for understanding the whole of the Book of Revelation. It has indeed been described as the central chapter or the pivot of the book.[168] Two signs are seen in heaven and are described in vv. 1–4. First, there is a woman who is clothed with the sun, with the moon at her feet and a crown of twelve stars on her head, and who is in labor pains, about to give birth, and then, secondly, a horrendous red dragon who is waiting to devor her child when born. This description sets the scene for the action that follows in vv. 5–6. The woman gives birth to a boy, destined to rule the nations (this is described in language borrowed from Ps 2, a psalm messianically interpreted in Judaism). The child is caught up to God, to his throne (v. 5). We seem to have here a "compression" of the life, ministry, death and resurrection of Jesus. The flow of thought has sprung from birth to

---

167. This seems assumed by Schlatter, *Johannes*, 272; Carson, *John*, 443; Preiss, *Life in Christ*, 19; Blank, *Krisis*, 284; Betz, *Paraklet*, 205; Beasley-Murray, *Lifting Up*, 75, and *John*, 213; Dietzfelbinger, *Sühnetod*, 68. Cf. Beale, *Revelation*, 660.

168. So both Adele Collins, *Combat Myth*, 231, and Kalms, *Sturz des Gottesfiendes*, 11–12, 18, 22.

ascension and enthronement.[169] Given the pagan myth of the goddess Leto about to give birth to Apollo and who is the object of murderous intent by the monster, Python, and the inclination of some emperors to identify themselves with Apollo, Rev 12:1–5 is a Christian counter-blast to imperial pretensions and is "politically subversive."[170]

In Rev 12:7–8, there is war in heaven between Michael and his angels and the dragon and his angels. We might instinctively assume a military battle, for by itself, 12:7–8 might suggest military warfare,[171] with the archangel Michael leading his angels against the dragon (who is also described in v. 9 as the ancient serpent and the one who deceives the whole world).[172] But it is clear that actually a juridical contest is primarily in mind, as vv. 9–11 make plain, for here military language shades over into juridical,[173] and these verses envisage the heavenly law court. In the English language too, military metaphors are used for legal realities: we speak of a legal "battle" taking place, and people talk about "fighting" to prove their innocence. We should not be surprised if military language occurs also in legal settings in the New Testament.

The heavenly law court is envisaged. The devil or the Satan[174] is described as "the accuser of our brothers . . . who accuses them day and night before our God" (12:10). The cry of triumph which goes up in heaven at Satan's defeat is because the great accuser of men and women before God has been thrown out. Satan has been active in the heavenly

---

169. Unless Caird, *Revelation*, 149–50, is right in taking the "birth" to be a symbolic reference to the enthronement—his royal "birthday." Caird is followed by Boxall, *Revelation*, 180.

170. Boxall, *Revelation*, 181.

171. Jörns, *Das hymnische Evangelium*, 119, suggests that the struggle with Michael has been weakened into a foil.

172. Weidemann, *Tod Jesu*, 442 (note 377), points out that the language used is reminiscent of John 8:44. There the devil is described as a murderer ἀπ' ἀρχῆς; here in Revelation he is the ὁ ὄφις ὁ ἀρχαῖος—in both passages Gen 3 is in mind. In addition, we may point to the fact that at John 8:44 he is described as speaking falsehood (τὸ ψεῦδος); here in Revelation he is the one who deceives (ὁ πλανῶν) the whole world—an agreement in sense, if not verbally.

173. Cf. Caird, *Revelation*, 155: "Although John depicts the battle between Michael and Satan in military terms, it was essentially a legal battle." (Cf. too the remark about the complementary nature of 19:11–21 and 20:4–6 made by Mealy, *After The Thousand Year*, 178, "There is no real incompatibility between the images of the last judgment as a battle and as a courtroom proceeding."); Beale, *Revelation*, 660, 662; Karrer, *Johannesoffenbarung*, 216.

174. Something of the meaning of "the Satan" as in Job 1–2 is glimpsed here.

law court. He has ceaselessly prepared his dossiers by which to accuse and incriminate men and women before God (cf. Job 2; Zech. 3), and secure the verdict of guilty against them. But now he has lost his case and has been cast out of the heavenly court.

But why has Satan now been cast out of the heavenly court? Verse 11 supplies the answer: "And they have conquered him because of the blood of the Lamb and because of the word of their witness and they did not love their lives unto death." The foundation of this victory in the heavenly law court is the cross ("the blood of the Lamb")! That victory is—so to speak—recapitulated or extended wherever Christ's followers maintain a faithful verbal witness to their Lord, even if it means surrendering their lives in his cause.

The archetypal victory is mentioned *first*[175]—the blood of the Lamb, the death of Jesus. This is (so to speak) prolonged or re-presented when Jesus' followers faithfully witness to Jesus and to the Father, even if necessary to the point where they are prepared to surrender their lives. The cross is seen as the victory, the primal victory. Jesus' followers may be victorious, but their victory is *derivative from and based upon his victory on the cross.*[176]

What we have, then, in 12:10–11 is a mythological picture of what Paul says in Rom 8:1 "There is now no condemnation to those who are in Christ Jesus"[177] (of course, even Paul's language is metaphorical and drawn from the law courts). The accuser in the heavenly law court is ejected from court, and one who is on our side, who loves us and died for us, has taken his place. His victory on the cross guarantees our acceptance, a favourable verdict, in this law court.

The victory over the devil is repeated where the followers of Jesus adhere to the testimony which Jesus himself gave and which the church witnesses to him, and where they are prepared to accept death in fidelity to that witness.[178] Hence, in the seven letters, the promises are made to ὁ

175. Cf. Charles, *Revelation* 1:329; Prigent, *Apocalypse,* 194.

176. Cf. Beasley-Murray, *Revelation,* 204; Smalley, *Revelation,* 328; Leivestad, *Christ the Conqueror,* 218; Jörns, *Hymnische Evangelium,* 114; Bauckham, *Climax,* 229, and *Theology,* 76–77; Taegar, *Gesiegt,* 38, 42; Knöppler, *Sühne,* 266–67.

177. Preiss, *Life in Christ,* 14, 55. See also Caird, *Revelation,* 155; Sweet, *Revelation,* 202; Mounce, *Revelation,* 235. Cf. Kiddle, *Revelation,* 232.

178. This would be strengthened if 14:18–20 was taken to refer to the martyrdom of God's faithful people, with the blood referring to them (and not to God's enemies), as Caird, *Revelation,* 189–94, impressively argues, followed by Sweet, *Revelation,* 232, but denied by Bauckham, *Climax,* 291–96.

νικῶν (2:7, 11, 17, 26; 3:5, 12, 21; and also the promise at 21:7; compare the plural form at 15:2 to describe those who have been faithful to Jesus Christ by not worshipping the beast and its image).

It is worth pointing out that while the victory of Jesus is cause for joyful celebration and, indeed, heaven and its inhabitants are bidden to rejoice (12:12a), it also is cause for some considerable discomfort, because the devil descends to earth "to make war against the rest of her [the woman seen at 12:1–5 and standing for the messianic community] seed, those who hold fast to the commands of God and who hold onto the testimony of Jesus" (12:17bc). "Woe to the earth and the sea, because the devil has gone down to you in great wrath, knowing that his time is short" (12:12cde). The following chapters then tell of how the devil wages war against the followers of Jesus. John's Gospel also knows that the followers of Jesus will incur hatred, persecution and even martyrdom at the hands of the world (John 15:18—16:4) and will need to be kept from the power of the evil one (17:15).

If in the Gospel of John the Holy Spirit is our Παράκλητος here on earth, in 1 John 2:1–2 the exalted Jesus is our Παράκλητος in heaven with the Father. He has taken the place of the great accuser!

There does seem to be an inter-relationship between these different sections of the three writings. It is as if pieces of a jigsaw fit together and complete the picture. It is not claiming too much, therefore, to accept that at some stage John of Patmos, whether personally or through the intermediary of tradition, had been in touch with this aspect of Johannine tradition. This should be added to the list of echoes of Johannine tradition to be founded in his work.[179]

179. It would be interesting to pursue the possibility that the transformation of imagery (or, to use Austin Farrer's phrase, "rebirth of images") was also a feature in common. Thus, for example, Judas is described in John 17:12 as "the son of perdition" which is surely an eschatological term (cf. 2 Thess 2:3) used here to describe an historical person, while in 1 John the false teachers are described with a similiar technique as antichrists (2:18; 4:3; cf. 2 John 7). In Revelation, the Warrior-Lion messianic figure is transformed into the slaughtered Lamb (5:1–12—see the brief but brilliant remarks on John of Patmos' artistry here by Caird, *Revelation*, 74–75), while the Warrior-God whose garments are stained with the blood of his enemies in Isa 63:1–6 is transformed into the Christ whose garments are stained with his own blood in Rev 19:13 (Among scholars who interpret 19:13 in this way are Preston—Hanson, *Revelation*, 120; Sweet, *Revelation*, 282–83; Aune, *Revelation* 3:1057, 1069; Boxall, *Revelation*, 274; Hanson, *Wrath*, 138–39; Torrance, *Apocalypse Today*, 160; Rissi, *Future*, 23–24; Rowland, *Open Heaven*, 434; van Daalen, *Revelation*, 151; Thompson, *Revelation*, 44, 85, 218 (note 31); Margaret Barker, *Revelation*, 308; Mealy, *Thousand Years*, 221–22; Hays, *Moral Vision*,

175; Royalty, *Streets of Heaven*, 214; Bredin, *Jesus, Revolutionary*, 214–15; Johns, *Lamb Christology*, 21, 184; and Friesen *Imperial Cults*, 190; while Knöppler, *Sühne*, 256 (note 230) says that this interpretation "is not to be excluded." Grayston, *Dying We Live*, 333, agrees that it is Christ's blood, but then says that the risen Christ comes as the avenger of blood. Holtz, *Christologie*, 172, lists Schlatter, Büchsel and Lutgert as taking the blood to be Christ's own, though he himself does not espouse this view. Caird, *Revelation*, 244–47, takes the blood to be that of the martyred saints. Bauckham, *Climax*, 233, is prepared to say "The distinctive feature of Revelation seems to be . . . its lavish use of militaristic language in a non-militaristic sense," and believes that while in 19:17 the military imagery is controlled by the judicial and that the slaughtered Lamb, God's witness, has become judge, "the blood of [God's] faithful witness to death still marks him" (*Theology*, 105–6). U. B. Müller, *Offenbarung*, 327, is far too dogmatic to brand this interpretation as "absurd." But this line of enquiry would take us beyond the scope of this work.

6

Appropriation of What Is Accomplished in the Cross

In the cross, Jesus drew all into a union with himself. Yet at the same time men and women must appropriate what has been already accomplished. They must respond freely, and when they do so, they assume the "place" which is already theirs, by Jesus' drawing them into a union with himself at the cross.

The Vine Discourse and the High Priestly prayer, both uttered to a large degree from the standpoint that the cross has taken place, illustrate the actualization of this union. Jesus says that he is the Vine and the disciples are the branches (he does not say that he is the trunk and they are the branches). He is the totality, the Vine. The disciples are part of him. This discourse sets forth the solidarity of Christ and his disciples: they are one "organism." It is, of course, true that we find side by side the indicative and imperative: the disciples abide in him, yet they are commanded to abide. There is also both promise and threat. There is the promise that if they abide in him, they will produce fruit and glorify the Father; there is the threat, that every useless branch will be cut off and burned. But this mixture tells us something about the nature of this union and this will be explored later.

In the High Priestly prayer, Jesus and the Father are one and Jesus and the disciples are one. The former unity is both the model and the motivating power for the latter. Jesus has drawn his followers both into union with himself and through him into union with the Father.

How, then, does it come about that the disciples, who abandoned Jesus at the arrest (16:32) but who were drawn into union with himself at the cross, actually come into that union?

There are, in the Fourth Gospel, statements which seem to attribute the receiving of salvation to election by God or to a believing response to Jesus, while there are statements which, if taken in isolation, seem to imply that the whole world will be saved.[1] We set these out as follows: There are statements that assert that salvation is *by election*. Some are given by the Father to Jesus (6:37, 39, 65; 10:29; 17:2, 6, 9, 24) or are drawn by the Father (6:44). Other statements seem to imply two groups of people which determines whether someone comes to Jesus or not (e.g., those "of the truth" 18:17; "of God" 8:47; "of my sheep" 10:26). Secondly, salvation comes *by faith*. Statements about the need to believe or the blessings to be given to those who believe are so numerous and so well known as not to need quotation. As illustrations merely, we refer to "This is the work of God, that you believe in the one whom he sent" (6:29) and "The person who believes has eternal life" (6:47). Numerically this is the largest category. Finally, there is the universalist type of saying. Into this category fall 1:29; 3:16–17; 4:42; 6:51; 12:32, 47; 14:31; 17:21, 23, while several "I am" sayings have a universal claim, though a condition is attached (e.g., 8:12).

When the context of many of these statements is examined, it would appear that the evangelist can combine such statements without any sense of incongruity. What, then, is the significance of this threefold pattern?

(a) The whole world, and nothing less, is the object of God's saving love. He wills to save all people through his Son. This is the purpose of the so-called universalist sayings.

(b) Salvation is God's work and gift alone—it is nothing that we do of ourselves. This is safeguarded by the election or predestinarian type sayings.[2]

1. Caird, *Will of God*, 117; Caird, *Judgment and Salvation*, 231–32.

2. Onuki, *Gemeinde*, 180, comments that the harder the struggle to persuade people to believe, the more an individual's coming to faith seems the victory of the absolutely supra-human decision of God. Such comments as 17:6, 9–10, 24, are apologetically orientated. For him, Johannine determinism is only to be understood in its relationship to the historical experiences of the Johannine church, namely the rejection of its message by contemporary Judaism, together with the intimidation, persecution, and even martyrdom which its members suffered (ibid., 36).

    (c) Faith must appropriate God's gift of salvation accomplished in Jesus. Faith reaches out to receive what God gives.

Justice must be done to these three strands, rather than subsuming two under one of them.[3]

    We shall now approach the question of appropriation from a different angle—the work of the Holy Spirit[4] and the response of faith and its consequences.

(1) THE WORK OF THE HOLY SPIRIT

Two of the Paraclete-Spirit sayings refer to the work of the Spirit vis-à-vis the unbelieving world,[5] 15:26–27 and 16:7–11. The Paraclete-Spirit is a witness of God against the world. In the great lawsuit, he takes the place of Jesus, now returned to the Father, and continues to press God's case against the world, though, since the incarnation, that case must now always be related to Jesus.

    According to 16:7–11, the Paraclete-Spirit has a triple case to prove and seeks to convince the world on the following three charges. The first charge relates to sin. The world must be convinced and persuaded of its error and sin in rejecting Jesus. The case rests on the fact that the Father sent, as his agent, his Son, to save the world, but the world did not accept him. The second charge concerns what is right. The world crucified Jesus as a wrongdoer. Jesus' return to the Father proves that he was in the right in his claims and that the world was wrong in the standards to which it clung. The world must be brought to acknowledge the truth of

---

3. As, e.g., do both Hofius and Kammler in their *Johannesstudien*. They both assert that only those elected by God in fact come to faith (e.g., 67, 80, for Hofius; 175 for Kammler).

4. That the post-Easter work of the Spirit is understood as necessary for salvation (so Kammler, *Johannesstudien*, 183) is worked out in detail by Bennema, *Saving Wisdom*.

5. Against Porsch, *Pneuma und Wort*, 281, who believes that the Spirit convinces the conscience of the disciples concerning the guilt of the world to strengthen their faith (he takes 15:26 in a similar way). Supporting the view espoused here are Carson, *John*, 530; Lincoln, *John*, 412, 418–19; Schultz, *Untersuchungen*, 148; Preiss, *Life in Christ*, 20; Dahl, *Johannine Church*, 139; Betz, *Paraklet*, 192–206; Johnston, *Spirit-Paraclete*, 141–46; Muller, *Parakletenvorstellung*, 69–70; Harvey, *Jesus on Trial*, 113–14; Trites, *Witness*, 117–20; Franck *Revelation Taught*, 59–65; Burge, *Anointed Community*, 7, 208–10; Metzner, *Sünde*, 219, 245, 279–80 (In addition. Metzner, *Sünde*, 93, draws attention to the parallelism between 15:22 and 26 (following Obuki, *Wahrheit*, 293–94).

his claims. The final charge has reference to judgment. Since the ruler of this world has been judged (12:31), the world must be brought to realize the error of giving allegiance to him, for this is rebellion against God and futile since there is no true life through the prince of this world. How does the Paraclete-Spirit carry out this task of convincing the world?—through the proclamation and message of the church.[6]

In different language, though still related to the cosmic lawsuit theme, 15:26–27 says that the Paraclete-Spirit will bear witness concerning Jesus. The word "bear witness" will include the kind of themes already touched on above. As the Spirit of Truth, Paraclete-Spirit reveals falsehood for what it is and reveals the truth that Jesus not only brings but is. He brings to men and women a true awareness of who Jesus is.

The saying at 15:27 reveals to us how the Paraclete-Spirit works: he will work through the church,[7] through disciples as they proclaim and preach Jesus as the Christ, the Son of God (cf. 20:30–31) and summon people to believe in him. Thus, while the world cannot receive the Paraclete-Spirit because it neither sees nor knows him (14:17), this is true only insofar as it persists in being the world. If it will let itself be persuaded and convinced, then the Paraclete-Spirit will come to it. The context of 15:18—16:4 suggests that the Johannine churches experienced hostility and rejection at the hands of the world, as their Lord and Master had.

The process of convincing the world, of bringing it from unbelief to belief, is described in the conversation with Nicodemus as birth ἄνωθεν, birth by the Spirit and water. Only the activity of the Spirit can lift a person out of the realm of "flesh" and into the realm of the Spirit, from below to above. For "what is born of flesh is flesh; and what is born of the Spirit is Spirit" (3:8; cf. 6:63: "The flesh does not benefit at all: it is the Spirit who gives life"). This new birth from above is no human achievement, but a work of God through the Spirit. A human being cannot create a new beginning, only God can, and his activity remains a mystery: "The wind blows where it wants to; you hear its sound but you do not know from where it comes or where it goes; so is everyone

---

6. Onuki, *Gemeinde*, 146–48; Frank, *Revelation Taught*, 60; Burge, *Anointed Community*, 208–10.

7. Cf. e.g., Schnackenburg, *John* 3:117–20; Lincoln, *John*, 412; Dahl, *Johannine Church*, 139; Schlier, *Begriff des Geistes*, 238; Trites, *Witness*, 139; Frank, *Revelation Taught*, 61.

who is born of the Spirit" (3:8). The mysterious movement of the wind within the natural world provides an analogy to the rebirth by the Spirit, a mystery that God has kept within his inscrutable purpose.

Thus, for Johannine Christianity, being lifted out of solidarity with the world, the realm of flesh, into union with Jesus and the sense of liberation and new life enjoyed as a result, seemed so miraculous that it could only be ascribed to God working through his Spirit in the lives of believers; it was in effect a new birth, a birth from the divine realm.[8]

(2) BELIEVING (AND KNOWING)

Constantly, Jesus summons men and women to believe in him. "Truly, truly, I say to you, that the person who hears my word and believes my Sender has eternal life" (5:24) may be taken as typical, since it stresses the word which Jesus proclaims, the need to hear it receptively and the necessity of recognizing that behind Jesus, the man of Nazareth, there stands (as it were) God who has sent him. The gift offered when such belief is aroused is nothing less than eternal life.

It is this faith that God requires, not a series of actions. "This is what God wants you to do—to believe in the one whom He has sent" (6:29)—so said Jesus in response to the enquiry couched in the plural— "What shall we do to do the works of God?" (v. 28).

There are, however, obstacles in the way of faith. The Galileans know him as the son of Joseph and are acquainted with his father and mother: how can he claim to be the bread descended from heaven and to give his flesh to eat (6:41, 52)? Can anything good come out of Nazareth (1:46) or Galilee (7:52)? Jesus seems to break God's law, so how can he be from God (5:16, 18a; 9:24) or claim to be one with God (10:30–33)? Yardsticks are produced by which to measure Jesus and by which he seems to be found wanting (7:25–27, 31, 40–44).

People want reputation and honor from one another (5:44), and the truth about a person is often painful and is so rejected (8:45). Even when confronted by the truth it is more comfortable to stay where one

---

8. Dunn, *Jesus and the Spirit*, 350, referring to the metaphor of living water, speaks of "a living religious experience which the Johannine community could attribute only to the Spirit"; Burge, *Anointed Community*, 170, speaks of "a life-changing encounter with the Spirit" as "one of the hall-marks of Johannine Christianity."

is (cf. Pilate). To leave the old solidarities and break out becomes too demanding (12:42–43).

Closely allied to faith/belief in Jesus is the idea of knowing him. "We have believed and know that you are the Holy One of God" (6:69): here faith and knowledge are synonymous. Eternal life comes via faith and may be described as knowing God and his Son, Jesus (17:3). Jesus said that people are to believe him or, if they cannot do that, then "believe the works that you may come to know and go on knowing that the Father is in me and I in the Father" (10:38),[9] whereas in the Farewell Discourse he can say "Do you not believe that I am in the Father and the Father is in me?" (14:10). In the High Priestly, within the same sentence, knowing and believing appear with the same object differently expressed: "They have received (the words which Jesus has passed on) and have truly come to know (ἔγνωσαν) that I came forth from you and have believed (ἐπίστευσαν) that you sent me." (17:8)

Jesus knows the Father, and this relationship is a prototype of the relations between Jesus and his disciples: "I am the Good Shepherd; and I know my own and my own know me, even as the Father knows me and I know the Father" (10:14–15;[10] cf. 10:27).

(3) BAPTISM

Since baptism into the name of Jesus was practiced from the earliest days of the church, and certain blessings were associated with being baptized (e.g., Acts 2:38; Rom. 6:1–4, etc.), we need to ask whether the fourth evangelist saw baptism as part of that process of appropriating what Jesus has done for us.

In the conversation with Nicodemus in chapter 3, Jesus says, "Truly, truly, I say to you, unless someone is born of water and the Spirit, they cannot enter the kingdom of God" (v. 5). I have argued elsewhere that here the evangelist is using baptismal language in order to describe the experience of conversion that led to and was linked with and was expressed in baptism.[11]

9. This rather cumbersome translation is an attempt to render γνῶτε καὶ γινώ σκητε—an aorist and present subjunctive active of the same verb.

10. This is the nearest Johannine parallel to the so-called "Johannine thunderbolt" in the Synoptic tradition [Q] (Matt 11:27/Luke 10:22).

11. Morgan-Wynne, *Baptism*, 121–26. Dunn, *Baptism*, 193, had previously con-

In context, the evangelist stresses the sovereign, free, unfettered activity of the Spirit.[12] Baptism as such is not the main focus of attention, but rather the work of the Spirit in opening up the possibility of the new birth.[13] Elsewhere, the evangelist can refer to the life-giving gift of the Spirit without reference to baptism, but under the imagery of flowing waters that quench thirst (7:37–39; 4:14). This gift of the Spirit has its objective basis in the descent from heaven and especially in the lifting-up on the cross and to glory of the Son of Man (3:13–15).[14] The need for faith is stressed in vv. 12, 15, 16, and 18 (as in 1:12–13 where the idea of (new) birth is mentioned, but no express mention of the Spirit or of baptism).

We may infer from the reference to water that the evangelist reveals an awareness of baptism and its association with that process of "birth from above" worked by the Spirit on the basis of what Jesus had done in his being lifted up and in response to faith. But for him the whole emphasis lay on the experience of spiritual birth, the beginning of a new existence, in the power of the Spirit.[15]

Some scholars have argued for a reference to baptism in 9:1–7, on the grounds that the man born blind is told to go and "wash" in the pool of Siloam (v. 7), which the evangelist interprets as meaning ἀπεσταλμένος ("Sent") and in this Gospel Jesus is the one sent by the Father, together with the fact that baptism was interpreted by at least Justin Martyr as "illumination," possibly as early as Heb 6:4 if φωτισθέντας in this verse is an allusion to baptism.[16] But the reference to "having been

---

sidered this viewpoint a very real possibility, though he favors taking the phrase as a hendiadys, with water being a symbol of the life-giving power of the Spirit (or possibly, water baptism and Spirit baptism being integral parts of Christian conversion-initiation—see 191–92).

12. Cf. e.g., Schnackenburg, *John* 1:369–70; Dunn, *Baptism*, 191.

13. Cf. e.g., Lincoln, *John*, 150–51; Dunn, *Baptism*, 193; Burge, *Anointed Community*, 167–69; Kammler, *Johannesstudien*, 154. Beasley-Murray, *Baptism*, 230, agrees, although he does see a reference to baptism in 3:5. Carson, *John*, 195, denies that the Holy Spirit is in mind, and draws an unconvincing distinction between the imparting of God's nature as "spirit" and the Holy Spirit in interpreting John 3:5.

14. See earlier on p. 84.

15. See Dunn, *Baptism*, 188–94, for a detailed discussion of John 3:1–8, and also my *Holy Spirit*, 24–34, for an examination of the link of religious experience and the Spirit in John's Gospel.

16. Hoskyns, *John*, 355, 363–65; Brown, *John* 1:380–82 and *NT Essays*, 64–66; Cullmann, *Early Christian Worship*, 102–5.

enlightened" in Hebrews is by no means certainly a specific reference to baptism and could as easily refer to the whole process of conversion[17] (of which baptism would be a part), and in any case, this is using a text outside of John to interpret John.

It should be noticed that Jesus expressly denies that the man was born blind because of sin committed by him or his parents, so that the flow of the whole story is turned away from the theme of sin/sins. The story is meant to illustrate Jesus as the light of the world: the miracle of healing is support for the claim made by Jesus in 8:12 and 9:5. As the Word made flesh, as the one sent from the Father, he is the bearer and transmitter of light (cf. 1:4, 8–9). We see no reason to import a reference to baptism into this story.[18]

We have earlier (p. 177) rejected the view that sees a reference to the sacraments contained in the outflow of blood and water from the crucified Jesus in 19:34–35.

Summarizing, we might say that what Jesus has done for all must be appropriated by all. Where what Jesus has done is met by the response of faith, there the Spirit of God so acts as to bring about a new birth, a new life with new possibilities.[19] This is no human achievement but the act of God through his Spirit applying to the believer the work of his Son on the cross. The believer is lifted out of one sphere of power, dominated by the prince of this world, into the new sphere of power, being in Christ.

---

17. Dunn, *Baptism*, 210.

18. In agreement with Schnackenburg, *John* 2:257–58; Beasley-Murray, *John*, 162; Carson, *John*, 365; Dunn, *Unity* 169; Metzner, *Sünde*, 112–14, which is a detailed and careful rebuttal of the theory of a reference in this story to the forgiveness of sins and baptism.

19. Indeed, Hofius, *Johannesstudien*, 75, can say that the new birth is the coming to faith, and draws attention to the parallel between vv. 3, 5 and 15–16, 18. Moloney, *John*, 99, thinks that originally v. 5 lacked "water and" and spoke of the need for rebirth in the Spirit for entry into the community, but these words were added to make an explicit reference to water baptism, "a public sign that externally marked the internal experience and commitment to the beliefs of the Johannine community" [I would myself speak of commitment to Jesus and then the beliefs of the community]. He had previously said (ibid., 93) that "from its [the Johannine community's] beginnings the gift of the Spirit 'from above' was accompanied by a ritual of rebirth solemnized by water baptism (vv. 3, 5)." Moloney's views are akin to, though not identical with, de la Potterie *Naitre*, 51–74 (= de la Potterie and Lyonnet, *Vie selon l'Esprit*, 31–63). The views of de la Potterie and Moloney are not the same as that of Bultmann, *John*, 138 (note 3) and many of his pupils, who see ὕδατοσ καὶ as due to a later ecclesiastically minded redactor.

We turn now to a consideration of *the results of the cross*. God did not send the Son into the world to condemn the world but to save it (3:17), but to save *for what*?

Firstly, there is *the gift of eternal life*.[20] Eternal life is the favorite phrase used by the evangelist to describe God's gift to believers through the work of his Son: "And as Moses lifted up the serpent in the desert, so the Son of Man must be lifted up in order that everyone who believes might have eternal life in him" (3:14–15). Because Jesus has drawn all into a union with himself at the cross, believers united to him enjoy the life bestowed on him by the Father (5:24–26; 6:57) and which it was his purpose to bring (10:10). Eternal life is not a gift which can be separated from the giver, for Jesus is himself life (cf. 14:6).

Negatively, believers no longer come under judgment (3:18); they avoid death (5:24; 8:51) and God's wrath (3:36), and will not perish (3:16; 10:28). On the positive side, a whole range of metaphors and non-metaphorical statements are employed—to enjoy the light of life (8:12); to drink living waters (4:14); to satisfy oneself with the bread of life (6:35); believers are set free from the bondage of sin (8:11–32, 34, 36) and become children of God (1:12–13); enter the kingdom of God (3:3); receive one grace after another (1:16); and will share the glory which Jesus has with the Father (17:22–24; cf. 12:26).

Eternal life embraces both present experience (3:36; 5:24; 6:47, etc.) and future hope (4:14; 6:27). There is no need to excise statements about believers being raised on the Last Day (e.g., 6:39–40, 44, 54).[21]

In a sense, John does not give us much detail in a description. His one formal definition perhaps gives us a clue to this: "Now this is eternal life, to know you [i.e., the Father], the only true God and Jesus Christ whom you have sent" (17:3). The Greek καί, here rendered "and," may be said to be both coordinating and explanatory. It coordinates Father and Son, for this Gospel heaps the highest honors on the Son (e.g., 1:18; 20:28; 5:23; 14:9; the absolute use of ἐγώ εἰμι; etc.), but equally the Son is the way to the Father and only through him can men and women come to the Father (e.g., 14:6; 1:18; 6:46, and 14:9),[22] so that καί is also

---

20. For full-scale studies of John's concept of life, see Pribnow, *Leben*; Mussner, *Leben*. See also Dodd, *Interpretation*, 144–50; Schnackenburg, *John* 2:352–61.

21. As Bultmann, *John*, 219, one-sidedly does. See Ashton, *Understanding*, 220–26, for a recent, balanced assessment of this issue.

22. Barrett, *John*, 504, succinctly puts it: "Knowledge of God cannot be severed

explanatory—knowing God means knowing his envoy, Jesus Christ, and through him knowing God.

Given that "knowing" here is primarily the knowing of personal experience, of personal relationships, it is not surprising that John stresses eternal life but does not attempt a detailed description. For the invitation to come to Jesus and through him to the Father is an invitation to a journey, a pilgrimage, a voyage of discovery which in the end is unceasing, for who can exhaust what is involved in knowing God? It would be entirely wrong to deduce from John's use of μένειν ἐν in the Vine Discourse that union with Christ was an inert response; rather, abiding in Christ has a dynamic quality about it, and growth and development are involved.

Secondly, there is *the unity of believers*. Individual believers do not function on their own. They, in being united to Christ, are also united to their fellow-believers. Much has been written in recent years on the individualism of the Fourth Gospel,[23] and rightly so, for this is a strong feature of its thought and approach. But, as we earlier pointed out, there is "a fellowship of the individualists," and the very sharp either/or in Johannine thought—of the world or not of the world, etc.—indicates, in all probability, a group deeply conscious of its separation from its milieu and its *bonding together* in that separation.[24] Hence, the reiterated love command, with Jesus' own love as the example and the power to fulfill that example (13:34–35; 15:12, 17), and hence the stress on unity as it emerges in the High Priestly prayer and elsewhere (17:20–26; 10:16; 11:51–52).

The fact that both the Shepherd and Vine Discourses, seen as containing pictures for the church in the Fourth Gospel, seem to stress more the individual sheep's or branch's relationship to the Shepherd or Vine than the relation of the sheep or branches to one another, should not be exaggerated. What is said is perfectly true, but it does not follow that the fourth evangelist sat lightly to the fellowship of the church. The sense of

---

from knowledge of his incarnate Son."

23. E.g., Moule, *Individualism*, 171–90.

24. E.g., Onuki, *Gemeinde*, 27. He rightly stresses that separation does not mean isolation from the world (64–65, against the position of Luise Schottroff). See also Wilckens, *Sohn Gottes*, 56–88, for a robust defense of a strong consciousness of the church in John.

"togetherness" would no doubt be heightened by the persecution experienced from the world (15:18—16:4; cf. 17:11).

The Johannine church is conscious of having been chosen and sent out by Jesus as his envoys to continue the mission entrusted to him by the Father (20:21; 17:18; 15:16). If that mission culminated in the cross, as we have argued, then it follows that the cross must be an integral part of its missionary message. They go as envoys of the Risen Lord who bears the marks of his cross (20:20).

The missionary task depends on what is already accomplished. It is the church's task to evangelize on the basis of what Jesus has already done in the cross (12:32). The church will help in bringing the "other sheep" into the one flock of the one shepherd (10:16), in bringing God's scattered children into one (11:51–52).

In chapter 4, we catch a glimpse of the missionary task of the church. Whatever may be the historical difficulties of John 4 as it now stands (in the light of Matt 10:5–6), it uses the picture of reaping a harvest of converts in connection with the Samaritans. The fields are already ripe and ready for harvesting (4:35), and already the reaper is gathering in for the harvest. Harvest home means joy for both sower and reaper alike (4:36). The disciples are reaping where they did not sow (4:38).[25]

The Samaritan woman appears as a prototype missionary in 4:28–30, 39[26] and may be an indication that in the Johannine congregations women played their part in evangelizing (cf. Mary Magdalene 20:17b–18).[27]

---

25. See Cullmann, *Samaria*, 186–94, for a fuller discussion (also Becker, *Johannesevangelium* 1:181–82). Cullman saw in the ἄλλοι of 4:38 an allusion to the Hellenists of Acts 8. Okure, *Mission*, 163, argues for the Father and Jesus being the "others"; and Neugebauer, *Textbezuge*, 135–41, believes that on the level of Jesus, the sender is the Father; the sower is the Samaritan woman; the reaper is Jesus; and the harvest is the Samaritan believers; but that on the level of the Johannine church, the sender is Jesus; the sowers must be the Samaritans; the reapers, the disciples; and the harvest to be reaped, other Samaritans. Robinson, *Twelve NT Studies*, 61–66, sees the "others" as John the Baptist and his disciples; cf. Carson, *John*, 230–31.

26. Lindars, *John*, 192, says of 4:27–42: "It is a model of the mission of the church"; cf. Becker, *Johannesevangelium* 1:179. See Okure, *Mission*, 183: "the passage presents the mission of the disciples as an integral and very dependent part of Jesus' own mission" (see also 181–91; 226–27, 228–35).

27. See Brown, *Community*, 183–98; Scott, *Sophia*, 174–24. Witherington, *Women*, 174–82, stresses that women are better disciples than the men in the Fourth Gospel.

The church's task is to bear witness to the world and in that task it is helped by the Paraclete-Spirit (15:26–27; see also 20:21–22). Perhaps, the more correct way of putting it is that it is the task of the Paraclete-Spirit to bear witness about Jesus to the world and he uses the activity of disciples to this end. The "word" of the disciples will be a means of bringing men and women to faith (17:20), just as the word of Jesus was potent to achieve this (17:8; cf. 6:63, 68–69). The message of the church is not only that the Word became flesh but that in the cross Jesus the Word Incarnate drew men and women into union with himself and so accomplished the salvation of the world.[28]

True worship, worship prompted by, guided by, illumined by the Spirit of Truth, takes place once Jesus has been lifted up and has sent the Paraclete-Spirit from the Father (4:21–24). Worship tied to geographical sites like Jerusalem or Gerizim will be transcended. The Paraclete-Spirit will enable believers to offer that worship based on truth—not only that the Word became flesh but that, lifted up on the cross, he has drawn all into union with himself.

Prior to the conversation with the Samaritan woman on the theme of worship, the evangelist had indicated that Jesus was in the process of superseding the Jewish cult: it is water placed in jars set aside for Jewish purificatory rites (2:6) which is transformed into wine at Cana, while after the cleansing of the temple, Jesus says, "Destroy this temple and I will raise it in three days" (2:19), which the evangelist interprets as a reference to the temple of Jesus' body (v. 21). Jesus' resurrection body will be the temple in which God can be worshipped.[29] The cleansing of the temple would thus be a sign of what is to come. (There may be a secondary reference to the church.[30]) We note that Jesus' death ("Destroy this temple"), in the view of the evangelist, is the necessary factor in the supersession of Jewish rites and the creation of the possibility of true worship.[31]

28. Against Bultmann, *John*, 494, who stresses just "the proclamation of the σάρξ γενόμενος."

29. So Barrett, *John*, 201; Beasley-Murray, *John*, 41; Carson, *John*, 182; Lincoln, *John*, 140–41 (this view is challenged by Lindars, *John*, 144).

30. So Barrett, *John*, 201; Schnackenburg, *John* 1:352: Brown, *John* 1:125 (possibly); denied by Carson, *John*, 182; Moloney, *John*, 83; and Lincoln, *John*, 141.

31. Cf. too 1:51 (shrines like Bethel are clearly superseded). In general, John seems interested in the theme of the supersession of Jewish festivals by Jesus (e.g., 7:37–38; 8:12 at Tabernacles).

Earlier, we maintained that while 3:5 contained language associated with baptism, for the evangelist the main emphasis fell on the sovereign, free role of God's Spirit, the receiving of whom imparted a new divine birth to a new mode of life—eternal life. Similarly, in 6:53–58, while Lord's Supper language is probably being used, the main emphasis lies on the necessity of Jesus' death for believers to share his life. However, we could deduce that leaders in the Johannine congregations did use the language of feeding on Christ and being nourished by him, plus the familiar idea of abiding in Christ and Christ in the believer (6:56), when preaching or giving meditations at the Lord's Supper. The Supper was a mode of encounter. The stress is on Christ, mediated by the Spirit (6:63). Within the Johannine community, language drawn from the senses seems to have been utilized—hear, see, touch (cf. 20:17 and 1 John 1:1) and taste—to describe fellowship with Christ, open to those who believe.[32]

Thirdly, we shall briefly mention *the role of the Paraclete-Spirit as teacher within the Christian community* (his role in bringing about the new birth and also his role in worship having been touched on). The Paraclete-Spirit only comes when Jesus has gone (16:7; 7:39). In 14:26 the Paraclete-Spirit has one function—to teach, a function which consists of[33] helping the disciples to remember (with deeper understanding) what Jesus has already said (εἶπον, aorist indicative—not what he will say). The evangelist gives us at least two clear examples of this at 2:22, 12:16, to which should be added also 13:7 (greater understanding, in the future, of the meaning of the foot washing). The remembering is not a "bare" recall, but a deeper understanding of the meaning of words and events and indeed the Old Testament background.

At first sight the opening sentence of the final Paraclete-Spirit saying in 16:12–15 might seem to suggest new revelation imparted by the Paraclete-Spirit. There are things that Jesus has not been able to pass on to the disciples, because of their lack of understanding, but the Paraclete-

---

32. Mussner, *Historical Jesus*, 7–47, deals with "to see" and "to hear," plus other terms, in what he calls "the Johannine mode of vision" or "understanding" Jesus (his other four terms are γινώσκειν, εἰδέναι, μαρτυρεῖν, and (ὑπο)μιμνήσκειν).

33. For καὶ as explanatory, see Bultmann, *John*, 626 (note 6); Barrett, *John*, 467; Brown, *John* 2:650–51; Schnackenburg, *John* 3:83; Lindars, *John*, 483; Becker, *Johannesevangelium* 2:469; Beasley-Murray, *John*, 261; Moloney, *John*, 413; Olsson, *Structure and Meaning*, 269; Porsch, *Pneuma und Wort*, 265; de la Potterie, *Vérité*, 1:377; Jonge, *Jesus*, 11; Franck, *Revelation Taught*, 42; Bennema, *Saving Wisdom*, 229.

Spirit will guide them into all the truth, vv. 12–13. But vv. 14–15 serve to
correct any such impression and ensure the correct balance—it is, rather,
a case of new insights based on the past revelation given in the ministry
of Jesus.[34] "He will glorify me, because he will take what belongs to me
(ἐκ τοῦ ἐμοῦ) and expound[35] it to you. All that the Father possesses
belongs to me. For this reason I said that he will take what belongs to
me and expound it to you." The revelation imparted by the incarnate
Word is sufficient, but the disciples' perception is inadequate and the
Paraclete-Spirit will have to help them. This he will do by illuminating
what has already been passed on in word and deed by Jesus, for all that
Jesus said and did came to him from the Father who bestowed everything on His Son (as the evangelist has made abundantly clear in the
Gospel previously). The harmony of the Paraclete-Spirit and the exalted
Jesus is conveyed by the fact that this interpretative ministry of the Spirit
depends on what he hears (v. 13 οὐ γὰρ λαλήσει ἀφ' ἑαυτοῦ, ἀλλ ὅσα
ἀκούει λαλήσει)—presumably from the exalted Jesus and the Father.

The same could be said of 16:25 where there is a contrast between
the present speaking which is done in a figurative manner (ἐν παροιμί
αις) and the future speaking in plain terms (παρρησία): both are
done by Christ. Clearly, he does the latter through the Paraclete-Spirit.
The "author" of the speaking is the same in both instances. The difference between figurative and clear speaking happens—in the light of
16:14–15—because the Paraclete-Spirit interprets and expounds what
has already been given.[36]

In the light of what we have said thus far, it is highly improbable
that what the Paraclete-Spirit will do in 16:13c refers to either charismatic prophecy in general or prediction of the End, with the Book of
Revelation as a particular example.[37] Either τὰ ἐρχόμενα refers to the

---

34. For a helpful discussion, see Dunn, *Jesus and the Spirit*, 351–52.

35. "Expound" is an attempt to get the interpretative nuance contained in ἀναγγέ
λλειν. The verb contains more than a mere declaration—see the research of de la
Potterie, *Vérité* 1:445–49.

36. So Bultmann, *John*, 587–88; Barrett, *John*, 495; Brown, *John* 2:735;
Schnackenburg, *John* 3:161; Lindars, *John*, 511; Beasley-Murray, *John*, 287; Haenchen,
John 2:245; Carson, *John*, 546–47; Olsson, *Structure and Meaning*, 271; Porsch, *Pneuma
und Wort*, 291; Onuki, *Gemeinde*, 156; Burge, *Anointed Community*, 214. What Lincoln,
John, 397, says on 14:26 about the work of the Paraclete-Spirit in unfolding the signifi-
cance of what Jesus said for new situations could be applied to 16:14–15 too.

37. Becker, *Johannesevangelium* 2:499; Betz, *Paraklet*, 190–92; Windisch, *Spirit-*

Passion (cf. the phrase in 18:4)[38] or ἀναγγελεῖ refers to *interpreting coming events in the light of what Christ has said and done in his ministry* (including his lifting up).[39] Barrett is prepared to accept that both interpretations were present in the evangelist's intentions.[40] In view of the evangelist's capacity for double entendre, this cannot be ruled out as a possibility. It might well be yet another instance of the evangelist seeing two possibilities, one of which the reader might not fully see until after a full reading of the Gospel and reflection on it. Certainly it fits in with the crucial importance of the cross in the Fourth Gospel if the Passion were in mind and if it was being stated that one of the Paraclete-Spirit's tasks was to expound and interpret its significance.

The Paraclete-Spirit, then, has, above all, a didactic role within the community of believers, [41] so that in a very real sense future believers are not at a disadvantage over against the first generation of believers (important as they are 15:27; 17:20)

Within the context of the Farewell Discourse, we must note that the Paraclete-Spirit has a consoling role. This does not depend on any particular translation of παράκλητος, but rather on what is said about his relationship to the disciples in the light of the imminent departure of Jesus. Jesus is going; he is leaving the world; he is returning to the Father. By contrast the disciples are left in the world, exposed to the attacks of the evil one and the persecution of men (17:14; 15:18—16:4). There is a danger that they might think of themselves as orphans without protector or defender (ὀρφανούς, 14:18). But in fact Jesus says that the Paraclete-Spirit, while at the moment alongside of them (παρ᾽ ὑμῖν), will be in them (ἐν ὑμῖν) (14:16-17). There is a careful distinction between the present "external" relationship of the Paraclete-Spirit to them (παρά)

Paraclete, 12; Hill, *NT Prophecy,* 151; Boring, *Continuing Voice,* 146, 178.

38. Lightfoot, *John,* 287 (apparently—he uses the phrase "events now imminent); Cadman, *Open Heaven,* 194–95; Kammler, *Johannesstudien,* 149. Cf. Temple, *Readings,* 291.

39. Hoskyns, *John,* 487 (the new order resulting from the departure of Jesus); Brown, John 2:716; Schnackenburg, *John* 3:135; Lindars, *John,* 505; Beasley-Murray, *John,* 284; Carson, *John,* 540; Thüsing, *Erhöhung,* 153; Olsson, *Structure and Meaning,* 270; Onuki, *Gemeinde,* 77. Lincoln, *John,* 421, comes close to this position.

40. Barrett, *John,* 490.

41. Kammler, *Johannesstudien,* 182, maintains that the concentration of the work of the Spirit on the word and faith is a consequence of the evangelist's theology of the cross.

and the future, intimate, indwelling relationship with them (ἐν). This gift of the Paraclete-Spirit to be in the disciples will be a comfort and a consolation (especially, furthermore, in the light of the fact that the Paraclete-Spirit's activities exactly parallel those attributed to Jesus in his ministry).[42] The coming of Paraclete-Spirit could be seen as the fulfillment of "I will not leave you as orphans, I will come to you" (14:18) in the present shape of the Farewell Discourse. Jesus goes, but the Spirit comes—as comforter and as teacher.

Fourthly, there are *the ethical consequences.* At the cross as an objective fact, we were drawn into union with Christ. When we appropriate this by faith, his life is given to us. The Christian life is living out this life in union with the exalted Christ.

Obedience to Christ's commands is the consequence of our union with Christ; it is the test of our love for him and of our discipleship (14:15, 21, 23). That Jesus makes us his friends does not eliminate the need for obedience: "You are my friends if you do what I command you" (15:14). And what are the commands of Jesus? He singles out one command above all else, one which is based on what he has done for us in the cross: "This is my command, that you love one another as I have loved you (καθὼς ἠγάπησα). No one has greater love than this: that someone lays down their life for their friends. You are my friends" (15:12–14a). The aorist indicative active in the καθὼς clause in all probability points to the cross, as is the case earlier in v. 9 which reads "As the Father has loved me, I also have loved (ἠγάπησα) you."[43] Compare 13:34–35: "I am giving you a new command, that you love one another. I command you that you also should love one another as I have loved you. All will know that you are my disciples by this fact—if you have love for one another." This is uttered in the context of the announcement of his glorification (= his death 13:31) and his departure (13:33 and 36). The newness of the command lies not so much in the idea of loving one another, as in the standard of love—"as I have loved you." The love of Jesus displayed supremely in his death on the cross is our standard but equally its motivating power.[44] Of themselves, Christians cannot do this but only in

---

42. Cf. the helpful summary by Brown, *John* 2:1140–41.

43. Schnackenburg, *John* 3:117; Beasley-Murray, *John*, 274; Moloney, *John*, 424; Lincoln, *John*, 405; Theobald, *Herrenworte*, 417.

44. Bultmann, *John*, 525–27; Barrett, *John*, 452; Brown, *John* 2:613–14; Schnackenburg, *John* 3:53–54, esp. 54; Lindars, *John*, 464; Becker, *Johannesevangelium*

living union with Christ—"Abide in me and I in you . . . apart from me you cannot do anything." This mutual love within the fellowship should make its impact on the world (13:35; cf. 17:21, 23).

Another characteristic of the Christian life also flows from what Christ did for us in the cross. We have seen that the foot washing symbolized Christ's service to his own in his death, without which they have no share in him (13:1–11). This service-in-his-death becomes the model for his followers: "You call me Master and Lord; and you say well, for I am [that]. If I, then, your Lord and Teacher, have washed your feet, you ought also to wash one another's feet. For I have given you an example that you also should do as I have done to you. Truly, truly I say to you, the servant is not greater than his master nor the agent greater than his sender" (13:13–16). Humility and willingness to be the servant should characterize those who confess Jesus as Lord and Master. The task grows out of the experience of salvation given in Jesus' death on the cross.

It is highly probable that in this ethical interpretation of the foot washing we have a development of the Johannine tradition. Secondary development it may be, but there is no need to attribute it to a different author from the evangelist, or to minimize its importance for lifestyle.

Other qualities of life in Christ which emerge are:

(a) *Joy*, springing from Christ's victory in the cross (16:33) and his return from death (16:20–22) to abide with his disciples and they in him (15:11). This must be set against a background of experiencing hatred and rejection of their message, even persecution and martyrdom (see especially 15:18—16:4; 16:20–22).[45]

Only by going to the Father can Jesus in the end bestow a lasting joy (17:13; cf. 14:28b), for then the disciple can experience free access in prayer to the Father through him and know the assurance of answered prayer (16:24).

(b) *Peace*, qualitatively different from that offered by the world (14:27), is exemplified by the risen Jesus' word, which, surely, in context, is much more than just a greeting; it is a word of forgiveness (20:19, 21). Peace stems from the continuing presence of Christ with his disciples (14:23) through the Paraclete-Spirit (14:26). Again, we

---

2:450–51 (though attributing the new command to the redactor); Beasley-Murray, *John*, 246–48.

45. Onuki, *Gemeinde*, 158, speaks of a "dialectic" of tribulation from a hostile world and the already present joy of Jesus who returns continually anew to his community.

need to bear in mind the contemporary situation of the Johannine church mentioned in the previous paragraph (hostility from a Pharisaic-dominated Judaism).

(c) *Holiness* (i.e., separation from the world hostile to its creator and consecration to God's service) can only take place "in the truth" 17:17—the truth that God wills to draw us into union with himself through his Son. The disciples' consecration rests on the prior consecration of Jesus who offered himself to God in perfect service, both in life and in death (17:19). It is only as disciples are caught up in union with him—in his obedience, sacrifice, and consecration—that there is opened to them the possibility of holiness. Thus, we may say that the Christian ethic and lifestyle stem from our union with Christ established in the cross—hence the emphasis on love, humility, joy, peace, and holiness.

SUMMARY

Men and women need to believe in Jesus as God's Son and Agent for salvation. This is constantly stressed by John and statements which imply election by God or which have a universalist flavor must not be explained in such a way as to weaken this stress on faith. In the act of their faith, the Holy Spirit is at work seeking to persuade men and women to leave behind unbelief and solidarity with the world and to trust in Jesus. The Spirit effects the birth from above, which is the transition from being of the world to being in Christ. The result of this movement from the sphere ruled over by the prince of this world to the sphere in Christ means true worship based on union with Christ and the experience of eternal life (i.e., knowing Christ and, through him, the Father) now and hereafter; and being committed to love one's fellow believers and to bearing witness about Christ to the world. Believers are taught by the Paraclete-Spirit within the community of believers and know his consoling and encouraging ministry. From our union with Christ spring the obligation to serve others and the qualities of joy, peace and holiness, thus marking believers off from a hostile and unbelieving world.

PART II:

THE JOHANNINE LETTERS

7

"The Death of Jesus in the Johannine Letters" in New Testament Scholarship From Bultmann to Painter

BULTMANN, IN A CONTRIBUTION in 1927 to the *Festgabe für Adolf Julicher*, entitled "Analyse des ersten Johannesbriefes," attempted to reconstruct a source used by the author. This source was akin to the revelatory discourse source that he postulated for the Gospel. The author of 1 John modified some of the gnostic tendencies of his source either by introducing glosses into it or by the material with which he surrounded the source (e.g., 1:5–10 came from the source; vv. 7b and 9b are glosses; and 2:1–2 further comments on it). Later, in "Die kirchliche Redaktion des ersten Johannesbriefes," his contribution to the *In Memoriam Ernst Lohmeyer* volume of 1951, Bultmann refined his analysis and argued for a church redactor who edited the letter. He now attributed to a church redactor 1:7b, because it disturbed both the rhythm of the verse and the flow of thought and jarred with 1:9 (199–201) and also 2:2 (201) and 4:10b (201). Later, in his commentary, *The Johannine Epistles* (1973), he continued to attribute to the church redactor both 1:7b and 9b (20–21) as well as 2:2 and 4:10—"The concept of ἱλασμός ('expiation') which is also foreign to the Gospel, belongs to the ecclesiastical theology" (23; cf. 68).

Thus, Bultmann in the end postulated a source; the Letter using and modifying the source; and a church redaction of the Letter. All statements about the cleansing and atoning significance of Jesus' death belong to the third stage and are really untypical of Johannine thought.

In 1937, C. H. Dodd argued for a difference of authorship between Gospel and Epistles (the article was entitled "The First Epistle of John and the Fourth Gospel"), and continued to hold to that in his commentary on *The Johannine Epistles,* published in 1946. Among the arguments which he put forward was the claim that there were various points "Where the Epistle represents a theological outlook nearer than that of the Gospel to primitive, or, popular Christianity" (*Epistles*, liii). Dodd believed that the Atonement was one such point: "The statements made in the Epistle about the redemptive efficacy of the death of Christ scarcely go beyond the terms of the primitive apostolic preaching" (*Epistles*, 1iv). Dodd referred to "expiation" (2:2; 4:10), not utilised in the Gospel, while the distinctive doctrine of the Gospel—descent and lifting up to glory, releasing the life in him to dwell in believers, and drawing all into the unity of the divine love—is absent in the letter (*Epistles,* liv; cf. xxxii—xxxiii).

Subsequent discussion often referred to possible differences of emphasis in the teaching about the death of Jesus, though there was far from agreement as to whether these were as great as had been alleged by Dodd or whether they demanded different authors of Gospel and Epistles or were an original letter and glosses. Thus, Vincent Taylor in *The Atonement in New Testament Teaching.* (2nd ed., 1945), while accepting different emphases, still adhered to common authorship of Gospel and Epistles: "Must we accept the principle that theologians are to be judged by their sermons, or the view that a brilliant teacher never returns to older and more traditional beliefs?" (133).

Rudolf Schnackenburg, the seventh edition of whose commentary (1984) was translated into English and appeared in 1992, was less than happy with driving a wedge between Gospel and Epistle as Dodd had done. He felt that while the atoning effect of Christ's death might not find so marked expression in the Gospel as in 1 John 2:2; 4:10, yet John 1:29, 36, and especially the use of ὑπέρ in John 6:51; 10:11, 15; 11:50–52; 15:13; 17:19; 18:14, attested it, and he compared the use of "savior of the world" in John 4:42 and 1 John 4:14, and the thought of God's loving action for a world in need of redemption in John 3:16 and 1 John 4:9–10 (35–38). By the 5th printing (1975), according to the *Ergänzungsheit* (335), Schnackenburg had revised his opinion and now accepted that there was a different author for the letters.

Wolfgang Nauck, *Die Tradition und der Charakter des ersten Johannesbriefes* (1957), argued for an original composition used by its own author in a letter. This original composition, marked by antitheses, was baptismal instruction (47), possibly used in Syria (42–43, 165). Forgiveness (1 John 1:9), cleansing (1:7), Jesus' blood (1:7), light/darkness (1:6–7), plus that of birth from God (2:9—3:10), all confirm for Nauck a setting in baptismal instruction (47–64). We need not discuss Nauck's theory of how 1 John reached its present shape. For our purposes it is sufficient that, against Bultmann, he accepted the same author for the alleged source and the Letter, and believed that, for 1 John, Jesus' blood not only effected cleansing once for all in baptism but cleanses now (98, 116, in comment on 1:7), mediated through the Lord's Supper (176).

Ulrich B. Müller in his monograph, *Die Geschichte der Christologie in der johanneischen Gemeinde* (1975), discussed the situation behind the Epistles and specifically the differences in attitude to the death of Jesus on the part of the author and his opponents (53–68, esp. 59–65). The opponents denied the saving death of Jesus on the Cross (because they overstressed the divinity of Jesus and saw him as a heavenly being who did not know suffering and death in the sense of the early Christian idea of atonement), whereas the author asserted Jesus' saving death. For him, Jesus' sonship implies his atoning death. Death is the decisive event of Jesus' coming in the flesh (56). When the author stresses confession or faith in Jesus as Son of God, he means Jesus' divine sonship which includes his saving death. Strangely, by contrast, Klaus Wengst did not treat the theme of the meaning of Jesus' death in 1 John, in his monograph, *Häresie und Orthodoxie im Spiegel des ersten Johannesbriefs* (1976).

John L. Bogart, *Orthodox and Heretical Perfectionism in the Johannine Community as evident in the First Epistle of John* (1977), endorsed Dodd's view concerning differences of emphasis between Gospel and Epistle concerning Jesus' death. The author of 1 John sought to refute heretical notions of sinlessness by the doctrine of Christ's expiation for sin (1:7; 2:2), wishing to bring the Johannine community back into line with mainline Christian thinking about Christ's death, and so silence the heretics within the community (35, 37).

Another commentator, I. Howard Marshall, *The Epistles of John* (1978), inclined to common authorship (41), and was convinced that the atoning significance of the death of Jesus was just as firmly embedded in the Gospel (John 1:29, 36; 10:11, 15, 17–18; 11:50–52) as in the Epistle (35, 41). Raymond E. Brown's monumental commentary, *The Epistles of John* (1982), dealt with the alleged differences of interpretation of Jesus' death in the Gospel and Epistle (26, 98–99). Brown's solution is that the Fourth Gospel presents Jesus' death as a glorification and ascension (an aspect on which the "secessionists," to use Brown's term, concentrated), but it contains minor indications that the sacrificial and vicarious character of Jesus' death was known and perhaps taken for granted, referring to 1:29; 11:51–52; 10: 15. The author of 1 John exploited this vein of Johannine tradition (1:7; 3:16; 2:2; 4:10).

Pierre Bonnard's commentary, *Les Épîtres Johanniques* (1983), is rather brief, but he did reject Bultmann's position on 1:7b with the comment that it cohered with the author's central proposal—the reality of Jesus' flesh and his death—so that one could attribute its deliberate use, if not its composition, to him in his fight against the triumphal spiritualism of the false prophets (41).

The Word series commentary on *1, 2, 3 John* by Stephen S. Smalley appeared in 1984. Smalley argued that sacrificial ideas are implicit in the Gospel (1:29, 36; 3:14–16; 10:11; 11:50–52; 12:24) and that in 1 John the sacrificial description of Christ's death developed the understanding of atonement in the Fourth Gospel for those inclined to play down or even deny the reality of the cross (25–26)

Among his many contributions to Johannine studies, John Painter dealt with "The 'Opponents' in 1 John," which is now chapter 13 in *The Quest for the Messiah* (1991). He believed that the opponents one-sidedly interpreted selected themes from the Johannine tradition, and this amounted to a distortion of that tradition. He thought that they may have argued that some were by nature God's children, participating in God's "light nature" through God's seed in them and so were sinless (110; 39), while others who received the anointing of the Spirit at baptism were sinless from their initiation (59 on 1:8). The author was "sure that he could demonstrate the error of those who claimed never to have sinned because this claim runs contrary to the message of forgiveness and cleansing in the Gospel, including the GJ [Gospel of John] tradition, GJ 1:29; 13:10; 15:3; 17:17 . . . the death of Jesus Christ the righteous was to make possible the forgiveness and cleansing of the sins of everyone in the world" (56). Painter reiterated his position in his large commentary, *1, 2 and 3 John*, in the Sacra Pagina Series, 2002.

Urban C. von Wahle, *The Johannine Commandments: 1 John and the Struggle for the Johannine Tradition* (1990), argues that the opponents behind 1 John had come to believe that what was important was the receiving of the Spirit (a radical pneumatology): Jesus' ministry had prepared for this, but he was no longer of any significance—hence the Elder's reference to their "going beyond" the accepted teaching (2 John 9). He also takes λύει as the original reading of 1 John 4:3 and translates it as "do away with Jesus." Their experience of the Spirit gave them knowledge of God, rendered any guidance by teachers as unnecessary, and all ethical instructions as otiose, for they had become sinless. He believes that, given this, they attributed no significance whatsoever to the death of Jesus. By contrast, the Elder insisted on the permanent significance of Jesus, his expiatory sacrifice on the cross (1:7; 2:2; 3:5, 16; 4:10; 5:6), his words, and the need to keep the commandments (specifically, to love one another).

Martinus C. de Boer, *Johannine Perspectives on the Death of Jesus* (1996; see also his articles "Jesus the Baptizer: 1 John 5:5–8 and the Gospel of John"; and "The Death of Jesus Christ and His Coming in the Flesh (1 John 4:2)"), in what he calls the time after the third crisis in the story of the Johannine community (the first crisis was expulsion from the synagogue; the second, martyrdoms; and the third, schism), alleges that the fourth edition of the Gospel together with the Epistles sought to combat those who accepted Jesus' heavenly origin, but not the necessity or relevance of his death. De Boer takes 1 John 5:6 to be a reference to Jesus' own baptising activity (John 3:22, 26; 4:1), which Johannine Christians took as baptising with the Spirit—an ability passed on to the disciples at John 20:22. The Elder seeks to correct a kind of baptismal triumphalism on the part of the secessionists and stresses the death of Jesus, taking ideas associated with baptism and transferring them to the death of Jesus (1 John 1:6—2:2) The sacrificial death of Jesus, not his baptising activity, was of crucial significance for 1 John (219–307).

SUMMARY

Bultmann's theory of an ecclesiastical redactor does not seem to have won support in the scholarly discussion of 1 John. There is a fair unanimity that the author of 1 John held an atoning view of the death of Jesus, though scholars are divided as to whether this view marks 1 John off from the Gospel or whether he is exploiting a view already present in the Gospel.

8

The Situation Behind the Johannine Letters

(A) GENERAL BACKGROUND

W E SHALL ASSUME THAT the Letters were written after the Gospel,[1] by someone other than the author of the Gospel, though from within the same circle.[2] It has become fashionable in recent years to speak of a "Johannine School."[3] Perhaps "school" evokes a more precise image than we can actually substantiate in the case of the Gospel and Letters. "Circle"[4] raises fewer questions and is perhaps the more neutral term.

The situation behind the writing of 1 and 2 John is clearly that of a breakaway movement from the Johannine churches—some "have gone out" and they have left the congregations (2:19; 4:1), and are conducting successful propaganda for their viewpoint (4:5). For a long time scholars have assumed that those who left did so because they moved

---

1. Exceptions to this are Grayston, *Epistles,* 12–14; Strecker, *Anfänge,* 34, 37, and *Letters,* xl–xlii; Schnelle, *Antidocetic Christology,* 52–63 (Strecker and Schnelle assume the order 2, 3 and 1 John, Fourth Gospel); and Knöppler, *Sühne,* 220. Griffith, *Idols,* 209, is inclined to the priority of 1 John.

2. E.g., Dodd, *Epistles,* xlvii—lvi; Schnackenburg, *Epistles,* 38, 41 (cautiously; cf. 4:66–67); Bultmann, *Letters,* 1; Houlden, *Epistles,* 38; Brown, *Epistles,* 30, 90, 101; Smalley, *1, 2, 3 John,* xxii; Painter, *1, 2 & 3 John,* 50–51, 60–61, 69, 73–77.

3. E.g., Culpepper, *Johannine School.*

4. E.g., Cullman, *Johannine Circle*; Brown, *Epistles,* 96, and Painter, *1, 2 & 3 John,* 76, accept a Johannine school and a broader Johannine community.

in what may be called some sort of Gnostic-docetic direction[5] and set up rival congregations. [6]

It would appear that the split arose over two interrelated issues. The first was *doctrinal*: There was a difference of opinion over the person of Jesus. The writer seems to emphasize that the messiah is *Jesus* (2:22; 5:1), and that the Son of God is *Jesus* (4:15; 5:5).[7] That is, it is the human figure of Jesus of Nazareth who is at the centre of discussion. The problem is to determine *in what way* the human figure is under discussion.

At 4:2 the writer gives a confession of faith which can distinguish true from false inspiration. The former is revealed by the confession: Ἰησοῦν Χριστὸν ἐν σαρκὶ ἐληλυθότα, which poses a problem of meaning and translation, since there are four possible renderings:

(a) confess that Jesus Christ has come in the flesh.[8] This would centre on the historical fact of the coming of Jesus, but that is hardly at issue.

(b) confess Jesus Christ as come in the flesh.[9]

(c) confess Jesus Christ come in the flesh (or Jesus Christ incarnate).[10]

In sense, (b) and (c) come very close together, and both stress the mode of Jesus Christ's coming. In (c) the whole phrase is the object of "confess," whereas perhaps in (b) Jesus Christ is the object, of whom "come in the flesh" is predicated.

(d) confess Jesus as the Christ come in the flesh.[11] In favor of this is the fact that it would represent an expansion of a traditional Jo-

---

5. For discussions which see some form of Docetism involved, see Brown, *Community*, 103–44; Painter, *Opponents*, 48–71 (= *Quest*, 371–99), and also *1, 2 & 3 John*, 88–93; and U. Schnelle, *Antidocetic Christology*, 76–83.

6. For alternative suggestions as to whether there were "opponents," and, if so, what their views were, see the Excursus: "The 'Opponents' in 1 John," at the end of this chapter.

7. Cf. John 20:30–31. Brown, *Community*, 111, alleges a real difference despite the similarity in wording.

8. So Schneider, *Kirchenbriefe*, 170; Houlden, *Epistles* (translation), 104; Malatesta, *Interiority and Covenant*, 285; Smith, *First, Second, & Third John*, 98; Painter, *1, 2 & 3 John*, (translation), 253.

9. Hauck, *Kirchenbriefe*, 139–40; Marshall, *Epistles*, 205; Schnackenburg, *Epistles*, 221.

10. Brown, *Epistles*, 493; Smalley, *1, 2, 3 John*, 222; Griffith, *Idols*, 186–87.

11. Law, *Tests*, 94; Dodd, *Epistles*, 96, 99; Houlden, *Epistles*, 106 (Comment); Lieu, *Authority*, 217; Painter, *1, 2 & 3 John*, 260 (Comment); Griffith, *Idols*, 186–87.

hannine confession "The Messiah is Jesus,"[12] in order to face a new and critical situation in the life of the churches. Against it from a grammatical point of view is that there ought to be a τὸν after Χριστὸν,[13] though New Testament writers ought not to be judged too strictly on this score, and exceptions to the need of an article before a participle or prepositional phrase exist. In response to the argument that the author uses "Jesus Christ" at 1:3; 2:1; 3:13; 5:6, 20, it could be maintained that these are, in fact, all other instances apart from the actual quotation of a traditional Johannine confession as at 2:22; 5:1; plus our passage. Thus, it could be that the author naturally used Jesus Christ except where he was quoting or modifying traditional material. Our decision on 4:2 may well rest, therefore, on whether we think that he is quoting traditional material or not. The use of ὁμολογεῖν favors the view that he is and just tilts the scales in favor of (d).

So, 4:2 confirms the impression left by 2:22; 5:1; and 4:15; 5:5 that the human figure of Jesus was under discussion. Actually, whichever translation of b–d we adopt, there is a stress on what we call the incarnation. Either there appear to be some who deny that a true incarnation took place, or there is a denial that there was a pre-existent Son of God who became incarnate as the man Jesus. In respect of the former possibility, the problem is now to determine what form the denial took. Was it a position that downplayed the humanity and overstressed the divinity of Jesus? Or was it a position that envisaged a divine being descending on a human figure and leaving him at the crucifixion? In respect of the second possibility, we would have a situation akin to that reflected in the Fourth Gospel where "the Jews" reject the claims of Jesus to be the divine Son of God come down to earth from God, from heaven, from above. Clearly, there is a considerable difference between these two interpretations of the evidence. We have accepted that the former is probably the more correct interpretation, but, in order not to hold up the flow of the discussion, we refer the reader to the excursus to this chapter for a more detailed discussion of the arguments.

What form, then, did the denial of the incarnation take? It is impossible to equate the views apparently reflected in 1 and 2 John with

12. So Neufeld, *Earliest Christian Confessions,* 71, 103–4, 106–7; more recently, Klauck, *Der erste Johannesbrief,* 233.

13. Cf. *BDF,* paras. 272, 412–13.

any known "heresy" from other sources for the second century[14] (e.g., the opponents of Ignatius of Antioch; or Cerinthus).[15] The reconstructed "identikit" does not fit with other deviant forms of Christianity known to us from roughly the same period or slightly later. In any case, it is methodologically more proper to start with the text rather than seeking some model outside of the text and imposing it upon the text.

In the eyes of the Elder, the doctrinal views of those who have withdrawn amount to a denial of the Son, a corollary of which is that they have no access to the Father (2:22–23) and that they, therefore, have forfeited life (5:11–12). For Johannine Christianity, it was absolutely vital that the Word/Son of God who was with the Father in the beginning had become flesh: he had entered the earthly, transitory realm and shared our human nature. The revelation of the unseen God and the salvation intended by him had been worked out in the flesh, in this world. Any lessening of this stress would be damaging to the very fabric of the Christian faith as understood in Johannine circles. Thus, any wrong approach in respect of the person of Christ would adversely affect the understanding of God. Christology and theology were inextricably linked together. To deny that the divine became incarnate in Jesus of Nazareth was, therefore, to undermine one's confidence in the truth of the revelation and salvation proclaimed in the Johannine gospel.

Within a certain intellectual milieu in the Graeco-Roman world which so emphasized the transcendence of the divine over against this world of time and space and flesh and blood, and which would find it difficult to see any sort of real union between "flesh" and "spirit," it is easy to imagine that some would find it difficult to accept a revelation of the divine "in the flesh." It might seem to them crude and absurd and impossible to associate the divine too strongly with the flesh. If some such had become members of the Johannine congregations and reflected on the emphasis that the Word was with God in the beginning, they might well accept a revelation through this Word/Son within the earthly sphere without, however, accepting the full Johannine doctrine of the incarnation. They might well argue that they had access to the Father.

14. So Schnackenburg, *Epistles*, 21–23; Brown, *Epistles*, 67.

15. Wengst, *Häresie und Orthodoxie*, 34, however, does see a close connection between the opponents in 1 John and Cerinthus, though they represent a tendency that Cerinthus expressly stated. Schnelle, *Antidocetic Christology*, 63–70, esp. 68, stresses the opponents' Docetism and their kinship with the teaching combated by Ignatius and Polycarp, but not with Cerinthus.

However, for the Elder access to the Father only came through the one who had come from the Father and had "become flesh." Thus, at 2:22–23 the phrase "the Son" must be taken in the sense which the Elder read into it and which would be so understood by those who still remained in the Johannine congregations, i.e., the pre-existent, incarnate, lifted up on a cross, and glorified Christ. Since the prime purpose of 1 John is a pastoral one rather than specifically to combat the opponents who had left the Johannine churches (we would expect more material and more detail if the latter purpose were the case), the Elder did not feel it incumbent upon him to spell out in detail all the arguments which had no doubt previously been thrashed out in discussion and debate and he felt content to use abbreviated references which would be picked up by the addressees.

Can 5:6 help us with its stress that Jesus Christ came by water and blood (and not just by water)? This obscure verse has been the subject of considerable discussion and any case which rested on it would run the risk of building on sand. We will anticipate our discussion of it in chapter 9 and state our conviction that it is probably a mistake to read a Cerinthian type Gnosticism behind this verse. It seems to stress that Jesus Christ was a real and genuine human being. If this is correct, it helps to reinforce the picture that has already emerged, and would suggest that the form which the denial of the incarnation took was some form of Docetism (without there being identity with Ignatius' opponents, as stated above).

The second cause of division was what we can call *ethical or behavioral.* The Elder levels some general charges against those who have withdrawn—they walk in the darkness (1:6), and they do not keep God's commands (2:4). In the end, the specific charge, reiterated in many passages, is that of hating the brothers (2:9, 11; 3:10; 4:19–21). Here we need to decode the language. In Semitic modes of expression, anything less than total love and commitment is "hate." So, behind the charge of hating the brothers is something less than showing them the love that should be shown to them (e.g., a practical example is given at 3:17–18—withholding help from someone in economic need). There may well have been a certain spiritual pride and a claim to possess greater knowledge than some of their fellow members (2:20–21, 26–27) and probably a claim that sin was no longer relevant in their lives (1:8, 10).[16] It is, of course,

16. While it is obviously true that faithful members of the Johannine congregations

possible that those who had withdrawn loved their own number and saw this as fulfilling Jesus' new command.[17]

There is currently a dispute as to whether those who had withdrawn arrived at their position and outlook either by pushing the insights, now contained for us in the Fourth Gospel, to extremes, and thus allowed the "divinity" of Christ to overshadow or swallow up his humanity, without holding on to the safeguards discernible in the Fourth Gospel; and they so interpreted the Johannine idea of spheres that abiding in Christ led to perfection;[18] or by taking some alien ideas (e.g., Gnostic ones) into the Johannine system.[19] We need not be drawn into this issue here (either view has to face the issue of "Gnostic" influence on the Fourth Gospel itself prior to the writing of the Epistles). Suffice to say that both the Elder and apparently those who had withdrawn claimed a perfectionism and this is one of the puzzles of the letter.[20] How can the Elder berate those who claimed to have no sin (1:8, 10), while at the same time claim that those born of God not only do not sin (3:6; 5:18) but cannot sin because God's seed abides in them (3:9)? Some sort of perfectionist teaching (however we explain it) formed part of instruction in the Johannine congregations—otherwise 3:6, 9, and 5:18 are inexplicable, and this seems confirmed by the οἴδαμεν ὅτι of 5:18. What is equally certain is that the form of this teaching as promulgated by those who

are being addressed in 1:6, 8, 10, as de la Potterie, *Vérité*, 2:907, 949–51, emphasises, it is equally probable that the author is exhorting them not to take up similar behaviour to that of the heretics (as de la Potterie, *Vérité* 2:907, acknowledges); cf. Brown, *Epistles*, 197, 225, 232, 238, 241–41. See Griffith, *Idols*, 116–24, for a denial that slogans of the secessionists are being quoted in 1:6—2:2 and for arguments that these statements fit in with a community debate over how to deal with sin within the community.

17. Cf. Lieu, *Authority*, 227 (note 40). Brown, *Epistles*, 273, also holds this to be a probability.

18. See especially Brown, *Community*, 106–20, esp. 106–7; Lieu, *Authority*, 225; Klauck, *Internal Opponents*, 58.

19. Bogart, *Perfectionism*, 135, believes that some Johannine Christians became gnostics and accepted views alien to the Fourth Gospel. Painter, *Opponents*, 49 (= *Quest*, 372) argues that the opponents were Gentile Christians who interpreted the Fourth Gospel not from within the conflict with Judaism but from their own Gentile background.

20. For discussions see Bogart, *Perfectionism*, and Griffith, *Idols*, 128–42 (Griffith maintains that in 3:4–10 sin is defined as lawlessness, i.e., the ultimate iniquity or rebellion characteristic of the End time, and insofar as Christians have been born of God they cannot commit that sin. It is also in respect of that sin of rebellion or apostasy that the writer forbids intercession in 5:16–20).

had withdrawn was unacceptable to the Elder (hence 1:8, 10). It may be that light will be shed on this by our study.

The issue of perfectionism itself raises the question of how sin was perceived in the mind of the Elder, and to that we now turn.

(B) THE TEACHING ON SIN

The same mode of thinking in terms of spheres of influence/power is characteristic of the Elder's writings as of the Gospel. We meet the light/ darkness, truth/falsehood, not of this world/of the world, life/death antitheses. We also meet a two spirits antithesis (4:6), but not so much a flesh/spirit contrast, probably because this would have played into the hands of his opponents,[21] and the Elder wished to affirm that Jesus was the Christ come in the flesh (4:2; 2 John 7).

We meet two of the three terms used in the Gospel for a personal agent of evil opposed to God. There is one reference to *the devil*. It is said in 3:8 that the sinner is "of the devil," because the devil sinned from the beginning. This statement is not elaborated and so we are left wondering what is the precise significance of ἀπ ἀρχῆς in this verse. Presumably, it is a reference to the idea of a pre-cosmic fall so that when the world began, the devil was already set on his course of opposition to God.[22] Throughout history he has built up his family that is distinguishable from the family of God precisely on this issue of sin (3:10). The devil has his children, then, with their distinctive characteristics.

The second term used is *the evil one*. An individual may be a child of the evil one and serve his ends. This is said of Cain who killed his brother, Abel. Cain's deeds were evil (πονηρὰ) and thus he showed his parentage (3:12). The evil one's efforts have been so successful that the Elder can say, "The whole world lies [in the grip of] the evil one" (5:19). However, there is one mightier than he, and God or Christ[23] is able to keep and preserve God's children from the attacks of the evil one (5:18b).

21. Cf. e.g., Painter, *Opponents*, 53 (= *Quest*, 377).

22. Houlden *Epistles*, 95; Smalley, *1, 2, 3 John*, 169; Marianne Thompson, *1–3 John*, 95; but Schnackenburg, *Epistles*, 174; and Brown, *Epistles*, 406, think of the events of Gen 1–4 (cf. Strecker, *Letters*, 100). Painter, *1, 2 & 3 John*, 229, also thinks that Genesis may be in mind (relying on John 8:44).

23. See Brown, *Epistles*, 620–22, for a full discussion of the various options for understanding ὁ γεννηθεὶς τοῦ Θεοῦ. Ultimately, it is divine help and aid that is in mind.

It is because of this protecting power that the Elder can write, rejoicing, to the "young men" of the churches because they have overcome the evil one (2:13–14). They are strong in the strength of Christ, and God's word abides in them (2:14).

There is no use of the phrase "the ruler of the world" (as in the Gospel), though we do meet the phrase "Greater is he who is in you than he who is in the world" (4:4), which is akin to it in sense.

The corporate dimension of sin is amply attested, as we have said, in 1 John. The world hates the followers of Jesus (3:13), and it does not understand or recognize what they truly are (namely, children of God, 3:1). Believers are warned not to love the world and its ways, its lifestyle and its attitude, for such love would conflict with their love for their Father (2:15). There follows a very negative evaluation of the world: "For everything that is in the world, the desire of the flesh, what the eye desires, pride in possessions, does not belong to the Father but belongs to the world, and the world and its desire(s) are passing away, but the one who does God's will remains forever" (vv. 16–17). This accords with the verdict of 5:19 quoted above. At the same time, readers are reminded of God's love for the world in sending his Son and of Jesus' atoning death for the sins of the world (4:9–10, 14; 2:1–2).

Alongside the expression "the world," we meet the use of the darkness-light contrast. There is no darkness in God; so, living in a way opposite to God's character may be described as walking in the darkness (1:5–6; 2:11). Darkness is personified in 2:11 in the statement: "the darkness has blinded his [i.e., the one who hates his brother] eyes."[24]

No doubt, style has determined the expression here and we could read devil or evil one for the sense.

Three facets of the understanding of sin in 1 John will now be mentioned, two occurring in formal definitions of sin. Firstly, "Everyone who commits sin also does lawlessness, for the sense of (καὶ) sin is lawlessness" (ἡ ἀνομία, 3:4). The term ἀνομία is intriguing, because there is certainly no conflict over the Mosaic Law reflected in the letter. It perhaps reflects the Jewish tradition within the Johannine churches.

---

24. We note that whereas in John 12:40 God is said to have blinded the eyes of the Jews (τετύφλωκεν in the Isa 6:9 quotation), here in 1 John it is the power of darkness, probably a sign of what Judith Lieu called an independent exegesis of Isa 6 within the Johannine tradition: *Blindness*, 91.

The normal usage of the Septuagint, in which ἀνομία is practically synonymous with ἁμαρτία,[25] would be inappropriate here, as the writer would then be guilty of tautology.[26] In early Judaism, ἀνομία can designate the hostility and revolt of the forces of evil against the kingdom of God—satanic power under whose influence sinful acts are committed,[27] a sense also present in the New Testament (2 Thess 2:3; Matt 7:23; 13:41; 24:12; cf. W reading of Mark 16:14) and Apostolic Fathers (*Did.* 16:3–4; *Barn.* 4:1–4; 18:1). As the devil is mentioned soon after 1 John 3:4 at 3:8 and the children of the devil at 3:10, there is good reason to suppose that this may be the sense of ἀνομία here.

Supremely, in this letter, the will and command of God is to believe in his Son, Jesus Christ, and to love one another (3:13). In the writer's eyes, those who have broken away do not observe this command, and belong, therefore, to the children of the devil and so are guilty of ἀνομία. They are setting at nought God's revealed will and are part of Satan's dominion.[28] They embody the spirit of anti-Christ, the godless figure expected at the end (2:18; 4:3). By his choice of ἀνομία the writer could well have wanted to show the readers the eschatological significance of the sin of unbelief as satanic power.[29]

Secondly, "All unrighteousness is sin" (5:17). We shall be considering the paragraph 5:16–17 later; here we extrapolate the formal statement in which ἀδικία is described as sin. Again, one suspects that the choice of terms reflects Jewish background. Previously in the letter, God has been described as δίκαιος (1:9), and also Jesus (2:1, 29). Jesus has revealed what is right in God's sight. Any deviation from this is unrighteousness and, therefore, sin. Those who have withdrawn from the congregation ignore what God has shown in His Son and so are guilty of

25. Schnackenburg, *Epistles*, 170–72; Brown, *Epistles*, 399; Smalley, *1, 2, 3 John*, 154; Painter, *1, 2 & 3 John*, 222; de la Potterie, *Péché*, 68; Dodd, *Bible and the Greeks*, 79–80.

26. Cf. Brown, *Epistles*, 399; de la Potterie, *Péché*, 74.

27. Schnackenburg, *Epistles*, 171; Brown, *Epistles*, 399–400; Strecker, *Letters*, 94; de la Potterie, *Péché*, 69–71; Griffith, *Idols*, 136–38.

28. Schnackenburg, *Epistles*, 171; Brown, *Epistles*, 400; Marshall, *Epistles*, 176–77; Smalley, *1, 2, 3 John*, 155. Cf. W. Gutbrod, νόμος, *TDNT* 4:1086; de la Potterie, *Péché*, 78–79; Nauck, *Tradition*, 16 (note 1).

29. Smith, *First John*, 83; Strecker, *Letters*, 94–95; de la Potterie, *Péché*, 83; Griffith, *Idols*, 142.

ἀδικία and sin. Though intercession is possible for some sins, wrongdoing is still serious and the writer wishes to stress this.[30]

Thirdly, we mention the idea of sin as falsehood. The truth-false-
hood antithesis runs through the epistle. We could say that it has both a
doctrinal and moral/ethical aspect. On the doctrinal side, anyone who
denies that the Messiah is Jesus is branded as the liar (ὁ ψεύστης) and
indeed the antichrist (2:22). Those who deny the reality of the incarnation are branded as false prophets and again also as antichrists (4:1–3).
Not to receive the witness which God has given to His Son (the writer
does not say when or in what form this witness occurred) is equivalent to
declaring God to be a liar (5:10) and incurs the disastrous consequences
of such a step—forfeiting life (5:11–12).

As to the moral/ethical side, the author seems to pick up or rebut certain claims made (presumably) by those who had withdrawn.[31]
These claims centre on knowing God (1:6) and not having sin (1:8, 10).
These claims prove false because those who make them are walking "in
darkness" (whereas God is light, 1:5) and do not, therefore, behave in
a manner commensurate with the claim (they "lie and do not do the
truth," 1:6). To claim not to have sinned is to be guilty of not only self-
deception but also in effect making God a liar (a self-evident impossibility), for God has declared men and women to be sinners in need of
being saved (1:8, 10).

A similar argument occurs at 2:4: "The one who says 'I know him'
but does not keep his commands is a liar and the truth is not in him."
Again, at 4:20, we read "If anyone says 'I love God' but hates his brother,
he is a liar." Conduct which breaks the new command renders false a
claim to love the God whose Son gave the command.

Arguably, the two sides of falsehood are related, since those who
have withdrawn deny (in the writer's eyes) the incarnation (4:2) and
possibly the death of Jesus (if 5:6 is to be taken in this way),[32] both

30. Schnackenburg, *Epistles*, 251–52: "He does not want to belittle failure to keep
the commandments"; cf. Brown, *Epistles*, 619; Griffith, *Idols*, 115.

31. Even if the rhetorical interpretation of 1:6—2:2 were correct and the statements
in 1:6–10 and 2:4–9 reflect discussion within the community about how to deal with sin
(see especially Griffith, *Idols*, 116–24), this would not alter the sense of what is actually
said about sin.

32. See chapter 9, subsection 6, for a full discussion of 5:6. If 5:6 is taken to refer to
the incarnation, then it would be a logical conclusion that the opponents denied both
the reality of and any saving significance of Jesus' death.

of which are the grounds for asserting that God is love (the incarnation—4:9–10; the death—3:16), an assertion which is itself the basis for demanding love to others ("Beloved, if God so loved us, we also ought to love one another," 4:11). It is this command, which, above all else, those who withdrew seem guilty of ignoring. So, the doctrinal and the ethical aspects of falsehood flow into and merge with each other.[33]

Other aspects of sin receive mention. The universality of sin is clearly assumed. To deny that one has sin is ruled out of court: if this claim, made by those who believe themselves to be "born" into a perfect existence, is denied, then it is clear *a fortiori* that pre-Christian existence must be sinful! Jesus Christ has in fact died for the sins of the whole world (2:2). If what Jesus has done has cleansing consequences (1:7), then clearly the writer is using a model that envisages sin as something defiling, tainting, rendering unclean (cf. 1:9 with its assertion that Jesus' blood cleanses us from all unrighteousness). In a verse reminiscent of John 5:24, we read in 3:14: "We know that we have passed from death to life because we love the brothers; the one who does not love remains in death." The phrase οἴδαμεν ὅτι confirms that the writer is reproducing well-known and accepted teaching. Sin is a feature of the sphere of death: the two go together.

Here is the place to consider the paragraph 5:16–17, deferred earlier. We meet here a gradation of sins: a distinction between a sin that leads to death and a sin that does not necessarily lead to death. Actually, the writer does not say what he has in mind in describing a certain kind of sin as a sin leading to death. His readers presumably knew what was intended. We are left in the dark, though it seems a reasonable assumption that those guilty of the sin leading to death are those who have embraced the false teaching and have denied the reality of the incarnation and the importance of the atoning death of Jesus and have withdrawn from fellowship with the Johannine Christians who were still loyal to the writer's proclamation, in short, are guilty of apostasy in the eyes of the author.[34]

---

33. Cf. Caird, "Letters of John," *IBD*, Vol. E–J, 949: "The intellectual and the moral belief in the incarnation and obedience to the commandment of love, are obverse and reverse of one coin"; Whitacre, *Johannine Polemic*, 141 "Their belief and behaviour are inseparably intertwined"; cf. Brown, *Epistles*, 368, 602. Griffith, *Idols*, 141–42, refers to the theological aspect and the sociological dimension of the apostasy.

34. So Dodd, *Epistles*, 136; Schneider, *Kirchenbriefe*, 186; Houlden, *Epistles*, 136; Brown, *Epistles*, 617–18; Smith, *First John*, 135 ("quite conceivably"); Painter, *1, 2, & 3*

The writer bans intercession for those guilty of such a sin leading to death—such prayer will not avail. The distinction envisaged (reminiscent of the Old Testament distinction between sins committed in ignorance and sins committed willfully and deliberately, "with a high hand")[35] grades sin according to a standard of seriousness, and this forces us to ask whether the writer has embarked on the first step of an ethical casuistry that could potentially have disastrous effects.

EXCURSUS: THE "OPPONENTS" IN 1 JOHN

For a long while, scholars have assumed that those who had left the Johannine congregations had moved in a Gnostic-Docetic direction and denied the relevance of sin in their lives together with the atoning significance of the death of Jesus. The case was built up as follows. Firstly, it was assumed that the secessionists were the ones who denied that Jesus was the messiah or Son of God, and that it was against them that the author affirmed that Jesus was the messiah come in the flesh (4:2). It was also assumed by many that they had a slogan "He came by water" (5:6), meaning that the divine Christ or Logos or Spirit descended on the human Jesus at his baptism and left him at or before the crucifixion. Against this view, the author maintained that Jesus came by water and blood, i.e., the author asserted the unity of the person of Jesus from his baptism in the river Jordan to the death on the cross.

Secondly, it was assumed that in 1:6—2:2; 2:6–11; 4:20, the author quoted slogans of the secessionists (in order to rebut them). They denied that they had sinned and claimed to know and love God and to walk in the light. The author brands them as guilty of "hating" their fellow Christians (e.g., 4:7–21) and being indifferent to their material needs (3:17).

John, 317–19; Wilckens, *Sohn Gottes*, 142. Marshall, *Epistles*, 247, and Smalley, *1, 2, 3 John*, 298, go more generally for behavior incompatible with being a child of God, while Schnackenburg, *Epistles*, 251, says that we cannot be sure that the author meant those who fall away into false teaching. Griffith, *Idols*, 143–46 takes "the sin unto death" as apostasy which puts one beyond the atonement achieved by Jesus and leads to spiritual death, and the "sin not unto death" as sins which break but do not destroy fellowship with God and with Christian believers and which can be forgiven by the atoning blood of Jesus (1:6—2:2).

35. Hauck, *Kirchenbriefe*, 152; Schneider, *Kirchenbriefe*, 186; Marshall, *Epistles*, 247; Smalley, *1, 2, 3 John*, 297–98; Smith, *First John*, 134; Strecker, *Letters*, 1, 2–3; Painter, *1, 2 & 3 John*, 319; Nauck, *Tradition*, 144–45.

Thirdly, they had left the congregation(s) and were gaining a hearing in the world outside the congregation(s) (2:19; 4:1, 5).

Over a number of years, there has been a growing number of dissentient voices directed against this "consensus" view, beginning with Pheme Perkins,[36] and including Judith M. Lieu,[37] and Ruth B. Edwards.[38] Both Perkins and Edwards considered that the rhetorical style of the author, who used antithetical and dualistic language together with abusive polemic, did not permit direct inferences about the precise historical situation in his congregations. Lieu contended that the opponents were not the main concern of the author at all, as shown by his failure to give a clear picture of their views and a detailed rebuttal of them and the fact that assurance of the readers is the main concern, while the moral debate is not explicitly related to those who had seceded. But it is T. M. Griffith[39] (himself a doctoral student of Professor Lieu), and H. Schmid,[40] who recently have worked out in most detail the alternative case,[41] while among others U. Wilckens has also rejected the "Gnostic" case in an important study on the opponents in 1 John, the Gospel of John and the letters of the Apocalypse.[42]

We shall make some general comments on the attempts to play down the importance of "opponents," then briefly consider the views of Griffith, K. Erlemann, Wilckens (all three of whom postulate a return to the Synagogue by disillusioned Jewish Christians) and Schmid, and offer comments on them, and, finally, turn to look at the suggestions of E. Stegemann and M. J. Edwards, who maintain a persecution setting behind 1 John.

To accept the reality of a recent secession does not mean that one sees the purpose of 1 John only in terms of rebutting opponents. That would be over-simplistic. We may agree that study of 1 John should not

36. Perkins, *Johannine Epistles*.

37. Lieu, *Authority*, 210–28; reiterated in *Theology*, esp. 12–16

38. Edwards, *Epistles*, esp. 64–67.

39. Griffith, *Idols*.

40. Schmid, *Gegner im 1. Johannesbrief?*

41. D. Neufeld, *Reconceiving Texts as Speech-Acts*, was not available to me. Apparently he argues that the purpose of 1 John is to transform the readers' expectations, speech and conduct, and the words of the text do not simply describe the author's or community's theological position, but enact belief (so the brief summary of Neufeld by Edwards, *Epistles*, 65).

42. Wilckens, *Gegner*.

be wholly dominated by the question of opponents and who they were.[43] Pastoral care, in terms of giving assurance and encouragement, is quite clearly also a major concern of the writer. Painter is surely right when he asserts, "Assurance of the believers and polemic against the views of the opponents are thus two strands running through 1 John."[44] It is not a question of either-or but of both-and.

We may readily accept that the secessionists are typified as apostates and all that the faithful Johannine Christians ought not to be. That fits in with Johannine dualism. Just as in the Gospel, Judas is an example of one who passes from the light into the darkness (e.g., John 13:30), so that would be true in a sense of the secessionists, except that the author of 1 John sees them as having been a "foreign body" within the Johannine congregations all along. In fact, the author of 1 John has written them off—they never really belonged, but were masquerading under false pretences within the true children of God (2:19).

On another issue, we may agree completely that the opponents are not clearly profiled. But that is not necessarily so unusual. We may think of how difficult it is to make out exactly what some of Paul's opponents believed—e.g., those mentioned in 2 Corinthians or Philippians. Furthermore, if either of these two letters was a unity as they now stand— and this is, of course, hotly disputed—then Paul did not launch into an attack until well into his letter! Rather than a lot of detail, the rhetoric of opponent "bashing" in ancient times could be very ferocious, as we know from the Qumran writings, and that is the case in 1 John—the secessionists are branded as "antichrists," "false prophets," "liars" and "children of the devil."

The fact that the secessionists are only specifically mentioned at 2:18–27 and 4:1–6 need not occasion all that much surprise. The major concern of the author of 1 John is with the congregation who remain. But that does not mean that the secessionists had not left behind them a potentially dangerous legacy.[45] Their ideas could not be waved away as with a magic wand. Those ideas could live on and still exercise a powerful influence. Part of the author's aim could, therefore, have been to get in some criticism of their views, even if not a point-by-point rebuttal.

43. Schmid, *Gegner*, 21.

44. Painter, *1, 2 & 3John*, 86.

45. Lieu, *Authority*, seems to ignore this possibility in her constant stress on the writer's concern to give assurance to the readers.

We turn now specifically to look at the views of the two authors previously mentioned. Griffith argues, firstly, that the phrases "If we say that" and "The person who says [that]" are to be found in secular philosophical school debates in discussions on ethical questions. Here, in 1 John, they introduce debates within the Johannine congregations about ethical conduct and how Christians stand in relation to sinful behavior.[46] They are in no way the slogans of the secessionists. (Incidentally, Strecker, who believed that the secessionists were Docetists, nonetheless accepted that they were not in mind in 1:6—2:11).[47]

Secondly, Griffith maintained that 2:22 is crystal clear and must control the discussion rather than the more obscure 4:1-3 and 5:6-8. What is said at 2:22 points to a denial that the messiah is Jesus[48] (cf. 4:15 and 5:1, where it is affirmed that the Son of God is Jesus). Griffith argues that the secessionists were Jewish Christians who were going back on their confession of faith in Jesus and had returned to the synagogue (he sees 5:20-21 as a highly effective rhetorical ending, with "idols" being used metaphorically and polemically for Judaism, akin to the no-holds-barred polemic of Qumran against fellow Jews).

He takes at 4:2 to be a way of saying that Jesus appeared in the sphere in which humanity lives (interpreting 4:3 as an abbreviation of this phrase and rejecting the variant reading λύει at 4:3). In support of this, he quotes the occurrence of an identical or very similar phrase in non-polemical contexts in the Letter of Barnabas 5:6-7, 10-11; the Testament of Benjamin 10:7-8 (a Christian interpolation); together with the long recension of Ignatius Smyrneans 6:1 and the Letter to Diognetus 5:8-9; 6:3; and even the Gospel of Thomas 28.

As for 5:6-8, the opponents are not mentioned at all (unlike at 4:1-6) and they are not in mind. The grammatical construction οὐ μόνον . . .

46. See Griffith, *Idols*, 119, 175-76, 185, for those scholars who had previously taken the moral discussions in 1 John as arising from the community's own concerns rather than from a schism, and/or queried the "Gnostic/ heretical" approach.

47. Strecker, *Letters*, 28-29, 33-34.

48. Griffith, *Idols*, 170-9, argues for a translation of Ἰησοῦς οὐκ ἔστιν ὁ Χριστός as "[denies] that the messiah is Jesus," on the grounds that ὁ Χριστός is the subject and the anarthous Ἰησοῦς is the predicate, the article having been dropped because Ἰησοῦς is placed before the verb. Curiously, this translation does not occur in modern translations and is not even discussed in the commentaries that I have consulted, despite the grammatical grounds for its justification (*BDF*. para. 429 discuss the presence of the negative and point out its redundancy by the canons of English, German, etc.). Is this a case of the Gnostic-Docetic theory dominating translation?

ἀλλά makes the emphasis fall on the last item, namely the blood = the death of Jesus. The author, in other words, stresses the death of Jesus.

There is no doubt that Griffith has presented his case very ably. In the end, like Agrippa in Acts 26:28, I am nearly persuaded, but certain things hold me back. In the first place, the ethical debate within the community could have been one in which—at the very least—the secessionists had participated, or indeed, could have sparked off. I do not think that in the end it is sufficient to say that the Johannine system itself with its black and white approach—abiding in Christ or not, not of the world or of it, from above or below—would engender such a debate without the kind of opponents hypothesized. (The same could be said, for example, of Paul's teaching on dying with Christ through faith union with Christ and baptism and rising to a new life alive to God in Christ, and indeed it did provoke the charge that his teaching encouraged sin, as Rom 6:1 shows.) In the end, someone raises the issue in their own mind and by their own behavior. Can we in the case of 1 John exclude the erstwhile members of the community from the debate?

Secondly, even if 2:22 is crystal clear,[49] it remains to be asked why add "come in the flesh" at 4:2, if those branded as antichrists and false prophets were objecting (on Griffith's view) to the high Christology of Johannine Christianity? They did not deny that the man Jesus was part of the human scene. In this sense, John 6:41, 52 reveal all too clearly the sticking point for people in a Jewish milieu. How could the son of Joseph and Mary be the bread of heaven come to earth? How could a human being offer his flesh to eat? Jewish Christians objecting to the Johannine high Christology would not dispute the manhood or humanity of Jesus. It was the "divinity" of Jesus which, it is alleged, was putting them off.

Thirdly, as to 5:6, why does the author throw the emphasis on to the blood = the death of Jesus? Are we being asked to envisage Jewish Christians who once had confessed Jesus crucified and risen, now reneging on that acceptance and repudiating the cross as the saving event? What then made them "reinstate" the cross as a stumbling block when once they had overcome it? Did objecting to a "high" Christology carry with it a complete denial of any saving efficacy of Jesus' death? Certainly, there is in 1 John itself no hint of persecution, which might

---

49. The use of ἀντίχριστος in 2:22 may have been influenced by the "antichrist" motif in the context (so Brown, *Epistles*, 353, and Schmid, *Gegner*, 113).

have browbeaten or compelled people to change their views (although John 15:18—16:4a forecasts such).

In the end, while acknowledging the skill with which the new view has been presented by Griffith, my verdict remains "not proven." We will now mention the view of K. Erlemann,[50] which in some respects is not far from that of Griffith. Erlemann believes that 1 John preceded the Gospel, reflecting a situation before the separation from the Synagogue had taken place. 1 John is in fact a witness to a stage in that process, when two rival groups disputed over the correct theological evaluation of Jesus of Nazareth (286). The author of 1 John formulates a binding christological confession and maintains the completed messianic work of Jesus, even if Christians continue to sin (288–89). Those attacked had withdrawn because they felt that the sinfulness of Christians belied the claim that Jesus was the promised messiah. The conflict in 1 John is one within a common Jewish–Jewish Christian sphere (294, 301), and for the author the opponents have returned back to their pre–conversion position and conformed to the mainstream Jewish position (295, 301). There is no need for us to repeat our arguments against Griffith's position.

Wilckens has also proposed abandoning the idea that the secessionists of 1 John were Docetists/Cerinthian Gnostics.[51] Those who had left the Johannine congregations felt that the Johannine confession of Jesus as Son of God damaged "the divinity of God" and broke the first commandment of the Decalogue. There is no one beside God, not even a Son.

Before considering his arguments, we might point out that while Wilckens expresses criticism of reconstructions of phases in the history of Johannine Christianity on the basis of literary-critical hypotheses of different layers within the Fourth Gospel (sometimes with alleged theological differences and tensions), he himself by implication has postulated a reaction by Johannine Jewish Christians to a development in Christology, presumably from a belief in Jesus as messiah within traditional Jewish categories of a human figure, to a belief in Jesus as the incarnation of the pre-existent Word/Son, who descended to earth, lived among us and then returned to the Father. This was seen by the Synagogue

---

50. Erlemann, *Trennungsprozess*.

51. Wilckens mentions with approval the works of Wurm, *Irrlehrer;* Thyen, *Johannesbriefe*, 186–200; Berger, *Implizierten Gegner,* 373–400, but does not mention any of the works of English speaking scholars mentioned in our survey.

authorities as a threat to Jewish monotheism (see John 5:18; 10:33–36; 19:7) and their arguments unsettled and persuaded some members of the Johannine congregations to leave and return to the Synagogue.

We may raise certain questions. Firstly, were these ex-Johannine Christians unaware of the "high" Christology of the Johannine congregations before they joined, or were they members before the "high" Christology was worked out and objected to this "development"? Secondly, how soon/late did this "high" Christology emerge? After all, Paul was probably teaching the pre-existence of Christ at least as early as the fifties (e.g., 1 Cor 8:6; 2 Cor 8:9; Rom 10:6), while if Phil 2:6–11 is at base a non-Pauline hymn used by Paul, then other thinkers were also using the pre-existence category. The Letter to the Hebrews (assuming its composition to be before 70 AD) would be another example of an early theologian using the pre-existence idea in his Christology (1:1–3; 10:5). There is *a priori* no need to assume necessarily a date late in the first century for the development of a "high" Christology within Johannine circles. This is not to argue for an early date for John's Gospel, merely to point out that Wilckens' assumptions need to be tested.

Wilckens sees John 6:60–71 as relevant to the discussion. He points out that some disciples in 6:60, 66 react to Jesus' claims in a way similar to the Jews of 6:41–42. The existing members of the Johannine churches should see in Peter's confession their own confession adumbrated. While one could easily see how the story could be so used, nevertheless the title "Holy One of God" does not of itself point to pre-existence with the Father, although of course at 10:36 Jesus speaks of the Father's consecrating him (ἡγίασεν) and sending him into the world. One might have expected something akin to the confession of Martha at 11:27, especially in the light of 20:30–31 and the overall stress on Sonship throughout the Gospel.

Basically, Wilckens puts forward two major arguments. Firstly, he maintains that 1 John 2:23 is an inappropriate argument if it were directed against a Cerinthian type Docetism, for Docetists could agree that to deny the Son involved not having the Father.[52] To this we may respond as follows. In 2:22 it is said that the liar is whoever denies that Jesus is the Christ. The one who denies the Father and the Son is in

---

52. Wilckens quotes with approval the comment of Thyen (*Johannesbriefe*, 194) that Gnostics would scarcely dispute the Sonship of Jesus for the sake of the truth of the confession of God.

reality in league with antichrist. Since "Jesus is the Christ" is a standard confession in the Johannine churches (1 John 5:1; cf. John 9:22; 20:31), it seems odd that this should be denied by members of the church. If, however, language is being used (as one would expect) by the insider to the insider, "Christ" and "Son" are used in v. 22 and "Son" in v. 23 in the sense understood by the author and the addressees, those who were still faithful members, i.e., the meaning is: whoever denies the Son—in the sense that we understand it.

Secondly, at 4:2 Wilckens takes the phrase ἐν σαρκὶ ἐληλυθότα to be akin to other expressions used in the Fourth Gospel like "to come from above," "to come from the Father," "to descend from heaven," or "to come into the world," and should be compared also with John 1:14. But, we may ask, why choose the term "flesh"? If the Elder wanted to affirm the divinity of Christ, why not say "come from God" or "come from above" or one of the other phrases just referred to? Would not these say better what Wilckens thinks the Elder is trying to say? The use of "flesh" focuses attention precisely on the *humanity* of Jesus.

We may also mention Wilckens' use of 5:6. He takes "come with water" as a reference to Jesus' baptism. But would not this be inappropriate if arguing against Jewish Christians allegedly offended by a "high" Christology? A story like Mark 1:9–11 or something akin to it, which seems to lie behind John 1:29–34, could be taken in an "adoptionist" sense, and, if "come with water" were a reference to the Jordan event, then it could be so taken. The author would be using a phrase with which his opponents on Wilckens' view could have agreed! But for the Elder, Jesus Christ was Son of God from the beginning.

Finally, a general point. Might we not have expected some reference to the fact that Old Testament had foreshadowed the Sonship of Jesus Christ? John 10:34, 36 shows that within the Johannine tradition there was precedent for this approach.

Despite the fact that Wilckens' view has the merit of producing a common front against which to place the Gospel and Letters, we are not convinced that he has established his case.

The case put forward by H. Schmid is very different and is an illustration of how some German scholars are adopting literary criticism approaches, in this case applied not so much to a piece of narrative but to an "epistle"[53] (using that designation without going into all the issues of whether it is an appropriate description). Schmid propounds the view that while there may have been some event of schism in the past, we can no longer reconstruct it. In fact, the opponents are much more of a literary construct.

Schmid operates on what he calls the principle of "intertextuality," by which he means that John's Gospel and 1 John belong to the same Johannine *Sinnsystem* (which we may paraphrase as "the thought system or mindset" characteristic of Johannine Christians) and can be used to explain each other mutually. Thus, for example, in both 2:18–27 and 4:1–6, the author of 1 John has particularly in mind the desertion of disciples mentioned in John 6:60–71, which itself is to be regarded as a piece of Johannine church history rather than an incident from the ministry of Jesus.

For Schmid, there are only two passages in 1 John where the opponents are specifically mentioned, namely 2:18–27 and 4:1–6, both of which are really excursuses set in passages concerned with ethical teaching (2:15–17, 28–31; and 3:11–24; 4:7–21 respectively). In discussing 2:18–27, Schmid points out that details concerning the opponents are sparse and incomplete and are set in the past. The opponents are simply a negative example to offset what the community ought to be; they are a peg on which to articulate a profiled exhortation to the members of the congregation. In this way, the readers are tested once more as to the seriousness of their following. The time for Christological clarification is past; the time for ethical testing has broken in, and the motive of the last hour makes the ethical theme all the more pressing. The readers need to reaffirm their link with the christological kerygma (what they have heard from the beginning), in order that they may have a firm basis for the ethical action and lifestyle commensurate with their belief.

In addition to John 6:6–71 (the desertion by many disciples), John 8:21–59 (an example of faith which does not last) is drawn in as intertextual reading for 1 John 4:1–6. The assurance of the reader is the main concern, not a rebuttal of the opponents' teaching (more and clearer detail would be necessary if that were the case). At 4:2, the Elder stresses the human existence of Jesus as the basic condition of redemption (there is no opposition between flesh and Spirit lurking in this verse).

---

53. Schmid, *Gegner*, spends 26–80 discussing literary theorists and how their approaches might be applied to 1 John.

The confession of 4:2 is made precise and developed in 5:6, with the emphasis resting on "with blood." Water and blood are symbols of the meaning of Jesus' coming for salvation (life linked to the sacrifice of the cross)—John 4:10–14; 7:37–39; 19:34–35 are drawn in on the intertextuality principle. Schmid sees 5:6 as the climax of Johannine Christology, a creative performance that invites the reader to work out the intertextual links and fill out and make concrete the symbolism.

Schmid quotes Griffith's argument[54] concerning the alleged "slogans" in 1:6—2:11 and 4:20, and accepts this: there is an internal group debate about the ethics of the Johannine system of thought. There is an ethical problem immanent within the Johannine system. 1 John deepens and develops the basic ethical lines set forth in John 13–17. Mutual love has to correspond to the asserted fellowship with God. 1 John turns against both a perfectionism, which emancipates itself from God's saving action, and a moral indifference.

The opponents serve to personalize the christological antithesis in 1 John, and they stand for apostasy and return to the world and show how pressing it is to overcome every possible form of ethical deficiency. Schmid says that the opponents are in the text, though not the main theme. The opponents are what the readers should never be.

What may be said in response to Schmid's case? In the first place, it ought to be said that quite a lot of what Schmid says would apply equally well if the so-called opponents had recently left the community and there was a vivid awareness of their views among those left, together with a fear of the continuing influence of their views (I am thinking of certain statements which Schmid makes: e.g., that the description of the opponents is related to the identity of the community; that the consequences of apostasy are held before the reader; that ethics cannot be separated from Christology, for they stand in closest union with Christology and the basic theological message; that the author builds reception of the letter into the antithetical scheme; that whoever disregards the ethical commands comes close to the one who denies the Christological confession; etc.). It is also puzzling to read that there is no reference to unity in 1 John, seen by Schmid as further proof that it is ethics and not the division of the congregation that is the issue. Surely, the constant appeals

---

54. Griffith had summarised a good many of his arguments in an article, *Non-Polemical Reading*, 253–76, before his book appeared in 2002.

to unity are precisely an appeal for unity among those who remain after the secession.

Secondly, many will feel that Schmid's reconstruction is too theoretical and cerebral, and does not do justice to that passion with which the text vibrates. The passion reflects the pressing urgency of a real situation, not an artificial literary construction dreamt up for the sake of exhortation. I find it significant that Klauck, writing before the "new look" had really got underway, could say that traces of a bitter controversy have entered too clearly into the text, and Painter remarks that "explicit references to the schism are few, but those that are present make clear the serious nature of the event."[55]

Thirdly, we may mention the principle of intertextuality. Schmid concedes that this may be applied both ways:[56] thus, 1 John 2:18–27 could actualize the disciple-story of John 6:60–71 into a potential departure from the Johannine system of thought, or the opponents motif of 1 John will be shaped into a scene of disciples departing in John 6:60–71.[57]

Now, clearly, whether the epistles were written before or after the Gospel, Johannine Christians would be acquainted with the kind of stories now incorporated into the Gospel. In principle, therefore, one could not deny the possibility that incidents in the ongoing life of Johannine Christians could be illustrated from incidents in the ministry of Jesus: one might see a contemporary incident through the "lens" of a past one, just as Second Isaiah saw the departure from Babylon as a new Exodus. It is an entirely different matter, however, to envisage artificial constructions for the sake of urgent exhortation. There are many good things in Schmid's book, especially his exegesis of passages, and his work stimulates even through disagreement. But I do not feel that he has made out his central thesis.

A further line of approach to the situation behind 1 John needs to be mentioned: that of persecution and the threat of martyrdom. Stegemann[58] argued that the final warning of 5:21 was a warning against cultic honoring of pagan images, in the context of martyrdom of Christians at the hands of the Roman state (288). He stresses the ter-

---

55. Klauck, *Der erste Johannesbriefe*, 35; Painter, *1, 2 & 3 John*, 86.

56. Schmid, *Gegner*, 76, 124, 161–62, 284.

57. Schmid, *Gegner*, 124, quotes L. Schenke as seeing the crisis of 1 John retrojected into the ministry of Jesus.

58. Stegemann, *Kindlein*, 284–94.

minology (291) and believes that those who had left the congregation had done so to save their own lives and not over the issue of doctrine (292)—hence the accusation that they do not love the brothers and sisters. Stegemann compares the situation with that revealed in Pliny's correspondence with the emperor Trajan (288). Edwards [59] has basically put forward the same viewpoint.

The case against this approach is surely that one would expect more specific allusions to the possibility of martyrdom for the sake of faithfulness to Jesus—3:16 is too oblique as a potential reference to martyrdom on the grounds of a Christian confession. We might also expect some reference to the state authorities, and possibly a reference to the way Jesus had conducted himself when he was on trial before the Roman as an example for Christians to follow.[60]

In the end, we have stayed with the majority view that some within the Johannine congregations had moved in a direction of weakening the emphasis on the humanity of Jesus, and it is that which prompted the author's christological assertions in 1 John.

59. Edwards, *Martyrdom*, 164–71.

60. Stegemann's view is firmly rejected by Wilckens, *Sohn Gottes*, 109 (note 48), as freely invented ("frei erfunden").

9

The Meaning of the Death of Jesus in the Johnannine Letters

W E WILL BEGIN BY noticing the stress which the Elder places on the initiative of God. On three occasions the phrase "God sent (His Son)" is used. These are: "God's love for us was revealed in the fact that God sent His only Son into the world that we might live through him" (4:9); "Love consists of this—not that we loved God but that he loved us and sent his Son to be the expiation for our sins" (4:10); "And we have seen and do bear witness that the Father sent the Son to be the Saviour of the world" (4:14).

The phrase about God's sending His Son raises the possibility of a formula—the sending formula—being current in the early church,[1] but the evidence is by no means conclusive,[2] and all we can say is that the suggestion is a possibility (cf. John 3:16–17). We would be on firmer ground with a more modest suggestion, that Johannine circles utilised such a mode of expressing its convictions that God was "behind" the total activity of Jesus. What Jesus did was an expression of God's love. The incarnation and the cross are thus grounded in His love for the world.

---

1. Maintained by Kramer, *Christ*, 112–14; Mussner, *Galaterbrief*, 271–72; Betz, *Galatians*, 205–6; Strecker, *Epistles*, 150. Schweizer, υἱός, *TDNT* 8:383, speaks of a traditional pattern of thought.

2. Thus, Schweizer, *Herkunft*, 68, sees Gal 4:4 as a Pauline formulation, while Wengst, *Christologische Formeln*, 59, denies the existence of a formula (according to Betz, *Galatians*, 206 (note 40)).

The subjective side of salvation—rebirth—is also attributed to God: the believer is begotten ἐκ τοῦ Θεοῦ and the mutual immanence formula is "God in believers—believers in God" (in the Gospel this formula is used of Christ and believers). It corresponds to this initiative of God the Father when the writer says, "We know that the Son of God has come and given us understanding in order that we might know him who is true" (5:20), where the phrase οἴδαμεν ὅτι makes appeal to common ground and tradition. We may also assume divine initiative in the opening sentence, which says that the eternal life which was with the Father was manifested to us (1:2).[3] This initiative of God in sending his Son, then, rests on his love (4:10) and reveals that love (4:9).

Another aspect of this love is that eternal life is God's gift through His Son: "This is the witness of God, that God has given eternal life to us, and this life is in his Son" (5:11). When Christ laid down his life for us, he revealed the true nature of love: "We know love by this fact, that he laid down his life for us; and we ought to lay down our lives for the brothers" (3:16). The Elder probably wished to indicate the love of both the Father and the Son.

It comes as no surprise, therefore, to read at 1:9: "If we confess our sins, God is faithful and just to forgive us our sins and cleanse us from all unrighteousness." God is faithful to his own saving nature, to his promise to save, and responds to the confession of sins. God is righteous, a God who wills to restore men and women to himself,[4] and sets us right with himself by cleansing us from our sins, through what his Son Jesus has done (1:7).

Secondly, there are two statements in chapter 3 whose literary structure seems to point to formal material which mentions the taking away of sins and the destruction of the works of the devil. The first opens with the phrase οἴδατε ὅτι, which obviously has the purpose of recalling what was already familiar to the addressees. Both have a subject plus ἐφανερώθη; and follow this with a ἵνα clause stating the purpose of the Son of God's being revealed. Traditional church formulae may well

---

3. Cf. the use of the passive ἐφανερώθη concerning the Son at 3:5, 8.

4. Cf. Isa 45:21 ("a righteous God and a Saviour"); Exod 34:6–7 ("abounding in steadfast love and faithfulness"—manifested in forgiveness); Deut 32:4 ("just and right is he"). Lieu, *Beginning*, 461–66, very helpfully explores the scriptural background to 1 John 1:9—2:2, and locates it in a tradition beginning with Exod 34:6 and continuing in some prophetic writings, the psalms, Qumran and Hellenistic Judaism. In 1 John, forgiveness is rooted in the character of God and is embodied in Jesus.

be utilised here by the Elder. "And you know that he[5] was revealed to take away sins, and there is no sin in him" (3:5). The purpose of Christ's appearance is to take away sins: ἵνα τὰς ἁμαρτίας ἄρῃ. We are reminded of John 1:29—"Behold the Lamb of God who takes away the sin of the world" (in fact, under the influence of John 1:29, ms 629 of 1 John.3:5 has ἁμαρτίαν). When dealing with John 1:29, we maintained that it was a theological tradition of the Johannine Churches on the basis of "and you know that etc." of 1 John 3:5. The Elder is appealing to common ground.[6]

We may legitimately assume that there is here an allusion to the death of Jesus and that the sacrificial understanding of Jesus is assumed (cf. 1:7; 2:2; 4:10).[7] To what is the aorist subjunctive active ἄρῃ referring here? It suggests a once-for-all action and would fit in with a view which ascribes decisive consequences to the cross. The Son of God appeared in order that he might at the cross take away sins. Christ's death is understood here as "a sacrifice of expiation,"[8] with Christ as the unblemished sacrifice ("and there is no sin in him" 3:5b). What meaning has αἴρειν here? To take away the guilt and condemnation or the stain, consequent upon sinning?[9] Or is it to take away the habit of sinning? Certainly the writer is aware of the fact that a sense of guilt and condemnation can seize the human heart with the consequent fear of meeting God (3:19–22). The antidote to this rests on God, on his character and nature, what he has done for us in sending his Son—to take away sins. Furthermore, God knows all circumstances, and his love is greater than our hearts. It is the knowledge of what God is like, based on the appearance of his Son, which can still the accusing voice within our hearts (cf. 4:17). Certainly, in 2:12–14, the Elder writes to the members of the whole community, calling them τεκνία and παιδία and drawing attention to the fact that their sins have been forgiven "because of his (?Christ's) name" (2:13) and they know the Father (2:14) as a result.

5. Ἐκεῖνος may have replaced "Son of God"; the designation "Christ" has been the theme of 2:28—3:3.

6. So Schnackenburg, *Epistles*, 172; Brown, *Epistles*, 401; Smalley, *Epistles*, 156; Strecker, *Letters*, 95; Painter, *1, 2 & 3 John*, 223.

7. Brown, *Epistles*, 401–2.

8. Strecker, *Letters*, 95–96; Jeremias, αἴρειν, *TWNT* 1:186.

9. While "take away" or "remove" is the predominant sense of αἴρειν, we cannot altogether exclude the possibility that the nuance of "take up and carry/bear" is included. Cf. Wilckens, *Johannes*, 40, on John 1:29.

Equally, it is true that the Elder wishes that members of the churches should grow in Christ-likeness and ultimately become like Christ at
his Parousia (3:2): they should be righteous like Christ (3:7; cf. 2:29) and
pure like him (3:3). The general principle is stated clearly at 2:6: "The
person who claims to abide in him should so conduct themselves as he
behaved."[10] Leaving sin behind and becoming more Christ-like till in
the end we see him as he is and are transformed fully into his likeness
is what the Elder hopes for himself and the addressees. Although he is
aware that Christians do in fact sin (2:1–2), the ideal is that Christians
should not (3:6; 5:18); indeed they ought not to, since God's seed abides
in them (3:9).

Accordingly, based on the general teaching of the letter and on the
context, we might be advised to assume that "taking away sins" involves
both the removal of the guilt and condemnation of sin[11] *and* of its hold
on us in terms of conduct and habits.[12] This would fit in with the kind of
teaching already seen in the Gospel, especially John 12:31; 1:29. The use
of the plural 'sins' (as opposed to the singular in John 1:29) may be due
to the pastoral situation—the Elder is addressing Christians directly and
reminding them of their own sins.[13]

The other statement which we are to consider in this category is,
"The Son of God appeared for this very purpose to destroy the works
of the devil" (λύσῃ τὰ ἔργα τοῦ διαβόλου, 3:8). Here we meet the
idea of conflict, struggle, and warfare. God's Son encounters and defeats
an antagonistic force: he destroys the works of the devil. Two questions
arise—what are the works of the devil? and how does the Son of God
destroy them?

The works of the devil include the falsehood by which he deceives
men and women and lures them away from their true allegiance to God
and so deprives them of life, which is what God wants for them. Thus, to
liberate and set men and women free must involve an element of exposure and unmasking of the falsity of the devil's and the world's approach.

---

10. The καθὼς ἐκεῖνος περιεπάτησεν must point to Jesus and his earthly lifestyle.

11. So Jeremias, αἴρειν, *TWNT* 1:185–86. Cf. Marshall, *Epistles*, 177, and Smalley,
Epistles, 156. Brown, *Epistles*, 402, speaks of "cleansing."

12. Westcott, *Epistles*, 103; Bultmann, *Letters*, 50; K. Grayston, *Dying, We Live*, 280.
For both/and, see Schnackenburg, *Epistles*, 172–73, while Smalley, *Epistles*, 156 also
veers in this direction.

13. Schnackenburg, *Epistles*, 173.

We have seen that in the Gospel the prince of this world is judged at the Cross (12:31) and the Spirit uses this to persuade men and women to change their allegiance (16:8–11). Another element in Jesus' victory is his obedience to God which proves the devil's impotence over him and inability to lure him away from God, an obedience which in the Fourth Gospel climaxes in the cross (14:30–31; 16:31–32). It would fit the aorist subjunctive active if the Elder did in fact have the cross in mind when he wrote that the Son of God came to destroy the works of the devil.[14]

We have already seen how the Elder expects this archetypal victory to be (as it were) re-enacted in the life of believers: "the young men" have conquered the evil one (2:13–14). The use of the perfect indicative active (νενικήκατε) may be explained by a later passage in the Letter: "Everyone[15] born of God overcomes (νικᾷ) the world. And this is the victory which has overcome the world—our faith. Who is the person who overcomes the world but the person who believes that Jesus is the Son of God?" (5:4–5).

When a person believes that the man Jesus is none other than the Son of God, then that person moves out of the realm of the world and breaks with the works of the devil, and becomes a child of God: he/she changes family allegiance. Henceforth they live by the strength of him who is greater than the devil (4:4) and they endeavour not to love "the things of the world" (2:15).

Thirdly, sacrificial ideas are applied to the death of Jesus. "The blood of Jesus, his [God's] Son, cleanses us from all sin" (1:7). Since the death of Jesus was not caused by loss of blood, the use of the term conveys either the notion of a violent death (e.g., the phrase "the blood of the prophets") or that of sacrifice. The subsequent use of "cleanse" fits in with the model of sacrifice, since in the Old Testament those sacrifices specifically intended to deal with sin "cleansed" the worshippers from their sense of uncleanness and defilement and made them clean and fit to appear before God.

So, we may say that the verse being considered assumes a sacrificial interpretation of the death of Jesus. In no way does this assume that Jesus

14. Houlden, *Epistles*, 96 and Smalley, *Epistles*, 170, believe that it is likely that the death of Jesus is in mind, while Schnackenburg, *Epistles*, 174, believes that the Elder is looking beyond the atoning death of Christ on the cross to the continuing battle against Satan's works (as does Painter, *1, 2, & 3 John*, 229, apparently). Marshall, *Epistles*, 184–85 and Brown, *Epistles*, 406–7 do not mention Jesus' death.

15. The Greek is literally the neuter (πᾶν τὸ)—a feature of Johannine style.

does something to appease an angry deity. The passages about God's love considered above rule out that suggestion entirely. In any case, in the Old Testament, the sacrificial system is the gracious gift of God to enable the defiled worshipper to appear before Him.

Twice the term ἱλασμός is used in connection with Jesus. Jesus (previously described as righteous) "is the ἱλασμός for our sins, not for our sins only but also for those of the whole world" (2:2). "Love is revealed in this, not that we loved God, but that he loved us and sent his Son to be the ἱλασμός for our sins" (4:10).

The term ἱλασμός is another term drawn from the sphere of sacrifice. Nowadays it is often paraphrased as the means by which sins are forgiven or removed. Such a paraphrase loses some nuance of the original, however laudable it may be in an age when the religious background of sacrifice is a "closed book" to so many. The older translation of propitiation is still supported by some scholars,[16] though many prefer expiation[17] as the means by which the defiling consequences of sins are wiped away or obliterated. If propitiation were to be retained, it must not undermine the emphasis on God's initiative outlined earlier. It is true that in the context assurance is given that we have an advocate (ὁ παρά κλητος) in the presence of the Father, and he presumably pleads our case, but that does not mean that he has to persuade an unwilling Father to forgive. The idea behind ἱλασμός coheres, therefore, with that of the blood that cleanses in 1:7.[18]

We notice that there appears in 2:2 to be something of a protest against any attempt to narrow down the effects of Christ's death to believers. If the sending formula were traditional and one of its accompanying phrases could have been "for our sins," as in 4:10, then there might have been the temptation to concentrate only on Christ's dying

16. Houlden *Epistles*, 62; Marshall, *Epistles*, 117–19; Smalley, *Epistles*, 38–40; Morris, *Apostolic Preaching*, 178–79 (in criticism of Dodd, *Bible*, 82–95) and Hill, *Greek Words*, 36–38, allow an element of propitiation.

17. E.g. Dodd, *Epistles*, 25; Thornton, *Propitiation or Expiation?* 53–55, esp. 54; Knöppler, *Sühne*, 229; Brown, *Epistles*, 220–21, prefers "atonement" to either; cf. Schnackenburg, *Epistles*, 88, "atoning sacrifice"; Büchsel, ἱλασμός, *TDNT* 3. 317–18 "setting aside of sin as guilt against God." Smith, *First, Second & Third John*, 107, and Painter, *1, 2 & 3 John*, 158–59, use expiation.

18. Strecker, *Letters*, 153, comments on 4:10: "The sending of the Son, an action proceeding from the Father, is the act that creates reconciliation between God and humanity."

for his own, given the sharp lines of demarcation drawn between the two "spheres." The Elder stresses that Jesus is the ἱλασμός not just for "our" sins but for "the sins of the whole world." He is, therefore, the savior of the world (4:14).

We have commented above on 3:5 and pointed out that there the sacrificial model is also utilised to illuminate the effects of Christ's death.

Fourthly, the use of ὁ παράκλητος for Jesus at 2:1 needs to be considered: "If anyone sins, we have a Paraclete with the Father, Jesus Christ the Righteous." Clearly it is the exalted Jesus who once was crucified, who is in mind in this passage. He has ascended, is in the presence of the Father, and acts as a παράκλητος on our behalf.[19] Both his quality of being righteous and the fact that he has atoned for our sins (ἱλασμός ἐστιν περὶ τῶν ἁμαρτιῶν ἡμῶν) fit him to carry out such an office or function.

When we interpreted John 12:31b, we suggested that it presupposed the kind of background glimpsed more fully in Rev 12:9–11, and we would now suggest that 1 John 2:1 also presupposes the same background. At the cross, Jesus has achieved the victory over the devil, as a result of which the devil is ejected from the heavenly law court. The great accuser has been thrown out. In his place (as it were), there steps Jesus Christ the Righteous One—not to act as an accuser but as an advocate. He is our "friend at court." He could be everyone's advocate, for his death is the expiation of the sins of the entire world.

The presupposition of this seems to demand something akin to what is found in the Gospel—that at the cross Jesus draws all into a union with himself. What we see in 1 John of the heavenly advocacy of Jesus demands, as its roots, what we see happening at the cross in the Gospel. Because he, the Righteous One, drew all into a unity with himself by identifying with them and because he has been exalted to the Father's side, he is the representative Advocate before the Father. Believers who have responded to him know this fact for themselves.

Fifthly, one of the assumptions of the Elder is that believers have been born of God[20] and, therefore, are called children of God (3:1, 10)

19. In the Farewell Discourse of the Gospel, the Spirit is with the disciples on earth. Cf. the apt description of the Friend at Court and the Friend from Court, coined by Bacon, *The 'Other' Comforter*, 274–82.

20. See Schnackenburg, *Epistles*, 162–69, for a link between the Spirit and the birth

and belong to God's family. He does not really explain how this takes place, but assumes it and draws implications from it. The analogy of birth is considered suitable to illustrate the passage from the family of the devil or of the world into God's family. A completely new beginning is necessary, of which natural birth supplies an illustration.

The idea of being "born of God" focuses attention on the "subjective" side of Christian experience. But it rests on what God has accomplished for us in his Son, Jesus Christ. Without his having dealt with our sins and destroyed the works of the devil, it would not be possible for the new "birth" to take place. Although nowhere explicitly said so, the Spirit is presumably the agent of this birth from God, using the word preached.[21] God gives the Spirit to every believer (3:24; 4:13—probably both these verses are traditional material).

Sixthly, we need to consider the passage 5:6 since an almost standard interpretation relates a major part of the verse to Jesus' death: "This is he who came with water and blood, Jesus Christ: not by water only but by water and blood." Many scholars have claimed that the secessionists asserted that the divine Christ descended on the human Jesus in the river Jordan but left him before the crucifixion. To counter this, it is said, the author asserts the unity of experience of the one person, Jesus Christ, from baptism to and including crucifixion (hence the emphasis "but by water and blood"[22]). (This would push the opponents into proximity to—though not necessarily identity with—Gnostic groups who taught such a view, e.g., Cerinthus[23]).

There is, however, a fatal weakness to this view, widespread as it is: for the writer, Jesus is the incarnate Son of God from the beginning of his life, not just at his baptism. Had he said that Jesus "came with water" and meant Jesus' own baptism in the Jordan, he would have conceded a

---

from God; cf. Mussner, *Leben*, 111–123; F. Büchsel, γεννάω, κτλ., *TDNT* 1:671; Brown, *Epistles*, 411.

21. Marshall, *Epistles*, 186–87; Smalley, *Epistles*, 172–74; Dunn, *Baptism*, 195–200, especially 198; S. Schutz, σπέρμα, *TDNT* 8:545. So too de la Potterie, *Vie selon l'Esprit*, 126–42, especially 141–42.

22. So Brooke, *Epistles*, xlv—xlix; Dodd, *Epistles*, 130; Schneider, *Kirchenbriefe*, 182; Bultmann, *Letters*, 80; Houlden, *Epistles*, 125–26; Marshall, *Epistles*, 231–35; Strecker, *Letters*, 74 (likely); Painter, *1, 2 & 3 John*, 305; Theobald, *Fleischwerdung*, 401–21.

23. E.g., Robinson, *Twelve NT Studies*, 134–36; Wengst, *Häresie und Orthodoxie*, 24–34.

major part of their argument![24] He would not be arguing sufficiently appositely against his opponents. Furthermore, one event seems in mind— a coming δι'ὕδατος καὶ αἵματος, *not* two separate events.[25]

Finally, "coming in water" refers to something done *by* Jesus, not something done to him.[26] This too tells against the dominant interpretation in the twentieth century.

An alternative view has been to argue that the Christian sacraments are in mind:[27] "water" stands for Christian baptism and "blood" for the Lord's Supper. There are two objections which may be raised against this position. In the first place, "blood" is not the most natural way of referring to the Lord's Supper. Secondly, to say that Jesus came with baptism and the Lord's Supper sounds slightly strange,[28] and did anyone accept baptism but deny the dominical gift of the Lord's Supper?[29]

Another group of scholars has suggested a link between this passage and John 19:34b where the spear thrust into Jesus' side occasioned an outflow of blood and water and, thus, 1 John 5:6 is held to refer to the death of Jesus.[30] This view envisages one event and explains the alteration of the order "blood and water" (John 19:34b) into "water and blood" (1 John 5:6) as due to the writer's desire to stress the atoning

---

24. Smalley, *Epistles*, 279; Richter, *Studien*, 124; Lieu, *Authority*, 218; Brown, *Community*, 113.

25. Brown, *Epistles*, 574, 577; Thompson, *1–3 John*, 133; Richter, *Studien*, 125; Schweizer, *Johanneische Zeugnis*, 344 (a unique event). Perhaps too much ought not to be made of this argument, for in the next phrase ἐν τῷ is used with both ὕδατι and αἵματι, but perhaps this may be due to emphasis.

26. De Boer, *Perspectives*, 259.

27. Westcott, *Epistles*, 182; Cullmann, *Early Christian Worship*, 110 (note 1).

28. Cf. Brown, *Epistles*, 575. See also Knöppler, *Sühne*, 231, for a denial of the sacramental interpretation.

29. It is true that Ignatius accuses some of absenting themselves from the Eucharist (Smyrna 6:2), but he also reveals that these Docetists celebrated their own Eucharist or love feasts (see W. Schoedel, *Ignatius of Antioch*, 240). Irenaeus, *AH* 1/13/1–5, affords evidence too of a kind of Eucharist amongst Marcosian Valentinians.

30. Barrett, *John*, 556; Brown, *Epistles*, 577–78; Klauck, *Der erste Johannesbriefe*, 296–97; Thompson, *1–3 John*, 134; Knöppler, *Sühne*, 232. Theobald, *Fleischwerdung*, 405, draws in both John 19:35 and 1:15 to support a reference in 1 John 5:6–8 to Jesus' baptism and death—he does so via the theme of witness, which occurs in both these verses in the gospel, namely of John the Baptist and the Beloved Disciple resp., a witness designed to stress the reality of the man Jesus in the events of his baptism and death as the reality of God.

death of Jesus.[31] It is a weakness of this view, however, that the language "He came by water and blood" does not strike one as the most natural way of referring to the event described in John 19:34b,[32] nor indeed of referring to the crucifixion as a whole[33] (as if he had not been with blood prior to this).

Two scholars have recently suggested that the opponents saw Jesus as one who brought the Spirit, though they argue in different ways. Von Walde took the wording of 5:6 to indicate that the opponents believed that Jesus came to give the Spirit.[34] He is vague on how Jesus might be thought to have prepared for the eschatological outpouring of the Spirit predicted in the OT (Joel 2:28–30; Isa 32:15, 19; Ezek 11:17, 19; 36:26–27; 39:29). He states that once that had happened, the opponents thought that the believer had no more essential need of Jesus: Jesus himself would then hold no permanent or continuing role in salvation.[35]

The cleansing of sins came through the Spirit and guidance by the Spirit was immediate and direct. Von Walde does not suggest why the opponents dismissed the significance of Jesus, especially when, within the Farewell Discourse, even without the Paraclete sayings, there is evidence of the idea of "a more abiding presence of Jesus" with his disciples than the resurrection appearances.[36]

On the basis of 2 John 9, von Walde accepts that the opponents denied that Jesus had come in the flesh.[37]

De Boer thinks that at 5:6 the Elder was quoting his opponents' view: they believed that Jesus came to baptize with the Spirit (symbolized by "water").[38] However, since the Elder wished to assert the need for Jesus' death, he joined "blood" (Jesus' death) to "water" (baptizing with the Spirit): the former was crucial and the key to water used in baptism.[39]

To our earlier criticisms of de Boer, we may here ask why, if "water" in 5:6 stood for Spirit in the opponents' slogan, did the Elder go on to

31. Thompson, *1–3 John*, 133, 135.

32. Smalley, *Epistles*, 278.

33. Richter, *Studien*, 125; cf. Painter, *1, 2 & 3 John*, 306.

34. Van Walde, *Commandments*, 117.

35. Ibid., 118

36. So Brown, *John* 2:730.

37. Van Walde, *Commandments*, 112 (Table).

38. De Boer, *Perspectives*, 245, 262, 265, 269.

39. Ibid., 269, 305.

refer to Spirit as an apparently "extra" factor along with water and blood in vv. 7–8 ("There are three who bear witness"). De Boer says that Spirit and water "are shared territory between the author and his adversaries and thus non-controversial,"[40] but this does not afford an answer to the question which we have posed.

In addition, de Boer's idea that the Elder took ideas associated with baptism and applied them to Jesus' death, in order to correct a kind of baptismal triumphalism, seems to put the cart before the horse. It was because the messiah had died for our sins (1 Cor 15:3) that the early church associated cleansing of sins with the act of baptism,[41] not vice versa.

There remains to be mentioned the view that the reference to "water" and "blood" is a way of referring to *a real person*.[42] "He came" would refer to Jesus' entry upon human life. He came as a completely real human being. There would be an anti-docetic thrust to this statement of 1 John 5:6 and, as such, it would fit in with the stress on Jesus' humanity elsewhere (e.g., 4:2–3). The success or failure of this view to convince depends on two factors: were water and blood regarded as components of a genuine human person in antiquity, and were there people who asserted that the Son of God only came with water?

E. Schweizer has argued that in both Greek and Jewish thought there was a widespread view that a person consisted of blood and water (he quotes many Greek texts from 500 BC to the second century AD; and also *Lev. Rab.* 15 and 4 Macc. 9:20 from the Jewish side).[43]

On the second question, G. Richter has drawn attention to the *Acts of Thomas* 165, where Judas says that the Lord was of one element, which, Richter claims, can only mean water,[44] and passages from Mandaean literature (e.g., Enosch-Uthra the redeemer is clothed in a garment made of cloud water and this veils his glory[45]). Richter's examples fall short of

40. Ibid., 305.

41. Beasley-Murray, *Baptism*, 100, 127–28. L. Hartmann, *Into the Name of the Lord Jesus*, 85, is more cautious, but accepts such a view when discussing 1 Cor 1:13; 6:11; Rom 6:1–14.

42. Richter, *Studien*, 122–34. Smalley, *Epistles*, 279, also believes that the Elder is here stressing Jesus' humanity, but for reasons which differ from those suggested by Richter (Jesus was "baptized in water and crucified in shed blood").

43. Schweizer, *Zeugnis*, 350–51.

44. Richter, *Studien*, 131.

45. Ibid., 130.

decisive proof,[46] though perhaps John 1:13 offers some support for the view that blood was associated with a genuine human birth.

No view is without its difficulties for us today, since we lack the information which the readers of 1 John possessed. Of the five views outlined, the third one (the link with John 19:34) and the final one (blood and water indicating a human being) seem, on balance, to be least unsatisfactory. Only on the alleged link up with John 19:34b would there be a reference to the meaning of the death of Jesus,[47] and this on the assumption that in the Johannine congregations, the blood and water were taken to mean the atoning death of Christ and the gift of the Spirit. On the view that water and blood refer to a real person, there is, however, no specific reference to Jesus' death.

SUMMARY

1 John grounds the death of Jesus in the will of God and in His love (4:9, 10, 14) and stresses that it reveals God's love (3:16). In this it is one with the Fourth Gospel.

The Letter also declares that the purpose of Jesus' death was to take away sins (3:5). Whatever the sense of "take away," the assertion is reminiscent of John 1:29. The conflict and victory motif is also linked with Jesus' death (3:8), and this also reminds us of teaching in the Fourth Gospel (12:31; 14:30).

Arguably, there are more sacrificial references in the Letter (1:7; 2:2; 3:5; 4:10), proportionately speaking, but the sacrificial understanding of Jesus' death is not absent from the Fourth Gospel (e.g., 1:29; 17:19).

Interestingly, the idea of Jesus as our Advocate in heaven (2:2) seems the obverse side of the coin whose reverse side is seen at John 12:31: the prince of this world is cast out of heaven, and Jesus takes his place as our Advocate.

While accepting that the Letter was written by a different author, we believe that Dodd may have overstressed differences in understanding

---

46. Brown, *Epistles*, 576, challenges Richter's theory and evidence.

47. Schnackenburg, *Epistles*, 233, suggests that the heretics may have assigned to Jesus the role of the first "pneumatic" (who was given the Spirit in his baptism), while the Elder focuses especially on the death as the soteriological event. But this separates the coming into two events.

Jesus' death in the Letter and the Gospel. The Letter remains within the range of understanding visible in the Fourth Gospel.

10

Final Summary
and Conclusions

|

A FTER OUR REVIEW OF scholarly discussion of the Fourth Gospel's understanding of the place of the cross, if any, in the salvation of men and women, we set out briefly the view that salvation is by revelation in the ministry of the incarnate Word.

Unquestionably, there is teaching to this effect in the Fourth Gospel, but it is not the whole story. John's concept of the hour shows that the cross is the climax of Jesus' ministry, and is sufficient proof that John does have a *theologia crucis*. The idea of Jesus' glory and glorification shows that the cross is a moment of glorification. The idea is somewhat elastic, but there is no question but that Jesus is glorified in the cross in a sense in which he was not before. Room must be found for this special stress on the cross in John's glorification concept (in agreement with Thüsing against his critics, especially Blank and Riedl). The "lifting up" passages with their dual reference to a literal lifting up (crucifixion) and metaphorical one (exaltation to the Father) confirm the importance of the cross for John. They prevent a rigid separation of the cross from the subsequent exaltation (compare the point about glorification in the cross and subsequently). That the cross is a triumphant return to the Father is clearly true (as many scholars stress), but that does not exhaust its significance.

The very inclusion of what is probably a traditional confession at 1:29 suggests that the evangelist wanted to emphasize Jesus' role in removing sin. By means of 2:13–22, John sets the remaining story under the sign of the cross, while 20:19–29 affirms the permanent significance of the cross (the Risen One is the one who was crucified).

We also mentioned the idea of a "work" to be accomplished by Jesus and which is clearly completed in the cross (4:34; 17:4; 19:30; cf. the cup to be drunk of 18:11). The Spirit can only come after the cross, seen in terms of Jesus' glorification and his return home to the Father (7:39; 14:16; 16:7).

There is a profound difference between discipleship before and after the cross. Both of these points raised the question of whether the change is due to the accomplishment of something decisive in the cross. In addition, a very significant point is the clear presentation of the inadequacy of faith before the cross. If the revelation given in the incarnate ministry has failed, does this mean that something further must be done to rectify the situation?

At this point in our study, we looked at the Johannine concept of sin. The evangelist envisages spheres or areas of power. Human beings are in either one of two spheres (light/darkness, with other antithetical pairs also used—Spirit/flesh; truth/falsehood, etc.), in which God and the devil exercise their power. The Johannine concept of the world amply illustrates that this sphere develops its own ethos, mores, and lifestyle in opposition to God. Men and women can break out of the one sphere and move into the other sphere, but in the end it is birth from above which enables this to take place.

In chapter 4, we examined Jesus' ministry under the themes of his mutual companionship with the Father and their shared purpose which is to extend the companionship which they enjoy to believers: believers are to be drawn into the blessings of that divine life existing between the Father and the Son.

Then, at last, we turned to look at the meaning of the cross in the Gospel. We first saw that the cross is deemed necessary for men and women to receive eternal life, at 3:14–15; 6:51c–58. Exactly *why* it is a divinely willed necessity is not expatiated upon there.

The cross is itself revelation. It discloses the close union between Jesus and the Father, such that Jesus is the divine presence on earth (8:28–29; 16:31–32), while it also reveals the Son's love for his own (13:1;

15:13) and in that love he reflects the Father's love for the world (3:16, with its double reference in "gave" to the incarnation and the cross). The reference in 15:13 to dying for one's friends is not in fact explained. His death benefits them, but it is not said how.

The passage 12:20–34 proved of crucial significance in our quest. Here there are a number of unquestionably Johannine terms—hour, glorify, lift up, alone, bearing fruit, judgment. The passage refers to the cross as the hour of glorification, and this is illustrated by the mini-parable about the seed dying and bearing much fruit. Jesus is like that seed: in his death, he will obtain a harvest of followers. So, to evade this hour of the cross would be to renege on the very purpose of his coming into the world. Giving full force to the double "now" of 12:31, we believe that the passage teaches us, firstly, that Jesus himself accepts the judgment appropriate for the world; secondly, that the prince of this world is ejected from the heavenly court, having lost his case; and, thirdly, that Jesus draws humanity into union with himself. The evangelist stresses that the "lifting up" must be related both to the cross and to a "lifting up" to the Father. Here is the closest we come to a rationale of the cross. Here is why Jesus is the Lamb of God who takes away the sin of the world and why he can be described as the good shepherd who gives his life for the sheep (10:11, 15) and the one whose death draws God's scattered children into one (11:51–52; cf. 10:16).

Fully obedient to the Father, Jesus finished his work (17:4) and is victorious over the power of evil, in the cross (14:31; 16:33). He thus enables believers, in union with himself, to pass from that "sphere" where evil's power reigns, to that where God's Spirit reigns. He can set people free by his truth (8:32).

On the threshold of his death, he consecrates himself like a sacrificial victim to the task ahead (17:19). The cleansing and consecrating power of his death is thus indicated. In addition, the foot washing sets forth in graphic form the necessity of what Jesus must do in his service on the cross. Otherwise, Peter can have no fellowship with him nor receive cleansing (13:1–11, esp. vv. 8, 10b).

Thus, Jesus becomes the savior of the world in his death. He becomes the ladder leading to heaven and opening up contact between God and individuals (1:51). From Christ's death there flow at-one-ment with God and the gift of the Spirit (19:34b).

If, as we claimed, each episode in the Gospel preaches the gospel of God's Word/Son incarnate, crucified/lifted up, then there is an answer to Ashton's argument that the absence of any reference to the cross and passion in 3:16–21, 31–36; 7:33–36; 8:21–27; 12:44–50 (which are seen as highly representative of the evangelist's views and where Jesus' death is referred to as departure, exaltation or ascent), is noteworthy and that this only goes to reinforce the thesis which he and so many others hold that revelation "is unquestionably the dominant theme of the Gospel" and that "every major motif in the Gospel is directly linked to the concept of revelation."[1] But, what if (we may ask) the evangelist wished to show that the truth revealed is that God wills to draw men and women into fellowship with himself and wills to do so through Jesus Christ, his Son and Word incarnate, and can in fact do so only through the cross, the lifting up and glorifying of Christ? What if it is that understanding which is presupposed behind the words inviting us to come to Jesus, to believe in him, to follow him, to feed on him, etc.? What if what Jesus reveals *in toto* is not simply that he is the revealer or that he is an enigma, but that he alone can draw us into union with the Father because he has representatively already done so? What if when the Johannine Jesus invites us to come to, and believe in, him, it is as One who was incarnate, lifted up on a cross and back to the Father, whither he has in his cross drawn us? The language of departing and ascending is important, for it is the way we must go to the Father (14:3–6). The Paraclete-Spirit now takes the written story of the words and deeds of Jesus and actualizes the offer of eternal life which Jesus makes, for men and women of each generation.

Finally, we surveyed how what has been accomplished in the cross is appropriated—through the work of the Spirit and through faith—and what the results are in eternal life, the fellowship of believers, the teaching ministry of the Paraclete-Spirit, and in lifestyle.

We then turned to the First Letter of John and adopted the position that it was written by a different person from the fourth evangelist, though from within the same Johannine stream of Christianity. After sketching the general background to the Letter and its teaching on sin, we examined its teaching on the death of Jesus. Like the Gospel, the First Letter grounds the death of Jesus in the saving initiative and purpose of God (4:9–10, 14; 3:16; 1:9).

1. Ashton, *Understanding*, 515.

Two sentences with a common structure ("He appeared" followed by a purpose clause) describe the purpose of Christ's coming to take away sins (cf. John 1:29) and to destroy the devil's works (cf. John 14:30–31; 16:33). Christ's victory once for all is to be repeated in his followers (2:13–14; 5:4–5).

Sacrificial ideas are applied to Jesus' death (1:7; 2:2; 4:10), proportionately more frequently than in the Gospel. The concept of Jesus as our Παράκλητος in heaven dovetails into the "myth" assumed as the background of John 12:31, the casting out from heaven of Satan. If Satan, as accuser, is cast out, the exalted Jesus takes his place as our advocate before the Father.

All this is the objective side of the subjective experience of being born from God, an idea which occurs in the Letter (cf. John 3:5; 1:13).

As stated earlier, it may be that Dodd exaggerated the differences between the Gospel and the Letter concerning the death of Christ. Although different authors are involved, they both drew on traditions of their churches.

II

What are the implications of our findings for our understanding of one section or circle of early Christianity, namely the Johannine churches? Let us first set out a working model which many scholars have accepted in the past:

The Johannine churches were deeply influenced by a towering theological and spiritual genius whom we know as the Beloved Disciple. On the Bultmannian view, this figure taught salvation by revelation. The Beloved Disciple's Gospel was edited by his disciples—no doubt, in the end, one was made responsible for this task. He may or may not be the same person who wrote the Letters. This Deutero-Johannine stage[2] saw

2. Taeger, *Johannesapokalypse*, believed that John of Patmos had contact with the Johannine tradition at this Deutero-Johannine stage. Taeger is mainly concerned to compare and contrast the theme of the water of life in the Gospel of John and the Book of Revelation. He then broadens out his study into an examination of eschatology in the Gospel, Letters, and Revelation. He shows that there are "realised eschatology" elements in Revelation and that John of Patmos stands close to the eschatology represented by John 5.28–29 and by 1 John, which he calls the Deutero-Johannine stage. He concludes that John of Patmos did belong to the Johannine circle. Taegar has followed this up with his article "Gesiegt!" 23–46: John of Patmos stresses Christ's victory in his death (from

a taking up of more traditional ways of looking at salvation through the death of Jesus. On the Bultmannian view, this stage made the Johannine version of the Gospel more acceptable to the church at large.

We have called into question the way in which an *exclusively* revelatory understanding of salvation (whether the cross is or is not included) in the Fourth Gospel has been maintained by scholars. On the contrary, something decisive happened at the cross for the salvation of men and women.

An alternative working model may be proposed: From its earliest days the Christian movement had to defend its conviction that Jesus was God's promised Messiah, in view of his shameful death on a Roman cross. That death, in the eyes of so many Jews, disproved any idea that Jesus was a prophet sent by God, let alone the Messiah. One way of trying to overcome the scandal of the cross was to prove that the death of Jesus was within the purposes of God as contained in the scriptures (i.e. the OT). We can see in the Johannine passion story (which, we believe, was independent of Mark's Gospel, but may have had some contacts with the special tradition of the passion story which came eventually into Luke's hands) how OT passages were quoted to show that the death of Jesus had been foreseen by God and foretold by him (see John 13:18 (quoting Ps 41:9); 15:25 (quoting Ps 69:4/35:19); 19:24 (Ps 22:18); 19:28 (Ps 22:15); 19:29 (Ps 69:21); 19:36 (Ps 34:20 or Exod 12:46/Num 9:12); and 19:37 (Zech 12:10). See also the two quotations, from Isa 53:1 and 6:9–10, used at 12:38–40. This is an impressive number and comes close to the so-called fulfillment quotations in Matthew's Gospel, which has significantly less direct quotations from the OT in the passion story than John's Gospel. This passion story came into what we call the Johannine stream of Christianity.

This Johannine Christianity emerged in Palestine or nearby in Greek-speaking Syria, influenced by the Beloved Disciple, whom we have described as a person of profound spirituality and brilliance as a theologian. Whether under external influences—the pressure to defend the messiahship and sonship of the crucified Jesus—or under the impact of his own experience as a believing Christian, the Beloved Disciple reflected on the meaning of the cross for men and women. In his public

---

the Gospel) and also believers' share in this victory (from the Epistles), but in speaking of a future victory of Christ, John exhibits a tendency which characterised the later stages of the theology of the Johannine circle. For an alternative suggestion, see note 3.

preaching and teaching, the Beloved Disciple maintained that the cross was decisive for the salvation of men and women, but equally that the ministry of the incarnate Word/Son of God was of crucial significance. The revelation of the Word/Son had not evoked a positive response and Christ died representatively in order to enable us to be where he is, with the Father.[3]

The interpretative preaching of the Beloved Disciple took episodes from the ministry of Jesus and set them forth in such a way that in and through them the glorified Christ summoned men and women to believe in him as the One who through his lifting up on the cross had become the Savior of the world, able to dispense eternal life. The form was that of revelation; the basis of the form was the cross. The form revealed Christ lifted up as the One able to give life.

When the Beloved Disciple died, his work was not completely finished, and so members of his circle "published" his work (see 21:24). It is possible that they may have added some material here and there in the Gospel, but to pursue that question would demand far more space than is appropriate here. What is rather unlikely is that they attempted to introduce far-reaching modifications of, or even opposing standpoints to, the theology already set forth in the work.[4]

The Letters were written by a member of the Johannine circle, indebted to the Beloved Disciple. The author made use of various traditional confessions (e.g., 3:5, 8; possibly a sending formula—4:9, 10, 14), and he used sacrificial concepts (expiation, 2:2; 4:10; cleansing by the blood of Christ, 1.7). The idea of Jesus as our Paraclete before the Father on the basis of his expiatory death coheres with the "myth" of the ejection of Satan from heaven at John 12:31 (cf. Rev 12:9–11).

We believe that it is something of an exaggeration to say that the Elder was deliberately seeking, on the subject of the significance of Christ's death for our salvation, to draw back the thought of the Beloved Disciple into more traditional channels and so make his master's thought

3. It would be probably at this stage (rather than later) that the author of the Book of Revelation or his predecessors had contact with the Johannine tradition, and this explains why there are certain common links between this book and the Fourth Gospel. The most notable, as far as the death of Jesus is concerned, is the "myth" of the ejection of Satan from heaven, brought about by the cross. Later, on the island of Patmos, John wrote the Book of Revelation.

4. See our comments in chapter 1, section B, sub-sections I and II.

more palatable to "orthodoxy." For the Beloved Disciple, the cross was and would continue to be central and crucial for our salvation.

III

If our study has correctly delineated John's theology of the cross, then the alleged difference between him on the one side and, let us say, Paul or the author of the Letter to the Hebrews in respect to their understanding of the meaning of Christ's death will have to be revised. Both the centrality of the cross in terms of the narrative structure of the Gospel and its theological significance in the fourth evangelist's thought rule out putting John in a different category from the other two in how they conceived the process of salvation. John takes his stand with Paul and Hebrews, and indeed other NT writers, as a theologian of the cross. As far as Johannine Christianity was concerned, the cross is fundamental for the salvation of all humanity. Jesus became the Savior of the world at the cross. It was there that he finished the work given him by the Father. Hence, he could utter the triumphant cry "It is finished." The cross is, therefore, the moment of his glorification, and it becomes his lifting up into the presence of the Father who sent him. Under the inspiration of the Paraclete-Spirit, John has suffused that shameful death on the cross with glory. His witness to the meaning of the cross takes its place among the many voices in the NT with their differing emphases, and has continued to exercise a profound influence on the way subsequent Christians, ancient and modern, have looked at the cross of Jesus.

Select Bibliography

A : THE GOSPEL OF JOHN

Appold, Mark L., *The Oneness Motif in the Fourth Gospel*. WUNT 1. Tübingen: Mohr Siebeck, 1976.

Ashton, John. *Understanding the Fourth Gospel*. Oxford: Clarendon, 1991.

———. ed. *The Interpretation of John*. London: SPCK, 1986.

Bacon, B. W. "The 'Other' Comforter." *The Expositor* 14 (8th series) (1917) 274–82.

Barrett, C. K., *Church, Ministry and Sacraments in the New Testament*. Exeter: Paternoster, 1985.

———. *Essays on John*. London: SPCK, 1982.

———. "Johannine Christianity." In *Jesus and the Word and Other Essays*, 93–118. Edinburgh: T. & T. Clark, 1995.

———. *The Gospel according to St. John*. 2nd ed. London: SPCK, 1978.

Bauckham, Richard. ed. *The Gospels for all Christians. Rethinking the Gospel Audiences*. Grand Rapids: Eerdmans, 1998.

———. *The Testimony of the Beloved Disciple: Narrative, History, and Theology in the Gospel of John*. Grand Rapids: Baker Academic, 2007.

Bauer, Walter. *Das Johannes-Evangelium*. HNT 6. 2nd ed. Tübingen: Mohr Siebeck, 1925.

Baum-Bodenbender, Rosel, *Hoheit in Niedrigkeit: Johanneische Christologie im Prozet Jesu vor Pilatus (Joh 18, 28–19, 16a)*. FzB 49. Würzburg: Echter, 1984.

Beasley-Murray, George R., *Baptism in the New Testament*. London: Macmillan, 1962.

———. "John 12.31–34. The Eschatological Significance of the Lifting up of the Son of Man." In *Studien zum Text and zur Ethik des Neues Testaments*, Festschrift für H. Greeven. Edited by Wolfgang Schrage, 70–81. Berlin: Topelmann, 1986.

———. *John*. WBC 36. Waco, TX: Word, 1987.

Becker, Jürgen. "Die Abschiedsreden Jesu im Johannesevangelium." *ZNW* 61 (1970) 215–46.

———. *Das Evangelium des Johannes*. 2 vols. Gütersloh: Mohn, 1979, 1981.

Bennema, Cornelis, *The Power of Saving Wisdom: An Investigation of Spirit and Wisdom in relation to the Soteriology of the Fourth Gospel*. WUNT 148. Tübingen: Mohr Siebeck, 2002.

Bergmeier, Roland, "ΤΕΤΕΛΕΣΤΑΙ Joh 19.30." *ZNW* 79 (1988) 284–90.

Betz, Otto, *Der Paraklet, Fürsprecher im häretischen Spätjudentum, im Johannes-Evangelium und in neu gefundenen gnostischen Schriften.* AGSU 11. Leiden: Brill, 1963.

Blank, Josef, *Krisis. Untersuchungen zur johanneischen Christologie und Eschatologie.* Freiburg: Lambertus, 1964.

Boer, Martinus C. de, *Johannine Perspectives on the Death of Jesus.* BET 17. Kampen: Pharos, 1996.

Boismard, M-E. *Du Baptême à Cana (Jean 1.19—2.11).* LD 18. Paris: Cerf, 1956.

———. "Le Lavement des pieds (Jean 13.1–17)." *RB* 71 (1964) 5–24.

Borgen, Peder. *Bread from Heaven: An Exegetical Study of the Concept of Manna in the Gospel of John and the Writings of Philo.* SNT 10. Leiden: Brill, 1965.

———. "John 6: Tradition, Interpretation and Composition." In *From Jesus to John. Essays on Jesus and New Testament Christology in Honour of Marinus de Jonge,* edited by Martinus C. de Boer, 268–91. JSNTSS 84, Sheffield: Sheffield Academic, 1993.

———. "Observations on the Midrashic Character of John 6." *ZNW* 54 (1963) 232–40.

Borig, Rainer, *Der wahre Weinstock. Untersuchungen zu Jo 15.1–10.* SANT 16. München: Kösel, 1967.

Boring, M. Eugene. *The Continuing Voice of Jesus: Christian Prophecy and Gospel Tradition.* Louisville, KY: Westminster/John Knox, 1991.

Bornkamm, Gunter, "Der Paraklet im Johannesevangelium." In *Festschrift für Rudolf Bultmann zum 65. Geburtstag überreicht,* 12–35. Stuttgart: Kohlhammer, 1949.

———. "Die eucharistische Rede im Johannesevangelium." *ZNW* 47 (1956) 161–69.

———. "Towards the Interpretation of John's Gospel: A Discussion of The Testament of Jesus by Ernst Kasemann (1968)." In *The Interpretation of John,* edited by John Ashton, 76–98. London: SPCK, 1986.

Braun, F-M. *Jean le Théologien et son Évangile dans l'Eglise ancienne.* EB. Paris: Gabalda, 1959.

———. *Jean le Théologien: Les grandes Traditions d'Israël. L'accord des Écritures d'après le quatrième Évangile.* EB. Paris: Gabalda, 1964.

Brown, Raymond E., *An Introduction to the Gospel of John.* Edited by Francis J. Moloney. ABRL. New York: Doubleday, 2003.

———. *New Testament Essays.* London: Chapman, 1967.

———. *The Community of the Beloved Disciple.* New York: Paulist, 1979.

———. *The Death of the Messiah. From Gethsemane to the Grave: A Commentary on the Passion Narratives of the Gospels.* ABRL. London: Chapman, 1994.

———. *The Gospel according to John I–XII.* AB 29. New York: Doubleday, 1966.

———. *The Gospel according to John XIII–XXI.* AB 29A. New York: Doubleday 1966.

Bühler, Pierre, "Ist Johannes ein Kreuzestheologe? Exegetische-systematische Bemerkungen zu einer noch offenen Debatte." In *Johannes-Studien. Interdisziplinare Zugange zum Johannesevangelium, Festschrift für Jean Zumstein,* edited by M. Rose, 191–207. Zurich: TVZ, 1991.

Bühner, Jan-A., *Der Gesandte und sein Weg im 4. Evangelium.* WUNT 2. Tübingen: Mohr Siebeck, 1977.

Bultmann, Rudolf. *The Gospel of John.* Translated by George R. Beasley-Murray, et al. Oxford: Blackwell, 1971.

————. *The Theology of the New Testament*, Vol. 2. Translated by K. Grobel. London: SCM, 1955, 1–92.

Burge, Gary M., *The Anointed Community: The Holy Spirit in the Johannine Tradition.* Grand Rapids: Eerdmans, 1987.

Burridge, Richard A. "About People, By People and For People." In *The Gospels for All Christians: Rethinking the Gospel Audiences*, edited by Richard Bauckham, 113–45. Grand Rapids: Eerdmans, 1998.

Cadman, W. H., *The Open Heaven: The Revelation of God in the Johannine Sayings of Jesus.* Edited by G. B. Caird. Oxford: Blackwell, 1969.

Caird, George B. "Judgment and Salvation: An Exposition of John 12.31–32." *CJT* 2 (1956) 231–37.

————. *New Testament Theology.* Completed and edited by L. D. Hurst. Clarendon: Oxford, 1994.

————. "The Glory of God in the Fourth Gospel: An Exercise in Biblical Semantics." *NTS* 15 (1968–69) 265–77.

————. "The Will of God in the Fourth Gospel." *ExT* 74 (1960–61) 115–17.

Carson, D. A., *The Gospel according to John.* Leicester: InterVarsity, 1991.

Charlier, J-P. *Le Signe de Cana.* Paris: Pensée Catholique, 1959.

Chibici-Revneanu, Nicole, *Die Herrlichkeit des Verherrlichten: Das Verständnis der δόξα im Johannesevangelium.* WUNT 2.231. Tübingen: Mohr Siebeck, 2007.

Corell, Alf, *Consummatum Est. Eschatology and Church in the Gospel of St. John.* London: SPCK, 1958.

Coloe, Mary L., *God Dwells With Us: Temple Symbolism in the Fourth Gospel.* Collegeville, MA: Liturgical, 2001.

Cosgrove, Charles H., "The Place where Jesus Is: Allusions to Baptism and Eucharist in the Fourth Gospel." *NTS* 35 (1989) 522–39.

Cullmann, Oscar, *Early Christian Worship.* Translated by A. S. Todd and J. B. Torrance. SBT 10. London: SCM, 1953.

————. "Samaria and the Origins of the Christian Mission." In *The Early Church.* Translated by A. J. B. Higgins, and S. Godman, 185–92. London: SCM, 1956.

————. *The Johannine Circle: Its Place in Judaism among the Disciples of Jesus and in Early Christianity. A Study in the Origin of the Gospel of John.* Translated by John Bowden. London: SCM, 1976.

Culpepper, R. Alan. *Anatomy of the Fourth Gospel: A Study in Literary Design.* Philadelphia: Fortress, 1983.

————. *The Johannine School: An Evaluation of the Johannine-School Hypothesis based on an Investigation of the Nature of Ancient Schools.* SBLDS 26. Missoula, MT: Scholars, 1975.

Dahl, Nils A. "Der Erstgeborene Satans und der Vater des Teufels (Polyk. 7.1 und Joh 8.44)." In *Apophoreta. Festschrift für Ernst Haenchen*, 70–84. BZNW 30. Berlin: Topelmann, 1964.

————. "The Johannine Church and History." In *Current Issues in New Testament Interpretation*, edited by Walter Klassen and Graydon F. Snyder, 124–42. London: SCM, 1962.

Dauer, Anton. *Die Passionsgeschichte im Johannesevangelium: Eine traditionsgeschichtliche und theologische Untersuchung zu Joh 18.1—19.30.* SANT 30. München: Kösel, 1972.

Davies, Margaret. (See also Pamment, Margaret) *Rhetoric and Reference in the Fourth Gospel.* JSNTSS 69. Sheffield: Sheffield Academic, 1992.

Dennis, John A. *Jesus' Death and the Gathering of True Israel: The Johannine Appropriation of Restoration Theology in the Light of John 11.47–52.* WUNT 2.217. Tübingen: Mohr Siebeck, 2006.

Dettwiler, Andreas, and Jean Zumstein, eds. *Kreuzestheologie im Neuen Testament.* WUNT 151. Tübingen: Mohr Siebeck, 2002.

Dibelius, Martin, "Joh 15.13. Eine Studie zum Traditionsproblem des Johannesevangelium." In *Festgabe fur A. Deissmann,* 168–86, Tübingen: Mohr Siebeck, 1927. Reprinted in Martin Dibelius, *Botschaft und Geschichte.* Edited by Gunter Bornkamm, Vol. 1, 204–20. Tübingen: Mohr Siebeck, 1953.

Dietzfelbinger, Christian, "Sühnetod im Johannesevangelium?" In *Evangelium–Schriftauslegung–Kirche, Festschrift für Peter Stuhlmacher,* edited by Jostein Adna et al., 65–76. Göttingen: Vandenhoeck & Ruprecht, 1997.

Dodd, C. H., *According to the Scriptures: The Substructure of New Testament Theology.* London: Nisbet, 1952.

———. *Historical Tradition in the Fourth Gospel.* Cambridge: Cambridge University Press, 1963.

———. *The Interpretation of the Fourth Gospel.* Cambridge: Cambridge University Press, 1958.

Dunn, James D. G. *Baptism in the Holy Spirit.* SBT 15. London: SCM, 1970.

———. *Jesus and the Spirit: A Study of the Religious and Charismatic Experience of Jesus and the First Christians as Reflected in the New Testament.* London: SCM, 1975.

———. "John VI—A Eucharistic Discourse?" *NTS* 17 (1970–71) 328–38.

———. "Let John be John: A Gospel for Its Time." In *The Christ and The Spirit, Volume 1. Christology,* 345–75. Edinburgh: T. & T. Clark, 1998.

———. "The Washing of the Disciples' Feet in John 13.1–20." *ZNW* 61 (1970) 247–52.

———. *Unity and Diversity in the New Testament.* London: SCM, 1977.

Dupont, Jacques, *Essai sur la Christologie de St. Jean.* Bruges: Abbaye de St. André, 1951.

Evans, Craig A., *Word and Glory: On the Exegetical and Theological Background of John's Prologue.* JSNTSS 89. Sheffield: Sheffield Academic, 1993.

Ferreira, Johan, *Johannine Ecclesiology.* JSNTSS 160. Sheffield: Sheffield Academic, 1998.

Feuillet, André, *Johannine Studies.* Translated by T. E. Crane. Staten Island, NY: Alba House, 1965.

Ford, Josephine Massyngbaerde. *Redeemer–Friend and Mother: Salvation in Antiquity and in the Gospel of John.* Minneapolis: Fortress, 1997.

Forestell, J. Terence. *The Word of the Cross: Salvation as Revelation in the Fourth Gospel.* AB 57. Rome: Biblical Institute, 1974.

Fortna, Robert T. *The Gospel of Signs: A Reconstruction of the Narrative Source underlying the Fourth Gospel.* SNTSMS 11. Cambridge: Cambridge University Press, 1970.

Fortna, Robert T., and Tom Thatcher, eds. *Jesus in Johannine Tradition.* Louisville, KY: Westminster/John Knox, 2001.

Franck, Eskil, *Revelation Taught: The Paraclete in the Gospel of John.* CB NTS 14. Lund: CWK Gleerup, 1985.

Freed, Edwin D., *Old Testament Quotations in the Gospel of John.* SNT 11. Leiden: Brill, 1965.

Frey, Jorg. "Die 'theologia crufixi' des Johannesevangelium." In *Kreuzestheologie im Neuen Testament*, edited by Andreas Dettwiler and Jean Zumstein, 169–238. WUNT 151. Tübingen: Mohr Siebeck, 2002.

———. "Probleme der Deutung des Todes Jesu in der neutestamentlichen Wissenschaft. Streiflichter zur exegetischen Diskussion." In *Deutungen des Todes Jesu im Neuen Testament*, edited by Jorg Frey and Jens Schröter, 3–50. WUNT 181. Tübingen: Mohr Siebeck, 2005.

———. "'Wie Mose Schlange in der Wüste erhöht hat . . .' Zur fruhjüdischen Deutung der 'ehernen Schlange' und ihrer christologischen Rezeption in Johannes 3, 14f." In *Schriftauslegung im antiken Judentum und im Urchristentum*, edited by Martin Hengel and Hermut Löhr, 153–205. WUNT 73. Tübingen: Mohr Siebeck, 1994.

Griesmer, Dirk F. *In den Prozetz verwickelt: Erzähltextanalytische und textpragmatische Erwägungen zur Erzählung vom Prozetz Jesu vor Pilatus (Joh 18.28—19.16a.b)*. EH 23.688. Frankfurt: Lang, 2000.

Grayston, Kenneth. *Dying, We Live: A New Enquiry into the Death of Christ in the New Testament*. 276–323. London: Darton, Longman & Todd, 1990.

Haacker, Klaus. *Die Stiftung des Heils: Untersuchungen zur Struktur des johanneischen Theologie*. ATh 47. Stuttgart: Calwer, 1972.

Haenchen, Ernst. *A Commentary on the Gospel of John*. Edited by Ulrich Busse and translated by Robert W. Funk. 2 Vols. Hermeneia Series. Philadelphia: Fortress, 1984.

Hahn, Ferdinand, "Die Hirtenrede in Joh 10." In *Theologia Crucis—Signum Crucis. Festschrift für Erik Dinkler*, edited by Carl Andresen and Gunter Klein, 185–200. Tübingen: Mohr Siebeck, 1979.

Hanson, Anthony T., *The Living Utterances of God: The New Testament Exegesis of the Old*. London: Darton, Longman and Todd, 1983.

———. *The Prophetic Gospel: A Study of John and the Old Testament*. Edinburgh: T. & T. Clark, 1991.

Harvey, A. E. *Jesus on Trial: A Study in the Fourth Gospel*. London: SPCK, 1976.

Hasitschka, Martin. *Befreiung von Sünde nach dem Johannesvanngelium. Eine bibeltheologische Untersuchung*. IBS 27. Innsbruck: Tyrolia, 1989.

Heckel, Ulrich. *Hirtenamt und Herrschaftskritik. Die urchristlichen Ämter aus johanneischer Sicht*. BTS 65. Neukirchen, Germany: Neukirchener, 2004.

Hegermann, H. "Er kam in sein Eigentum. Zur Bedeutung des Erdenwirkens Jesu im vierten Evangelium." In *Der Ruf Jesu und die Antwort der Gemeinde. Festschrift für Joachim Jeremias*, edited by Eduard Lohse et al., 112–31. Göttingen: Vandenhoeck & Ruprecht, 1970.

Hengel, Martin. *The Johannine Question*. Translated by John Bowden. London: SCM, 1989.

Higgins, A. J. B. *Jesus and the Son of Man*. London: Lutterworth, 1964.

Hill, David. *New Testament Prophecy*. Basingstoke, UK: Marshall, Morgan & Scott, 1979.

Hofius, Otfried, and H-C. Kammler. *Johannesstudien: Untersuchungen zur Theologie des vierten Evangelium*. WUNT 88. Tübingen: Mohr Siebeck, 1996.

Hollis, H. "The Root of the Johannine Pun ΥΨΩΘΗΝΑΙ." *NTS* 35 (1989) 475–78.

Hoskyns, Edwyn C. *The Fourth Gospel*. Edited by Francis N. Davey. 2nd ed. London: Faber & Faber, 1947.

Hübner, Hans. "EN APXH EΓΩ EIMI." In *Israel und seine Heilstraditionen im Johannesevangelium: Festgabe für Johannes Beutler zum 70. Geburtstag*, edited by Michael Labahn et al., 107–22. Paderborn, Germany: Schöningh, 2004.

Hultgren, Arland J. "The Johannine Footwashing (13.1–11) as Symbol of Eschatological Hospitality." *NTS* 28 (1982) 539–46.

Jeremias, Joachim, "Joh. 6.51c–58—redaktionall?" *ZNW* 54 (1952–53) 256–57.

Johnston, George., *The Spirit-Paraclete in the Gospel of John.* SNTSMS 12. Cambridge: Cambridge University Press, 1970.

Jonge, Marinus de. *Jesus: Stranger from Heaven and Son of God.* Edited and translated by John E. Steely. Missoula, MT: Scholars, 1977.

Kammler, H.-C. "Die 'Zeichen' des Auferstandenen: Uberlegungen zur Exegese von Joh 20.30–31." In *Johannesstudien: Untersuchungen zur Theologie des vierten Evangeliums*, edited by O. Hofius and H.-C. Kammler, 191–211. WUNT 88. Tübingen: Mohr Siebeck, 1996.

Käsemann, Ernst. "The Structure and Purpose of the Prologue to John's Gospel." In *New Testament Questions of Today*, translated by W.J. Montague, 138–67. London: SCM, 1969.

———. *The Testament of Jesus: A Study of the Gospel of John in the Light of Chapter 17.* Translated by Gerhard Kroedel. London: SCM, 1968.

Klaiber, Walter. "Die Aufgabe einer theologischen Interpretation des 4. Evangeliums." *ZThK* 82 (1985) 300–24.

Knöppler, Thomas. *Die theologia crucis des Johannesevangeliums: Das Verständnis des Todes Jesu im Rahmen der johanneischen Inkarnations- und Erhöhungschristologie* WMANT69. Neukirchen, Germany: Neukirchener, 1994.

———. *Sühne im Neuen Testament: Studien zum urchristliche Verständnis der Heilsbedeutung des Todes Jesu.* WMANT 88. Neukirchen, Germany: Neukirchener, 2001.

Koester, Craig R. *Symbolism in the Fourth Gospel. Meaning, Mystery, Community.* 2nd ed. Minneapolis: Fortress, 2003.

Kohler, Herbert, *Kreuz und Menschwerdung im Johannesevangelium: Ein exegetisch-hermeneutischer Versuch zur johanneischen Kreuzestheologie.* AThANT 72. Zurich: TVZ, 1987.

Kollmann, Hanjo-Christoph. *Die Kreuzigung Jesu nach Joh 19, 16–22. Ein Beitrag zur Kreuzestheologie des Johannes im Vergleich mit den Synoptikern.* EH XXIII.710. Frankfurt: Lang, 2000.

Kostenberger, Andreas J. *The Missions of Jesus and the Disciples according to the Fourth Gospel: With Implications for the Fourth Gospel's Purpose and the Mission of the Contemporary Church.* Grand Rapids: Eerdmans, 1998.

Kovacs, Judith L. "Now Shall the Ruler of This World be Driven Out: Jesus' Death as Cosmic Battle in John 12.20–36." *JBL* 114 (1995) 227–47.

Kuhl, Josef. *Die Sending Jesu und der Kirche nach Johannes-Evangelium.* St. Augustine: Steyler, 1967.

Kuhn, Heinz-Wolfgang, "Jesus als Gekreuzigter in der frühchristlichen Verkundigung bis zur Mitte des 2. Jahrhunderts." *ZThK* 72 (1975) 1–46.

Labahn, Michael, et al., eds. *Israel und seine Heilstraditionen im Johannesevangelium. Festgabe für Johannes Beutler zum 70. Geburtstag.* Paderborn, Germany: Schöningh, 2004.

Lang, Manfred. *Johannes und Synoptiker: Eine redaktionsgeschichtliche Analyse von Joh 18–20 vor dem markinischen und lukanischen Hintergrund*. Göttingen: Vandenhoeck & Ruprecht, 1999.

Cordula Langner. "Was für ein Konig ist Jesus?" In *Israel und seine Heilstraditionen im Johannesevangelium*, edited by Michael Labahn et al., 247–68. Paderborn, Germany: Schöningh, 2004.

Lazure, Noël. *Les Valeurs Morales de la Théologie Johannique (Évangile et Epîtres)*. EB. Paris: Gabalda, 1965.

Leenhardt, Franz J. "La structure du chapitre 6 de l'évangile de Jean." *RHPR* 39 (1959) 1–13.

Leon-Dufour, X. "Le mystere du Pain de Vie (Jean VI)." *RSR* 46 (1958) 481–523.

Leroy, Herbert, *Rätsel und Missverstandnis. Ein Beitrag zur Formgeschichte des Johannesevangeliums*. BBB 30. Bonn: Hanstein, 1968.

Lieu, Judith M. "Blindness in the Johannine Tradition." *NTS* 34 (1988) 83–95.

Lightfoot, R. H. *St. John's Gospel: A Commentary*. Edited by C. F. Evans. Oxford: Oxford University Press, 1956.

Lincoln, Andrew T. *The Gospel according to Saint John*. BNTC. London: Continuum, 2005.

———. *Truth on Trial: The Lawsuit Motif in the Fourth Gospel*. Peabody, MA: Hendrickson, 2000.

Lindars, Barnabas. *Jesus Son of Man: A Fresh Examination of the Son of Man Sayings in the Gospels in the Light of Recent Research*. London: SPCK, 1983.

———. *The Gospel of John*. NCB. London: Oliphants, 1972.

———. "The Passion in the Fourth Gospel." In *God's Christ and His People: Festschrift for Nils A. Dahl*, edited by Jacob Jervell and Wayne A. Meeks, 71–86. Oslo: Universitatsverlaget, 1977.

———. 'Word and Sacrament in the Fourth Gospel.' *SJT* 29 (1976) 49–63.

Lindemann, Andreas. "Gemeinde und Welt im Johannesevangelium." In *Kirche, Festschrift für Gunter Bornkamm*, edited by Dieter Lührmann and Georg. Strecker, 133–61. Tübingen: Mohr Siebeck, 1980.

Loader, William, *The Christology of the Fourth Gospel. Structure and Issues*. Frankfurt: Lang, 1989.

Lohse, Eduard, "Wort und Sakrament im Johannesevangelium." *NTS* 7 (1960–61) 110–25.

Longenecker, Bruce W. "The Unbroken Messiah: A Johannine Feature and its Social Functions." *NTS* 41 (1995) 428–41.

Luz, Ulrich. "Theologia Crucis als Mitte der Theologie im Neuen Testament." *EvTh* 34 (1974) 116–41.

Maddox, Robert, "The Function of the Son of Man in the Gospel of John." In *Reconciliation and Hope: New Testament Essays on Atonement and Eschatology, presented to L. L. Morris*, edited by Robert J. Banks, 186–204. Exeter: Paternoster, 1974.

Marsh, John, *Saint John*. Pelican Gospel Commentaries. Harmondsworth, UK: Penguin, 1968.

Martyn, J. Louis, *History and Theology in the Fourth Gospel*. New York: Harper & Row, 1968.

———. *The Gospel of John in Christian History: Essays for Interpreters*. New York: Paulist, 1979.

Meeks, Wayne A. "The Man from Heaven in Johannine Sectarianism." *JBL* 91 (1972) 44–72.

———. *The Prophet-King: Moses Traditions and the Johannine Christology.* SNT 14. Leiden: Brill, 1967.

Menken, Maarten J. "Die jüdischen Feste im Johannesevangelium." In *Israel und seine Heilstraditionen im Johannesevangelium*, edited by Michael Labahn et al., 269–86. Paderborn, Germany: Schöningh, 2004.

———. "John 6.51c–58: Eucharist or Christology?" *Biblica* 74 (1993) 1–26.

———. *Old Testament Quotations in the Fourth Gospel: Studies in Textual Form.* CBET 15. Kampen, the Netherlands: Pharos, 1996.

Metzer, Rainer. *Das Verständnis der Sünde im Johannesevangelium.* WUNT 122. Tübingen: Mohr Siebeck, 2000.

Michl, J. "Der Sinn der Fusswaschung." *Biblica* 40 (1959) 697–708.

Mohr, Till A. *Markus- und Johannespassion: Redaktions- und traditionsgeschichtliche Untersuchung der Markinischen und Johanneischen Passionstradition.* AThANT 70. Zürich: TVZ, 1982.

Moloney, Francis J. "Israel, the People and the Jews in the Fourth Gospel." In *Israel und seine Heilstraditionen im Johannesevangelium*, edited by Michael Labahn et al., 351–64. Paderborn, Germany: Schöningh, 2004.

———. *The Gospel of John.* Sacra Pagina 4. Collegeville, MN: Liturgical, 1998.

———. *The Johannine Son of Man.* Rome: Las-Roma, 1976.

Morgan-Wynne, John Eifion, "A Note on John 14.17b." *BZ* 23 (1979) 93–96.

———. "The Cross and the Revelation of Jesus as ἐγώ εἰμι in the Fourth Gospel (John 8.28)." In *Studia Biblica* 1978 Vol. II, edited by Elizabeth A. Livingstone, 219–26. JSNTSS 2. Sheffield: JSOT, 1980.

———. "References to Baptism in the Fourth Gospel." In *Baptism, The New Testament and the Church: Historical and Contemporary Studies in Honour of R. E. O. White*, edited by Stanley E. Porter & Anthony R. Cross, 116–35. Sheffield: Sheffield Academic, 1999.

Morris, Leon. L., *The Gospel according to John.* NICNT. Grand Rapids: Eerdmans, 1971.

Motyer, Stephen. *Your Father the Devil? A New Approach to John and "the Jews."* PBM. Carlisle, UK: Paternoster, 1997.

Moule, Charles F. D. "The Individualism of the Fourth Gospel." *NT* 5 (1962) 171–90.

Muller, Theophil, *Das Heilsgeschehen im Johannesevangelium: Eine exegetische Studie, zugleich der Versuch einer Antwort an Rudolf Bultmann.* Zürich: Gotthelf, 1963.

Müller, Ulrich B. "Die Bedeutung des Kreuzestodes Jesu im Johannesevangelium. Erwägung des Kreuzestheologie im Neuen Testament." *KuD* 21 (1975) 49–71.

———. "Die Parakletenvorstellung im Johannesevangelium." *ZTK* 71 (1974) 31–78.

———. "Zur Eigentumlichkeit des Johannesevangelium. Das Problem des Todes Jesu." *ZNW* 88 (1997) 24–55.

Mussner, Franz. ZΩH. *Die Anschauung vom "Leben" im vierten Evangelium unter Berucksichtigung der Johannesbrief.* MTS 1. Historische Abteilung 5. München: Zink, 1952.

———. *The Historical Jesus in the Gospel of St. John.* Translated by W. J. O'Hara. QD 19. London: Burns & Oates, 1967.

Neugebauer, J., "Die Textbezuge von Joh 4.1–42 und die Geschichte der johanneischen Grue." *ZNW* 84 (1993) 135–41.

Nicholson, Godfrey C. *Death as Departure: The Johannine Descent-Ascent Schema.* SBLDS 63. Chico, CA: Scholars, 1983.

Nissen, Johannes. "Community and Ethics in the Gospel of John." In *New Readings in John*, edited by Johannes Nissen and Sigfred Pedersen, 194–212. Sheffield: Sheffield Academic, 1999.

———. "Mission in the Fourth Gospel: Historical and Hermeneutical Perspectives." In *New Readings in John*, edited by Johannes Nissen and Sigfred Pedersen, 213–31. Sheffield: Sheffield Academic, 1999.

Obermann, Andreas. *Die christologische Erfüllung der Schrift im Johannesevangelium.* WUNT 83. Tübingen: Mohr Siebeck, 1996.

Obuki, Y. *Die Wahrheit im Johannesevangelium.* Bonn: Hanstein, 1972.

Odeberg, Hugo. *The Fourth Gospel Interpreted in its Relation to Contemporaneous Religious Currents in Palestine and the Hellenistic-Oriental World.* Uppsala: Almqvist, 1929.

Okure, Teresa. *The Johannine Approach to Mission. A Contextual Study of John 4.1–42.* WUNT 31. Tübingen: Mohr Siebeck, 1988.

Olsson, Birger, *Structure and Meaning in the Fourth Gospel: A Text-Linguistic Analysis of John 2.1–11 and 4.1–41.* CB NT series 6. Lund: CWK Gleerup, 1974.

Onuki, Takashi, *Gemeinde und Welt im Johannesevangelium. Ein Beitrag zur Frage nach den theologischen und pragmatischen Funktion des johanneischen "Dualismus."* WMANT 56. Neukirchen, Germany: Neukirchener, 1984.

Orchard, Helen C. *Courting Berayal: Jesus as Victim in the Gospel of John.* JSNTSS 161: GCT 5. Sheffield: Sheffield Academic, 1998.

Osten-Sacken, Peter von der. "Leistung und Grenze der johanneischen Kreuzestheologie." *EvTh* 36 (1976) 154–76.

Painter, John. "Sacrifice and Atonement in the Gospel of John." In *Israel und seine Heilstraditionen im Johannesevangelium*, edited by Michael Labahn et al., 287–313. Paderborn, Germany: Schöningh, 2004.

———. *The Quest for the Messiah: The History, Literature and Theology of the Johannine Community.* Edinburgh: T. & T. Clark, 1991.

Pamment, Margaret (see also Davies, Margaret). "The Meaning of doxa in the Fourth Gospel." *ZNW* 74 (1983) 12–16.

Porsch, Felix, *Pneuma und Wort: Ein exegetischer Beitrag zur Pneumatologie des Johannesevangeliums.* FTS 16. Frankfurt: Knecht, 1974.

Potterie, Ignace de la, "Jesus roi et juge d'après Jean 19.13." *Biblica* 41 (1960) 217–47.

———. *La Vérité dans Saint Jean, Tome I: Le Christ et la vérité. L'Esprit et la vérité.* AB 73. Rome: Biblical Institute, 1977.

———. *La Vérité dans Saint Jean. Tome II: Le croyant et la vérité.* AB 74. Rome: Biblical Institute, 1977.

———. "Naitre de l'eau et naitre de l'Esprit." *Sc.Ec.* 14 (1962) 351–74.

———. *The Hour of Jesus: The Passion and the Resurrection of Jesus according to John: Text and Spirit.* Translated by Gregory Murray. Slough: St. Paul, 1989.

Preiss, Theo. *Life in Christ.* SBT 13. Translated by H. Knight. London: SCM, 1957.

Pribnow, H. *Die Begriffe vom Leben in vierten Evangelium.* Greifswald: Mamberg, 1934.

Rahner, Johanna, *"Er aber sprach vom Tempel seines Leibes." Jesus von Nazaret als Ort der Offenbarung Gottes im vierten Evangelium.* BBB 117. Bodenheim: Philo, 1998.

Regensberger, David. *Overcoming the World: Politics and Community in the Gospel of John.* London: SPCK, 1989. (USA Title: *Johannine Faith and Liberating Community.* Philadelphia: Westminster, 1988).

Richter, Georg. "Blut und Wasser aus der durchbohrten Seite Jesu (Joh.19.34b)." *MTZ* 21 (1970) 1–21.

———. *Die Fusswaschung im Johannesevangelium: Geschichte und Deutung.* BU1. Regensburg: Pustet, 1967.

———. *Studien zum Johannesevangelium.* Edited by Josef Hainz. BU 13. Regensburg: Pustet, 1977.

———. "Zur Formgeschichte und literarischen Einheit von Joh 6.31–58." *ZNW* 60 (1969) 21–55.

Riedl, Johannes. *Das Heilswerk Jesu nach Johannes.* Freiburg: Herder, 1973.

Rigsby, B. H. "The Cross as an Expiatory Sacrifice in the Fourth Gospel." *JSNT* 15 (1982) 51–80.

Ringe, Sharon H. *Wisdom's Friends: Community and Christology in the Fourth Gospel.* Louisville, KY: Westminster John Knox, 1999.

Robinson, John A.T., "The Significance of the Footwashing." In *Neotestamentica et Patristica: Eine Freundesgabe für O. Cullmann,* edited by Amos Wilder et al., 144–47. Leiden: Brill, 1962.

Ruckstuhl, Eugen. *Die literarische Einheit des Johannesevangeliums: der gegenwartige Stand der einschlägigen Forschung.* Freiburg: Paulusverlag, 1951.

———. "Abstieg und Erhöhung des johanneischen Menschensohns." In *Jesus und Menschensohn, für A. Vögtle,* edited by Rudolf Pesch et al., 315–43. Freiburg: Herder, 1975.

Ruiz, Miguel R. *Der Missionsgedanke des Johannesevangeliums: Ein Beitrag zur johanneischen Soteriologie und Ekklesiologie.* FzB 55. Wurzburg: Echter, 1987.

Sanders, J. N., *The Gospel according to St. John.* Edited by B. A. Masten. BNTC. London: A. & C. Black, 1968.

Schenke, Ludger "Die formale und gedankliche Struktur von Joh 6.26–58." *BZ* 24 (1980) 21–41.

Schlatter, D. A. *Der Evangelist Johannes: Wie er spricht, denkt und glaubt.* Stuttgart: Calwer, 1930.

Schlier, Heinrich, "Zum Begriff des Geistes nach Johannesevangelium." In *Neutestamentliche Aufsätze: Festschrift für Josef Schmid,* edited by Josef Blinzer et al., 233–39. Regensburg: Pustet, 1963.

Schlund, Christine. *"Kein Knochen soll gebrochen werden." Studien zu Bedeutung und Funktion des Pesachfests in Texten des frühen Judentums und im Johanessevangelium.* WMANT 107. Neuchirchen, Germany: Neukirchener, 2005.

Schnackenburg, Rudolf. *The Gospel according to St. John.* Vol. 1. Translated by Kevin Smyth. London: Burns & Oates, 1968.

———. *The Gospel according to St. John.* Vol. 2. Translated by Cecily Hastings et al. London: Burns & Oates, 1980.

———. *The Gospel according to St. John.* Vol. 3. Translated by D. Smith and G. A. Kon. New York: Crossroad, 1982.

Schneider, Johannes, "Zur Frage Komposition von Joh 6.27–58 (59)—Die Himmelsbrotrede." In *In Memoriam Ernst Lohmeyer,* edited by W. Schmauch, 131–42. Stuttgart: Evangelische, 1951.

Schnelle, Udo, "Die Abschiedsrede im Johannesevangelium." *ZNW* 80 (1989) 64–79.

————. *Antidocetic Christology in the Gospel of John: An Investigation of the Place of the Fourth Gospel in the Johannine School.* Translated by Linda M. Maloney. Minneapolis: Fortress, 1992.

Scholtissek, Klaus. "'Geschrieben in diesem Buch' (Joh 20.30). Beobachtungen zum kanonischen Anspruch des Johannesevangelium." In *Israel und seine Heilstraditionen im Johannesevangelium.* Edited by Michael Labahn et al. 207–26. Paderborn, Germany: Schöningh, 2004.

Schulz, Siegried. *Untersuchungen zur Menschensohn-Christologie im Johannesevangelium, zugleich ein Beitrag zur Methodengeschichte der Auslegung des 4.Evangeliums.* Göttingen: Vandenhoeck & Ruprecht, 1957.

————. *Das Evangelium nach Johannes.* NTD 4. Göttingen: Vandenhoeck & Ruprecht, 1975.

Schürman, Heinz. "Joh 6.51c. Ein Schlüssel zur grossen johanneischen Brotrede." *BZ* 2 (1958) 244–62.

Schweizer, Eduard. "Das johanneische Zeugnis vom Herrenmahl." *EvTh* 12 (1952–53) 341–63.

————. "Das Herrenmahl im Neuen Testament." In *Neotestamentica,* Zürich: Zwingli, 1963.

Scott, Martin. *Sophia and the Johannine Jesus.* JSNTS 71. Sheffield: JSOT, 1992.

Segovia, Fernando F. *Love Relationships in the Johannine Tradition: Agape/Agapan in 1 John and the Fourth Gospel.* SBLDS 58. Chico, CA: Scholars, 1982.

————. "John 13.1–20. The Footwashing in the Johannine Tradition." *ZNW* 73 (1982) 31–51.

————. "The Theology and Provenance of John 15.1–17." *JBL* 101 (1982) 115–28.

Smith, D. Moody. *Johannine Christianity: Essays on its Setting, Sources and Theology.* Edinburgh: T. & T. Clark, 1987.

Snaith, Norman H. "The Meaning of 'The Paraclete.'" *ExT* 57 (1945–46) 47–50.

Söding, Thomas. "Die Offenbarung des Logos. Biblische Theologie und Religionsgeschichte im johanneischen Spektrum." In *Israel und seine Heilstraditionen im Johannesevangelium,* edited by Michael Labahn et al. 387–415. Paderborn, Germany: Schöningh, 2004.

Stibbe, Mark W. G. *John as Storyteller: Narrative Criticism and the Fourth Gospel.* SNTSMS 73. Cambridge: Cambridge University Press, 1992.

Strathmann, Hermann. *Das Evangelium nach Johannes.* NTD 4. Göttingen: Vandenhoeck & Ruprecht, 1959.

Straub, Esther. "Der Irdische als der Auferstandene. Kritische Theologie bei Johannes ohne ein Wort vom Kreuz." In *Kreuzestheologie im Neuen Testament,* edited by Andreas Dettwiler and Jean Zumstein, 239–64. WUNT 151. Tübingen: Mohr Siebeck, 2002.

Taylor, Vincent. *The Atonement in the New Testament.* 2nd ed. London: Epworth, 1945.

————. *Jesus and His Sacrifice: A Study of the Passion-Sayings in the Gospels.* London: Macmillan, 1951, 218–49.

Theobald, Michael. *Die Fleischwerdung des Logos: Studien zum Verhaltnis des Johannesprologs zum Corpus des Evangeliums und zu 1Joh.* NA 20. Münster: Aschendorff, 1988.

————. *Herrenworte im Johannesevangelium.* HBS 34. Freiburg: Herder, 2002.

Thomas, John C. *Footwashing in John 13 and the Johannine Community.* JSNTSS 61. Sheffield: JSOT, 1991.

Thompson, Marianne M. *The God of the Gospel of John*. Grand Rapids: Eerdmans, 2001.

———. *The Humanity of Jesus in the Fourth Gospel*. Philadelphia: Fortress, 1988.

Thüsing, Wilhelm, *Die Erhöhung und Verherrliching Jesu im Johannesevangelium*. NA 21.1–2. 3rd ed. Münster: Aschendorff, 1979.

Thyen, Hartwig. "Entwicklungen innerhalb der johanneischer Theologie und Kirche im Spiegel von Joh 21 und der Lieblingsjungertexte des Evangeliums." In *L'Évangile de Jean: sources, rédaction, theologie*, edited by Marinus de Jonge, 259–99. BETL 44. Louvain: Louvain University Press, 1977.

———. "Johannes 10 im Kontext des vierten Evangeliums." In *The Shepherd Discourse of John 10 and its Context*, edited by Johannes Beutler and Robert T. Fortna, 115–34. SNTSMS 67. Cambridge: Cambridge University Press, 1991.

———. "Johannes 13 und die 'kirchliche Redaktion' des vierten Evangeliums." In *Tradition und Glaube: Festschrift für Karl-Georg Kuhn*, edited by Gert Jeremias et al., 343–67. Göttingen: Vandenhoeck & Ruprecht, 1971.

———. "'Niemand hat grössere Liebe als die, dass er sein Leben für seine Freunde hingibt.' (Joh 15.13). Das johanneische Verständnis des Kreuzestodes Jesu." In *Theologia crucis—Signum crucis, Festschrift für E. Dinkler*, edited by Carl Andresen and Gunter Klein, 467–81. Tübingen: Mohr Siebeck, 1979.

Trites, Allison A., *The New Testament Concept of Witness*. SNTSMS 31. Cambridge: Cambridge University Press, 1977.

Turner, Max B. "Atonement and the Death of Jesus in John—Some Questions to Bultmann and Forestell." *EQ* 62 (1990) 99–122.

Van Unnik, Wilhelm C. "The Quotation from the Old Testament in John 12.34." *NT* 3 (1959) 174–79.

Vergote, A. "L'exaltation du Christ en croix selon le quatriéme Evangile." *ETL* 28 (1952) 5–23.

Weidemann, Hans-Ulrich. *Der Tod Jesu im Johannesevangelium: Die erste Abschiedsrede als Schlüsseltext für den Passions- und Osterbericht*. BZNW 122. Berlin: de Gruyter, 2004.

Wengst, Klaus, *Bedrängte Gemeinde und verherrlichter Christus: Ein Versuch über das Johannesevangelium*. BThSt 5. 2nd ed. Neukirchen, Germany: Neukirchener, 1983.

Whitacre, Richard A. *Johannine Polemic: The Role of Tradition and Theology*. Chico, CA: Scholars, 1982.

Wikenhauser, Alfred. *Das Evangelium nach Johannes*. RNT 4. Regensburg: Pustet, 1961.

Wilckens, Ulrich. "Christus traditus se ipsum tradens." In *Gemeinschaft am Evangelium, Festschrift für Wiard Popkes*, edited by E. Brandt et al., 363–84. Leipzig: Evangelische Verlagsanstalt, 1996.

———. "Der eucharistische Abschnitt der johanneischen Rede vom Lebensbrot (Joh 6.51c–58)." In *Neues Testament und Kirche: Festschrift für R. Schnackenburg*, edited by Joachim Gnilka, 220–48. Freiburg: Herder, 1974.

———. *Das Evangelium nach Johannes*. NTD 4. Göttingen: Vandenhoeck & Ruprecht, 1998.

———. *Der Sohn Gottes und seine Gemeinde. Studien zur Theologie der johanneischen Schriften*. FRLANT 200. Göttingen: Vandenhoeck & Ruprecht, 2003.

Wilkens, Wilhelm. "Das Abendmahlzeugnis im vierten Evangelium." *EvTh* 18 (1958) 354–80.

———. *Die Entstehungsgeschichte des vierten Evangeliums*. Zollikon: EVZ, 1958.

————. *Zeichen und Werke: Ein Beitrag zur Theologie des vierten Evangeliums in Erzahlungs- und Redestoff.* AThANT 55. Zürich: TVZ, 1969.

Windisch, Hans. *The Spirit-Paraclete in the Fourth Gospel.* Translated by J. W. Cox. Facet Books: Biblical Series 20. Philadelphia: Fortress, 1968.

Wink, Walter. "'The Son of Man' in the Gospel of John." In *Jesus in Johannine Tradition,* edited by Robert T. Fortna and Tom Thatcher, 117–24. Louisville: Westminster/ John Knox, 2001.

Witherington III, Ben. *Women in the Earliest Churches.* SNTSMS 59. Cambridge: Cambridge University Press, 1988.

Woll, D. Bruce. *Johannine Christianity in Conflict: Authority, Rank and Succession in the First Farewell Discourse.* SBLDS 60. Chico, CA: Scholars, 1981.

Yee, Gale A. *Jewish Feasts and the Gospel of John.* Wilmington, DE: Glazier, 1989.

Zemke, C. "Der sogenannte Logos-Hymnus im johanneischen Prolog." *ZNW* 58 (1967) 45–68.

Zumstein, J., "Die johanneische Interpretation des Todes Jesu." In *Kreative Erinnerung. Relecture und Auslegung im Johannesevangelium,* J. Zumstein, 219–39. AThANT 84. 2nd ed. Zürich: TVZ, 2004.

B: THE FIRST EPISTLE OF JOHN

Berger, Klaus. "Die implizierten Gegner: Zur Methode des Erschlietzens von 'Gegnern' in neutestamentliche Texten." In *Kirche. Festschrift für G. Bornkamm,* edited by Dieter Lührmann and Georg Strecker, 373–400. Tübingen: Mohr Siebeck, 1980.

de Boer, Martinus C. "Jesus the Baptizer: 1 John 5.5–8 and the Gospel of John." *JBL* 107 (1988) 87–106.

————. "The Death of Jesus Christ and His Coming in the Flesh (1 John 4.2)." *NT* 33 (1991) 326–46.

Bogart, John, *Orthodox and Heretical Perfectionism in the Johannine Community as Evident in the First Epistle of John.* SBLDS 33. Missoula, MT: Scholars, 1977.

Bonnard, Pierre, *Les epîtres johanniques.* Commentaire du Nouveau Testament 13C. Geneva: Labor et Fides, 1983.

Brooke, A. E. *The Johannine Epistles.* ICC. Edinburgh: T. & T. Clark, 1912.

Brown, Raymond E. *The Epistles of John.* AB 30. New York: Doubleday, 1982.

Bultmann, Rudolf. "Analyse des ersten Johannesbriefes." In *Festgabe für A. Jülicher,* edited by Rudolf Bultmann and Hermann F. von Soden, 138–58. Tübingen: Mohr Siebeck, 1927.

————. "Die kirchliche Redaktion des ersten Johannesbriefes." In *In Memoriam Ernst Lohmeyer,* edited by Werner Schmauch, 189–201. Stuttgart: Evangelisches, 1951.

————. *The Johannine Epistles.* Translated by R. P. O'Hara et al. Hermeneia. Philadelphia: Fortress, 1973.

Caird, George B. "Letters of John." In *The Interpreter's Dictionary of the Bible,* Vol.E–J. Edited by George Arthur Buttrick. Nashville, TN: Abingdon, 1962.

Conzelmann, Hans. "Was von Anfang war." In *Neutestamentliche Studien für Rudolf Bultmann,* edited by Walter Eltester, 194–201. BZNW 21. Berlin: Topelmann, 1954.

Dodd, C. H. *The Johannine Epistles.* Moffatt New Testament Commentary. London: Hodder & Stoughton, 1946.

Dunn, James D. G., *Baptism in the Holy Spirit.* SBT 2.15. London: SCM, 1971.

Edwards, M. J. "Martyrdom and the First Epistle of John." *JTS* 31 (1989) 164–71.

Edwards, Ruth B. *The Johannine Epistles.* NT Guides. Sheffield: Sheffield Academic, 1996.

Erlemann, K. "1Joh und der judisch-christliche Trennungsprozess." *TZ* 55 (1999) 285–302.

Griffith, Terry M. "A Non-Polemical Reading of 1 John: Sin, Christology and the Limits of Johannine Christianity." *Tyndale Bulletin* 49 (1998) 253–76.

———. *Keep Yourselves from Idols: A New Look at 1 John.* JSNTSS 233. Sheffield: Sheffield Academic, 2002.

Hauck, Friedrich. *Die Kirchenbriefe.* NTD 10. Göttingen: Vandenhoeck & Ruprecht, 1957.

Houlden, J. Leslie. *A Commentary on the Johannine Epistles.* BNTC. London: A. & C. Black, 1973.

Klauck, Hans-Josef. *Der erste Johannesbrief.* EKKNT 23.1. Neukirchen, Germany: Neukirchener, 1991.

———. "Internal Opponents: the Treatment of the Secessionists in the First Epistle of John." *Concilium* 200 (1988) 55–65.

Law, Robert. *The Tests of Life: A Study of the First Epistle of St. John.* Edinburgh: T. & T. Clark, 1909.

Lieu, Judith M. "Authority to become Children of God." *NT* 23 (1981) 210–28.

———. *The Theology of the Johannine Epistles.* Cambridge: Cambridge University Press, 1991.

———. "What was from the Beginning: Scripture and Tradition in the Johannine Epistles." *NTS* 39 (1993) 458–77.

Malatesta, Edward. *Interiority and Covenant: A Study of* εἶναι ἐν *and* μένειν ἐν *in the First Letter of Saint John.* AnBib 69. Rome: Biblical Institute, 1978.

Marshall, I. Howard. *The Epistles of John.* NICNT. Grand Rapids: Eerdmans, 1978.

Müller, Ulrich B. *Die Geschichte der Christologie in der johanneischen Gemeinde.* SBS 77. Stuttgart: KBW, 1975.

Nauck, Wolfgang. *Die Tradition und der Charakter des ersten Johannesbriefes. Zugleich ein Beitrag zur Taufe im Urchristentum und in den alten Kirche.* WUNT 3. Tübingen: Mohr Siebeck, 1957.

Painter, John. *The Quest for the Messiah: The History, Literature and Theology of the Johannine Community.* Edinburgh: T. & T. Clark, 1991.

———. *1, 2, and 3 John.* Sacra Pagina 18. Collegeville, MN: Litugical, 2002.

Perkins, Pheme. *The Johannine Epistles.* NT Message 21. Wilmington, DE: Glazier, 1979.

De la Potterie, Ignace, "Le Peche, c'est l'iniquite (1Jn 3.4)." In Ignace de la Potterie and Stanislaus Lyonnet, *La Vie selon l'Esprit. Condition du Chrétien*, 65–83. Unam Sanctam 55. Paris: Cerf, 1965.

Robinson, John A. T. *Twelve New Testament Studies.* SBT 34. London: SCM.

Schmid, H. *Gegner im 1. Johannesbrief? Zu Konstruktion und Selbstreferenz im johanneischen Sinnsystem.* BWANT 159. Stuttgart: Kohlhammer, 2002.

———. "How to read the First Epistle of John Non-Polemically." *Bib* 85 (2004) 24–41.

Schnackenburg, Rudolf. Die *Johannesbriefe.* HTKNT 13.3. 7th ed. Freiburg: Herder, 1984 (= *The Johannine Epistles.* Translated by Reginald and Ilse Fuller. Tunbridge Wells, UK: Burns & Oates, 1992).

Schneider, Johannes, *Die Kirchenbriefe*. NTD 10. Göttingen: Vandenhoeck & Ruprecht, 1961.

Smalley, Stephen S. *1, 2, 3 John*. WBC 51. Dallas, TX: Word, 1984.

Smith, D. Moody. *First, Second, and Third John*. Interpretation. Louisville: John Knox, 1991.

Stegemann, E., "Kindlein, hutet euch vor den Gottesbildern!" *TZ* 41 (1985) 284–94.

Strecker, Georg, "Die Anfange der johanneische Schule." *NTS* 32 (1986) 31–47.

———. *The Johannine Letters*. Translated by Linda M. Mahoney. Hermeneia. Minneapolis: Fortress, 1996.

Thompson, Marianne M. *1–3 John*. IVP NT Commentary Series. Downers Grove, IL: InterVarsity, 1992.

Thornton, T. C. G. "Propiation or Expiation? Ἱλαστήριον and ἱλασμός in Romans and 1 John." *Ex.T.* 80 (1968) 53–55.

Thyen, Hartwig, "Johannesbriefe." *TRE* 17 (1988) 186–200.

von Walde, Urban C. *The Johannine Commandments: 1 John and the Struggle for the Johannine Tradition*. New York: Paulist, 1990.

Wengst, Klaus. *Häresie und Orthodoxie im Spiegel des ersten Johannesbriefes*. Gütersloh, Germany: Mohn, 1976.

Westcott, Brooke Fosse. *The Epistles of St. John*. 2nd ed. Cambridge and London: Macmillan, 1886.

Wilckens, Ulrich. "Die Gegner im 1 und 2 Johannesbrief, 'die Juden' im Johannesevangelium und die Gegner in den Ignatiusbriefen und den Sendschreiben der Apokalypse." In *Religionsgeschichte des Neuen Testament. Festschrift für Klaus Berger*, edited by Andreas von Dobbeler et al., 477–500. Tübingen: Francke, 2000.

Wurm, Alois. *Die Irrelehrer im ersten Johannesbrief*. BS 8.1. Freiburg: Herder, 1903.

C: THE BOOK OF REVELATION[1]

Aune, David E. *Revelation 1–5*. WBC 52A. Dallas, TX: Word, 1997.

———. *Revelation 6–16*. WBC 52B. Nashville, TN: Thomas Nelson, 1998.

———. *Revelation 17–22*. WBC 52C. Nashville, TN: Thomas Nelson, 1998.

Barker, Margaret. *The Revelation of Jesus Christ*. Edinburgh: T. & T. Clark, 2000.

Bauckham, Richard. *The Climax of Prophecy: Studies on the Book of Revelation*. Edinburgh: T. & T. Clark, 1993.

———. *The Theology of the Book of Revelation*. Cambridge: Cambridge University Press, 1993.

Beale, G. K. *The Book of Revelation*. NIGTC. Grand Rapids: Eerdmans, 1999.

Beasley-Murray, George R. *The Book of Revelation*. NCB. London: Oliphants, 1974.

Böcher, Otto, *Kirche in Zeit und Endzeit: Aufsätze zur Offenbarung des Johannes*. Neukirchen, Germany: Neukirchener, 1983.

Boxall, Ian, *The Revelation of Saint John*. BNTC. London: Continuum, 2006.

Caird, George B., *The Revelation of St. John the Divine*. BNTC. London: A. & C. Black, 1966.

Charles, R. H. *The Revelation of St. John*. 2 Vols. ICC. Edinburgh: T. & T. Clark, 1920.

1. See chapter 5, Excursus 2.

Collins, Adela Yarbro. *The Combat Myth in the Book of Revelation*. HDR 9. Missoula, MT: Scholars, 1976.

Hemer, Colin J. *The Letters to the Seven Churches of Asia in their Local Setting*. BRS. Grand Rapids: Eerdmans, 2001.

Hoffmann, Matthias Reinhard. *The Destroyer and the Lamb: The Relationship between Angelomorphie und Lamb Christology in the Book of Revelation*. WUNT 2.203. Tübingen: Mohr Siebeck, 2005.

Holtz, Traugott. *Die Christologie der Apokalypse des Johannes*. TU 85. Berlin: Akademie, 1962.

Johns, Loren L. *The Lamb Christology of the Apocalypse of John. An Investigation into Its Origins and Rhetorical Force*. WUNT 2.167. Tübingen: Mohr Siebeck, 2003.

Jörns, Klaus-Peter, *Das hymnische Evangelium. Untersuchungen zu Aufbau, Funktion und Herkunft der hymnischen Stücke in der Johannesoffenbarung*. SNT 5. Gütersloh: Mohn, 1971.

Kalms, Jürgen U. *Der Sturz des Gottesfiendes: Traditionsgeschichtliche Studien zu Apokalypse 12*. WMANT 93. Neukirchen, Germany: Neukirchener, 2001.

Karrer, Martin. *Die Johannesoffenbarung als Brief: Studien zu ihrem literarischen, historischen und theologischen Ort*. FRLANT 140. Göttingen: Vandenhoeck & Ruprecht, 1986.

Kiddle, Martin, *The Revelation of St. John*. MNTC. London: Hodder and Stoughton, 1940.

Kraft, Heinrich, *Die Offenbarung des Johannes*. HNT 16A. Tübingen: Mohr Siebeck, 1974.

Kraybill, J.Nelson. *Imperial Cult and Commerce in John's Apocalypse*. JSNTSS 132. Sheffield: Sheffield Academic, 1996.

Leivestad, Ragnar. *Christ the Conqueror: Ideas of Conflict and Victory in the New Testament*. London: SPCK, 1954.

Lohse, Eduard. *Die Offenbarung des Johannes*. NTD 11. Göttingen: Vandenhoeck & Ruprecht, 1976.

Mealy, J. Webb. *After the Thousand Years: Resurrection and Judgment in Revelation 20*. JSNTSS 70. Sheffield: Sheffield Academic, 1992.

Mounce, Robert H. *The Book of Revelation*. NICNT. Rev. ed. Grand Rapids: Eerdmans, 1997.

Preston, Ronald H and Hanson, Anthony T. *The Revelation of Saint John the Divine*. TBC. London: SCM, 1949.

Prigent, Pierre. *L'Apocalypse de Saint Jean*. CNT XIV. Geneva: Labor et Fides, 1988.

Rissi, Mathias. *The Future of the World: An Exegetical Study of Revelation 19.11—22.15*. SBT 2.23. London: SCM, 1972.

Roloff, Jürgen. *Revelation*. A Continental Commentary. Translated by J. E. Alsup. Minneapolis: Fortress, 1993.

Royalty, Jr., Robert M. *The Streets of Heaven: The Ideology of Wealth in the Apocalypse of John*. Macon, GA: Mercer University Press, 1998.

Slater, Thomas B. *Christ and Community: A Socio-Historical Study of the Christology of Revelation*. JSNTSS 178. Sheffield Academic, 1999.

Smalley, Stephen S. *The Revelation to John: A Commentary on the Greek Text of the Apocalypse*. Downers Grove, Illinois: IVP, 2005.

Sweet, John P. M. *Revelation*. Westminster Pelican Commentaries. Philadelphia: Westminster, 1979.

Taegar, Jens-W. *Johannesapokalypse und johanneischer Kreis*. Berlin: Topelmann, 1989.

————. "'Gesiegt! O himmlische Musik des Wortes!'—Zur Entfaltung des Siegesmotivs in den johanneischen Schriften." *ZNW* 65 (1994) 23–46.

Thompson, Leonard L. *The Book of Revelation: Apocalypse and Empire*. Oxford-New York: Oxford University Press, 1990.

Torrance, Thomas F. *The Apocalypse Today*. London: SPCK, 1960.

D: OTHER NEW TESTAMENT & EARLY CHRISTIAN LITERATURE

Betz, Hans Dieter. *Galatians*. Hermeneia. Philadelphia: Fortress, 1979.

Caird, George B. *The Language and Imagery of the Bible*. Duckworth Studies in Theology. London: Duckworth, 1980.

Collins, John J. "The Son of God Text from Qumran." In *From Jesus to John: Essays on Jesus and New Testament Christology in Honour of Marinus de Jonge*, edited by Martinus C. de Boer, 65–82. JSNTSS 84. Sheffield: Sheffield Academic, 1993.

Dunn, James D. G., ed. *Jews and Christians: The Parting of the Ways AD 70 to 135*. Grand Rapids: Eerdmans, 1999.

————. *The Partings of the Ways Between Christianity and Judaism and their Significance for the Character of Christianity*. London: SCM, 1991.

Hartmann, Lars. *Into the Name of the Lord Jesus*. Edinburgh: T. & T. Clark, 1997.

Hays, Richard B. *The Moral Vision of the New Testament: A Contemporary Introduction to New Testament Ethics*. Edinburgh: T. & T. Clark, 1996.

Hengel, Martin. *The Atonement: The Origin of the Doctrine in the New Testament*. Translated by John Bowden. Philadelphia: Fortress, 1971.

Hill, David. *Greek Words and Hebrew Meanings*. SNTSMS 5. Cambridge: Cambridge University Press, 1967.

Horbury, William. "The Benediction of the Minim and Early Jewish-Christian Controversy." *JTS* 33 (1982) 19–61.

Jeremias, Joachim. *The Eucharistic Words of Jesus*. Translated by Norman Perrin. London: SCM, 1966.

Käsemann, Ernst. *New Testament Questions of Today*. Translated by W. J. Montague. London: SCM, 1969.

Katz, Steven T. "Issues in the Separation of Judaism and Christianity after 70 CE: A Reconsideration." *JBL* 103 (1984) 43–76.

Kimelman, Reuben. "Birkat Ha-Minim and the Lack of Evidence for an Anti-Christian Jewish Prayer in Late Antiquity." In *Jewish and Christian Self-Definition*, Vol. 2, edited by E. P. Sanders et. al., 226–44. Philadelphia: Fortress, 1981.

Kramer, Werner. *Christ Lord Son of God*. Translated by B. Hardy. SBT 50. London: SCM, 1966.

Lindars, Barnabas. *New Testament Apologetic*. London: SCM, 1967.

Metzger, Bruce M. *A Textual Commentary on the Greek New Testament*. Corrected edition. London: United Bible Societies, 1975.

Morris, Leon. *The Apostolic Preaching of the Cross*. 2nd ed. London: Tyndale, 1956.

Moule, C. F. D. *The Origin of Christology*. Cambridge: Cambridge University Press, 1977.

Mussner, Franz. *Der Galaterbrief*. HTKNT 9. Freiburg: Herder, 1974.

Overman, J. Andrew. *Matthew's Gospel and Formative Judaism: The Social World of the Matthean Community.* Minneapolis: Fortress, 1990.

Perrin, Norman. *Jesus and the Language of the Kingdom.* London: SCM, 1976.

Porter, J. R. "The Legal Aspects of the Concept of 'Corporate Personality' in the OT." *VT* 15 (1965) 361–80.

Porter, Stanley E. "Two Myths: Corporate Personality and Language/Mentality Determinism." *SJT* 43 (1990) 289–307.

Rogerson, John W. "The Hebrew Conception of Corporate Personality: A Re-examination." *JTS* 21 (1970) 1–16.

Rowland, Christopher. *The Open Heaven: A Study of Apocalyptic in Judaism and Early Christianity.* London: SPCK, 1982.

Schoedel, William R. *Ignatius of Antioch.* Hermeneia. Philadelphia: Fortress, 1985.

Schweizer, Eduard. "Zur Herkunft der Präexistenzvorstellung bei Paulus." *Ev.Th.* 19 (1959) 65–70.

Stanton, Graham N. *A Gospel for a New People: Studies in Matthew.* Edinburgh: T. & T. Clark, 1992.

Wengst, Klaus, *Christologische Formeln und Lieder des Urchristentums.* Gütersloh, Germany: Mohn, 1972.

Wright, N. T. *The Climax of the Covenant: Christ and Law in Pauline Theology.* Edinburgh: T. & T. Clark, 1991.

(E) DICTIONARIES, GRAMMARS & CONCORDANCES

Bauer, Walter. *A Greek-English Lexicon of the New Testament.* Translated and adapted by William F. Arndt and F. Wilbur Gingrich. Chicago: University of Chicago Press and Cambridge: Cambridge University Press, 1957.

Blass, Friedrich and Albert Debrunner. *A Greek Grammar of the New Testament and Other Early Christian Literature.* Translated and revised by Robert W. Funk. Cambridge: Cambridge University Press and Chicago: University of Chicago Press, 1961.

Brooks, James A., and Carlton L. Winberry. *A Syntax of New Testament Greek.* Washington: University Press of America, 1979.

Buttrick, George Arthur, ed. *Interpreter's Dictionary of the Bible,* 4 vols. Nashville, TN: Abingdon, 1963.

Denis, A-M., and Y. Janssens, eds. *Concordance Grecque des Pseudepigraphes d'Ancien Testament.* Louvain: Université Catholique de Louvain, 1987.

Kittel, Gerhard, and Gerhard Friedrich, eds. *A Theological Dictionary of the New Testament.* Translated by Geoffrey W. Bromiley. 10 Vols. Grand Rapids: Eerdmans, 1964–76.

Liddell, Henry George, and Robert Scott. *A Greek-English Lexicon.* Revised and augmented by Sir Henry Stuart Jones with the asistance of Robert McKenzie. Oxford: Clarendon, 1968.

Robertson, A. T. *A Grammar of the Greek New Testament.* Nashville, TN: Broadman, 1934.

Index of Author

Appold, M. L., 14, 38, 88, 165, 166
Ashton, J., 6, 15, 28, 37–39, 55, 77,
    88, 91, 105, 170, 200, 257
Aune, D. E, 19

Bacon, B. W., 24
Barker, Margaret, 19
Barrett, C. K., 27, 40, 52, 54, 57, 59,
    61, 68, 71, 72, 75–78, 84, 89, 90,
    93, 110, 114–15, 118, 120, 129,
    133, 135–36, 139–41, 143, 147,
    154, 159, 162, 165–68, 171–73,
    178, 181, 200, 203–207, 249
Bauckham, R., 41, 46, 50, 73, 138,
    141, 159, 170, 189, 191
Bauer, W., 120, 157
Beale, G. K., 187–88
Beasley–Murray, G. R 19, 27, 38,
    54, 55, 61, 64, 68, 71– 73, 78,
    84, 85, 90, 101, 114, 118, 120,
    129, 136, 141, 145, 147–48, 150,
    158–59, 162, 165–66, 168, 170,
    172, 175, 177–78, 181, 187, 189,
    198–99, 203–208, 251
Becker, J., 24, 25, 31, 37, 38, 41, 42,
    59, 61, 64, 72, 85, 89–91, 95,
    110, 132, 136, 141, 144–47,
    149, 158–59, 165–66, 168, 170,
    172–73, 175, 177, 202, 204, 205,
    207
Bennema, C., 9, 55, 106, 109, 194,
    204
Berger, K., 234
Bertram, G., 84
Betz, H. D., 241

Betz, O., 72, 151, 168, 187, 194, 205
Beutler, J.,
Bittner, W., 107
De Boer, M. C., 25, 26, 38, 39, 68,
    74, 85, 87, 140, 160–62, 178–79,
    216, 249–50
Blank, J., 11, 17, 27, 28, 38, 39, 59,
    68, 71, 73, 81–83, 113, 150, 187,
    254
Bocher, O., 140, 177
Bühler, P., 6, 63, 145
Bogart, J., 214, 223
Boismard, M–E., 64, 157
Bonnard, P., 215
Borgen , P., 67, 133–34, 136, 139
Borig, R, 121, 144, 147
Boring, M. E., 206
Bornkamm, G., 15, 135–36, 168
Boxall, I., 188, 190
Bredin, M., 191
Brooke, A. E., 248
Brooks, J. A., 76
Brown, R. E., 27, 41, 52, 54–56, 59,
    61, 66, 67, 70, 71, 74–78, 80, 84,
    85, 89, 93, 94, 101, 109–10, 118,
    120–21, 125, 129, 136, 140–41,
    143–45, 147, 149, 153, 158–60,
    162, 165–66, 168, 170, 172–78,
    181–82, 186, 198, 202–207,
    215, 218–19, 223–26, 228, 233,
    243–46, 248–50, 252
Büchsel, F., 246, 248
Bühner, J–A., 67, 126
Bultmann, R., 3, 4, 6, 13, 20, 22, 24,
    37, 38, 41, 44, 55, 59, 61, 64,

68, 72, 73, 75, 77, 78, 90, 93, 99,
  101–102, 110, 118, 120–21, 129,
  136, 141, 145, 148–49, 156–60,
  165–66, 168, 170–73, 175, 177,
  199, 200, 203–205, 207, 212,
  217–18, 244, 248
Burge, G., 59, 61, 129, 168, 181,
  194–96, 205
Burridge, R., 138

Cadman, W. D., 17, 128, 139, 147,
  155, 158–59, 172, 206
Caird, G. B., 17, 69, 82, 109, 128,
  139–40, 150, 188–91, 193, 227
Carroll, J. T., 36, 38
Carson, D., 20, 52, 54, 55, 57, 59, 64,
  67–70, 72–74, 77, 78, 80, 84,
  85, 87, 89, 90, 93, 101, 114–15,
  120, 129, 136–37, 139, 145, 147,
  158–59, 161, 163, 165–67, 170,
  172–73, 175, 177–78, 181–82,
  187, 194, 198–99, 202–203,
  205–6
Charles, R. H., 189
Charlier, J–P., 64
Chibici–Revneanu, Nicole, 3, 21, 22,
  41, 67, 68, 70, 72–79, 83, 138,
  148, 181
Collins, Adele Y., 187
Collins, J. J., 49, 52
Coloe, Mary, 41, 51
Conzelmann, H., 118, 178
Correll, A., 160
Cosgrove, C. H., 135
Cullmann, O., 60, 160, 198, 202,
  218, 249
Culpepper, R. A., 42, 44, 71, 73, 106,
  136, 159, 172, 218

Daalen, D. H., van, 190
Dahl, N. A., 19, 67, 114, 194–95
Dauer, A., 68–70, 100–101, 110, 120,
  175, 18
Davies, Margaret (see also
  Pamment) 44, 45, 54, 95, 128,
  156, 178–79
Delling, G., 100

Dennis, J. A., 37,41, 51, 53, 91, 145,
  148, 153–54, 163, 165–66, 173
Dettwiler, A., 6
Dibelius, M., 144
Dietzfelbinger, C., 34, 38–39, 42, 187
Dodd, C. H., 10, 27, 38, 40, 44, 62,
  67, 83, 89–91, 93, 99, 101, 121–
  22, 126, 129, 136, 142, 156–57,
  168, 172, 175, 178, 181, 200,
  213, 218–19, 225, 228, 246, 248
Dunn, J. D. G., 51, 53, 85, 129,
  135–36, 138–40, 159–60, 181,
  196–99, 205, 248
Dupont, J., 67

Edwards, M. J., 230, 240
Edwards, Ruth, 230
Erlemann, K., 230, 234

Farrer, A., 190
Ferreira, J., 71, 147
Feuillet, A., 136
Ford, Josephine M., 8, 105, 147, 181
Forestell, J. T., 7, 38, 55, 90, 143, 163,
  172
Fortna, R. T., 100, 157
Franck, E., 55, 168, 194–95, 204
Freed, E. D., 67
Frey, J., 34, 35, 38, 39, 41, 84–86, 91,
  96, 119, 163–64, 180–81
Friesen, S. J., 191

Grayston, K., 12, 38, 90, 171, 191,
  218, 244
Green, J. B, 36, 38
Gniesmer, D. F., 13, 38, 41, 45, 53,
  95, 120, 176, 180–82
Griffith, T. M., 218, 223, 226–28,
  230, 232–34, 238
Gutbrod, W., 226

Haacker, K., 163
Hahn, F., 30, 39, 167
Hanson, A. T., 142, 153, 181, 190
Hartmann, L., 251
Harvey, A. E., 194
Hasitschka, M., 89, 91, 92, 96, 109,
  113, 178

Hauck, F., 219, 229
Hays, R. B., 190
Haenchen, E., 24, 25, 38, 60, 61,
    77, 90, 118, 136, 141, 145, 153,
    157–59, 170, 173, 177, 205
Heckel, U., 91, 92
Hegermann, H., 29, 39
Hemer, C. J., 140
Hengel, M., 31, 41, 45, 144
Higgins, A. B. J., 173
Hill, D., 206, 246
Hofius, O., 20, 38, 84 –86, 96, 145,
    153–54, 178, 194, 199
Hollis, H., 88
Holtz, T., 19
Horbury, W., 53
Hoskins, E. C., 57, 67, 101, 110,
    120–21, 147, 167, 170, 172–73,
    181–82, 198, 206
Houlden, J. L., 218–19, 224, 228,
    245–46, 248
Hübner, H., 54
Hultgren, A. J., 158–59

Jeremias, J., 48, 133, 136, 243–44
Johns, L. J., 191
Johnston, G., 168, 181, 194
Jonge, M. de, 204
Jorns, K-P., 188–89

Kaiber, W., 30, 39
Kalms, J. U., 187
Kammler, C., 20, 62, 88, 96, 109,
    116, 119, 129, 150, 178, 194,
    198, 206
Karrer, M., 140, 188
Käsemann, E., 13–15, 28, 31, 38, 39,
    65, 66, 77, 81, 88
Katz, S., 53
Kiddle, M., 189
Kimelman, R., 45, 53
Klauck, H-J., 96, 178, 220, 223, 239,
    249
Knöppler, T., 13, 31, 32, 39, 41, 59,
    64, 66, 70, 84, 89, 91, 95, 96,
    105, 136–37, 140, 145, 154, 159,
    161, 163, 165, 167, 170, 175,
    178–80, 189, 191, 218, 246, 249

Koester, C. R., 21, 38, 52, 72, 89,
    136, 138
Kohler, H., 31, 39, 65, 90, 95, 96, 145
Kollmann, H–C., 83, 153, 159, 165,
    167, 176
Kostenberger, A. J., 109
Kramer, W., 241
Kuhl, J., 145, 147, 156
Kuhn, H. W., 29, 39

Lang, M., 44, 175
Law, R, 219
Langner, C., 121
Lazure, N., 147
Lee, Dorothy A., 20, 134, 136–38
Leenhardt, F–J., 13
Leivestad, R., 18
Leon–Dufour, X., 136
Leroy, H., 13
Lieu, Judith, 219, 223, 230–31, 242,
    24
Lightfoot, R. H., 206
Lincoln, A. T., 52, 53, 61, 63, 64, 69,
    70, 71, 72, 74, 76, 78, 84, 85,
    87, 90, 96, 101, 110, 118, 120,
    128–29, 136, 139, 145, 147,
    156, 158–59, 163–67, 172–73,
    177–82, 194, 203, 205–7
Lindars, B., 19, 27, 38, 48, 52, 54, 59,
    61, 71, 72, 75, 80, 84, 85, 89, 90,
    93, 101, 107, 109, 118, 120, 129,
    134, 136, 139, 141, 147, 158–59,
    162–63, 165–66, 170, 172–73,
    175, 177–78, 181–82, 202–7
Lindemann, A., 30, 39, 90
Loader, W., 6, 38, 44, 87, 141, 150,
    163
Lohse, E., 136
Luz, U., 29, 39

Maddox, R., 173
Malatesta, E., 219
Maloney, F. J., 48, 54, 55, 57, 58, 59,
    61, 64, 67–70, 72, 73, 75, 78, 80,
    84, 85, 87, 88, 90, 96, 101–102,
    114, 116, 118, 120, 129, 136,
    139, 141, 147, 162, 165, 167–68,

170, 172–73, 177, 181–82, 199, 203–204, 207

Marsh, J., 73

Marshall, I. H., 215, 226, 228–29, 244–46, 248

Martyn, J. L., 53

Mealy, J. W., 188, 190

Meeks, W., 44, 77, 138, 157, 181

Menken, M. J. J., 50, 93, 139, 145, 173, 180

Metzner, R., 20, 38, 43, 46, 90–92, 96, 113–14, 119, 172, 180, 194, 199

Michl, J., 158–5

Mohr, T., 17

Morgan–Wynne, J. E., 48, 102, 143, 197–98

Morris, L., 67, 68, 72, 74, 84, 85, 90, 93, 120, 130, 145, 171, 178, 246

Motyer, S., 51

Moule, C. F. D., 126, 156, 201

Mounce, R. H., 189

Müller, T., 16, 90, 91, 163, 170

Müller, U. B., 5, 6, 29, 34, 37, 38, 41, 163, 168, 191, 194, 214

Mussner, F., 16, 38, 90, 135, 163, 179, 204, 241, 248

Nauck, W., 214, 226, 229

Neufeld, D., 230

Neufeld, V. H., 220

Neugebauer, J., 202

Nicholson, G. C., 14, 38, 40, 58, 62, 85, 86, 88, 138, 141

Nielsen Helge K., 37–39, 92

Nissen, J., 145, 147

Obermann, A., 38, 50, 96–98, 100–101, 134, 180

Obuki, Y., 194

Odeburg, H., 139

Okure, Teresa, 41, 44, 109, 147, 153, 202

Olsson, B., 55, 59, 63, 147, 172, 204–6

Onuki, T., 8, 71, 73, 109, 144, 146–48, 156–57, 159, 178, 193, 195, 201, 205–207

Orchard, Helen C., 37, 38, 138

Osten–Sacken, P. Von der, 30

Overman, A., 53

Painter, J., 9, 38, 95, 137, 139, 144, 153, 172, 215, 218–19, 224–25, 228–29, 231, 243, 246, 248, 250

Pamment, Margaret (see, Davies, Margaret), 67, 71, 74, 88

Perkins, Pheme 23

Perrin, N., 63

De la Potterie, I., 54, 55, 59, 155, 171, 181, 199, 204–205, 223, 225–26, 24

Preiss, T., 154, 157, 187, 189, 194

Preston, R. H. (and A. T. Hanson), 140, 190

Pribnow, H., 200

Prigent, P., 189

Porsch, F., 55, 61, 109, 129, 168, 181, 194, 204–5

Porter, J. R., 154

Porter, S. E., 154

Rahner, Joanna, 8, 38, 93–95

Regensberger, D. K., 8, 136

Richter, G., 23, 24, 31, 38, 133, 135–36, 158–59, 177, 249–51

Riedle, J., 11, 28, 38–40, 60, 68, 70, 71, 74, 75, 81–83, 90, 96, 98, 99, 109, 113, 125, 143, 145, 152, 154, 173, 176, 254

Rigsby, B. H., 19

Ringe, Sharon, 106

Rissi, M., 190

Robertson, A. T., 92, 117

Robinson, J. A. T., 159, 162, 166, 202, 248

Roloff, J., 140

Rowland, C., 190

Royalty, R. M., 191

Rogerson, J. W., 154

Ruckstuhl, E., 11, 38, 133, 14

Ruiz, M. R., 92

Sanders, J. N., 77, 101, 149, 181

Schenke, L., 40, 136

Schlatter, A., 93, 120, 147, 150, 158, 187

Schlier, H., 195
Schlund, Christine, 180
Schmid, H., 91, 230–31, 233, 236–39
Schnackenburg, R., 18, 27, 48, 52,
    54, 57, 61, 64, 66, 67, 71–73,
    78, 80, 84, 85, 88–93, 100–101,
    110, 113–14, 118–20, 123, 129,
    135–36, 139, 141, 143–45, 147,
    149, 151, 153, 158–59, 162–63,
    166, 168, 171–73, 175, 177–78,
    181–82, 195, 198–200, 203–
    207, 213, 218, 221, 224–26, 228,
    243–47, 252
Schneider, J., 136, 158, 219, 228–29,
    248
Schnelle, U., 30, 31, 39, 41, 62, 95,
    144, 159, 218–19, 221
Schoedel, W., 249
Scholtissek, K., 86
Schotroff, Luise, 31, 201
Schröter, J., 34, 35, 39
Schultz, S., 5, 37, 41, 141, 172–73,
    194, 248
Schürmann, H., 16, 38, 134–36
Schweitzer, E., 134, 136–37, 168,
    177, 241, 249, 251
Scott, M., 202
Segovia, F. F., 109, 144, 158–59, 161
Smalley, S. S., 189, 215, 218, 225–26,
    228–29, 243–46, 248–51
Smith, D. M., 219, 226, 228–29, 246
Snaith, N., 168
Stanton, G. N., 53
Stegemann, E., 230, 239–40
Stibbe, M., 42, 167
Strathmann, H., 70, 72, 73, 80, 120,
    149
Straub, Esther, 35, 36, 38, 64, 116
Strecker, G., 218, 224, 226, 229, 232,
    241, 243, 246, 248
Sweet, J. P., 189–90

Taegar, J–W., 189, 258
Taylor, V., 5, 37, 170, 213
Theobald, M., 12, 25, 38, 42, 54, 85,
    86, 89, 91, 102–105, 108, 122,
    134, 146–47, 152–53, 163, 166–
    67, 173–74, 207, 248–49

Thompson, L. L., 190
Thompson, Marianne M.,
    19, 65, 137, 139, 159, 162–63, 178,
    224, 249–50
Thomas, C., 42, 159, 161
Thornton, T. C. G., 246
Thüsing, W., 16, 27, 39, 56, 60–62,
    66, 68–72, 74, 75, 77, 78, 80, 81,
    83–86, 88, 94, 109, 125, 128–29,
    142–43, 145, 147–48, 152–53,
    159, 162, 170, 172, 176, 178,
    206, 254
Thyen, H., 31, 39, 40, 144, 158, 235
Torrance, T. F., 190
Trites, A. A., 168, 194–95
Turner, M. M., 20, 91

Van Unnik, W. C., 52
Vergote, A., 10, 38, 83
Vögtle, A., 11
Vouga, F., 6, 7, 12, 37, 38
Von Walde, U. C., 216, 250

Weidemann, H., 26, 69, 74, 84, 95,
    102, 109, 114–15, 120, 122, 146,
    151, 167, 177, 180–82, 188
Wengst, K., 30, 31, 39, 53, 221, 241,
    248
Westcott, B. F., 120, 244, 249
Whitacre, R. A., 67, 109, 228
Wikenhauser, A. S., 73, 120, 149,
    170
Wilckens, U., 33, 34, 38, 39, 41, 42,
    54, 64–66, 73, 83,89, 90, 92, 95,
    109, 128, 135–36, 139, 144–45,
    147, 153, 158, 167, 172–73, 181,
    201, 228, 230–31, 234–36, 243
Wilkens, W., 22, 23, 38, 66, 108–
    109, 135, 152, 163
Wimbrey, C. L., 7
Windisch, H., 205
Wink, W., 156
Witherington, B., 202
Wright, N. T., 154
Wurm, A., 234

Yee, Gale, 51

Zemke, C., 54
Zumstein, J., 6, 32, 33, 38, 39, 65, 71,
    83, 96, 102, 113, 134, 157–60,
    167, 175–77, 180–81

Index of Ancient Documents

OLD TESTAMENT

Genesis

1–4	224
3	188
3:4	114
4	114
40:13	88
40:19	88
40:20–22	88

Exodus

4:9	186
12:4	186
12:22	101, 180
12:46	176, 259
16:13–14	48
16:15	133
17:1–7	185–87
17:2	186
17:7	186
18:13	186
34:6–7	242
34:6	242

Numbers

9:12	180, 259
20:11	186
21:8–9	88
21:9	84

Deuteronomy

6:4	49
18:15–18	46
18:15	47
32:4	242

2 Samuel

7:12–16	49

Job

1–2	114, 188
21:33	153

Psalms

2	187
2:7	49
22:15	259
22:18	259

Psalms (cont.)

34:20	176, 180, 259
41:9	259
42:6–7	62
69:4	259
69:9	92–93
69:21	101, 259
78:15–16	174
78:20	174
78:24	48
89:26–29	49
89:37	52
118:22	97

Isaiah

6:9–10	259
6:9	225
6:10	67
12:3	174
25:6	64
32:15, 19	250
40:3	97
41:22–23	108
43:5	164
43:10–13	108
44:8	108
45:21	108, 242
48:3–6	108
49:12	164
52:13	88, 184
53	20
53:1	67, 259
54:13	133
63:1–6	190

Jeremiah

23:2–3	164

31:1–6	
(LXX 38.1–6)	153
31:3	
(LXX 38:3)	152–53
31:12	64

Ezekiel

11:17, 19	250
34:12	164
36:26–27	250
37:21	164
39:29	250
47:12	174

Hosea

2:2	64
11:4	152–53
14:7	64

Joel

2:28–30	250
2:19, 24	64
3:18	64

Amos

9:13–14	64

Zechariah

9–14	142
9:9	71
12:10	176, 180, 259
13:7	142
14:8	174

APOCRYPHA

4 Ezra

13:47   164

Wisdom of Solomon

2:23–24   114

PSEUDEPIGRAPHA

4 Maccabees

9:20   251

Psalms of Solomon

8:34   164

1 Enoch

10:19   64

Testament of Benjamin

10:7–8   232

2 Baruch

29:5   64

NEW TESTAMENT

Matthew

7:23   226
10:39   148
11:27   199
12:38–40   94
13:41   226
16:17   137
16:19   91, 122
16:25   148
18:18   91, 122

24:12   226
26:31   142
26:52   99

Mark

1:9–11   236
8:30   88
8:31   63, 84
8:35   148
9:12   63
9:31   63
10:33–34   63
10:45   63, 88
14:27   142
14:36   99
14:58   94
16:14   226

Luke

9:24   148
10:22   197
17:25   84
17:33   148
22:19   162
22:20   162
24:26   84

John

1:1–18   40, 88, 89
1:1–2   124
1:1   54
1:3–4   127
1:3   116, 127
1:4   127, 199
1:6–8   92
1:10   116, 127
1:12–14   21

John (cont.)

1:12–13	21, 123, 198, 200
1:12	89
1:14	32, 65, 66, 75, 77, 80, 124–25, 128–29, 236
1:15	92, 249
1:16	200
1:17	105, 128
1:18	18, 54, 89, 124, 129, 155, 200
1:19–51	88, 89, 91
1:23	97
1:26	47
1:29–34	236
1:29	4, 6, 9, 10, 16, 18–20, 24, 25, 31, 33, 37, 88–92, 112, 163, 180, 193, 213, 215, 243–44, 252, 255, 258
1:30	25
1:31	25, 47, 100
1:33	47
1:34	89, 179
1:36	89–91, 213, 215
1:41	46, 88
1:43	46
1:45	48, 88
1:49	46
1:51	50, 88, 172–74, 182, 203, 256
2:1–11	95
2:4	15, 56, 57, 64, 65
2:6	203

2:11	65, 66, 75, 129
2:13–22	15, 30, 92, 255
2:13	22
2:14–22	30, 95
2:14–16	93
2:16	93
2:17–22	95
2:17	48, 92, 97
2:18	94
2:19	43, 93, 94, 203
2:20	46, 94
2:21–22	32, 60
2:21	94, 203
2:22	72, 88, 93, 94, 204
2:24–25	106
3:1–2	95
3:3	191. 200
3:3–8	123
3:5	22, 24, 135, 178, 197–99, 204, 258
3:6–11	135
3:8	195–96
3:12–15	15
3:12	198
3:13	50, 84, 85
3:14–21	31
3:14–16	215
3:14–15	10, 16, 48, 50, 84–86, 127, 132, 141, 145, 182, 200, 255
3:14	11, 86
3:15–16	199
3:15	179, 198
3:16–21	6, 257
3:16–17	171, 193, 241

John (cont.)

3:16	84, 127, 130, 145, 183, 198, 200, 213
3:17	91, 200
3:18–19	117, 149
3:18	199–200
3:19–20	116
3:22	216
3:26	216
3:27–30	92
3:28	46
3:31–36	257
3:31–32	6
3:32	54
3:33	128
3:34–35	130
3:34	102, 129
3:35	66, 75, 126, 129–30, 172
3:36	119, 200
4:1	216
4:6	56
4:9	60
4:10	14
4:13–14	127
4:14	88, 173, 178, 200
4:21–24	60, 203
4:21–23	59
4:24	59
4:22	166
4:25–26	46
4:27–42	202
4:28–30	202
4:34–36	147
4:34	21, 98, 99 140, 255
4:35	202
4:36	147
4:38	147, 202
4:39–42	147
4:39	202
4:42	155, 193, 213
4:48	106–107
4:50	107
4:52–53	56
4:53	107
5:1–9	98
5:16	196
5:17	49
5:18	49, 196, 235
5:19–47	50
5:19–27	61, 66
5:19–20	125
5:20	126, 130
5:23	200
5:24–26	200
5:24	61, 119, 127, 196, 200, 228
5:25	60
5:26	127
5:28–29	61, 62
5:30	125
5:33–35	92
5:36	98
5:39	50, 117, 119
5:40	50, 119
5:41	73, 129
5:43	117
5:44	73, 116, 118, 129, 196
5:45–47	48
5:46–47	119
6:2	107
6:4	22

John (cont.)

6:26	107
6:27	173–74, 182, 200
6:28	196
6:29–30	133
6:29	196
6:31–58	9, 24
6:31–51	133, 135
6:31	97, 133
6:32–58	133
6:32–51	133
6:32–35	50, 127, 133, 136
6:32–33	136
6:34	134
6:35	133–37, 200
6:36–47	133
6:37	136, 165, 193
6:39–40	61, 200
6:40	136–37
6:41–51	135
6:41–42	235
6:41	107, 133–34, 196, 233,
6:42	49
6:44	61, 107, 136, 153, 165, 193, 200
6:45	97, 136
6:46	155, 200
6:47	127, 136–37, 200
6:48–51	48, 133, 136
6:48–50	49
6:49–51	134, 136
6:50–51	136

6:51–58	24, 32, 127, 132–33, 135–36, 139, 141, 182, 255
6:51–52	134
6:51	10, 16, 18, 24, 134–37, 140, 162–63, 173, 182, 193, 213
6:52–58	133
6:52	107, 134–35, 137, 196, 233
6:53–58	7, 134–35, 137–38
6:54–58	178
6:54	61, 137, 139, 200
6:55–57	139
6:56	204
6:57	200
6:58	48
6:60–71	135, 235, 237, 239
6:60–63	138
6:60	138, 235
6:61–63	15
6:62	77, 138, 155
6:63	54, 60, 135, 138, 195, 203–4
6:64–65	107
6:65	107, 193
6:66	107, 235
6:68–69	203
6:68	54
6:69	109, 197
6:70–71	113–14
7:4	65
7:6	57, 65

John (cont.)

7:7	116
7:18	73, 116, 118
7:19	27
7:21	98
7:25–43	118
7:25–27	196
7:25	103
7:27–28	48
7:27	47
7:30	15, 56, 59
7:31–36	6
7:31	196
7:32	103
7:33–36	32, 257
7:33–34	103
7:35–36	104
7:35	103
7:37–39	174, 185, 198
7:37–38	50, 71, 127, 173–74, 178, 203
7:37	174
7:38	174
7:39	32, 60, 71–73, 75, 81, 82, 88, 96, 101, 173–74, 178, 182, 204, 255
7:40–44	196
7:41–42	47
7:43	47
7:52	196
8:11–32	200
8:12	127, 193, 199–200, 203
8:14	48
8:16	125, 129
8:20–21	104
8:20	15, 56, 59
8:21–59	232
8:21–29	146
8:21–27	6, 257
8:21–24	119
8:21–22	85
8:21	85, 104, 119–20, 150–51
8:22	85, 119, 141
8:24–25	146
8:24	119, 141–42, 150–51
8:26	54, 125–26, 128
8:28–29	7, 141–42, 183, 255
8:28	9, 54, 85, 108, 125–26, 142–43, 169
8:29	90, 125, 129, 142, 155, 169–70
8:31–58	107
8:31–36	128
8:31–32	90
8:31	54, 55, 107
8:32	4, 116, 128, 171, 256
8:34	115, 119, 200
8:36	49, 200
8:37–40	48
8:39	113
8:40	54, 119
8:41	113
8:42	49
8:44	113–15, 224
8:45	196
8:46	90, 170

John (cont.)

8:47	193	10:26	165, 193
8:48	108	10:27	197
8:49–50	73	10:28	200
8:51	200	10:29	48, 165, 193
8:54	73, 75, 80	10:30	129
8:56–58	68	10:32–38	50
8:56	48	10:33–38	49
9:1–7	198	10:33–36	235
9:5	127, 199	10:33	49
9:7	198	10:34	97
9:22	47	10:36	49, 170, 236
9:24	149, 196, 236	10:38	126, 197
9:29	149	10:40–42	92
9:34	47	11:4	66, 67, 72, 74,
9:39–41	149		75, 80, 81 129
9:39	117, 149	11:9	56
9:40–41	149	11.27	235
10:10	127	11:40	66, 75, 80, 129
10:11	6, 7, 10, 16, 24,	11:45–53	72, 120
	143, 162–63,	11:45	72
	166, 182, 213,	11:46	72
	215, 256	11:47–52	37
10:11–18	9, 12, 143, 165	11:47	72
10:12	143, 165	11:48–52	165
10:14	10, 163, 166	11:49–53	165
10:15	6, 7, 16, 24, 143,	11:49–52	65, 164, 167,
	162–63, 166,		182
	182, 256	11:50–52	10, 156, 163,
10.15–16	164, 167, 182		166, 213, 215
10:16	65, 153, 156,	11:50	16, 164
	163, 166,	11:51–52	9, 24, 32, 162,
	201–202, 256		164, 182,
10:17–18	95, 125–26, 167,		201–202, 215,
	180, 215		256
10:17	6	11:51	24
10:18	6, 126	11:52	69, 153
10:24–38	47	11.53	72
		11:55	22

John (cont.)

12:13	97
12:15	97
12:16	60, 71, 72, 75, 81, 88, 94, 204
12:20–36	65
12:20–34	145, 147, 157, 163–65, 167–68, 179, 256
12:20–22	146
12:23–34	9
12:23	15, 27, 51, 52, 56, 57, 62, 65, 68–70, 74, 75, 81, 82, 129, 146, 153, 169
12:24–26	146
12:24–25	15, 23, 46
12:24	16, 68, 110, 146–47, 153, 155, 166, 215
12:25–26	74
12:25	148
12:26	129, 148, 155, 200
12:27–36	31
12:27–28	62, 148
12:27	68, 146, 148
12:28	27, 30, 73–75, 81, 148
12:31–34	19
12:31–33	68
12:31–32	16–18, 148, 153, 155, 164, 166, 182
12.31	68, 69, 73, 115, 148, 150–52, 154, 168, 183, 187, 195, 244–45, 247, 252, 256, 258, 260
12:32–34	85
12:32–33	15
12:32	9, 17, 25, 51, 146–48, 151–54, 159, 164–65, 193, 202
12:33	14, 32, 51, 52, 60, 85, 88
12:34	24, 52, 84, 85, 138
12:35–36	127
12:36	97
12:37–43	108, 147
12:38–40	97
12:38	52, 97, 100
12:40	225
12:41	48, 50, 67
12:42–43	47, 116, 197
12:43	73, 129
12:44–50	6, 257
12:47–50	55
12:47	193
12:48	61, 117
12:49	125–26
13:1–20	158
13:1–17	31
13:1–11	157, 162, 208, 256
13:1–3	100, 158
13:1	14, 15, 58, 59, 63, 77, 87, 99, 103–104, 143–45, 183, 255

John (cont.)

13:2	108, 114, 121
13:3	59, 104, 121
13:4–5	157
13:4	100
13:5	178
13:6–11	108, 157
13:7	103, 158, 182, 204
13:8	16, 158, 160, 256
13:10	19, 121, 182, 215, 256
13:12–20	158, 161
13:12–17	157
13:13–16	208
13:14–15	24
13:16–17	206
13:16	43, 157
13:18	97, 100, 108, 180, 259
13:19	108–9
13:20	43
13:21–30	108
13:23	54
13:27	114
13:30	231
13:31–38	102
13:31–32	30, 70, 105, 153
13:31–14:31	26
13:32	69, 70, 82
13:33	103–105, 109, 207
13:34–35	143–44, 156–57, 201, 207
13:34	143–44
13:35	208
13:36–38	162
13:36	103, 207
14:1–3	61, 103, 110, 129, 158
14:2–3	104
14:2	153
14:3–6	257
14:4–6	105
14:5	108
14:6	105, 109, 128, 155, 200
14:7	179
14:8–11	108
14:8–9	162
14:9–10	129
14:9	179, 200
14:10–11	126
14:10	172, 197
14:12	76, 103
14:13–14	103
14:13	76, 81
14:15	207
14:16–17	130
14:16	255
14:17	102, 105, 115, 195
14:18	105, 206–7
14:20	126
14:21	207
14:23	103, 105, 207–8
14:26	55, 71, 75, 88, 106, 204–205, 208
14:27	96, 116, 208
14:28	58, 104–105, 108, 208
14:29	26, 108–9

John (cont.)

14:30–31	26, 168, 245, 258
14:30	115, 169, 252
14:31	24, 100, 108, 151, 167, 169, 183, 193, 256
15:1–15	8
15:2	147
15:3	4, 19, 54, 121, 161–62
15:5	147
15:7	55
15:8	69, 76, 81
15:9–16	144
15:9–10	126
15:9	207
15:10	55, 130, 167
15:11	208
15:12–14	207
15:12–13	105
15:12	144, 156, 201
15:13–14	24
15:13	7, 13, 24, 144–45, 162–63, 182–83, 213, 256
15:14–15	105, 144
15:14	207
15:15	54, 126
15:16	103, 153, 202
15:17	23, 201
15:18—16:4	47, 195, 202, 206, 208, 234
15:18–25	117
15:18–21	61
15:18	115
15:19	116
15:21	116
15:22	117, 194
15:23–24	116
15:23	52
15:24	117
15:25	97, 100, 180, 259
15:26–27	141, 166, 194–95, 203
15:26	194
15:27	195, 206
16:1–4	51, 61
16:2–3	118
16:7–11	166, 194
16:7	62, 71, 138, 204, 255
16:8–11	168, 245
16:9	116, 119
16:10	6, 70
16:11	73, 115, 150–51, 168–69, 183
16:12–15	61, 138, 204
16:12–13	205
16:13–15	55, 106
16:13	171, 205
16:14–15	43, 60, 72–73, 205
16:14	75–76, 81
16:16–24	8
16:20–22	208
16:20	116
16:21	56
16:22	96
16:23–24	106
16:25	103
16:26–27	103
16:27	130
16:28	58

John (cont.)

16:29–33	109
16:29–32	162
16:31–32	141, 183, 245, 255
16:31	109
16:32–33	96
16:32	58, 96, 109–10, 125, 129, 142, 146, 155, 193
16:33	16, 168–69, 177, 183, 208, 256, 258
17:1–5	79–80
17:1	15, 65, 70–71, 73–75, 79–81, 129, 169
17:2–3	79
17:2	70, 79–80, 127, 151, 165, 193
17:3	127–28, 197, 200
17:4	70–71, 75, 79, 81, 98–99, 176, 255–56
17:5	70, 77–81, 124, 129
17:6–8	76
17:6	193
17:7–19	61
17:8	54, 197, 203
17:9–10	193
17:9	75, 79, 193
17:10	75–76, 81
17:11	202
17:12	97, 100
17:13	208
17:14	116, 206
17:15	115, 151
17:17	4, 16, 55, 128, 209
17:18	76, 92, 202
17:19	5, 16, 24, 153, 162–63, 170–71, 182–83, 209, 213, 252, 256
17:20–26	156, 201
17:20–23	103
17:20–21	78, 92
17:20	55, 122, 166, 203, 206
17:21–23	126
17:21	70, 79, 193, 208
17:22–24	200
17:22	78, 81, 129
17:23	77, 79, 92, 169, 193, 208
17:24	77–78, 81, 104, 110, 124, 126, 129–30, 154, 159, 165, 167, 193
17:25	116, 130
17:26	130
18:1–11	109
18:1–10	120
18:4–9	180
18:4	99, 206
18:5–6	175
18:8	144, 175
18:9	180
18:10	183
18:11	99, 181, 255
18:14	163, 213
18:15–18	109, 162
18:17	193

John (cont.)

18:18	109
18:19–24	176
18:19	109, 146
18:20	119
18:25–27	109, 162
18:28	120, 180
18:30	120
18:32	180
18:35	120
18:37	128
18:38	114, 117
19:1–3	176
19:4	117
19:5	176
19:6	117
19:7	235
19:9–10	120
19:9	48
19:11	120
19:13	181
19:14	56, 176
19:15	182
19:16	141
19:17	49
19:20	176
19:24	52, 97, 100, 180, 259
19:25–27	110
19:25–26	167
19:25	57
19:26–27	110, 167, 180
19:27	56
19:28–30	98–99, 101
19:28	52, 97–101, 180
19:29	259
19:30	21, 24, 30, 52, 71, 98–99, 101, 176, 255
19:31–39	23
19:31–37	22
19:31–34	176
19:31	100
19:34–35	22, 33, 176–77, 199, 237
19:34	4, 8, 16, 26, 96, 174, 177, 179, 181–82, 185, 249–50, 252–53
19:35	100, 177, 179, 249
19:36–37	97, 100, 176–77, 180
19:36	52, 180, 259
19:37	96, 180, 259
20:11–18	95
20:17–18	202
20:17	204
20:19–29	31, 96, 255
20:19–23	95
20:19	95, 208
20:20–21	96
20:20	202
20:21–22	203
20:21	76, 202, 208
20:22	91, 173, 181, 216
20:23	43, 91, 122
20:24	95
20:25	96
20:27	96
20:28	96, 200

John (cont.)

20:30–31	43, 46, 48, 107, 137, 195, 219, 235
20:31	127, 236
21:19	76
21:21	40

Acts

5:35–39	46
8	202
26:28	232

Romans

6:1–14	251
8:1	189
10:6	235
14:9	87

1 Corinthians

1:13	251
6:11	251
8:6	235
11:24	162
15:3	162, 251

2 Corinthians

8:9	235

Galatians

1:16	137
4:4	241

Ephesians

6:12	137

Philippians

2:6–11	28, 34, 235

2 Thessalonians

2:3	190, 226

Hebrews

1:1–3	235
6:4	198
10:5	235

1 Peter

3:18	162

Revelation

2:7	190
2:11	190
2:17	190
3:5	190
3:12	190
3:20	140
3:21	190
5:1–12	190
12:1–5	190
12:9–11	247
12:12	190
12:17	190
15:2	190
19:11–21	188
19:13	190
19:17	191
20:4–6	188
21:7	190

1 John

1:1	204
1:2	242
1:3	220
1:5–10	212
1:5–6	225
1:5	179, 227

1 John (cont.)

1:6–2:11	232, 238
1:6–2:2	216, 223, 227–29
1:6–10	227
1:6–7	214
1:6	222–23, 227
1:7	163, 178, 212, 214–16, 242–43, 245–46, 252, 258, 260
1:8	215, 222–23, 227
1:9—2:2	242
1:9	212, 214, 226, 228, 242, 257
1:10	222–23, 227
2:1–2	151, 190, 212, 225, 244
2:1	220, 226, 247
2:2	163, 178, 213–16, 220, 228, 243, 246, 253, 258, 260
2:4–9	227
2:4	222, 227
2:6–11	229
2:6	244
2:9–3:10	214
2:9	222
2:11	222, 225
2:12–14	243
2:13–14	225, 245, 258
2:13	243
2:14	225, 243
2:15–17	237
2:15	225, 245
2:16–17	225
2:18–27	231, 237, 239
2:18	190, 226
2:19	218, 230–31
2:20–21	222
2:22–23	221–22
2:22	219–20, 227, 232–33, 235–36
2:23	235–36
2:26–27	222
2:28—3:3	243
2:28–31	243
2:29	226, 244
3:1	225, 247
3:2	78
3:4–10	223
3:4	225–26
3:5	33, 178, 216, 242–43, 247, 252, 260
3:6	223, 244
3:8	224, 226, 242, 244, 252, 260
3:9	223
3:10	222, 224, 247
3:12	224
3:13	220, 225–26
3:14	228
3:16	163, 215–16, 227, 242, 257
3:17–18	222
3:17	229
4:1–6	231, 237
4:1–3	227, 232
4:1	218, 230
4:2–3	251
4:2	216, 219–20, 224, 227, 229, 232, 236–38

1 John (cont.)

4:3	190, 216, 226, 232
4:4	225, 245
4:5	218, 230
4:6	224
4:7–21	229, 237
4:9–10	163, 213, 225, 228, 257
4:9	241–42, 252, 260
4:10	178, 212–13, 215–16, 241–43, 246, 252, 258, 260
4:11	227
4:13	248
4:14	179, 213, 225, 241, 247, 252, 257, 260
4:15	219–20, 232
4:17	243
4:19–21	222
4:20	227, 229, 238
5:1	219–20, 232, 235
5:4–5	245, 258
5:5	219–20
5:6–17	226, 228
5:6–8	231–32, 249
5:6	216, 220, 222, 227, 229, 233, 237–38, 248–51
5:7–8	251
5:10	227
5:11–12	221, 227
5:11	242
5:16–20	223
5:17	226
5:18	223–24, 244
5:19	224
5:20–21	232
5:20	220, 242
5:21	239

2 John

7	190, 224
9	216, 250

Dead Sea Scrolls

4Q 246	49

RABBINIC WRITINGS

Exod Rab 3.13 186
Lev Rab 15   251
PsJonathan Targ
(NUM 20.11)   186

EARLY CHRISTIAN WRITINGS

Barnabas

4:1–4	226
5:6–7, 10–11	232
18:1	226

Didache

16:3–4	226

Gospel of Thomas

28	232

Ignatius: Letter to the Smyrneans

6:1	232
6:2	249

Irenaeus: Adv, Haer.

1:13:1–5	249

Justin Martin: Dialogue with Trypho

16.4	52
89:1–2	52
90:1	52

Letter to Diognetus

5:8–9	232
6:3	232